The following guides by Dawn Apgar are available from Springer Publishing to assist social workers with studying for and passing the ASWB® examinations necessary for licensure.

Bachelors

The Social Work ASWB® Bachelors Exam Guide: A Comprehensive Guide for Success, Second Edition

Test focuses on knowledge acquired while obtaining a Baccalaureate degree in Social Work (BSW). A small number of jurisdictions license social workers at an Associate level and require the ASWB Associate examination. The Associate examination is identical to the ASWB Bachelors examination, but the Associate examination requires a lower score in order to pass.

Masters

The Social Work ASWB® Masters Exam Guide: A Comprehensive Guide for Success, Second Edition

Test focuses on knowledge acquired while obtaining a Master's degree in Social Work (MSW). There is no postgraduate supervision needed.

Clinical

The Social Work ASWB® Clinical Exam Guide: A Comprehensive Guide for Success, Second Edition

Test focuses on knowledge acquired while obtaining a Master's degree in Social Work (MSW). It is usually taken by those with postgraduate supervised experience.

Advanced Generalist

The Social Work ASWB® Advanced Generalist Exam Guide: A Comprehensive Guide for Success, Second Edition

Test focuses on knowledge acquired while obtaining a Master's degree in Social Work (MSW). It is usually taken by those with postgraduate supervised nonclinical experience.

Dawn Apgar, PhD, LSW, ACSW, has helped thousands of social workers across the country pass the ASWB® examinations associated with all levels of licensure. In recent years, she has consulted in numerous states to assist with establishing licensure test preparation programs.

Dr. Apgar has done research on licensure funded by the American Foundation for Research and Consumer Education in Social Work Regulation and has served as chairperson of her state's social work licensing board. She is a past President of the New Jersey Chapter of NASW and has been on its National Board of Directors. In 2014, the Chapter presented her with a Lifetime Achievement Award. Dr. Apgar has taught in both undergraduate and graduate social work programs and has extensive direct practice, policy, and management experience in the social work field.

Social Work ASWB® Advanced Generalist Exam Guide

A Comprehensive Study Guide for Success

Second Edition

Dawn Apgar, PhD, LSW, ACSW

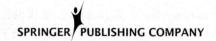
SPRINGER PUBLISHING COMPANY

Springer Publishing Company, LLC

11 West 42nd Street
New York, NY 10036
www.springerpub.com

Acquisitions Editor: Debra Riegert
Composition: diacriTech, Chennai

ISBN: 978-0-8261-4717-2
ebook ISBN: 978-0-8261-4719-6

17 18 19 20 21 22 / 5 4 3 2 1

The author and the publisher of this Work have made every effort to use sources believed to be reliable to provide information that is accurate and compatible with the standards generally accepted at the time of publication. The author and publisher shall not be liable for any special, consequential, or exemplary damages resulting, in whole or in part, from the readers' use of, or reliance on, the information contained in this book. The publisher has no responsibility for the persistence or accuracy of URLs for external or third-party Internet websites referred to in this publication and does not guarantee that any content on such websites is, or will remain, accurate or appropriate.

Library of Congress Cataloging-in-Publication Data
 Names: Apgar, Dawn, author. | Association of Social Work Boards.
Title: Social work ASWB advanced generalist exam guide : a comprehensive
  study guide for success / Dawn Apgar, PhD, LSW, ACSW.
Description: Second edition. | New York, NY : Springer Publishing Company,
  LLC, [2018] | Includes index.
Identifiers: LCCN 2017044819 | ISBN 9780826147172 | ISBN 9780826147196 (ebook)
Subjects: LCSH: Social workers—Certification—United States. | Social
  service—United States—Examinations--Study guides. | Social
  service—United States—Examinations, questions, etc.
Classification: LCC HV40.52 .A7347 2018 | DDC 361.3076—dc23 LC record available at
https://lccn.loc.gov/2017044819

Contact us to receive discount rates on bulk purchases.
We can also customize our books to meet your needs.
For more information please contact: sales@springerpub.com

Printed in the United States of America by Gasch Printing.

To Bill, Ryan, and Alex

You remind me what is important, support me so I can do it all, and
always inspire me to be a better person

Contents

Preface

Congratulations on getting to this point in your social work career. The decision to become licensed is significant, and passing the licensing examination demonstrates that you have the basic knowledge necessary to safely practice. Social workers are employed in all kinds of settings including hospitals, correctional facilities, mental health and addictions agencies, government offices, and private practices. It is essential that those served have some assurance that these practitioners are competent to provide the services that they are charged with delivering.

Regulation through certification and licensure helps to assure that social workers will interact in an ethical and safe manner, and there is oversight to address actions that are not consistent with this standard.

Passing the licensing exam is only one step in becoming certified or licensed, but it is usually the most difficult challenge faced after graduating with your degree.

This guide aims to assist in helping you through this process in several important ways. It will:

1. Increase your knowledge of the Association of Social Work Boards (ASWB®) examination, **including the new blueprints used for all tests taken on or after January 2, 2018**

2. Provide valuable test-taking strategies that will assist in developing a good study plan and in analyzing question wording in order to select the correct answer

3. Summarize content areas that may be included on the examination as per the Knowledge, Skills, and Abilities (KSA) statements published by ASWB, which are used by test developers to formulate actual questions

4. Supply sample questions that can be used to simulate an actual examination experience

Although there are other test preparation materials produced, this guide provides all these essential elements in a single, manageable, and easy-to-use guide.

Individuals who are studying for the social work licensing examination have a primary concern and request. They are worried that they do not know important information about the tests that will prove to be a barrier to passing, and they want a "place" to go that will have all the necessary materials in a single location. They want to focus their efforts on studying for the exam— not hunting around for what needs to be studied!

This guide was created based on this important information, and it has been gathered from thousands of social workers just like you. Although it is not produced by or affiliated with ASWB in any way, and does not guarantee a passing score on the examinations, the test-taking techniques have been developed and used successfully by others who were faced with the same challenge that you are—others who are now certified and licensed social workers! They found this information so helpful in passing because the skills that it takes to be a good social worker in practice can be very different than the skills that it takes to pass the examination.

Best wishes as you study for the examination. And remember that there is never only one way to achieve a goal, so use this guide in a way that works for you as you prepare. In choosing this guide as your roadmap, you have taken an important first step on the journey of passing the examination for certification and licensure.

New in the Second Edition

The new edition of this popular guide reflects the new blueprint for the ASWB Advanced Generalist examination for those taking the exam on or after January 2, 2018. Revisions include new and enhanced material on the Knowledge, Skills, and Abilities (KSAs) statements added by ASWB in the four content areas and incorporates the information from the *Diagnostic and Statistical Manual of Mental Disorders* (5th ed., DSM-5), which was added to the exam in July 2015. Lastly, this new edition links questions in the practice examination to material being tested within the four content areas, making it possible to diagnose areas which require further study.

Many new knowledge areas that have been incorporated into the revised blueprint are found in this new edition, including those in the following list.

Unit I: Human Development, Diversity, and Behavior in the Environment

1. HUMAN GROWTH AND DEVELOPMENT

- Theories of human development throughout the lifespan (e.g., physical, social, emotional, cognitive, behavioral)—new material on cognitive development
- Theories of spiritual development throughout the lifespan
- Theories of racial, ethnic, and cultural development throughout the lifespan
- The effect of aging on biopsychosocial functioning
- Factors influencing self-image (e.g., culture, race, religion/spirituality, age, disability, trauma)—new material added
- Parenting skills and capacities
- Addiction theories and concepts—new material added
- Strengths-based and resilience theories—new material added

- Psychoanalytic and psychodynamic approaches—new material on psychosexual stages of development and object relations
- Indicators and dynamics of abuse and neglect throughout the lifespan—new material on physical abuse added

2. FUNCTIONING OF VARIOUS SYSTEMS
- Family dynamics and functioning and the effects on individuals, families, groups, organizations, and communities
- Models of family life education in social work practice

3. EFFECTS OF THE ENVIRONMENT ON SYSTEMS' BEHAVIOR
- Person-in-environment (PIE) theory
- The impact of the environment (e.g., social, physical, cultural, political, economic) on individuals, families, groups, organizations, and communities
- Role theories
- Social and economic justice
- The impact of globalization on clients/client systems (e.g., interrelatedness of systems, international integration, technology, environmental or financial crises, epidemics)

4. DIVERSITY, DISCRIMINATION, AND STEREOTYPES
- The effect of disability on biopsychosocial functioning throughout the lifespan
- The influence of sexual orientation on behaviors, attitudes, and identity
- The impact of transgender and transitioning process on behaviors, attitudes, identity, and relationships
- Systemic (institutionalized) discrimination (e.g., racism, sexism, ageism)
- The principles of culturally competent social work practice
- Sexual orientation concepts
- Gender and gender identity concepts

Unit II: Intervention Processes and Techniques for Use Across Systems

5. BIOPSYCHOSOCIAL HISTORY AND COLLATERAL DATA
- The components of a biopsychosocial assessment
- Biopsychosocial responses to illness and disability
- Biopsychosocial factors related to mental health
- The indicators of mental and emotional illness throughout the lifespan—new material added
- Co-occurring disorders and conditions
- The impact of caregiving on families
- The impact of physical and mental illness on family dynamics—new material on the impact of mental illness
- The indicators of behavioral dysfunction
- The indicators of feigning illness—new material added
- The indicators of traumatic stress and violence

- The effects of life events, stressors, and crises on individuals, families, groups, organizations, and communities—new material added
- The impact of out-of-home placement (e.g., hospitalization, foster care, residential care, criminal justice system) on clients/client systems
- The indicators, dynamics, and impact of exploitation across the lifespan (e.g., financial, immigration status, sexual trafficking)
- Criminal justice systems

6. ASSESSMENT METHODS AND TECHNIQUES

- Methods to incorporate the results of psychological and educational tests into assessment
- Methods to obtain sensitive information (e.g., substance abuse, sexual abuse)
- Communication theories and styles
- Methods to assess the client's/client system's strengths, resources, and challenges (e.g., individual, family, group, organization, community)
- The indicators of motivation, resistance, and readiness to change— new material added
- Methods to assess motivation, resistance, and readiness to change
- Methods to assess the client's/client system's coping abilities
- The use of the Diagnostic and Statistical Manual of the American Psychiatric Association—more in-depth descriptions of the diagnoses in the *DSM-5*

7. INTERVENTION PLANNING AND IMPLEMENTATION

- The principles and techniques of interviewing (e.g., supporting, clarifying, focusing, confronting, validating, feedback, reflecting, language differences, use of interpreters, redirecting)—new material added
- The criteria used in the selection of intervention/treatment modalities (e.g., client/client system abilities, culture, life stage)—new material added
- The components of intervention, treatment, and service plans
- The impact of immigration, refugee, or undocumented status on service delivery
- The phases of intervention and treatment
- The client's/client system's role in the problem-solving process
- Methods to obtain and provide feedback—new material added
- The principles of active listening and observation—new material added
- Verbal and nonverbal communication techniques—new material added
- Techniques for harm reduction for self and others
- Theories of trauma-informed care
- Methods and approaches to trauma-informed care

- Anger management techniques
- Cognitive and behavioral interventions—new material added
- Partializing techniques—new material added
- Assertiveness training
- Psychoeducation methods (e.g., acknowledging, supporting, normalizing)
- Family therapy models, interventions, and approaches—new material added
- Mindfulness and complementary therapeutic approaches
- Techniques used for follow-up

Unit III: Intervention Processes and Techniques for Use With Larger Systems

10. SUPERVISION AND ADMINISTRATION

- Fund-raising and development
- The relationship between formal and informal power structures in the decision-making process
- Methods to create, implement, and evaluate policies and procedures for social worker safety
- Models of supervision and consultation (e.g., individual, peer, group)
- The components of a safe and positive work environment
- The process of interdisciplinary and intradisciplinary team collaboration—new material added on intradisciplinary team collaboration
- The basic terminology of professions other than social work (e.g., legal, educational)
- Methods to develop, review, and implement crisis plans
- Quality assurance, including program reviews and audits

11. RECORD-KEEPING AND REPORTING

- The elements of client/client system reports
- The principles and processes for developing formal documents (e.g., proposals, letters, brochures, pamphlets, reports, evaluations)

Unit IV: Professional Relationships, Values, and Ethics

12. PROFESSIONAL VALUES AND ETHICAL ISSUES

- Legal and/or ethical issues related to the practice of social work, including responsibility to clients/client systems, colleagues, the profession, and society
- Professional values and principles (e.g., competence, social justice, integrity, and dignity and worth of the person)
- Client/client system competence and self-determination (e.g., financial decisions, treatment decisions, emancipation, age of consent, permanency planning)
- Self-disclosure principles and applications
- Legal and/or ethical issues regarding documentation

- Legal and/or ethical issues regarding termination
- Legal and/or ethical issues related to death and dying
- Research ethics (e.g., institutional review boards, use of human subjects, informed consent)
- Ethical issues in supervision and management—new material added

14. PROFESSIONAL DEVELOPMENT AND USE OF SELF
- The social worker's role in the problem-solving process
- Social worker self-care principles and techniques
- The effect of the client's developmental level on the social worker–client relationship
- Burnout, secondary trauma, and compassion fatigue
- The influence of the social worker's own values and beliefs on interdisciplinary collaboration

In addition, the Advanced Generalist Exam Guide includes expanded, more in-depth content from that found in the Masters Exam Guide in the 34 KSAs in the following list.

Unit I: Human Development, Diversity, and Behavior in the Environment

1. HUMAN GROWTH AND DEVELOPMENT
- Theories of human development throughout the lifespan (e.g., physical, social, emotional, cognitive, behavioral)
- Theories of spiritual development throughout the lifespan
- The effect of aging on biopsychosocial functioning
- Factors influencing self-image (e.g., culture, race, religion/spirituality, age, disability, trauma)
- Addiction theories and concepts
- Strengths-based and resilience theories
- Psychoanalytic and psychodynamic approaches

2. FUNCTIONING OF VARIOUS SYSTEMS
- Theories of group development and functioning

3. EFFECTS OF THE ENVIRONMENT ON SYSTEMS' BEHAVIOR
- Person-in-environment theory

4. DIVERSITY, DISCRIMINATION, AND STEREOTYPES
- The effects of discrimination and stereotypes on behaviors, attitudes, and identity

Unit II: Intervention Processes and Techniques for Use Across Systems

5. BIOPSYCHOSOCIAL HISTORY AND COLLATERAL DATA
- The components of a biopsychosocial assessment
- Biopsychosocial factors related to mental health
- The indicators of mental and emotional illness throughout the lifespan
- The effects of life events, stressors, and crises on individuals, families, groups, organizations, and communities

- The effects of physical, sexual, and psychological abuse on individuals, families, groups, organizations, and communities
- The effects of addiction and substance abuse on individuals, families, groups, organizations, and communities

6. ASSESSMENT METHODS AND TECHNIQUES

- The indicators of motivation, resistance, and readiness to change
- Methods to assess motivation, resistance, and readiness to change

7. INTERVENTION PLANNING AND IMPLEMENTATION

- The principles and techniques of interviewing (e.g., supporting, clarifying, focusing, confronting, validating, feedback, reflecting, language differences, use of interpreters, redirecting)
- Methods to involve clients/client systems in intervention planning
- The criteria used in the selection of intervention/treatment modalities (e.g., client/client system abilities, culture, life stage)
- The components of intervention, treatment, and service plans
- The phases of intervention and treatment
- Methods to obtain and provide feedback
- Methods and approaches to trauma-informed care
- Family therapy models, interventions, and approaches

Unit III: Intervention Processes and Techniques for Use With Larger Systems

8. PROGRAM DEVELOPMENT AND RESEARCH

- Data collection and analysis methods

10. SUPERVISION AND ADMINISTRATION

- The effects of policies, procedures, regulations, and legislation on social work practice and service delivery
- Employee recruitment, training, retention, performance appraisal, evaluation, and discipline
- The components of case management

11. RECORD-KEEPING AND REPORTING

- The principles of case recording, documentation, and management of practice records

Unit IV: Professional Relationships, Values, and Ethics

12. PROFESSIONAL VALUES AND ETHICAL ISSUES

- Professional objectivity in the social worker–client/client system relationship

14. PROFESSIONAL DEVELOPMENT AND USE OF SELF

- The principles and techniques for building and maintaining a helping relationship—new material on the process of engagement in social work
- The dynamics of diversity in the social worker–client/client system relationship

Introduction

About the Examination

Generally, when social workers are getting ready to take the Association of Social Work Boards (ASWB®) tests, they are anxious not only about knowing the content, but also about the examinations themselves. They have many questions about the number of questions that will be asked and the number of correct answers required to pass. Becoming familiar with the examination basics will assist in making you more comfortable with the examination conditions and structure, thereby reducing your anxiety about the unknown.

In order to ensure that the examinations are based on necessary knowledge and skills, ASWB conducts a practice analysis every 5 to 7 years. The first analysis was completed in 1981 and the most current collected data between 2015 and 2016 to construct the blueprint for all examinations taken after January 2, 2018. The structure of this guide and the material contained in it are based on this new blueprint.

10 THINGS THAT YOU SHOULD KNOW ABOUT THE ASWB EXAMINATIONS

1. All of the ASWB examinations have the same format, meaning that each has the same number of questions that each test-taker is given the same amount of time to complete. There are **170 multiple-choice questions** and you will have **4 hours** from the time that you start answering the questions. You can take a brief restroom break or stand to stretch, but the clock does not stop and these activities will be included in your 4-hour limit, so you want to be judicious with your time.

2. Although you will be answering a total of 170 questions, **20 of these questions are nonscored items** that are being piloted for possible inclusion as scored questions on future ASWB examinations. Thus, only 150 questions will determine whether you pass or not. However, you will never know which 20 are pilot items because they are mixed in with scored items, so you will need to try to select the right answers on all 170 questions.

3. You **do not want to leave any questions blank**; answer all 170 questions in the 4 hours.

4. The examination is **computerized**, but requires no specialized computer knowledge. There is a brief computer tutorial that will assist you when you first sit down and look at the screen, and spending time getting to feel comfortable with the device at that time is a good idea, since it will not count toward your 4-hour time limit.

5. You will be taking your examination at a **testing center with others who are being tested in different disciplines** and may be taking shorter or longer examinations, so do not be concerned if they finish before or after you.

6. Testing center activities are **closely monitored**, and you will need to leave all of your belongings, including your watch, in a provided locker. You can ask for earplugs, scrap paper, or a pencil, but will not be able to bring anything into the room with you. The room may be hot or cold, so you should dress in comfortable layers. All testing accommodations related to documented disabilities must be approved by your state licensing board and arranged in advance with ASWB. Some states allow for extra time or foreign language dictionaries as accommodations for those who do not have English as a first language.

7. You will leave the testing center with an unofficial copy of your examination results. It will tell you how many questions you were asked and how many you got correct in each of the four areas or domains. You will never know which specific answers were correct and incorrect. You will also not find out the correct answers for those that you answered incorrectly. **The exam is pass/fail**, and a passing score can be used for certification or licensure in any state.

8. Although the Knowledge, Skills, and Abilities (KSAs) are in four content areas and you may structure your studying to learn all the related material in a given domain before moving on to the next, **the questions on the examination are in random order** and skip across topics. There is not a separate section of questions labeled Human Development, Diversity, and Behavior in the Environment, or so on. You may have a human behavior question followed by one on ethics, so you really need to clear your head between questions and avoid

trying to relate them to one another in any way. Each question stands alone as a way to assess knowledge related to a distinct KSA.

9. Social workers always want to know how many questions of the 150 scored items they will need to answer correctly to pass the exam. Although this sounds like an easy question, it is not! Not all questions on the ASWB examinations are the same level of difficulty as determined by the pilot process, so individuals who were randomly assigned harder versions of the exams will need to answer fewer questions correctly than those who were lucky enough to have easier questions. This method ensures that the examination is fair for all those who are taking it, regardless of which questions were chosen. **The number of questions that you have to get correct generally varies from 93 to 106 of the 150 scored items**. You will find out how many needed to be answered correctly only after you are finished with your examination and it is immediately scored electronically. When you examine your unofficial test results, which are provided in a printout prior to leaving the testing center, you will be able to gauge the difficulty of your examination. If you needed to get closer to 93 correct, you had harder questions, and if you needed to get 106 or above correct, you had easier ones.

10. **If you do not pass the examination, you will not have the same questions repeated on any of your examinations in the future**. Other questions in the four areas will be selected. As the four domains are so broad, you may find that the topics of the questions may be quite different than those on a previous examination. To be adequately prepared, it is best to go back and study all the KSAs listed for a content area and not just those that may have caused you problems. If you do not pass, you will have to wait 90 days before taking the examination again.

If you have questions about the examination or scoring, such as the process for sending your passing exam score to another state in which you want to be licensed, visit the ASWB website at www.aswb.org for additional information and necessary forms. The *ASWB Examination Candidate Handbook*, which is free and located on this website, provides additional information about registering for the examination that may be useful.

Test-Taking Strategies and Tips

Social workers studying for the ASWB examinations always want to know techniques that will assist them in studying wisely and answering questions correctly. Remember that there are no replacements for good old-fashioned work, and test-taking strategies are not enough on their own to eliminate all of the incorrect answers. Usually, applying test-taking strategies can help you dismiss two of four possible multiple-choice responses and it is your knowledge of the content area that will be needed to select the correct answer from the two that are remaining. Thus, you will need to make sure that you are well versed in the examination content in order to pass the examination.

However, there are two types of strategies that may assist. The first concerns things to remember when developing your study plan. These are important pieces of information that may help when you are trying to decide what to learn and how to learn it. The second includes those tips that can assist you when actually answering the questions. These tips are important to remember after you have learned all the needed content and are tasked with applying it in the proper way to select the correct answer.

As both of these strategy types are keys to success on the examinations, they are outlined here.

10 ESSENTIAL STRATEGIES FOR STUDY SUCCESS

Strategy 1

This is an examination to assess knowledge of social work content, so you will need to make sure that you can describe an overview of the key concepts and terms related to each of the KSAs. You will know if you are ready to take the examinations when you are able to briefly explain these areas to someone who does not have any prior knowledge of them. The difference between passing and not passing the examinations almost always is a result of gaps in knowledge, not application of test-taking strategies, so you need to make sure that the bulk of your studying is aimed at filling in knowledge gaps or refreshing information already learned.

Strategy 2

You will never be "ready" to take the ASWB examination. Not unlike other standardized examinations, such as the Scholastic Aptitude Test (SAT) or Graduate Record Examination (GRE), you cannot judge readiness as knowing everything about the content areas. The ASWB examinations are not designed for test-takers to "know it all" in order to pass. Often, picking a test date is the hardest task; as with the SAT or GRE, a deadline for admission to college or graduate school forces individuals to select a date even when they do not feel ready. For the ASWB examination, you will need to select a date in the next few weeks or months, perhaps dictated by job opportunities or promotions predicated on being licensed. You will walk into the examination without feeling totally ready, but this is typical of others who have passed.

Strategy 3

You need to limit your study materials to this guide or other key resources that summarize material. This is not the time to go back and read your textbooks! There are so many topics that you are asked to know about under each KSA that you cannot and are not expected to know everything related to the topic. This guide is geared to provide important information on these areas "under one roof." It will be hard enough to read through all this material. You should only use outside materials if something in this guide is unclear or you feel that you need more than the information included, perhaps because you never learned this area in the first place. In these instances, you can use free resources on the Internet or any other documents that have no more than a paragraph summarizing key points. Remember, you do not need to read a book on Freud to understand his work and its importance in explaining human development.

Strategy 4

Although individuals like to study from sample questions, this is not advisable. There are many reasons why using this technique will hurt you on the examinations, but here are just a few:

1. Although it makes individuals feel better when they get an answer correct on a sample test, getting an answer correct is not a valid

indicator of really knowing the content in the KSA for which the question was developed. Studying from the KSAs and the topics within them will ensure that you are able to answer any question, not just the one that is in a sample test.

2. Your answers to sample questions inappropriately influence your decisions on the actual examinations when asked about similar topics. For example, you may see an answer that is similar to one that was correct or incorrect in a practice test and you will be more apt or less apt to select it based upon this prior experience. However, the question in the "real" examination will not be exactly the same as the one on the practice test, and you must evaluate all four answers independently without any undue bias that may be caused by your practice question experience.

3. The sample questions that you study are not going to be on your examination and probably are not even written by those who developed items for your test. Thus, the idea that many social workers have of wanting to "get into the head" of the individuals writing the exam or understand their logic is not valid—though it might make them good clinicians in real life!

Strategy 5

If you have access to sample questions, such as those in the last section of this guide, you should use them to create a "mock" examination. Most people have trouble resisting the urge to look at the answer key to see if they were correct immediately after selecting a response. However, a far better way to use these questions is to pretend that they are an actual examination.

1. After you are done studying the content and think you are ready to take the ASWB examination, select a 4-hour period where you can create a quiet environment without interruptions.

2. Answer the questions as you would on the actual examination—using the strategies and having to pick one answer—even if you are not completely sure that it is correct.

3. If you do not take unnecessary breaks, you will see that you can easily get through 170 questions in the 4 hours allotted. This experience should relieve some of your anxiety about the timed nature of the examination.

4. See which answers that you got correct and incorrect. The "mock" examination is not to be used to determine whether you are ready to take the actual test—even if getting 93 to 106 puts you in the range of having the knowledge to pass the actual examination. Instead, it gives you some idea of the length of the examination and how long you will need to focus, while giving you the confidence that you can get most of the answers correct within the time period allotted.

Strategy 6

It probably has been a long time since you had to sit for a 4-hour examination—if ever! Our lives are hectic, and we rarely get a chance to really focus on a single task or have the luxury of thinking about a single topic in a way that allows us to really understand it. Thus, many people find it helpful to study in 4-hour blocks of time rather than for a few minutes here and there. This may be difficult, but it will be beneficial because it will get you prepared to not lose your concentration or focus during such a long period. Remember, runners do not start with marathons, they need to build their strength and endurance over time before they can tackle 26.2 miles. Your preparation is similar: You do not want the first time that you have to sit and engage in critical thinking to be your actual examination.

Strategy 7

There is always a time lag between the generation of new social work content and when it appears on the ASWB examinations. It takes time to write and pretest questions on new material. For example, when the Health Insurance Portability and Accountability Act (HIPAA) of 1996 was passed, there were several years before questions related to this law were asked. Although the *Diagnostic and Statistical Manual of Mental Disorders (DSM-5)* was published in 2013, ASWB announced that it would not be included on examinations until July 2015. This lag is good and bad. The good news is that you do not have to know the "latest and greatest" in all content areas. It is hard to keep completely up to date in a profession that is changing so rapidly. Now for the bad news! For many, especially if they are working in a particular specialty area, some of the content or answers may appear to be dated. This is often the case in the area of psychopharmacology, because new medications are being approved and used rapidly. Remember the time lapse in your studying, and do not rely on breaking news or even practices in your own agency as information sources.

Strategy 8

As you think about what is important to learn or remember when you are reviewing this guide, you should recognize that social workers who have attended social work programs at different schools, as well as courses within a program taught by various instructors, have passed the examinations. Thus, although there is always information to add to a KSA related to experience or depth of knowledge, there are "core" elements included in any overview or lecture on the topic, regardless of school or professor. These elements are the ones that have to be learned and remembered because they are the basis of the knowledge being tested. In addition, there are also "core" or essential areas that contain information that is seen as critical to competent practice. Can you imagine a social worker leaving an undergraduate or graduate program without reviewing the signs of child abuse and neglect and his or her duty as a mandatory reporter? Of course not! This is a "core" topic that often is the basis of examination questions. The list of these areas is not fixed, but includes confidentiality, assessment of danger to self and others, cultural competence, and so on. You should ask yourself when studying, "Is this something that every social worker needs to know, regardless of setting or specialization?" If so, it may be essential to include it in your review of a topic because it is likely to be included on the examination.

Strategy 9

When studying, it is not necessary to memorize the content because you will not have to recall a term or definition from memory. The ASWB examinations are not tests geared to test your memory. Instead, they require you to be able to pick the one of several answers that most directly relates to the topic or is the best based on your knowledge of the content area. Thus, it is much more important that you understand each of the KSAs and are not focused on memorizing fancy terms or facts. If you stumble when asked a question about something that you are saying about a KSA, or cannot go off script when discussing these areas, you may be just memorizing the material instead of really understanding it.

Strategy 10

Often, social workers are focused on using the clinical and other jargon that they learned in their MSW programs; however, they may be unable to explain what these concepts mean in plain and understandable terms. For example, when asked what should happen when meeting with a client for the first time, social workers often use phrases such as "You need to build rapport," "It is essential that you start where a client is," or "Social workers should show empathy as to what a client is going through." Though all true, these statements give little insight into any real actions that a social worker should take in this first meeting. What should a social worker do to "build rapport"? How would a client know if a social worker was being "empathetic"? What would a social worker be doing or saying? Having to explain the KSAs to someone who knows little about social work practice and will ask you lots of questions about the content area can be a far better strategy than studying with a social work colleague who will not challenge you when you use jargon or technical terms without having to explain the basics.

20 TIPS YOU NEED TO USE TO ANSWER QUESTIONS CORRECTLY

Tip 1

This is an examination of your knowledge of social work content. Often, what we learn in the classroom and how we might act in practice based upon practice wisdom and clinical judgments are different. **When selecting an answer, you should base it upon the content that you studied from this guide and what you learned in the classroom.** Each question is written to make sure that you know requisite information about the KSAs. Thus, ask yourself— "What did I study in the guide that relates to this question?" or "Which KSA is being tested and what do I know about this content area?" If you are inappropriately asking, "What would I do in this case vignette?" or "How should I handle this situation?" you will be drawing upon your practice experience rather than the existing knowledge in a domain that is the basis for selecting the correct answer.

Remember, there is only one correct answer for each question. Since everyone has different practice experience, basing your answers on what you see or do in the field may lead you to a different response than someone else taking the examination. However, the textbook or existing body of knowledge on the KSAs is universal, regardless of setting or practice experience. Basing your responses on the information that is taught in the classroom and in social work textbooks, as outlined in this guide, will ensure that you get to the same correct response as others.

Tip 2

You may have a negative opinion about the need to take a standardized 4-hour examination after having successfully graduated from your social work program and even gotten the requisite clinical experience. However, it is a requirement for licensure and seen as a way of determining whether social workers possess the knowledge needed to practice safely. Just as the SAT and GRE are viewed as ways of determining the ability to perform in college or graduate school, the ASWB examinations are seen as indicators of proper social work preparation to successfully practice at various levels. You probably know individuals who have done well on the SAT and GRE and did not do well in postsecondary education and vice versa.

The use of standardized tests in social work and other life areas "is what it is" and **it will hurt your performance if you "fight" the use of such examinations**—in other words, do not approach the test with negative attitudes and resentment about having to take it.

It is important to approach the examination with a positive attitude and realize that your performance on this examination will not define your social work career. Passing it should not be viewed as an end in itself, but rather a step in the licensure process—just as the SAT is a step in the college acceptance process. Being resentful about the use of standardized testing as an indicator of competence or future performance will only get in your way.

Tip 3

Although there may be some questions that require you to simply "recall" content in a content area, many of them will be focused on you "applying" information to a particular situation or scenario. These questions come in the form of case vignettes and are often the ones in which social workers make mistakes. In practice, social workers often alter their actions based on many contextual variables. However, remember that the questions on the examination are about the application of social work knowledge within the KSAs, and this knowledge does not change regardless of the setting in the vignette. **You should not get "lost" in the scenario**. For example, the core components of a discharge plan are the same if it is prepared for a client leaving the hospital, a drug treatment facility, or an inpatient psychiatric treatment setting. The content within the components (i.e., history/assessment, treatment provided, follow-up needed) may be different, but each discharge plan has to contain information in these critical areas.

Thus, you need to stay focused on the content being tested and remember that it is not necessary to have worked in all the settings mentioned in the vignettes (schools, hospitals, drug treatment centers, nursing homes, etc.) to pass the examination; the KSAs or core social work content being tested is universal, regardless of venue.

Tip 4

The ASWB examination that you are taking is used for licensure in virtually every state. The correct answer to a question is the same for all social workers taking the examination. However, the systems of care and laws in each state differ; thus, responses to situations may be varied in real-life, everyday work. This is not the case on the examination, as **there is only one correct answer to each question**. Thus, if you are thinking about "rules" or laws that apply in your state, or resources that may be available, you are likely to get yourself in trouble on the examination because these vary between states and cannot influence your answer selection.

A simple way to avoid unconsciously using state-specific information when answering questions is to think of a state that you envision is very different than your own and ask yourself, "What answer would a social worker living in [insert name of state here] pick as the correct answer?" If your response is, "I don't know because I am not sure how things are done there," you are mistakenly drawing upon practice systems and rules that may differ between states and should not be considered. However, if your response is, "It would be the same as mine," you have considered the core social work content that applies to practice in all states.

Tip 5

Standardized examinations are often difficult and test-takers often find themselves struggling to identify the correct answer from several listed. In these instances, social workers can make a common mistake such as selecting the answer that has catchy social work phrases, such as "from a client's perspective" or "focus on a client's strengths and skills." Although these are important social work concepts, you need to make sure that these answers fit the scenario or question asked. **The "best" answer is not always the correct answer.** If you are judging answers solely based on the inclusion of important social work terms—independent of what the question is really asking—you will often be drawn to the "best" answers (judged to be so solely based on the inclusion of important social work terms or concepts), but they may not be correct. Remember, you always want to ask yourself, "What is the right answer to this question on the examination?"

Tip 6

If you are asked to select between four listed terms, diagnoses, or theories, and you do not know with certainty what all the terms listed mean or the criteria for all of the named diagnoses, you should only choose between those that you know. When they are uncertain about the answer to a question, social workers often mistakenly think that it must be the term, diagnosis, or theory listed that they do not know and will gravitate toward selecting this answer. It seems to make logical sense in their minds—"I am uncertain of the answer to the question and I am uncertain as to what this answer means, so they must go together." Although common, this logic is problematic.

Instead, you should concentrate on choosing between the answers that you know. **Only in instances in which you are able to eliminate with 100% certainty the three choices that you know—which is almost never the case— should you choose the "mystery" term, diagnosis, or theory.**

Tip 7

You will have plenty of time to answer the questions. Although the examination is timed, most people finish with a half-hour or more left in the 4 hours. However, you may be nervous about the time and feel rushed due to your anxiety. Use your time wisely, reading carefully and applying the tips described. You should answer the questions in the order in which they are listed. Skipping around will waste time. The most time that you will spend on a question is determining what the question is asking, so not answering a question after you have done this analysis serves no purpose because you will not have an epiphany or any more information that will be helpful to you later in the examination than you do at that moment. You need to select an answer and move on. You also will need to commit to an answer after having read the question no more than two to three times and applying the strategies. Individuals who run out of time are "stuck" because they are waiting for the feeling of certainty in their answers that does not come in these types of standardized examinations.

Tip 8

Look for qualifying words in examination questions. These words are often capitalized, but not always. Examples of qualifying words are "best," "next," "least," "most," "first," and "not." Whenever you see a qualifying word, it is the key to selecting the correct answer from the others and is directly related to the answer. Thus, when you read each of the response choices or answers, you should put the qualifying word in front of it to ensure that you are focusing on what, in this question, is important. You will repeat the qualifying word before reading each answer. By repeating the word before each response choice, you are making sure that you are focusing on what is important when selecting between the answers.

Tip 9

The examinations require you to have basic knowledge about many theories, practice models, and perspectives related to social work practice. A theory is a set of interrelated concepts that are organized in a way that explain aspects of everyday life. A practice model is a way in which a theory is operationalized. And a perspective is a point of view that is usually broader and at a higher level of abstraction (i.e., strengths perspective). Having a basic understanding of various theories, practice models, and perspectives, as well as the terms that are rooted in them, is necessary. Sometimes there are recall questions about theories, practice models, or perspectives, but knowledge in these areas is often tested through questions related to case vignettes. For example, the last sentence before the response choices or answers may state, "Using a systems approach, a social worker can expect this recent medical diagnosis to...." Examining the response choices or answers through the "lens" of systems theory is essential to selecting the correct answer. Systems theory states that individuals are in continual interaction with their environment and that parts within a system are interrelated. Thus, when one subsystem is affected, they are all affected. In this example, you would need to have this knowledge in order to select the correct answer, and you would be looking for the response choice that reflects the medical diagnosis affecting others in the family or other aspects of a client's life beyond health.

You do not have to be an expert in all theories, practice models, or perspectives. Instead, your knowledge base needs to be "an inch deep, but a mile wide." You do not need to know the material in great depth, but you do need to have basic knowledge about a lot of paradigms.

Remember to always make sure that you are determining whether a question asks you to use a particular theory, practice model, or perspective when selecting the correct answer. If so, it is not about what might be best to address the problem; instead, identify which answer most closely relates to the paradigm identified.

When studying the theories, practice models, and perspectives, make sure to also focus on their related terms. Sometimes questions do not specify paradigms, but use related terms that you would only know if you studied them.

Tip 10

Perhaps the biggest mistake that social workers make when taking the examinations is adding material to the questions. This is done unconsciously when social workers mistakenly think of a client or situation in their own lives that is similar to what is described in a question. Unfortunately, when this occurs, information related to this real-life client or situation is added to the information that you are considering when selecting the correct response choice or answer, even when it is not actually included in the question. For example, if a man is described as psychotic, you may inappropriately think that he is a danger to himself or others because you recently worked with someone who was psychotic and was exhibiting harm to self or others. However, being psychotic does not necessarily mean that you are posing any danger. This added information may cause you to choose the incorrect information.

In order to determine whether you are adding material to a question, ask yourself what a non-social worker might answer. If the non-social worker's answer would be different from your answer, you may be adding material based on practice experience, not what is stated in the question. Remember, the question has all the information needed to select the correct answer. **You should stay with the material in the question and not add information based upon practice experience.**

Tip 11

Look for quotation marks throughout the question or clues in the last sentence before the response choices, because both are often the keys to selecting the correct answers. For example, a case vignette may describe a client who walks into the first therapy session and states, "I don't have to tell you anything and I don't want to be here," followed by a question for a social worker's best actions. Although this question does not explicitly state that it is asking how to best address resistance, it is implied by the client's verbal statement as described in the quoted statement. These words are there for a reason and are usually important clues to the KSA being tested or the critical information needed to select between correct and incorrect answers.

In addition, a case vignette may ask you to use a particular practice modality or theoretical approach to select the correct response choice. The "lens" that you should use is often mentioned in the last sentence before the answers are listed. For example, a case vignette that ends with "using a task-centered treatment approach, a social worker should …" requires you to look at the response choices to see which relates to an intervention that is brief, highly structured, and focused on quick results in which a client can take a very active role. The correct answer would be very different if a social worker, responding to the same case vignette, was asked to use a "psychodynamic model."

Tip 12

Many of the response choices to questions on the examination often begin with verbs. **If you are debating between multiple answers, the verb choices can often provide some clues**. For example, some answers describe a social worker doing something for a client that he or she should be doing or for which he or she should be taking responsibility. These response choices often begin with the word "provide" when the question asks what a social worker should do in a particular situation.

In addition, some verbs may denote less of an empowerment approach, which may help rule them out. "Explore" and "engage" are active verbs that usually indicate that a social worker is relying on a client to come up with the answer or be responsible for the treatment process. "Ignore" or "wait" may indicate that a social worker is not taking critical information into account or acting when needed.

Although examining the verb used in the response choices is only one piece of information that should be used when selecting the correct response choice, and may not be as critical in some instances as other selection criteria, it is a vital tool to consider when two response choices appear equally viable.

Tip 13

Often, questions on the examinations require social workers to identify what they would do "first" or "next" or to pick out the issue or problem that is "most" important in a case scenario. In practice, such decisions are often somewhat subjective and driven by practice wisdom that takes into account many clinical and contextual factors. However, for the examination, all social workers must select the same correct answer. **A useful framework for prioritizing client needs and addressing them sequentially is Maslow's hierarchy of needs.**

Although it is unlikely that Maslow's hierarchy of needs would ever be explicitly asked about on the examination, it is a tool that will be used repeatedly in questions that want the social worker to prioritize problems or order actions based on client need.

A social worker should always address health and safety issues before moving on to issues that relate to self-esteem and relationships. Thus, when the question includes the qualifying word "first," the answers should be considered in light of the health and safety needs of a client. Social workers should also provide concrete services to meet basic needs, such as housing, employment, and transportation, before moving up the hierarchy. Maslow's framework indicates that without health, safety, and basic needs being met first, a client cannot meet his or her higher level needs.

Tip 14

Another critical tool available to select the correct answer is the problem-solving process (i.e., engagement, assessment, planning, intervention, evaluation, and termination). Understanding the goal of each phase and the tasks to be completed therein is critical because many questions on the examination focus on making sure that things are happening in the correct order. For example, if the question is about the first session or meeting with a client, the activities of a social worker should be focused on engagement. Engagement includes finding out why a client is there and why he or she is seeking services now, explaining the role of a social worker and what to expect in treatment, listening to a client as he or she explains his or her situation, and explaining the limits of confidentiality. Including a reference to a specific session in the question is a clue for a social worker in determining what stage of the problem-solving process a social worker and client are in and what activities are appropriate for this stage.

When a question asks what actions a social worker should take when interacting with a client, attention should be paid to what part of the problem-solving process a social worker and client are theoretically engaged in. A social worker's response may be quite different if it is the beginning of the process versus the end. Although questions will rarely explicitly state the phase, it can be identified by what has occurred, such as "when gathering information on the problem" to indicate assessment or "when developing the contract" to indicate planning. Also, it may be useful to classify response choices into these stages in order to select what comes "first" or "next."

Tip 15

If the age of a client or others is included in a case vignette, it is usually relevant to selecting the correct response choice. For example, having an imaginary friend at age 4 is very different than having one at age 34. Imaginary friends in childhood are an extension of pretend play and part of Piaget's preoperational stage. However, having one in later life might be an indicator of psychosis resulting from a hallucination or delusion. Thus, in the former instance, a social worker would view this behavior as typical, which would require no special intervention, whereas in the latter, a social worker may need to do a mental status examination or refer for a psychiatric evaluation.

When studying, a social worker does not need to memorize the exact age at which an individual leaves one stage of development or reaches a milestone. However, when mentioned in a question, the age can be a useful hint as to where a client is in the life course and what may be expected.

Tip 16

Often, questions on the examinations aim to assess whether a social worker is appropriately placing a client as the priority and respecting his or her right to self-determination. Questions may focus on conflicts between meeting a client's needs versus adhering to practices or policies created by an agency. When there is a barrier to meeting a client's needs, a social worker should always take responsibility for trying to remove the barrier.

Answers indicating that a social worker should provide advice to a client because he or she has better solutions to a client's problems are never correct.

In practice, a social worker may often encounter practices or policies that limit a client's alternatives or rights to self-determination, and fighting to change these "rules" may seem unrealistic and futile. However, whether or not a social worker will be successful does not change the mandate to challenge them. Do not dismiss an answer just because it seems difficult to achieve.

A client is the expert on his or her situation and should be regarded as such. The supervisor in case vignettes is there to ensure that a client receives the most effective and efficient services possible—not to make things easier for a social worker or enforce agency mandates.

Always look at the answers through the lens of what is best for a client. The self-determination of a client is only limited in situations that would cause harm to a client or others. The correct response choice is always the one that puts a client first.

Tip 17

It is essential that the question is thoroughly understood before looking at the answers. The most difficult part of selecting the correct answer is understanding the knowledge area or concept that is being tested. In order to ensure that proper attention is given to understanding the question, a multistep process should be undertaken.

1. Read the question exactly as it is written, paying attention to qualifying words and those in quotes. Do not look at the response choices yet!

2. Ask "What is this question about?" to determine which of the KSAs is being tested.

3. Think about the important concepts related to the KSA; they will be essential in selecting the correct answers from the incorrect ones.

4. Examine the question again to confirm that your assumption about which KSA is being tested is correct and to determine how the important concepts related to the KSA are relevant to the question.

5. Now look at the response choices for the first time! Read each carefully.

6. Eliminate any that do not appear to be correct. If more than one response choice appears to be viable, go back and read the question again—looking only at the remaining viable responses. It is difficult to eliminate three of four possible answers immediately, so this process may involve multiple iterations. Each time a response choice is eliminated, read the question and the answers that are left. Going back to the question each time you are unable to dismiss all but one

response choice will assist in selecting the correct answer for that particular question.

Tip 18

It is critical not to be influenced to select a response choice simply because it has social work "buzz words" such as "rapport," "empathy," "support system," "joining with a client," "strengths perspective," "from a client's perspective," and so on. Often, social workers have a hard time eliminating response choices that contain terms that are important to effective service delivery. These are key concepts that are the cornerstone of competent social work services. However, a word or catch phrase does not make a response choice correct. An answer may not be correct because the other parts of it are inadequate, false, or simply do not address what the question is asking. When you see these social work "buzz words" in a response choice, it is essential to read the rest of the answer critically. You might want to ask yourself whether the answer would still be as appealing if a synonym was used in place of the "buzz word." The entire answer has to stand on its merits as correct, even when the actual term that is making it so appealing is omitted.

Tip 19

Often, social workers view the examinations as a vehicle by which to demonstrate their clinical knowledge and skills. They view all client behaviors through a psychotherapeutic lens and are inappropriately quick to attribute actions to symptomology of disorders or dysfunction. Social workers also are more apt on the ASWB examinations to wrongly view clinical attributes as the focus of treatment or intervention.

For example, if a client has just experienced unsuccessful infertility treatments, she may be likely to feel depressed, frustrated, and hopeless. These are typical reactions to her inability to get pregnant as a result of this medical intervention. The presence of these feelings does not mean that they must be the focus of social work treatment or clinically analyzed and diagnosed. Perhaps the client simply needs support for pursuing alternative methods for becoming a mother, such as through adoption or surrogacy.

You should not be quick to diagnose a client with a disorder on the examinations unless ALL the required clinical criteria are present. You should

also not make all client feelings or behaviors clinical issues to be addressed as part of an intervention or treatment.

The ASWB examinations, including the Clinical Examination, are taken by social workers employed in all types of settings and roles. Clinical work does not always imply the need for psychotherapy. Unless the setting or type of intervention to be employed is explicitly stated in a case vignette, you should use a more generalist approach to selecting the correct answer.

Tip 20

Most questions do not ask a social worker to "solve the problem" or even take action that will directly lead to resolving the issue or situation. For example, a question may ask what a social worker should do FIRST when having an issue with his or her supervisor or not getting a verbal response from a colleague. Although speaking directly to a supervisor or putting the request to a colleague in writing may likely not result in an acceptable outcome, such as getting a client a service, they are required steps in ensuring adherence to chain of command or appropriate documentation procedures. It is also important to remember that it is possible to speak to your supervisor first, even if it won't achieve the desired outcome, and then go to an agency directly immediately after—perhaps even the same day—in order to follow the proper chain of command.

Social workers like to get results, and this desire can cause them to choose answers that will make a difference even when questions are not asking for resolution.

There are not long waiting lists, scarce resources, or delays in referrals in examination case vignettes unless they are explicitly stated. In actual practice, social workers encounter these realities daily and often base their decisions and actions to ensure results despite these constraints. These factors should not influence selecting a response choice unless they are explicitly stated in the question.

Assessing Examination Difficulties

If you are having difficulty answering practice questions or even passing the examinations, it is useful to try to diagnose what is causing your problem. You should reexamine the tips outlined in this guide to see what strategies may be helpful in preparing for the examinations and/or answering questions. You also might want to relook at the self-assessment to determine which content areas require more studying.

Although strategies are important, failing the examinations is almost always a result of gaps in knowledge of social work content.

The ASWB examinations are very reliable. Thus, if you study using the same strategy or methods, you are likely to get the same results.

Just like in social work practice, a thorough assessment is critical to ensuring a strategy or intervention is created to address the targeted problem(s). A social worker should spend time analyzing what is causing the difficulties before taking an examination again. For example, difficulties with anxiety will not be addressed by "hitting the books." In addition, knowledge gaps cannot be filled by simply reviewing the test-taking strategies.

Although social workers who have failed the examinations may be anxious to start studying so that they can take the tests again in 90 days, it is worth spending time critically reflecting on the strategies used to study and answer questions so that corrections can be made before trying again.

Dealing With Test Anxiety

Perhaps one of the biggest issues that social workers have to address when preparing for and actually taking the examinations is anxiety. Although not designed to be an exhaustive resource on how to address test anxiety, this guide would be incomplete if it did not provide some guidance to social workers to assist with anxiety during this stressful time in their professional development.

It is important to acknowledge that anxiety can be useful during this process because it helps you prioritize studying and preparing above other demands placed upon you in everyday life. There are no magic ways to instill the necessary knowledge in your brain besides good old-fashioned studying. Anxiety can be a motivator to keep going over the material even when there are more interesting things you could be doing!

Remember, everyone who is studying for the examinations is feeling the same way. This stress is typical, and you are not alone in feeling anxious.

However, it is essential to manage this anxiety, and there are several strategies that can help.

1. *Make a Study Plan and Work the Plan*
   A great way to instill confidence is being able to walk into the testing center having prepared the way that you set out to do. A study plan will help you break the material into smaller manageable segments and avoid last-minute cramming.

2. *Don't Forget the Basics*
   You need to make sure that you don't neglect your biological, emotional, and social needs leading up to and on the day of the examination. Get plenty of rest, build in relaxation time to your study plan, and eat well to give you energy during this exhausting process.

3. *Familiarize Yourself With the Test Environment*
Before the day of the examination, drive to the testing center so you know how to get there. Arrive early so you are not rushed. Take your time reviewing the tutorial on the computer before you start the examination.

4. *Use Relaxation Techniques*
Breathe and give yourself permission to relax during the examination. You may need to shut your eyes and stretch your neck or stand up several times during the 4-hour exam to help you to refocus.

5. *Put the Examination Into Perspective*
Rarely do people get the score that they want the first time taking any standardized test. Taking the SATs or GREs more than once is the rule rather than the exception. Social workers often attach too much meaning to whether or not they pass the examination the first or second time. They walk into the testing center feeling their entire career rests on the results. This is not true. There are many outstanding social workers who have had to take the test multiple times. Remember that you will be able to retake the examination if you do not pass—this is not your only chance. Not passing is not in any way reflective of your ability to practice social work. You will eventually pass, whether it is this time or another, so don't let the test define you. Avoid thinking in "all or nothing" terms.

6. *Expect Setbacks*
The road to licensure is not different than other journeys in life and not usually without unexpected delays or even disappointments. It is important to see these as typical parts of the process and not ends in themselves. Try to figure out why these setbacks in studying or passing are occurring and how you can use this information as feedback for making improvements. You did not get a social work degree without some disappointments and challenges. Studying for and passing the examination will also not be easy, but you will be successful if you keep focused and learn from challenges encountered.

7. *Reward Yourself*
You don't have to wait until you pass in order to celebrate. Build some enjoyment into the test-taking experience by creating little incentives or rewards along the way. Go out to dinner after having studied for 4 hours on a Saturday afternoon. Get up early and study before work so you can enjoy a movie when you get home. Improving your attitude about the test-taking experience can actually help you study more and improve your performance on the examination.

8. *Acknowledge and Address the Anxiety*

    Ignoring the anxiety that accompanies this process will not help. It is impossible to completely eliminate it through any of the techniques mentioned. However, you do need to assess whether it is manageable and can be addressed by some of these suggestions or if it is interfering so significantly with the learning process that you are "blanking out" or having problems in other areas of your life because of its presence. If this is the case, you may need more intensive anxiety reduction interventions. Repeatedly studying the content over and over will not reduce your anxiety. Although most people can develop their own strategies for anxiety management, others need outside help. Usually, individuals who need the assistance of others are those who have experienced debilitating anxiety in other areas of life prior to taking the examinations. No matter what the severity—anxiety management is a critical part of every study plan!

Examination Content

Although it is impossible to identify the information that will be tested in your examination, ASWB provides a listing of all content areas that are used as the basis for all question construction. These areas are identified by social workers in the field via a practice analysis conducted by ASWB. Through this process, a listing of topics that describe the KSAs that are important to the job of a social worker are used to make sure that questions focus on the areas of critical importance to social workers.

Although there is a separate set of KSAs for each of the four ASWB examinations (Bachelors, Masters, Advanced Generalist, and Clinical), there is tremendous overlap across these tests. Sometimes a KSA is not listed in the same content area or is described slightly differently (e.g., "theories of human development" versus "developmental theories"). However, upon review, you will see a tremendous overlap across the examinations.

This is good news, because doing well on one ASWB examination often means that you will do well on another. It is always easier to refresh your memory about a topic area than to learn it for the first time!

You do not have to be an expert in each of the KSAs, but you will need to recall critical content, as well as key concepts and terms that may be related to the area. Many people question whether they know enough or are ready to take the examination. With regard to content, it is challenging because individuals often define readiness by being an expert or highly skilled in each area.

For the examinations, you can use the following as a guide to assessing your readiness in having the requisite knowledge.

1. Would you be able to summarize the most relevant points related to the content area in a 5-minute "lecture" on the topic?

2. Do you understand the relevancy to social work practice and how social workers use this information to make decisions when interacting with clients?

3. Do you know how this content area relates to the assessment and treatment of clients? Does it in any way impact problems or issues that they may be experiencing?

In order to get the right answers, your exam questions may require you to broadly apply the overall key theme related to a theory or area (e.g., the understanding that what happens to a client early in life can influence later functioning) or specific terms associated with the area, even if the construct is not mentioned (e.g., picking a response that best represents "family homeostasis"). In order to help you to determine the areas in which you need to concentrate in your preparation for the examination, you should review KSAs, listed in the Self-Assessment in this guide. They are the basis for individual test questions.

If you feel that you have the requisite knowledge, you may only need to quickly review by reading through the content outlined in the subsequent pages of this guide. If you have gaps in content, you should mark the sections in this guide that relate to the topic and go over them in detail so you can get to the point that you have enough knowledge to recall the key concepts and terms. If you have never heard of the concept or recall little about its relevance to social work practice, do not worry—everyone has gaps in knowledge, but this just means that you will have to spend some extra time learning about the topic.

There are different learning styles and you will need to determine which one best fits you because researchers have shown that individuals perform better on examinations if they use study techniques that are consistent with their styles of learning.

The following are some suggested techniques for each learning style that can help fill in content gaps that may exist.

VISUAL LEARNERS

Visual learners learn best through what they see. Although lectures can be boring for visual learners, they benefit from the use of diagrams, PowerPoint slides, and charts.

- Use colored highlighters in this guide to draw attention to key terms.
- Develop outlines or take notes on the concepts in the guide.
- Write talking points for each of the KSAs on separate white index cards.

- Create a coding schema of symbols and write them in this guide next to material and terms that require further study.
- Study in an environment that is away from visual distractions such as television, people moving around, or clutter.

AUDITORY LEARNERS

Auditory learners learn best through what they hear. They may have difficulty remembering material that they read in this guide, but can easily recall it if it is read to them.

- Tape record yourself summarizing the material as you are studying it—listen to your notes as a way to reinforce what you read.
- Have a study partner explain the relevant concepts and terms related to the KSAs.
- Read the text from this guide aloud if you are having trouble remembering it.
- Find free podcasts or YouTube videos on the Internet on the content areas that are short and easy to understand to assist with learning.
- Talk to yourself about the content as you study—emphasizing what is important to remember related to each KSA.

KINESTHETIC OR HANDS-ON LEARNERS

Kinesthetic learners learn through tactile approaches aimed at experiencing or doing. They need activities and physical activities as a foundation for instruction.

- Make flashcards on material because writing it down will assist with remembering the content.
- Use as many different senses as possible when studying—read material when you are on your treadmill, use highlighters, talk aloud about content, and/or listen to a study partner.
- Develop mnemonic devices to aid in information retention (e.g., EAPIET or *EAt PIE T*oday is a great way to remember the social work problem-solving process—Engaging, Assessing, Planning, Intervening, Evaluating, and Terminating).
- Write notes and important terms in your guide margins.
- Ask a study partner to quiz you on material—turn it into a game and see how many KSAs you can discuss or how long you can talk about a content area before running out of material.

One important thing to remember is that success on the examination does not require a lot of memorization of material, but rather the ability to recall terms when you see them and to draw upon your knowledge of multiple concepts to select the correct course of action in hypothetical vignettes or scenarios. Thus, spend your time really understanding the KSAs and not just being able to recite definitions.

Self-Assessment

In order to help you determine the areas in which you need to concentrate in your preparation for the examination, please review the KSAs that describe the discrete knowledge components that may be tested as part of the examination and are the basis for individual test questions.

If you are not able to recall basic content and/or key terms, indicate the need to study this area thoroughly by circling "1." If you have some basic information about the content and/or key terms, indicate the need to fill in knowledge gaps by circling "2." If you are able to summarize the key concepts and terms, as well as answer questions about its applicability to social work practice and impacts on client functioning, you may be well prepared and can circle "3." Adequate preparation should not be indicated until you can synthesize material from multiple content areas and can discuss all aspects of the KSAs easily and fluidly.

Association of Social Work Boards'
Content Outline for Advanced Generalist Examination

3	2	1
Well Prepared	Somewhat Prepared	Not Prepared

I. Human Development, Diversity, and Behavior in the Environment (23%)

Human Growth and Development

Theories of human development throughout the lifespan   3   2   1
(e.g., physical, social, emotional, cognitive, behavioral)

(*continued*)

The indicators of normal and abnormal physical, cognitive, emotional, and sexual development throughout the lifespan	3	2	1
Theories of sexual development throughout the lifespan	3	2	1
Theories of spiritual development throughout the lifespan	3	2	1
Theories of racial, ethnic, and cultural development throughout the lifespan	3	2	1
The effects of physical, mental, and cognitive disabilities throughout the lifespan	3	2	1
Basic human needs	3	2	1
The principles of attachment and bonding	3	2	1
The effect of aging on biopsychosocial functioning	3	2	1
The impact of aging parents on adult children	3	2	1
Gerontology	3	2	1
Personality theories	3	2	1
Theories of conflict	3	2	1
Factors influencing self-image (e.g., culture, race, religion/ spirituality, age, disability, trauma)	3	2	1
Parenting skills and capacities	3	2	1
Feminist theory	3	2	1
Addiction theories and concepts	3	2	1
Systems and ecological perspectives and theories	3	2	1
Strengths-based and resilience theories	3	2	1
Crisis intervention theories	3	2	1
Psychoanalytic and psychodynamic approaches	3	2	1
Indicators and dynamics of abuse and neglect throughout the lifespan	3	2	1
Theories of conflict	3	2	1

Functioning of Various Systems

The family life cycle	3	2	1
Family dynamics and functioning and the effects on individuals, families, groups, organizations, and communities	3	2	1
Models of family life education in social work practice	3	2	1
Theories of couples development	3	2	1
Theories of group development and functioning	3	2	1

Effects of the Environment on Systems' Behavior

Person-in-environment (PIE) theory	3	2	1

The interplay of biological, psychological, social, and spiritual factors	3	2	1
The dynamics of interpersonal relationships	3	2	1
Psychological defense mechanisms and their effects on behavior and relationships	3	2	1
The indicators of psychosocial stress	3	2	1
The effect of poverty on individuals, families, groups, organizations, and communities	3	2	1
The impact of the environment (e.g., social, physical, cultural, political, economic) on individuals, families, groups, organizations, and communities	3	2	1
Role theories	3	2	1
Social and economic justice	3	2	1
The impact of globalization on clients/client systems (e.g., interrelatedness of systems, international integration, technology, environmental or financial crises, epidemics)	3	2	1

Diversity, Discrimination, and Stereotypes

The effect of disability on biopsychosocial functioning throughout the lifespan	3	2	1
The effect of culture, race, and ethnicity on behaviors, attitudes, and identity	3	2	1
The effects of discrimination and stereotypes on behaviors, attitudes, and identity	3	2	1
The influence of sexual orientation on behaviors, attitudes, and identity	3	2	1
The impact of transgender and transitioning process on behaviors, attitudes, identity, and relationships	3	2	1
Systemic (institutionalized) discrimination (e.g., racism, sexism, ageism)	3	2	1
The principles of culturally competent social work practice	3	2	1
Sexual orientation concepts	3	2	1
Gender and gender identity concepts	3	2	1

II. Intervention Processes and Techniques for Use Across Systems (32%)

Biopsychosocial History and Collateral Data

The components of a biopsychosocial assessment	3	2	1
The components and function of the mental status examination	3	2	1

(continued)

Biopsychosocial responses to illness and disability	3	2	1
Biopsychosocial factors related to mental health	3	2	1
Basic medical terminology	3	2	1
The indicators of mental and emotional illness throughout the lifespan	3	2	1
Co-occurring disorders and conditions	3	2	1
Symptoms of neurologic and organic disorders	3	2	1
The types of information available from other sources (e.g., agency, employment, medical, psychological, legal, or school records)	3	2	1
The impact of caregiving on families	3	2	1
The dynamics and effects of loss, separation, and grief	3	2	1
The impact of physical and mental illness on family dynamics	3	2	1
The indicators of behavioral dysfunction	3	2	1
The indicators of feigning illness	3	2	1
The indicators of somatization	3	2	1
Body image and its impact (e.g., identity, self-esteem, relationships, habits)	3	2	1
The indicators of traumatic stress and violence	3	2	1
The effects of life events, stressors, and crises on individuals, families, groups, organizations, and communities	3	2	1
The impact of out-of-home placement (e.g., hospitalization, foster care, residential care, criminal justice system) on clients/client systems	3	2	1
The impact of out-of-home displacement (e.g., natural disaster, homelessness, immigration) on clients/client systems	3	2	1
The indicators and risk factors of the client's/client system's danger to self and others	3	2	1
The impact of stress, trauma, and violence	3	2	1
The effects of physical, sexual, and psychological abuse on individuals, families, groups, organizations, and communities	3	2	1
The indicators, dynamics, and impact of exploitation across the lifespan (e.g., financial, immigration status, sexual trafficking)	3	2	1
The characteristics of perpetrators of abuse, neglect, and exploitation	3	2	1

The indicators of addiction and substance abuse	3	2	1
The effects of addiction and substance abuse on individuals, families, groups, organizations, and communities	3	2	1
Criminal justice systems	3	2	1
Common psychotropic and non-psychotropic prescriptions and over-the-counter medications and their side effects	3	2	1

Assessment Methods and Techniques

The factors and processes used in problem formulation	3	2	1
Methods of involving clients/client systems in problem identification (e.g., gathering collateral information)	3	2	1
Techniques and instruments used to assess clients/ client systems	3	2	1
Methods to incorporate the results of psychological and educational tests into assessment	3	2	1
Methods to assess ego strengths	3	2	1
Methods to assess organizational functioning (e.g., agency assessments)	3	2	1
Methods to obtain sensitive information (e.g., substance abuse, sexual abuse)	3	2	1
Communication theories and styles	3	2	1
Risk assessment methods	3	2	1
Methods to assess the client's/client system's strengths, resources, and challenges (e.g., individual, family, group, organization, community)	3	2	1
The indicators of motivation, resistance, and readiness to change	3	2	1
Methods to assess motivation, resistance, and readiness to change	3	2	1
Methods to assess the client's/client system's communication skills	3	2	1
Methods to assess the client's/client system's coping abilities	3	2	1
The indicators of the client's/client system's strengths and challenges	3	2	1
Methods used to assess trauma	3	2	1
Placement options based on assessed level of care	3	2	1
The use of the Diagnostic and Statistical Manual of the American Psychiatric Association	3	2	1

(continued)

Intervention Planning and Implementation

The principles and techniques of interviewing (e.g., supporting, clarifying, focusing, confronting, validating, feedback, reflecting, language differences, use of interpreters, redirecting)	3	2	1
Methods to involve clients/client systems in intervention planning	3	2	1
Cultural considerations in the creation of an intervention plan	3	2	1
The criteria used in the selection of intervention/ treatment modalities (e.g., client/client system abilities, culture, life stage)	3	2	1
The components of intervention, treatment, and service plans	3	2	1
Psychotherapies	3	2	1
The impact of immigration, refugee, or undocumented status on service delivery	3	2	1
Discharge, aftercare, and follow-up planning	3	2	1
The phases of intervention and treatment	3	2	1
The client's/client system's role in the problem-solving process	3	2	1
Problem-solving models and approaches (e.g., brief, solution-focused methods or techniques)	3	2	1
Methods to engage and motivate clients/client systems	3	2	1
Methods to engage and work with involuntary clients/ client systems	3	2	1
Methods to obtain and provide feedback	3	2	1
The principles of active listening and observation	3	2	1
Verbal and nonverbal communication techniques	3	2	1
The concept of congruence in communication	3	2	1
Limit setting techniques	3	2	1
The technique of role play	3	2	1
Role modeling techniques	3	2	1
Techniques for harm reduction for self and others	3	2	1
Methods to teach coping and other self-care skills to clients/client systems	3	2	1
Client/client system self-monitoring techniques	3	2	1
Methods of conflict resolution	3	2	1
Crisis intervention and treatment approaches	3	2	1
Theories of trauma-informed care	3	2	1
Methods and approaches to trauma-informed care	3	2	1

Anger management techniques	3	2	1
Stress management techniques	3	2	1
Cognitive and behavioral interventions	3	2	1
Strengths-based and empowerment strategies and interventions	3	2	1
Client/client system contracting and goal-setting techniques	3	2	1
Partializing techniques	3	2	1
Assertiveness training	3	2	1
Task-centered approaches	3	2	1
Psychoeducation methods (e.g., acknowledging, supporting, normalizing)	3	2	1
Group work techniques and approaches (e.g., developing and managing group processes and cohesion)	3	2	1
Family therapy models, interventions, and approaches	3	2	1
Couples interventions and treatment approaches	3	2	1
Permanency planning	3	2	1
Mindfulness and complementary therapeutic approaches	3	2	1
Techniques used for follow-up	3	2	1
Techniques used to evaluate a client's/client system's progress	3	2	1
The indicators of client/client system readiness for termination	3	2	1
Consultation approaches (e.g., referrals to specialists)	3	2	1
Methods to assess the availability of community resources	3	2	1

III. Intervention Processes and Techniques for Use With Larger Systems (18%)

Program Development and Research

Methods to establish program objectives and outcomes	3	2	1
Methods of service delivery	3	2	1
Methods to establish service networks or community resources	3	2	1
The effects of program evaluation findings on services	3	2	1
Methods to evaluate agency programs (e.g., needs assessment, formative/summative assessment, cost-effectiveness, cost-benefit analysis, outcomes assessment)	3	2	1

(continued)

The principles and features of objective and subjective data	3	2	1
Basic and applied research design and methods	3	2	1
Data collection and analysis methods	3	2	1
Methods to assess reliability and validity in social work research	3	2	1
Methods to develop and evaluate measurable objectives for client/client system intervention, treatment, and/or service plans	3	2	1
Methods, techniques, and instruments used to evaluate social work practice	3	2	1
Evidence-based practice	3	2	1

Methods for Social Change

Theories of social change and community development	3	2	1
Community organizing and social planning methods	3	2	1
Techniques for mobilizing community participation	3	2	1
The impact of social institutions on society	3	2	1
The impact of the political environment on policy-making	3	2	1
Concepts of social policy development and analysis	3	2	1
Techniques to inform and influence organizational and social policy	3	2	1
Theories and methods of advocacy for policies, services, and resources to meet clients'/client systems' needs	3	2	1
Primary, secondary, and tertiary prevention strategies	3	2	1

Supervision and Administration

Governance structures	3	2	1
Theories of organizational development and structure	3	2	1
The effects of policies, procedures, regulations, and legislation on social work practice and service delivery	3	2	1
Leadership and management techniques	3	2	1
Fiscal management techniques	3	2	1
Fund-raising and development	3	2	1
Asset-building approaches (e.g., collaborative relationships, human capital, resources)	3	2	1
The relationship between formal and informal power structures in the decision-making process	3	2	1
Educational components, techniques, and methods of supervision	3	2	1
Methods to identify learning needs and develop learning objectives for supervisees	3	2	1

Case recording for practice evaluation or supervision	3	2	1
Methods to create, implement, and evaluate policies and procedures for social worker safety	3	2	1
Models of supervision and consultation (e.g., individual, peer, group)	3	2	1
The supervisee's role in supervision (e.g., identifying learning needs, self-assessment, prioritizing, etc.)	3	2	1
Employee recruitment, training, retention, performance appraisal, evaluation, and discipline	3	2	1
The impact of transference and countertransference within supervisory relationships	3	2	1
The components of a safe and positive work environment	3	2	1
The components of case management	3	2	1
The elements of a case presentation	3	2	1
Time management approaches	3	2	1
Methods of networking	3	2	1
The process of interdisciplinary and intradisciplinary team collaboration	3	2	1
The basic terminology of professions other than social work (e.g., legal, educational)	3	2	1
Methods to create, implement, and evaluate policies and procedures that minimize risk for individuals, families, groups, organizations, and communities	3	2	1
Methods to develop, review, and implement crisis plans	3	2	1
Quality assurance, including program reviews and audits by external sources	3	2	1
Accreditation and/or licensing requirements	3	2	1
Professional development activities to improve practice and maintain current professional knowledge (e.g., in-service training, licensing requirements, reviews of literature, workshops)	3	2	1

Record-Keeping and Reporting

The principles of case recording, documentation, and management of practice records	3	2	1
The elements of client/client system reports	3	2	1
The principles and processes for developing formal documents (e.g., proposals, letters, brochures, pamphlets, reports, evaluations)	3	2	1

(*continued*)

IV   Professional Relationships, Values, and Ethics (27%)

Professional Values and Ethical Issues

Legal and/or ethical issues related to the practice of social work, including responsibility to clients/client systems, colleagues, the profession, and society	3	2	1
Professional values and principles (e.g., competence, social justice, integrity, and dignity and worth of the person)	3	2	1
Techniques to identify and resolve ethical dilemmas	3	2	1
Client/client system competence and self-determination (e.g., financial decisions, treatment decisions, emancipation, age of consent, permanency planning)	3	2	1
Techniques for protecting and enhancing client/client system self-determination	3	2	1
The client's/client system's right to refuse services (e.g., medication, medical treatment, counseling, placement, etc.)	3	2	1
Professional boundaries in the social worker–client/client system relationship (e.g., power differences, conflicts of interest, etc.)	3	2	1
Ethical issues related to dual relationships	3	2	1
Professional objectivity in the social worker–client/client system relationship	3	2	1
Self-disclosure principles and applications	3	2	1
Legal and/or ethical issues regarding documentation	3	2	1
Legal and/or ethical issues regarding termination	3	2	1
Legal and/or ethical issues related to death and dying	3	2	1
Research ethics (e.g., institutional review boards, use of human subjects, informed consent)	3	2	1
Ethical issues in supervision and management	3	2	1

Confidentiality

The principles and processes of obtaining informed consent	3	2	1
The use of client/client system records	3	2	1
Legal and/or ethical issues regarding confidentiality, including electronic information security	3	2	1
Legal and/or ethical issues regarding mandatory reporting (e.g., abuse, threat of harm, impaired professionals, etc.)	3	2	1

Professional Development and Use of Self

The components of the social worker–client/client system relationship	3	2	1
The social worker's role in the problem-solving process	3	2	1
Methods to clarify the roles and responsibilities of the social worker and client/client system in the intervention process	3	2	1
The principles and techniques for building and maintaining a helping relationship	3	2	1
The concept of acceptance and empathy in the social worker–client/client system relationship	3	2	1
The dynamics of power and transparency in the social worker–client/client system relationship	3	2	1
The impact of transference and countertransference in the social worker–client/client system relationship	3	2	1
The impact of domestic, intimate partner, and other violence on the helping relationship	3	2	1
The dynamics of diversity in the social worker–client/client system relationship	3	2	1
The effect of the client's developmental level on the social worker–client relationship	3	2	1
Social worker self-care principles and techniques	3	2	1
Burnout, secondary trauma, and compassion fatigue	3	2	1
The influence of the social worker's own values and beliefs on the social worker–client/client system relationship	3	2	1
The influence of the social worker's own values and beliefs on interdisciplinary collaboration	3	2	1

Unit I

Human Development, Diversity, and Behavior in the Environment (23%)

Human Growth and Development

1

THEORIES OF HUMAN DEVELOPMENT THROUGHOUT THE LIFESPAN (E.G., PHYSICAL, SOCIAL, EMOTIONAL, COGNITIVE, BEHAVIORAL)

Social work theories are general explanations that are supported by evidence obtained through the scientific method. A theory may explain human behavior by describing how humans interact with each other or react to certain stimuli. Because human behavior is so complex, numerous theories are utilized to guide practice.

Many factors influence people and their behaviors. The first influence is *individual characteristics* or differences that are unique to each client, such as knowledge, attitudes, beliefs, general personality style, and disposition. There are also *interpersonal factors* that impact how clients behave and feel. These may include social support, social cohesion, work relationships, friendships, and/or religious belonging. A third influence comes from *institutional factors*. These are the rules, regulations, and informal structures in the organizations where clients live and work. Institutional rules may include prohibition of certain behaviors (i.e., smoking), dress expectations, and/or rules about social interaction. A fourth influence is *community factors*, which come from the social environment in which clients live, including social resources/networks and community norms. The last influence is *public policy*, which may mandate regulations and laws such as wearing seatbelts, not using drugs, and/or limits on physical aggression. These hierarchical factors are the basis of the ecological perspective or model.

In social work, there are many theoretical perspectives that help to explain the human behavior of clients, including, but not limited to, systems, conflict, rational choice, social constructionist, psychodynamic, developmental, social behavioral, and humanistic perspectives.

Systems: Systems are made up of interrelated parts; each part impacts all other parts, as well as the system as a whole. The dynamic interactions within, between, and among systems produce both stability and change.

Conflict: Clients try to advance their own interests over the interests of others as they compete for scarce resources. Power is unequally divided and some social groups dominate others. Members of non-dominant groups become alienated from society. Social change is driven by conflict.

Rational Choice: Clients are rational and goal-directed and human interaction involves exchange of social resources, such as love, approval, information, money, and physical labor. Clients have self-interest and try to maximize rewards and minimize costs. Power comes from unequal resources in exchanges.

Social Constructionist: Social reality is created when clients, in social interaction, develop a common understanding of their world. Clients are influenced by social processes that are grounded in customs, as well as cultural and historical contexts.

Psychodynamic: Unconscious, as well as conscious, mental activity serves as the motivating force in human behavior. Early childhood experiences are central and clients may become overwhelmed by internal or external demands. Defense mechanisms are used to avoid becoming overwhelmed.

Developmental: Human development occurs in defined, age-related stages that build upon one another and are distinct. Human development is a complex interaction of biological, psychological, and social factors.

Social Behavioral: Human behavior is learned when clients interact with the environment through association, reinforcement, and imitation. All human problems can be formulated as undesirable behavior and can be changed through techniques such as classical and operant conditioning.

Humanistic Perspective: Each client is unique and is responsible for the choices he or she makes. Clients have the capacity to change themselves because human behavior is driven by a desire for growth, personal meaning, and competence. Behaving in ways that are not consistent with the true self causes clients anxiety.

Social Development

Human beings are inherently social. Developing competencies in this domain enhances a person's mental health, success in work, and ability to achieve in life tasks.

Erik Erikson was interested in how children socialize and how this affects their sense of self. He saw personality as developing throughout the life course and looked at identity crises as the focal point for each stage of human development.

According to Erikson, there are eight distinct stages, with two possible outcomes. Successful completion of each stage results in a healthy personality and successful interactions with others. Failure to successfully complete a stage can result in a reduced ability to complete further stages and, therefore, a more unhealthy personality and sense of self. These stages, however, can be resolved successfully at a later time.

Trust Versus Mistrust

From birth to 1 year of age, children begin to learn the ability to trust others based upon the consistency of their caregiver(s). If trust develops successfully, the child gains confidence and security in the world around him or her and is able to feel secure even when threatened. Unsuccessful completion of this stage can result in an inability to trust, and therefore a sense of fear about the inconsistent world. It may result in anxiety, heightened insecurities, and feelings of mistrust in the world around them.

Autonomy Versus Shame and Doubt

Between the ages of 1 and 3, children begin to assert their independence by walking away from their mother, picking which toy to play with, and making choices about what they like to wear, to eat, and so on. If children in this stage are encouraged and supported in their increased independence, they become more confident and secure in their own ability to survive in the world. If children are criticized, overly controlled, or not given the opportunity to assert themselves, they begin to feel inadequate in their ability to survive, and may then become overly dependent upon others while lacking self-esteem and feeling a sense of shame or doubt in their own abilities.

Initiative Versus Guilt

Around age 3 and continuing to age 6, children assert themselves more frequently. They begin to plan activities, make up games, and initiate activities with others. If given this opportunity, children develop a sense of initiative, and feel secure in their ability to lead others and make decisions. Conversely, if this tendency is squelched, either through criticism or control, children develop a sense of guilt. They may feel like nuisances to others and will therefore remain followers, lacking self-initiative.

Industry Versus Inferiority

From age 6 to puberty, children begin to develop a sense of pride in their accomplishments. They initiate projects, see them through to completion, and feel good about what they have achieved. If children are encouraged and reinforced for their initiative, they begin to feel industrious and feel confident in their ability to achieve goals. If this initiative is not encouraged but instead restricted, children begin to feel inferior, doubting their abilities, and failing to reach their potential.

Identity Versus Role Confusion

During adolescence, the transition from childhood to adulthood is most important. Children are becoming more independent, and begin to look at the future in terms of career, relationships, families, housing, and so on. During this period, they explore possibilities and begin to form their own identities based upon the outcome of their explorations. This sense of who they are can be hindered, which results in a sense of confusion ("I don't know what I want to be when I grow up") about themselves and their role in the world.

Intimacy Versus Isolation

In young adulthood, individuals begin to share themselves more intimately with others and explore relationships leading toward longer term commitments with others outside the family. Successful completion can lead to comfortable relationships and a sense of commitment, safety, and care within a relationship. Avoiding intimacy and fearing commitment and relationships can lead to isolation, loneliness, and sometimes depression.

Generativity Versus Stagnation

During middle adulthood, individuals establish careers, settle down within relationships, begin families, and develop a sense of being a part of the bigger picture. They give back to society through raising children, being productive at work, and becoming involved in community activities and organizations. By failing to achieve these objectives, individuals become stagnant and feel unproductive.

Ego Integrity Versus Despair

As individuals grow older and become senior citizens, they tend to slow down and explore life as retired people. It is during this time that they contemplate accomplishments and are able to develop a sense of integrity if they are satisfied with the progression of their lives. If they see their lives as being unproductive and failing to accomplish life goals, they become dissatisfied with life and develop despair, often leading to depression and hopelessness.

On a micro level, social development is learning how to behave and interact well with others. Social development relies on emotional development or learning how to manage feelings so they are productive and not counterproductive.

On a macro level, social development is about a commitment that development processes need to benefit people, particularly, but not only, the poor. It also recognizes the way people interact in groups and society, and the norms that facilitate such interaction.

Social development implies a change in social institutions. Progress toward an inclusive society, for example, implies that individuals treat each other fairly in their daily lives, whether in the family, workplace, or public office. Social cohesion is enhanced when peaceful and safe environments within neighborhoods and communities are created. Social accountability exists to the extent that individuals' voices are expressed and heard. Reforms aimed at improving rights and more participatory governance are part of the process by which institutional change is achieved.

Emotional Development

Emotional milestones are often harder to pinpoint than signs of physical development. This area emphasizes many skills that increase self-awareness and self-regulation. Social skills and emotional development are reflected in the ability to pay attention, make transitions from one activity to another, and cooperate with others.

During childhood, there is a lot happening during playtime. Children are lifting, dropping, looking, pouring, bouncing, hiding, building, knocking down, and more. Children are busy learning when they are playing. Play is the true work of childhood.

During play, children are also learning that they are liked and fun to be around. These experiences give them the self-confidence they need to build loving and supportive relationships all their lives.

Cognitive Development

Cognitive development focuses on development in terms of information processing, conceptual resources, perceptual skill, language learning, and other aspects of brain development. It is the emergence of the ability to think and understand.

A major controversy in cognitive development has been "nature and nurture," that is, the question of whether cognitive development is mainly determined by a client's innate qualities ("nature"), or by his or her personal experiences ("nurture"). However, it is now recognized by most experts that this is a false dichotomy: There is overwhelming evidence from biological and behavioral sciences that, from the earliest points in development, gene activity interacts with events and experiences in the environment.

There are six levels of cognition:

1. *Knowledge*: rote memorization, recognition, or recall of facts
2. *Comprehension*: understanding what the facts mean
3. *Application*: correct use of the facts, rules, or ideas
4. *Analysis*: breaking down information into component parts
5. *Synthesis*: combination of facts, ideas, or information to make a new whole
6. *Evaluation*: judging or forming an opinion about the information or situation

Ideally, in order for a client to learn, there should be objectives at each of these levels. Clients may have goals to learn in any of three domains of development:

1. *Cognitive*: mental skills (knowledge)
2. *Affective*: growth in feelings or emotional areas (attitude or self)
3. *Psychomotor*: manual or physical skills (skills)

Jean Piaget was a developmental psychologist best known for his theory of cognitive development. His stages address the acquisition of knowledge and how humans come to gradually acquire it. Piaget's theory holds that children learn though interaction with the environment and others.

Piaget also developed a theory of moral development, but the work by Lawrence Kohlberg is best known in this area. He agreed with Piaget's theory of moral development in principle, but wanted to develop the ideas further.

Stage	Age	Characteristics
1. Sensorimotor	0–2 years	a. Retains image of objects b. Develops primitive logic in manipulating objects c. Begins intentional actions d. Play is imitative e. Signals meaning—infant invests meaning in event (i.e., babysitter arriving means mother is leaving) f. Symbol meaning (language) begins in last part of stage

(continued)

Stage	Age	Characteristics
2. Preoperational	2–7 years	a. Progress from concrete to abstract thinking b. Can comprehend past, present, future c. Night terrors d. Acquires words and symbols e. Magical thinking f. Thinking is not generalized g. Thinking is concrete, irreversible, egocentric h. Cannot see another point of view i. Thinking is centered on one detail or event Imaginary friends often emerge during this stage and may last into elementary school. Although children do interact with them, most know that their friends are not real and only pretend they are real. Thus, having an imaginary friend in childhood does not indicate the presence of a disorder. It is a normal part of development and social workers should normalize behavior with parents who are distressed about this activity during this developmental stage.
3. Concrete Operations	7–11 years	a. Beginnings of abstract thought b. Plays games with rules c. Cause and effect relationship understood d. Logical implications are understood e. Thinking is independent of experience f. Thinking is reversible g. Rules of logic are developed
4. Formal Operations	11 through maturity	a. Higher level of abstraction b. Planning for future c. Thinks hypothetically d. Assumes adult roles and responsibilities

Kohlberg believed that moral development parallels cognitive development. Kohlberg's theory holds that moral reasoning, which is the basis for ethical behavior, has six identifiable developmental constructive stages—each more adequate at responding to moral dilemmas than the last. Kohlberg suggested that the higher stages of moral development provide the person with greater capacities or abilities in terms of decision making and that these stages allow people to handle increasingly complex dilemmas. He grouped his six stages of moral reasoning into three major levels. A person must pass through each successive stage of moral development without skipping a stage.

Level	Age	Stage	Orientation
Preconventional	Elementary school level (before age 9)	1	Child obeys an authority figure out of fear of punishment. Obedience/ punishment.
Conventional (follow stereotypic norms of morality)	Early adolescence	2	Child acts acceptably as it is in her or his best interests. Conforms to rules to receive rewards.
		3	Person acts to gain approval from others. "Good boy/good girl" orientation.
		4	Obeys laws and fulfills obligations and duties to maintain social system. Rules are rules. Avoids censure and guilt.
Postconventional (this level is not reached by most adults)	Adult	5	Genuine interest in welfare of others; concerned with individual rights and being morally right.
		6	Guided by individual principles based on broad, universal ethical principles. Concern for larger universal issues of morality.

Learning theory is a conceptual framework describing how information is absorbed, processed, and retained during learning. Cognitive, emotional, and environmental influences, as well as prior experience, all play a part in how understanding, or a worldview, is acquired or changed, as well as how knowledge and skills are retained.

There are many learning theories but all can be conceptualized as fitting into four distinct orientations:

1. Behaviorist (Pavlov, Skinner)—learning is viewed through change in behavior and the stimuli in the external environment are the locus of learning. Social workers aim to change the external environment in order to bring about desired change.

2. Cognitive (Piaget)—learning is viewed through internal mental processes (including insight, information processing, memory, and perception) and the locus of learning is internal cognitive structures. Social workers aim to develop opportunities to foster capacity and skills to improve learning.

3. Humanistic (Maslow)—learning is viewed as a person's activities aimed at reaching his or her full potential, and the locus of learning is

in meeting cognitive and other needs. Social workers aim to develop the whole person.

4. Social/Situational (Bandura)—learning is obtained between people and their environment and their interactions and observations in social contexts. Social workers establish opportunities for conversation and participation to occur.

Behavioral Development

Behavioral theories suggest that personality is a result of interaction between the individual and the environment. Behavioral theorists study observable and measurable behaviors, rejecting theories that take internal thoughts and feelings into account.

These theories represent the systematic principles of learning to the analysis and treatment of behaviors. Behaviors determine feelings. Thus, changing behaviors will also change or eliminate undesired feelings. The goal is to modify behavior.

The focus is on observable behavior—a target symptom, a problem behavior, or an environmental condition, rather than on the personality of a client.

There are two fundamental classes of behavior: respondent and operant.

1. Respondent: involuntary behavior (anxiety, sexual response) that is automatically elicited by certain behavior. A stimulus elicits a response.

2. Operant: voluntary behavior (walking, talking) that is controlled by its consequences in the environment.

Best known applications of behavior modification are Sexual Dysfunctions, phobic disorders, compulsive behaviors (i.e., overeating, smoking), and training of persons with Intellectual Disabilities and/or Autism Spectrum Disorder.

It is impractical for those using behavior modification to observe behavior when clients are not in residential inpatient settings offering 24-hour care. Thus, social workers train clients to observe and monitor their own behaviors. For example, clients can monitor their food intake or how many cigarettes they smoke. Client self-monitoring has advantages (i.e., inexpensive, practical, and therapeutic) and disadvantages (i.e., clients can collect inadequate and inaccurate information or can resist collecting any at all).

There are several behavioral paradigms.

A. RESPONDENT OR CLASSICAL CONDITIONING (Pavlov): Learning occurs as a result of pairing previously neutral (conditioned) stimulus with an unconditioned (involuntary) stimulus so that the conditioned stimulus eventually elicits the response normally elicited by the unconditioned stimulus.

Unconditioned Stimulus ⟶ Unconditioned Response

Unconditioned Stimulus + Conditioned Stimulus ⟶ Unconditioned Response

Conditioned Stimulus ⟶ Conditioned Response

B. OPERANT CONDITIONING (B. F. Skinner): Antecedent events or stimuli precede behaviors, which, in turn, are followed by consequences. Consequences that increase the occurrence of the behavior are referred to as reinforcing consequences; consequences that decrease the occurrence of the behavior are referred to as punishing consequences. Reinforcement aims to increase behavior frequency, whereas punishment aims to decrease it.

Antecedent ⟶ Response/Behavior ⟶ Consequence

Operant Techniques:

1. **Positive reinforcement:** Increases probability that behavior will occur—praising, giving tokens, or otherwise rewarding positive behavior.

2. **Negative reinforcement:** Behavior increases because a negative (aversive) stimulus is removed (i.e., remove shock).

3. **Positive punishment:** Presentation of undesirable stimulus following a behavior for the purpose of decreasing or eliminating that behavior (i.e., hitting, shocking).

4. **Negative punishment:** Removal of a desirable stimulus following a behavior for the purpose of decreasing or eliminating that behavior (i.e., removing something positive, such as a token or dessert).

Specific Behavioral Terms:

1. **Aversion therapy:** Any treatment aimed at reducing the attractiveness of a stimulus or a behavior by repeated pairing of it with an aversive stimulus. **An example of this is treating alcoholism with Antabuse.**

2. **Biofeedback:** Behavior training program that teaches a person how to control certain functions such as heart rate, blood pressure, temperature, and muscular tension. Biofeedback is often used for Attention-Deficit/Hyperactivity Disorder (ADHD) and Anxiety Disorders.

3. **Extinction:** Withholding a reinforcer that normally follows a behavior. Behavior that fails to produce reinforcement will eventually cease.

4. **Flooding:** A treatment procedure in which a client's anxiety is extinguished by prolonged real or imagined exposure to high-intensity feared stimuli.

5. **In vivo desensitization:** Pairing and movement through a hierarchy of anxiety, from least to most anxiety-provoking situations; takes place in "real" setting.

6. **Modeling:** Method of instruction that involves an individual (the model) demonstrating the behavior to be acquired by a client.

7. **Rational emotive therapy (RET):** A cognitively oriented therapy in which a social worker seeks to change a client's irrational beliefs by argument, persuasion, and rational reevaluation and by teaching a client to counter self-defeating thinking with new, nondistressing self-statements.

8. **Shaping:** Method used to train a new behavior by prompting and reinforcing successive approximations of the desired behavior.

9. **Systematic desensitization:** An anxiety-inhibiting response cannot occur at the same time as the anxiety response. Anxiety-producing stimulus is paired with relaxation-producing response so that eventually an anxiety-producing stimulus produces a relaxation response. At each step a client's reaction of fear or dread is overcome by pleasant feelings engendered as the new behavior is reinforced by receiving a reward. The reward could be a compliment, a gift, or relaxation.

10. **Time out:** Removal of something desirable—negative punishment technique.

11. **Token economy:** A client receives tokens as reinforcement for performing specified behaviors. The tokens function as currency within the environment and can be exchanged for desired goods, services, or privileges.

THE INDICATORS OF NORMAL AND ABNORMAL PHYSICAL, COGNITIVE, EMOTIONAL, AND SEXUAL DEVELOPMENT THROUGHOUT THE LIFESPAN

Human growth, development, and learning become progressively complex over time and are influenced through a variety of experiences and interactions. Growth, development, and learning proceed in predictable patterns reflecting increasingly complex levels of organization across the life course. Each developmental stage has distinctive characteristics; however, each builds from the experiences of earlier stages. The domains of development are integrated within the child, so when one area is affected, other areas are also affected. Development proceeds at varying rates from child to child, as well as across developmental domains for individual children, reflecting the unique nature of each. Because growth and development are generally predictable, social workers should know the milestones of healthy development and the signs of potential delay or disability.

Child Development

Child development refers to the physical, mental, and socioemotional changes that occur between birth and the end of adolescence, as a child progresses from dependency to increasing autonomy. It is a continuous process with a predictable sequence, yet having a unique course. Individuals do not progress at the same rate, and each stage is affected by the preceding types of development. Because these developmental changes may be strongly influenced by genetic factors and events during prenatal life, genetics and prenatal development are usually included as part of the study of child development.

Infants and Toddlers (Age 0–3)

Healthy Growth and Development

- Physical—grows at a rapid rate, especially brain size
- Mental—learns through senses, exploring, playing, communicates by crying, babbling, then "baby talk," simple sentences
- Social–Emotional—seeks to build trust in others, dependent, beginning to develop a sense of self

Key Health Care Issues

- Communication—provide security, physical closeness; promote healthy parent–child bonds
- Health—keep immunizations/checkups on schedule; provide proper nutrition, sleep, skin care, oral health, routine screenings
- Safety—ensure a safe environment for exploring, playing, sleeping

Examples of age-specific care for infants and toddlers:

- Involve child and parent(s) in care during feeding, diapering, and bathing
- Provide safe toys and opportunities for play
- Encourage child to communicate—smile, talk softly to him or her
- Help parent(s) learn about proper child care

Young Children (Age 4–6)

Healthy Growth and Development

- Physical—grows at a slower rate; improving motor skills; dresses self, toilet trained
- Mental—begins to use symbols; improving memory; vivid imagination, fears; likes stories
- Social–Emotional—identifies with parent(s); becomes more independent; sensitive to others' feelings

Key Health Care Issues

- Communication—give praise, rewards, clear rules
- Health—keep immunizations/checkups on schedule; promote healthy habits (good nutrition, personal hygiene, etc.)
- Safety—promote safety habits (use bike helmets, safety belts, etc.)

Examples of age-specific care for young children:

- Involve parent(s) and child in care—let child make some food choices
- Use toys and games to teach child and reduce fear
- Encourage child to ask questions, play with others, and talk about feelings
- Help parent(s) teach child safety rules

Older Children (Age 7–12)

Healthy Growth and Development

- Physical—grows slowly until a "spurt" at puberty
- Mental—understands cause and effect, can read, write, do math; active, eager learner
- Social–Emotional—develops greater sense of self; focuses on school activities, negotiates for greater independence

Key Health Care Issues

- Communication—help child to feel competent, useful
- Health—keep immunizations/checkups on schedule; give information on alcohol, tobacco, other drugs, sexuality
- Safety—promote safety habits (playground safety, resolving conflicts peacefully, etc.)

Examples of age-specific care for older children:

- Allow child to make some care decisions (in which arm do you want vaccination?)
- Build self-esteem—ask child to help you do a task, recognize his or her achievements, and so on
- Guide child in making healthy, safe lifestyle choices
- Help parent(s) talk with child about peer pressure, sexuality, alcohol, tobacco, and other drugs

Adolescent Development

The development of children ages 13 through 18 years old is a critical time as children develop the ability to understand abstract ideas, such as higher math concepts, and develop moral philosophies, including rights and privileges, and move toward a more mature sense of themselves and their purpose.

Healthy Growth and Development

- Physical—grows in spurts; matures physically; able to reproduce
- Mental—becomes an abstract thinker (goes beyond simple solutions, can consider many options, etc.); chooses own values
- Social–Emotional—develops own identity; builds close relationships; tries to balance peer group with family interests; concerned about appearances, challenges authority

Key Health Care Issues

- Communication—provide acceptance, privacy; build teamwork, respect
- Health—encourage regular checkups; promote sexual responsibility; advise against substance abuse; update immunizations
- Safety—discourage risk-taking (promote safe driving, violence prevention, etc.)

Examples of age-specific care for adolescents:

- Treat more as an adult than child—avoid authoritarian approaches
- Show respect—be considerate of how treatment may affect relationships
- Guide teen in making positive lifestyle choices (i.e., correct misinformation from teen's peers)
- Encourage open communication between parent(s), teen, and peers

Adult Development

Adult development refers to the changes that occur in biological, psychological, and interpersonal domains of human life from the end of adolescence until the end of life. These changes may be gradual or rapid, and can reflect positive, negative, or no change from previous levels of functioning.

Young Adults (Age 18–35)
Healthy Growth and Development

- Physical—reaches physical and sexual maturity, nutritional needs are for maintenance, not growth
- Mental—acquires new skills, information; uses these to solve problems
- Social–Emotional—seeks closeness with others; sets career goals; chooses lifestyle, community; starts own family

Key Health Care Issues

- Communication—be supportive and honest; respect personal values
- Health—encourage regular checkups; promote healthy lifestyle (proper nutrition, exercise, weight, etc.); inform about health risks (heart disease, cancer, etc.); update immunizations
- Safety—provide information on hazards at home, work

Examples of age-specific care for young adults:

- Support the person in making health care decisions
- Encourage healthy and safe habits at work and home
- Recognize commitments to family, career, community (time, money, etc.)

Middle Age Adults (Age 36–64)
Healthy Growth and Development

- Physical—begins to age; experiences menopause (women); may develop chronic health problems
- Mental—uses life experiences to learn, create, solve problems
- Social–Emotional—hopes to contribute to future generations; stays productive, avoids feeling "stuck" in life; balances dreams with reality; plans retirement; may care for children and parents

Key Health Care Issues

- Communication—keep a hopeful attitude; focus on strengths, not limitations
- Health—encourage regular checkups and preventive exams; address age-related changes; monitor health risks; update immunizations
- Safety—address age-related changes (effects on sense, reflexes, etc.)

Examples of age-specific care for middle adults:

- Address worries about future—encourage talking about feelings, plans, and so on
- Recognize the person's physical, mental, and social abilities/contributions
- Help with plans for a healthy active retirement

Older Adults (Age 65–79)

Healthy Growth and Development

- Physical—ages gradually; natural decline in some physical abilities, senses
- Mental—continues to be an active learner, thinker; memory skills may start to decline
- Social–Emotional—takes on new roles (grandparent, widow or widower, etc.); balances independence, dependence; reviews life

Key Health Care Issues

- Communication—give respect, prevent isolation, encourage acceptance of aging
- Health—monitor health closely; promote physical, mental, social activity; guard against depression, apathy; update immunizations
- Safety—promote home safety; especially preventing falls

Examples of age-specific care for older adults:

- Encourage the person to talk about feelings of loss, grief, and achievements
- Provide information, materials, and so on, to make medication use and home safe
- Provide support for coping with any impairments (avoid making assumptions about loss of abilities)
- Encourage social activity with peers, as a volunteer, and so on

Elders (Age 80 and Older)

Healthy Growth and Development

- Physical—continues to decline in physical abilities; at increasing risk for chronic illness, major health problems
- Mental—continues to learn; memory skills and/or speed of learning may decline; confusion often signals illness or medication problem

■ Social–Emotional—accepts end of life and personal losses; lives as independently as possible

Key Health Care Issues

■ Communication—encourage the person to express feelings, thoughts, avoid despair; use humor, stay positive

■ Health—monitor health closely, promote self-care; ensure proper nutrition, activity level, rest; reduce stress, update immunizations

■ Safety—prevent injury, ensure safe living environment

Examples of age-specific care for adults ages 80 and older:

■ Encourage independence—provide physical, mental, and social activities

■ Support end-of-life decisions—provide information, resources, and so on

■ Assist the person in self-care—promote medication safety; provide safety grips, ramps, and so on

THEORIES OF SEXUAL DEVELOPMENT THROUGHOUT THE LIFESPAN

Many people cannot imagine that everyone—babies, children, teens, adults, and older adults—are sexual beings. Some inappropriately believe that sexual activity is reserved for early and middle adulthood. Teens often feel that adults are too old for sexual intercourse. Sexuality, though, is much more than sexual intercourse. Humans are sexual beings throughout life.

Sexuality in infants and toddlers—Children are sexual even before birth. Males can have erections while still in the uterus, and some boys are born with an erection. Infants touch and rub their genitals because it provides pleasure. Little boys and girls can experience orgasm from masturbation, although boys will not ejaculate until puberty. By about age 2, children know their own gender. They are aware of differences in the genitals of males and females and in how males and females urinate.

Sexuality in children (age 3–7)—Preschool children are interested in everything about their world, including sexuality. They may practice urinating in different positions. They are highly affectionate and enjoy hugging other children and adults. They begin to be more social and may imitate adult social and sexual behaviors, such as holding hands and kissing. Many young children play "doctor" during this stage, looking at other children's genitals and showing theirs. This is normal curiosity. By age 5 or 6, most children become more modest and private about dressing and bathing.

Children of this age are aware of marriage and understand living together, based on their family experience. They may role play about being married or having a partner while they "play house." Most young children talk about marrying and/or living with a person they love when they get older. Most sex play at this age happens because of curiosity.

Sexuality in preadolescent youth (age 8–12)—Puberty, the time when the body matures, begins between the ages of 9 and 12 for most children. Girls begin to grow breast buds and pubic hair as early as 9 or 10. Boys' development of the penis and testicles usually begins between 10 and 11. Children become more self-conscious about their bodies at this age and often feel uncomfortable undressing in front of others, even a same-sex parent.

Masturbation increases during these years. Preadolescent boys and girls do not usually have much sexual experience, but they often have many questions. They usually have heard about sexual intercourse, homosexuality, rape, and incest, and they want to know more about all these things. The idea of actually having sexual intercourse, however, is unpleasant to most preadolescent boys and girls.

Same-gender sexual behavior can occur at this age. Boys and girls tend to play with friends of the same gender and are likely to explore sexuality with them. Same-gender sexual behavior is unrelated to a child's sexual orientation.

Some group dating occurs at this age. Preadolescents may attend parties that have guests of both genders, and they may dance and play kissing games. By age 12 or 13, some young adolescents may pair off and begin dating and/ or "making out." Young women are usually older when they begin voluntary sexual intercourse. However, many very young teens do practice sexual behaviors other than vaginal intercourse, such as petting to orgasm and oral sex.

Sexuality in adolescent youth (age 13–19)—Once youth have reached puberty and beyond, they experience increased interest in romantic and sexual relationships and in genital sex behaviors. As youth mature, they experience strong emotional attachments to romantic partners and find it natural to express their feelings within sexual relationships. There is no way to predict how a particular teenager will act sexually. Overall, most adolescents explore relationships with one another, fall in and out of love, and participate in sexual intercourse before the age of 20.

Adult sexuality—Adult sexual behaviors are extremely varied and, in most cases, remain part of an adult's life until death. At around age 50, women experience menopause, which affects their sexuality in that their ovaries no longer release eggs and their bodies no longer produce estrogen. They may experience several physical changes. Vaginal walls become thinner and vaginal intercourse may be painful because there is less vaginal lubrication and the entrance to the vagina becomes smaller. Many women use estrogen replacement therapy to relieve physical and emotional side effects of menopause. Use of vaginal lubricants can also make vaginal intercourse easier. Most women are able to have pleasurable sexual intercourse and to experience orgasm for their entire lives.

Adult men also experience some changes in their sexuality, but not at such a predictable time as with menopause in women. Men's testicles slow testosterone production after age 25 or so. Erections may occur more slowly once testosterone production slows. Men also become less able to have another erection after an orgasm and may take up to 24 hours to achieve and sustain another erection. The amount of semen released during ejaculation also decreases, but men are capable of fathering a baby even when they are in their 80s and 90s. Some older men develop an enlarged or cancerous prostate gland. If the doctors deem it necessary to remove the prostate gland, a man's ability to have an erection or an orgasm is normally unaffected.

Although adult men and women go through some sexual changes as they age, they do not lose their desire or their ability for sexual expression. Even among the very old, the need for touch and intimacy remains, although the desire and ability to have sexual intercourse may lessen.

THEORIES OF SPIRITUAL DEVELOPMENT THROUGHOUT THE LIFESPAN

Many models attempt to explain the impact of spirituality and/or religious beliefs on behavior. Many of them describe this impact along a continuum as follows, with some individuals changing during their life course and others remaining at the same point.

Individuals are unwilling to accept a will greater than their own.

Behavior is chaotic, disordered, and reckless. Individuals tend to defy and disobey, and are extremely egoistic. They lack empathy for others. Very young children can be at this stage. Adults who do not move beyond this point in the continuum may engage in criminal activity because they cannot obey rules.

Individuals have blind faith in authority figures and see the world as divided simply into good and evil and right and wrong.

Children who learn to obey their parents and other authority figures move to this point in the continuum. Many "religious" people who have blind faith in a spiritual being and do not question its existence may also be at this point. Individuals who are good, law-abiding citizens may never move further in the continuum.

Scientific skepticism and questioning are critical, because an individual does not accept things on faith, but only if convinced logically.

Many people working in a scientific and technical field may question spiritual or supernatural forces because they are difficult to measure or prove scientifically. Those who do engage in this skepticism move away from the simple, official doctrines.

The individual starts enjoying the mystery and beauty of nature and existence.

The individual develops a deeper understanding of good and evil, forgiveness and mercy, compassion and love. Religiousness and spirituality differ significantly from other points in the continuum and things are not accepted on blind faith or out of fear. The individual does not judge people harshly or seek to inflict punishment on them for their transgressions. This is the stage of loving others as one loves oneself, losing attachment to ego, and forgiving enemies.

Basic principles of all models move from the "egocentric," which are associated particularly with childhood, to "conformist," and eventually to "integration" or "universal."

There is a positive relationship between spirituality and overall mental health, as well as with regard to certain problems or disorders. For example, there is a positive association between church attendance and lower levels of depression. Similar relationships have been found between spirituality and anxiety or stress. There may also be a positive effect on Posttraumatic Stress Disorder (PTSD) because religion and spirituality may be beneficial in dealing with the aftermath of trauma. In these instances, clients may have religious openness and a readiness to face existential questions. In addition, traumatic experiences can lead to a deepening of religion or spirituality.

Those who share the same religious values as clients and their families may also serve as cohesive support networks. These religious and spiritual communities can provide tangible assistance in addition to being psychologically viewed by clients as supportive.

Some of the mechanisms by which spirituality assists include enhanced coping styles and locus of control, as well as providing social supports and a social network. Clients who are spiritual may use a more collaborative approach when coping (i.e., relying on a higher being to cope with stress), which is associated with the greatest improvement in mental health. Spirituality may also allow clients to reframe or reinterpret events that are seen as uncontrollable, in such a way as to make them less stressful and/or more meaningful.

Lastly, emotions encouraged in many spiritual traditions, including hope, contentment, love, and forgiveness, may be beneficial to clients in promoting positive mental health.

THEORIES OF RACIAL, ETHNIC, AND CULTURAL DEVELOPMENT THROUGHOUT THE LIFESPAN

Ethnicity refers to the idea that one is a member of a particular cultural, national, or racial group that may share culture, religion, race, language, or place of origin. Two people can share the same race but have different ethnicities.

The meaning of **race** is not fixed; it is related to a particular social, historical, and geographic context. The way races are classified has changed in the public mind over time; for example, at one time racial classifications were based on ethnicity or nationality, religion, or minority language groups. Today, society classifies people into different races primarily based on skin color.

Cultural identity is often defined as the identity of a group or culture of an individual who is influenced by his or her self-identification with that group or culture. Certain ethnic and racial identities may also bestow privilege.

Cultural, racial, and ethnic identities are important. They may instill feelings of shared commitment and values and a sense of belonging that may otherwise be missing.

Cultural, racial, and ethnic identities are passed from one generation to the next through customs, traditions, language, religious practice, and cultural values. Current events, mainstream media, and popular literature also influence cultural, racial, and ethnic identities.

Cultural, racial, and ethnic identities play a particularly large role among minority youth because they experience the contrasting and dominant culture of the majority ethnic group. Youth who belong to the majority ethnic culture may not even recognize or acknowledge their cultural, racial, and ethnic identities.

Following is a three-stage model for adolescent cultural and ethnic identity development. These stages do not correspond to specific ages, but can occur at any time. Individuals may spend their entire lives at a particular stage.

- The first stage, **unexamined cultural, racial, and ethnic identity**, is characterized by a lack of exploration of culture, race, and ethnicity and cultural, racial, and ethnic differences—they are rather taken for granted without much critical thinking. This is usually the stage reserved for childhood when cultural, racial, and ethnic ideas provided by parents, the community, or the media are easily accepted. Children at this stage tend not to be interested in culture, race, or ethnicity and are generally ready to take on the opinions of others.

- The second stage of the model is referred to as the **cultural, racial, and ethnic identity search** and is characterized by the exploration and questioning of culture, race, and ethnicity in order to learn more about them and to understand the implications of belonging. During this stage, there is questioning of where beliefs come from and why they are held. For some, this stage may arise from a turning point in their lives or from a growing awareness of other cultures, races, and ethnicities. It can also be a very emotional time.

- Finally, the third stage of the model is **cultural, racial, and ethnic identity achievement**. Ideally, people at this stage have a clear sense of their cultural, racial, and ethnic identity and are able to successfully navigate it in the contemporary world, which is undoubtedly very interconnected and intercultural. The acceptance of cultural, racial, and ethnic identity may play a significant role in important life decisions and choices, influencing attitudes and behavior. This usually leads to an increase in self-confidence and positive psychological development.

The classic model of cultural, racial, and ethnic identity development refers to identity statuses rather than stages, because stages imply a linear progression of steps that may not occur for all.

- **Preencounter:** At this point, the client may not be consciously aware of his or her culture, race, or ethnicity and how it may affect his or her life.

- **Encounter:** A client has an encounter that provokes thought about the role of cultural, racial, and ethnic identification in his or her life. This may be a negative or positive experience related to culture, race, and ethnicity. For minorities, this experience is often a negative one in which they experience discrimination for the first time.

- **Immersion–Emersion:** After an encounter that forces a client to confront cultural, racial, and ethnic identity, a period of exploration follows. A client may search for information and will also learn through interaction with others from the same cultural, racial, or ethnic groups.

- **Internalization and Commitment:** At this point, a client has developed a secure sense of identity and is comfortable socializing both within and outside the group with which he or she identifies.

THE EFFECTS OF PHYSICAL, MENTAL, AND COGNITIVE DISABILITIES THROUGHOUT THE LIFESPAN

The impacts of disabilities on human development are extremely varied depending upon the manifestations of the disability and when it occurs during the life course. Some disabilities are short-term, whereas others are lifelong. Critical to mitigating the negative impacts is the development of coping skills that strengthen a client's ability to deal with his or her limitations. Support (formal and informal) is also critical.

There may also be positive effects of disabilities because familial bonds may be stronger or individuals may develop skills to compensate for other tasks that cannot be performed.

Disability is a normal phenomenon in the sense that it exists in all societies. Although medical explanations remain primary in defining disability, the history of disability took an important turn in the latter half of the 20th century that has significantly influenced responses to it. Disability rights scholars and activists rejected the medical explanation for disability, since such explanations of permanent deficit did not advance social justice, equality of opportunity, and rights as citizens. Rather, these leaders proposed the intolerance and rigidity of social institutions, rather than medical conditions, as the explanation for disability. Words such as "inclusion," "participation," and "nondiscrimination" were introduced into the disability literature and reflected the notions that people who did not fit within the majority were disabled by stigma, prejudice, marginalization, segregation, and exclusion. This notion of disability requires the modification of societal structures to include all, rather than "fixing" individuals with varying abilities.

BASIC HUMAN NEEDS

Maslow's hierarchy of needs implies that clients are motivated to meet certain needs. When one need is fulfilled, a client seeks to fulfill the next one, and so on. This hierarchy is often depicted as a pyramid. This five-stage model can be divided into basic (or deficiency) needs (i.e., physiological, safety, social, and esteem) and growth needs (self-actualization).

- Deficiency needs—also known as D-Needs
- Growth needs—also known as "being needs" or B-Needs

Deficiency Needs

- Physiological
- Safety
- Social
- Esteem

Maslow called these needs "deficiency needs" because he felt that these needs arise due to deprivation. The satisfaction of these needs helps to "avoid" unpleasant feelings or consequence.

Growth Needs

- Self-actualization

These needs fall on the highest level of Maslow's pyramid. They come from a place of growth rather than from a place of "lacking."

A client must satisfy lower-level basic needs before moving on to meet higher-level growth needs. After meeting lower levels of needs, a client can reach the highest level of self-actualization, but few people do so.

Every client is capable and has the desire to move up the hierarchy toward a level of self-actualization. Unfortunately, progress is often disrupted by failure to meet lower level needs. Life experiences, including divorce and loss of job, may cause a client to fluctuate between levels of the hierarchy.

Physiological needs: These needs maintain the physical organism. These are biological needs such as food, water, oxygen, and constant body temperature. If a person is deprived of these needs, he or she will die.

Safety needs: There is a need to feel safe from harm, danger, or threat of destruction. Clients need regularity and some predictability.

Social needs: Friendship, intimacy, affection, and love are needed—from one's work group, family, friends, or romantic relationships.

Esteem needs: People need a stable, firmly based level of self-respect and respect from others.

Self-actualization needs: There is a need to be oneself, to act consistently with whom one is. Self-actualization is an ongoing process. It involves developing potential, becoming, and being what one is capable of being. It makes possible true objectivity—dealing with the world as it is, rather than as one needs it to be. You are free to really do what you want to do. There are moments when everything is right (peak experience); a glimmer of what it is like to be complete. One is in a position to find one's true calling (i.e., being an artist, writer, musician). Only 1% of the population consistently operates at this level.

On the examination, Maslow's hierarchy of needs is often not explicitly asked about, but it can be applied when asked about the order of prioritizing problems or issues with a client. A client with an acute medical problem should focus on getting a medical evaluation first; a victim of domestic violence should prioritize medical and safety issues; and a refugee must initially meet basic survival needs (shelter, food, income, clothing, etc.) before working on fulfilling higher level needs.

THE PRINCIPLES OF ATTACHMENT AND BONDING

Attachment theory originated with the seminal work of John Bowlby. Bowlby defined attachment as a lasting psychological connectedness between human beings that can be understood within an *evolutionary* context in which a caregiver provides safety and security for a child. Bowlby suggests that children come into the world biologically preprogrammed to form attachments with others, because this will help them to survive. They initially form only one primary attachment (monotropy) and this attachment figure acts as a secure base for exploring the world. Disrupting this attachment process can have severe consequences because the critical period for developing attachment is within the first 5 years of life.

There is another major theory of attachment that suggests attachment is a set of *learned behaviors*. The basis for the learning of attachments is the provision of food. A child will initially form an attachment to whoever feeds it. This child learns to associate the feeder (usually the mother) with the comfort of being fed and, through the process of classical conditioning, comes to find contact with the mother comforting. The child also finds that certain behaviors (i.e., crying, smiling) bring desirable responses from others and through the process of operant conditioning learns to repeat these behaviors in order to get the things he or she wants.

In both of these theoretical approaches, parents have important impacts on their children's attachment system. Insecure attachment systems have been linked to psychiatric disorders and can result in clients reacting in a hostile and rejecting manner as children or adults.

These theories are, however, criticized because there are cultural influences that may impact on attachment and the ways in which children interact with caregivers. Much of Bowlby and others' work has not fully considered these differences.

THE EFFECT OF AGING ON BIOPSYCHOSOCIAL FUNCTIONING

The process of human aging is complex and individualized, causing biological, psychological, and social changes. Biological aging is characterized by progressive age-changes in metabolism, organ functioning, and so on. It is a natural and irreversible process with biological changes that occur with age in the human body affecting mood, attitude, and social activity.

Social work with older adults is based on comprehensive assessments aimed at gathering information about the quality of their biopsychosocial functioning. Social workers evaluate older adults' capacity to function effectively in their environments and determine what resources are needed to improve interpersonal functioning. The purpose of biopsychosocial assessments is to gather information on functional capacity or everyday competence— the ability of older adults to care for themselves, manage their affairs, and live independent, quality lives in their communities. Assessments may also include diagnostic medical and physical evaluations.

During the life course, many events occur in older adulthood that can affect subjective and objective well-being. Some of the most significant are the onset of voluntary or involuntary retirement, loss of a spouse, and/or onset of disability. These can have negative effects, including having a lower income and an increased likelihood of living in poverty at an older age. A client's educational level and social class before these events occurred greatly influences their impacts. Women and those from ethnic minorities are at the greatest risk for adverse outcomes.

Experiencing loss, especially later in life, has physical, psychological, and social impacts. Maintaining a proper diet, with exercise, is important throughout the life course, but especially in older adulthood. Loss can result in sadness, isolation, and a breakdown in physical or emotional support that can cause neglect in maintaining a healthy lifestyle and/or the engagement in substance use and other maladaptive behaviors. Maintaining social support is essential as loss of family and friends due to death or disability in older adulthood occurs.

Although the negative impacts of aging and/or disability have received a lot of attention, there can be positive effects as well. Becoming a grandparent and/or receiving an inheritance are positive events that can occur in older adulthood. In addition, studies have indicated that there are some positive effects of caring for adults who are older and/or those with disabilities. Families' connections can be strengthened and satisfaction from helping another can result from fulfilling these caregiving roles.

THE IMPACT OF AGING PARENTS ON ADULT CHILDREN

For social workers, there is an increasing need to provide services and supports to adult children as they become caregivers for their parents. In these new roles, adult children may need direct assistance with maintaining adequate nutrition, decent housing, economic stability, and access to appropriate medical care for both their parents and themselves. However, of even greater concern to adult children are a multitude of psychosocial stressors that come with the transitioning of roles and the expectations placed upon them. In these instances, there are often blurred familial roles, boundaries, and expectations.

The responsibility of caring for the aging parent often falls to adult children who are generally accepting of this responsibility. Their reasons for doing so may include fulfilling expectations, religious beliefs, sense of duty, financial rewards, altruism, and/or respect/love.

Adult children may need the assistance of social workers due to feelings of guilt, fatigue, sadness, anxiety, and/or frustration. These feelings are compounded when the assistance of adult children is not appreciated by their aging parents. Often adult children need help getting other family members to share the burden and/or getting their parents' affairs in order.

Seeing parents grow old forces adult children to confront feelings about their own mortality. Feelings can include denial, hostility, resentment, hatred of their parents or themselves, helplessness, fear, anger, and sadness. Clients may have any or all of these emotions at one time and the emotions may vary in range and intensity. In some instances, adult children may feel in a bind and begin to seek reasons for reducing their commitment to their older family members. A social worker can provide help in sorting out these feelings, finding their roots, and reframing them into empowerment, opportunity, and choice.

Clients may want help in areas such as communication (i.e., understanding requests for assistance/resistance of their parents), self-care (i.e., developing coping skills and attending to their own needs), and/or resource identification (i.e., finding services to assist in meeting child/parent needs).

Social workers need to be sensitive to client needs in these situations, since the transforming role of child to adult child of aging parents will most likely leave a client on shaky ground, especially if the role was not expected or anticipated. A social worker may need to act as a consultant, advocate, case manager, catalyst, broker, mediator, facilitator, instructor, mobilizer, and/or clinician in these situations as the family dynamic is complex and the needs are great.

GERONTOLOGY

Aging is scientifically defined as the accumulation of diverse deleterious changes occurring in cells and tissues with advancing age that are responsible for an increased risk of disease and death. Life expectancy is defined as the average total number of years that a human expects to live. The lengthening of life expectancy is mainly due to the elimination of most infectious diseases occurring in youth, better hygiene, and the adoption of antibiotics and vaccines.

The notion that aging requires treatment is based on the false belief that becoming old is undesirable. Aging has at times received a negative connotation and become synonymous with deterioration, approaching pathology, and death. Society should learn to value old age to the same extent as it presently values youth.

There are physical changes that naturally occur. In older adulthood, age-related changes in stamina, strength, or sensory perception may be noticed and will vary based on personal health choices, medical history, and genetics.

Social workers understand that old age is a time of continued growth and that older adults contribute significantly to their families, communities, and society. At the same time, clients face multiple biopsychosocial–spiritual–cultural challenges as they age: changes in health and physical abilities; difficulty in accessing comprehensive, affordable, and high-quality health and behavioral health care; decreased economic security; increased vulnerability to abuse and exploitation; and loss of meaningful social roles and opportunities to remain engaged in society. Social workers are well positioned and trained to support and advocate for older adults and their caregivers.

PERSONALITY THEORIES

Personality theories attempt to explain both personality characteristics and the way these characteristics develop and impact behavior/functioning. Theories that have this aim can be categorized as biological, behavioral, psychodynamic, humanist, or trait focused.

Biological

Biological theories suggest that genetics are responsible for personality. Research on heritability suggests that there is a link between genetics and personality traits.

Behavioral

Behavioral theories suggest that personality is a result of interaction between the individual and the environment. Behavioral theorists study observable and measurable behaviors, rejecting theories that take internal thoughts and feelings into account.

Psychodynamic

Psychodynamic theories emphasize the influence of the unconscious mind and childhood experiences on personality.

Humanist

Humanist theories emphasize the importance of free will and individual experience in the development of personality. Humanist theorists emphasized the concept of self-actualization, which is an innate need for personal growth that motivates behavior.

Trait

Trait theories posit that the personality is made up of a number of broad traits. A trait is basically a relatively stable characteristic that causes an individual to behave in certain ways.

THEORIES OF CONFLICT

Conflict theory, derived from the works of Karl Marx, posits that society is fragmented into groups that compete for social and economic resources.

Social order is maintained by consensus among those with the greatest political, economic, and social resources.

According to conflict theory, inequality exists because those in control of a disproportionate share of society's resources actively defend their advantages. The masses are bound by coercion by those in power. This perspective emphasizes social control, not consensus and conformity. Groups and individuals advance their own interests, struggling over control of societal resources.

There is great attention paid to class, race, and gender in this perspective since they relate to the most pertinent and enduring struggles in society.

Conflict theorists challenge the status quo, encourage social change, and believe rich and powerful people force social order on the poor and the weak. Conflict theorists note that unequal groups usually have conflicting values and agendas, causing them to compete against one another. This constant competition between groups forms the basis for the ever-changing nature of society.

FACTORS INFLUENCING SELF-IMAGE (E.G., CULTURE, RACE, RELIGION/SPIRITUALITY, AGE, DISABILITY, TRAUMA)

Self-image is how a client defines himself or herself, which is often tied to physical description (i.e., tall, thin), social roles (i.e., mother, student), personal traits (i.e., worthy, generous), and/or existential beliefs (i.e., one with the world, a spiritual being). It is how a client sees himself or herself.

Self-esteem refers to the extent to which a client accepts or approves of this definition. Self-esteem always involves a degree of evaluation that may produce positive or negative feelings. Thus, self-image and self-esteem are linked throughout the life cycle.

Clearly, age has a profound impact on behavior and attitudes. Most developmental theorists trace physical, psychosocial, and other changes across the life course, marking distinctions in these areas by age. Interestingly, though, although behavior analysts have contributed to research on aging, the focus has largely been on remedying age-related deficits, rather than a concern with aging as a developmental process. Thus, although there is much documented that confirms that behavior changes with advancing years, there is less known about the sources of those changes.

Age can influence health behaviors, social/emotional patterns, mobility, cognitive functioning, economic well-being, independence, and other areas of life. Ensuring that a client's quality of life is not adversely impacted by these changes is critical to ensuring the maintenance of a positive self-image.

Generally, self-esteem is relatively high in childhood, drops during adolescence, rises gradually throughout adulthood, and then declines sharply in old age.

Childhood: Young children have relatively high self-esteem, which gradually declines over childhood. This high self-image may be because children's self-views are unrealistically positive. As children develop cognitively, they begin to base their self-evaluations on external feedback and social comparisons, and thus form a more balanced and accurate appraisal of their academic competence, social skills, attractiveness, and other personal characteristics.

Adolescence: Self-esteem continues to decline during adolescence, perhaps due to a decrease in body image and other problems associated with puberty, as well as the increasing ability to think abstractly coupled with more academic and social challenges.

Adulthood: Self-esteem increases gradually throughout adulthood, peaking sometime around the late 60s. This increase is tied to assuming positions of power and status that might promote feelings of self-worth. Adulthood also brings an increasing level of maturity and adjustment, as well as emotional stability.

Older Adulthood: Self-esteem declines in old age, beginning to drop around age 70. This decline may be due to loss of employment due to retirement, loss of a spouse or friends, and/or health problems.

Overall, males and females follow essentially the same course during the life cycle. However, there are some interesting gender differences. Although boys and girls report similar levels of self-esteem during childhood, a gender gap emerges by adolescence, with adolescent boys having higher self-esteem than adolescent girls. This gender gap persists throughout adulthood, and then narrows and perhaps even disappears in old age.

Individuals tend to maintain their ordering relative to one another, with those who have relatively high self-esteem at one point in time tending to have relatively high self-esteem years later.

Research on self-image indicates that persons with disabilities may or may not suffer loss of self as they go through a process in which they try to operate in the same manner as they did before their impairments or as typically as possible. Central to the self-image is a client's ability to view himself or herself as a person first and the disability as just one of the characteristics in his or her personality. Hence, impairment is reduced to, or interpreted as, one characteristic that is different among several similar characteristics in a person.

PARENTING SKILLS AND CAPACITIES

Although there are very few actual cause-and-effect links between specific actions of parents and later behavior of children, there are four distinct parenting styles that seem to impact behavior later in life.

Authoritarian Parenting

Children are expected to follow the strict rules established by the parents. Failure to follow such rules usually results in punishment. Authoritarian parents fail to explain the reasoning behind these rules.

Authoritarian parenting styles generally lead to those who are obedient and proficient, but are lower in happiness, social competence, and self-esteem.

Authoritative Parenting

Like authoritarian parents, those with an authoritative parenting style establish rules and guidelines that their children are expected to follow. However, this parenting style is much more democratic. Authoritative parents are responsive to their children and willing to listen to questions. When children fail to meet the expectations, these parents are more nurturing and forgiving rather than punishing.

Authoritative parenting styles generally tend to result in those who are happy, capable, and successful.

Permissive Parenting

Permissive parents have very few demands on their children. These parents rarely discipline their children and are generally nurturing and communicative with their children, often taking on the status of a friend more than that of a parent.

Permissive parenting often results in children who rank low in happiness and self-regulation, experiencing problems with authority and tending to perform poorly in school.

Uninvolved Parenting

An uninvolved parenting style is characterized by few demands, low responsiveness, and little communication. Although these parents fulfill basic needs, they are generally detached from their children's lives.

Those who have experienced uninvolved parenting styles rank lowest across all life domains. They tend to lack self-control, have low self-esteem, and are less competent than their peers.

FEMINIST THEORY

Feminist theory analyzes the status of women and men in society with the purpose of using that knowledge to better women's lives. Feminist theorists question the differences between women and men, including how race, class, ethnicity, sexuality, nationality, and age intersect with gender. Themes that are studied include discrimination, objectification (especially sexual objectification), oppression, stereotyping, and so on. Feminist theory is used in the fields of social work, sociology, economics, education, and others.

Feminism is a political, cultural, or economic movement aimed at establishing equal rights and legal protection for women.

ADDICTION THEORIES AND CONCEPTS

There are many risk factors for alcohol and other drug abuse, including, but not limited to:

1. *Family*: Parents, siblings, and/or spouse use substances; family dysfunction (i.e., inconsistent discipline, poor parenting skills, lack of positive family rituals and routine); family trauma (i.e., death, divorce)

2. *Social:* Peers use drugs and alcohol; social or cultural norms condone use of substances; expectations about positive effects of drugs and alcohol; drugs and alcohol are available and accessible

3. *Psychiatric:* Depression, anxiety, low self-esteem, low tolerance for stress; other mental health disorders; feelings of desperation; loss of control over one's life

4. *Behavioral:* Use of other substances; aggressive behavior in childhood; impulsivity and risk-taking; rebelliousness; school-based academic or behavioral problems; poor interpersonal relationships

Different models are believed to explain the causes of substance abuse.

1. *Biopsychosocial model:* There are a wide variety of reasons why people start and continue using substances. This model provides the most comprehensive explanation for the complex nature of substance abuse disorders. It incorporates hereditary predisposition, emotional and psychological problems, social influences, and environmental problems.

2. *Medical model:* Addiction is considered a chronic, progressive, relapsing, and potentially fatal medical disease.

   ■ Genetic causes: Inherited vulnerability to addiction, particularly alcoholism
   ■ Brain reward mechanisms: Substances act on parts of the brain that reinforce continued use by producing pleasurable feelings
   ■ Altered brain chemistry: Habitual use of substances alters brain chemistry and continued use of substances is required to avoid feeling discomfort from a brain imbalance

3. *Self-medication model:* Substances relieve symptoms of a psychiatric disorder and continued use is reinforced by relief of symptoms.

4. *Family and environmental model:* Explanation for substance abuse can be found in family and environmental factors such as behaviors shaped by family and peers, personality factors, physical and sexual abuse, disorganized communities, and school factors.

5. *Social model:* Drug use is learned and reinforced from others who serve as role models. A potential substance abuser shares the same values and activities as those who use substances. There are no controls that prevent use of substances. Social, economic, and political factors, such as racism, poverty, sexism, and so on, contribute to the cause.

Whatever the root causes, a client's substance abuse problem must be addressed before other psychotherapeutic issues. A social worker should also rule out symptoms being related to a substance abuse problem before attributing them to a psychiatric issue.

Substance Use Disorder

Substance Use Disorder in *Diagnostic and Statistical Manual of Mental Disorders* (5th ed.; *DSM-5*) combines the *DSM-IV* categories of Substance Abuse and Substance Dependence into a single disorder measured on a continuum from mild to severe. Each specific substance (other than caffeine, which cannot be diagnosed as a Substance Use Disorder) is addressed as a separate use disorder (Alcohol Use Disorder, Stimulant Use Disorder, etc.). Mild Substance Use Disorder in *DSM-5* requires two to three symptoms from a list of 11. Drug craving is added to the list, and problems with law enforcement is eliminated because of cultural considerations that make the criteria difficult to apply.

Non-Substance-Related Disorders

Gambling Disorder is the sole condition in a new category on behavioral addictions. Its inclusion here reflects research findings that Gambling Disorder is similar to Substance-Related Disorders in clinical expression, brain origin, comorbidity, physiology, and treatment.

There are also many other addictions that involve the use of something besides drugs and alcohol. An addiction is any behavior that a client feels powerless to control and interferes with his or her normal daily life. Addictions can have serious physical, emotional, and psychological consequences.

Sexual addiction is often misunderstood because, although it is perfectly acceptable to enjoy sexual activity, letting desires dictate daily life can cause shame and embarrassment. Sexual addiction often involves compulsive and promiscuous sexual behavior, porn addiction, and/or excessive masturbation.

Though essential for survival, food can also be the focus of addiction. Consuming excessive amounts of food is used by some to fill voids related to loneliness, shame, or lack of self-worth. This addiction can result in obesity or the development of an eating disorder. Some clients who have eating disorders also get addicted to exercise, such as running, to control their weight. Computer usage is also related to other addictions, such as online gambling and shopping.

Essentially, people can become addicted, dependent, or compulsively obsessed with any activity, substance, object, or behavior that gives pleasure. These activities, substances, objects, or behaviors produce beta-endorphins in the brain, producing a "high," leading to an addictive cycle. Those who are addicted will become obsessed with an activity, substance, object, or behavior and will seek it out, often to the detriment of work or interpersonal relationships. They will compulsively engage in the activity even if they do not want to do so. Cessation of the activity results in withdrawal symptoms of irritability, craving, and restlessness. Those with addictions do not appear to have control as to when, how long, or how much they will continue the activity, use of the substance or object, or behavior (loss of control). Individuals with addictive behaviors deny problems resulting from the addiction, even though others can see the negative effects. They usually have low self-esteem because there are psychological factors associated with other addictions as well.

Goals of Treatment

1. Abstinence from substances

2. Maximizing life functioning

3. Preventing or reducing the frequency and severity of relapse

The harm reduction model refers to any program, policy, or intervention that seeks to reduce or minimize the adverse health and social consequences associated with substance use without requiring a client to discontinue use. This definition recognizes that many substance users are unwilling or unable to abstain from use at any given time and that there is a need to provide them with options that minimize the harm that continued drug use causes to themselves, to others, and to the community.

Recovery is an ongoing process, and relapse occurs when attitudes, behaviors, and values revert to what they were during active drug or alcohol use. Relapse most frequently occurs during early stages of recovery, but it can occur at any time. Prevention of relapse is a critical part of treatment.

Stages of Treatment

1. Stabilization: Focus is on establishing abstinence, accepting a substance abuse problem, and committing oneself to making changes

2. Rehabilitation/habilitation: Focus is on remaining substance-free by establishing a stable lifestyle, developing coping and living skills, increasing supports, and grieving loss of substance use

3. Maintenance: Focus is on stabilizing gains made in treatment, relapse prevention, and termination

A social worker should be aware of the signs and symptoms of use, as well as withdrawal. For example, use of cocaine can be associated with dilated pupils, hyperactivity, restlessness, perspiration, anxiety, and impaired judgment.

Delirium tremens (DTs) is a symptom associated with alcohol withdrawal that includes hallucinations, rapid respiration, temperature abnormalities, and body tremors.

Wernicke's encephalopathy and Korsakoff's syndrome are disorders associated with chronic abuse of alcohol. They are caused by a thiamine (vitamin B_1) deficiency resulting from the chronic consumption of alcohol. A person with Korsakoff's syndrome has memory problems. Treatment is administration of thiamine.

Treatment Approaches

1. *Medication-assisted treatment* interventions assist with interfering with the symptoms associated with use. For example, methadone, a synthetic narcotic, can be legally prescribed. A client uses it to detox from opiates or on a daily basis as a substitute for heroin. Antabuse is a medication that produces highly unpleasant side effects (flushing, nausea, vomiting, hypotension, and anxiety) if a client drinks alcohol, it is a form of "aversion therapy." Naltrexone is a drug used to reduce cravings for alcohol; it also blocks the effects of opioids.

2. *Psychosocial or psychological interventions* modify maladaptive feelings, attitudes, and behaviors through individual, group, marital, or family therapy. These therapeutic interventions also examine the roles that are adopted within families in which substance abuse occurs; for example, the "family hero," "scapegoat," "lost child," or "mascot" (a family member who alleviates pain in the family by joking around).

3. *Behavioral therapies* ameliorate or extinguish undesirable behaviors and encourage desired ones through behavior modification.

4. *Self-help groups* (Alcoholics Anonymous, Narcotics Anonymous) provide mutual support and encouragement while becoming

abstinent or in remaining abstinent. Twelve-step groups are utilized throughout all phases of treatment. After completing formal treatment, the recovering person can continue attendance indefinitely as a means of maintaining sobriety.

SYSTEMS AND ECOLOGICAL PERSPECTIVES AND THEORIES

A system is a whole comprising component parts that work together. Applied to social work, systems theory views human behavior through larger contexts, such as members of families, communities, and broader society.

Important to this theory is the concept that when one thing changes within a system, the whole system is affected.

Systems tend toward equilibrium and can have closed or open boundaries.

Applications to Social Work

1. Social workers need to understand interactions between the micro, mezzo, and macro levels.

2. Problems at one part of a system may be manifested at another.

3. Ecomaps and genograms can help to understand system dynamics.

4. Understanding "person-in-environment" (PIE) is essential to identifying barriers or opportunities for change.

5. Problems and change are viewed within larger contexts.

Some System Theory Terms

Closed system	Uses up its energy and dies
Differentiation	Becoming specialized in structure and function
Entropy	Closed, disorganized, stagnant; using up available energy
Equifinality	Arriving at the same end from different beginnings
Homeostasis	Steady state
Input	Obtaining resources from the environment that are necessary to attain the goals of the system
Negative entropy	Exchange of energy and resources between systems that promote growth and transformation
Open system	A system with cross-boundary exchange
Output	A product of the system that exports to the environment

Subsystem	A major component of a system made up of two or more interdependent components that interact in order to attain their own purpose(s) and the purpose(s) of the system in which they are embedded
Suprasystem	An entity that is served by a number of component systems organized in interacting relationships
Throughput	Energy that is integrated into the system so it can be used by the system to accomplish its goals

STRENGTHS-BASED AND RESILIENCE THEORIES

The strengths perspective is based on the assumption that clients have the capacity to grow, change, and adapt (**humanistic approach**). Clients also have the knowledge that is important in defining and solving their problems (clients or families are experts about their own lives and situations); they are resilient and survive and thrive despite difficulties.

Strength is any ability that helps an individual (or family) to confront and deal with a stressful life situation and to use the challenging situation as a stimulus for growth. Individual strengths include, but are not limited to, cognitive abilities, coping mechanisms, personal attributes, interpersonal skills, or external resources. Families may have other strengths such as kinship bonds, community supports, religious connections, flexible roles, strong ethnic traditions, and so on.

Strengths vary from one situation to another and are contextual. What may be an appropriate strength or coping mechanism in one situation may not be appropriate in another. Ideally, in a given situation, a client selects an appropriate way to cope by drawing from a repertoire of coping mechanisms or strengths. The appropriateness of a particular coping mechanism may vary according to life course stage, developmental tasks, kinds of stressors, situation, and so on. Having a variety of coping mechanisms and resources enables flexibility in the way a client copes with stresses.

The strengths perspective focuses on understanding clients (or families) on the basis of their strengths and resources (internal and external) and mobilizing the resources to improve their situations. There is a systematic assessment of all the strengths and resources available to meet desired goals.

Methods to enhance strengths include:

- Collaboration and partnership between a social worker and client
- Creating opportunities for learning or displaying competencies
- Environmental modification—environment is both a resource and a target of intervention

A social worker should always use a strengths perspective when interacting with clients. Central to this perspective is the use of supportive communication throughout the problem-solving process. A social worker should be instilling hope in a client when engaging with him or her so a client believes that change is possible.

Supportive techniques include ensuring that the positives are included in an assessment of a client's situation. It also includes using positive phrasing when communicating with a client or on a client's behalf. Opportunities for growth and development should be seen in the face of adversity and challenges. A social worker should always take a "glass half full" approach.

Supportive techniques also require a nonjudgmental attitude. A client should not be fearful of being judged or feel that he or she will be condemned or retaliated against for expressing viewpoints or acting in a certain way.

Empathic communication is an essential supportive technique. A client should feel that a social worker understands what he or she is going through. A social worker should be warm and friendly, treating a client as a valuable partner in the problem-solving process. Making a client realize his or her quality attributes helps boost his or her self-image.

CRISIS INTERVENTION THEORIES

A "crisis" is an acute disruption of psychological homeostasis in which a client's usual coping mechanisms fail and there is evidence of distress and functional impairment. While there are many theories used to explain and address crises, there are seven critical stages through which clients typically pass on the road to crisis stabilization, resolution, and mastery. These stages are essential, sequential, and sometimes overlapping in the process of crisis intervention:

1. *Plan and conduct a thorough biopsychosocial–spiritual–cultural and lethality/imminent danger assessment*

   A social worker must conduct a biopsychosocial–spiritual–cultural assessment covering a client's environmental supports and stressors, medical needs and medications, current use of drugs and alcohol, and internal and external coping methods and resources. Assessing lethality is first and foremost.

2. *Make psychological contact and rapidly establish the collaborative relationship*

   In a crisis, a social worker must do this quickly, generally as part of assessment.

3. *Identify the major problems, including crisis precipitants*

   A social worker should determine from a client why things have "come to a head." There is usually a "last straw," but a social worker should also find out what other problems a client is concerned about.

It can also be useful to prioritize the problems in terms of which problems a client wants to work on first.

4. *Encourage an exploration of feelings and emotions*

A social worker should validate a client's feelings and emotions and let him or her vent about the crisis. The use of active listening skills, paraphrasing, and probing questions is essential. A social worker should also challenge maladaptive beliefs.

5. *Generate and explore alternatives and new coping strategies*

A social worker and a client must come up with a plan for what will help improve the current situation. Brainstorming possibilities and finding out what has been helpful in the past are critical.

6. *Restore functioning through implementation of an action plan*

This stage represents a shift from a crisis to a resolution. A client and a worker will begin to take the steps negotiated in the previous stage. This is also where a client will begin to make meaning of the crisis event.

7. *Plan follow-up*

Follow-up can take many forms as it can involve phone or in-person visits at specific intervals. A postcrisis evaluation may look at a client's current functioning and assess a client's progress.

PSYCHOANALYTIC AND PSYCHODYNAMIC APPROACHES

Psychodynamic theories explain the origin of the personality. Although many different psychodynamic theories exist, they all emphasize unconscious motives and desires, as well as the importance of childhood experiences in shaping personality.

Psychodynamic approaches aim to help clients review emotions, thoughts, early life experiences, and beliefs in order to gain insight into their lives and their present-day problems. Recognizing recurring patterns helps clients see the ways in which they avoid distress and/or develop defense mechanisms as methods of coping so that they can take steps to change these patterns.

In order to keep painful feelings, memories, and experiences in the unconscious, clients tend to develop defense mechanisms, such as denial, repression, rationalization, and others. Social workers using psychodynamic approaches encourage clients to speak freely about their emotions, desires, and fears in order to reveal vulnerable feelings that have been pushed out of conscious awareness. According to psychodynamic theory, behavior is influenced by unconscious thought; vulnerable or painful feelings are resolved by the use of defense mechanisms.

The therapeutic relationship is central to psychodynamic approaches because it takes an intimate look at interpersonal relationships so that clients can see relationship patterns. It also empowers clients, through insight and self-awareness, to transform dysfunctional dynamics.

Psychoanalytic Theory

Originally developed by Sigmund Freud, a client is seen as the product of his past and treatment involves dealing with the repressed material in the unconscious. According to psychoanalytic theory, personalities arise because of attempts to resolve conflicts between unconscious sexual and aggressive impulses and societal demands to restrain these impulses.

Freud believed that behavior and personality derive from the constant and unique interaction of conflicting psychological forces that operate at **three different levels of awareness:** the preconscious, the conscious, and the unconscious.

The **conscious** contains all the information that a client is paying attention to at any given time.

The **preconscious** contains all the information outside of a client's attention but readily available if needed—thoughts and feelings that can be brought into consciousness easily.

The **unconscious** contains thoughts, feelings, desires, and memories of which clients have no awareness but that influence every aspect of their day-to-day lives.

Freud proposed that personalities have three components: the id, the ego, and the superego.

- **Id:** A reservoir of instinctual energy that contains biological urges such as impulses toward survival, sex, and aggression. The id is unconscious and operates according to the **pleasure principle**, the drive to achieve pleasure and avoid pain.
- **Ego:** The component that manages the conflict between the id and the constraints of the real world. Some parts of the ego are unconscious, whereas others are preconscious or conscious. The ego operates according to the reality principle—the awareness that gratification of impulses has to be delayed in order to accommodate the demands of the real world. The ego's role is to prevent the id from gratifying its impulses in socially inappropriate ways.

Ego-Syntonic/Ego-Dystonic:

- Syntonic = behaviors "insync" with the ego (no guilt)
- Dystonic = behavior "dis-n-sync" with the ego (guilt)

The ego's job is to determine the best course of action based on information from the id, reality, and the superego. When the ego is comfortable with its conclusions and behaviors, a client is said to be ego-syntonic. However, if a client is bothered by some of his or her behaviors, he or she would be ego-dystonic (ego alien).

Inability of the ego to reconcile the demands of the id, the superego, and reality produces conflict that leads to a state of psychic distress known as anxiety.

Ego strength is the ability of the ego to effectively deal with the demands of the id, the superego, and reality. Those with little ego strength may feel torn between these competing demands, whereas those with too much ego strength can become too unyielding and rigid. Ego strength helps maintain emotional stability and cope with internal and external stress.

- **Superego:** The moral component of personality. It contains all the moral standards learned from parents and society. The superego forces the ego to conform not only to reality, but also to its ideals of morality. Hence, the superego causes clients to feel guilty when they go against society's rules.

Psychosexual Stages of Development

Freud believed that personality solidifies during childhood, largely before age 5. He proposed five stages of psychosexual development: the oral stage, the anal stage, the phallic stage, the latency stage, and the genital stage. He believed that at each stage of development, children gain sexual gratification or sensual pleasure from a particular part of their bodies. Each stage has special conflicts, and children's ways of managing these conflicts influence their personalities.

If a child's needs in a particular stage are gratified too much or frustrated too much, the child can become fixated at that stage of development. **Fixation** is an inability to progress normally from one stage into another. When the child becomes an adult, the fixation shows up as a tendency to focus on the needs that were overgratified or overfrustrated.

Freud believed that the crucially important **Oedipus complex** also developed during the phallic stage. The Oedipus complex refers to a male child's sexual desire for his mother and hostility toward his father, whom he considers to be a rival for his mother's love. Freud thought that a male child who sees a naked girl for the first time believes that her penis has been cut off. The child fears that his own father will do the same to him for desiring his mother—a fear called **castration anxiety**. Because of this fear, the child represses his longing for his mother and begins to identify with his father. The child's acceptance of his father's authority results in the emergence of the superego.

In psychoanalytic psychotherapy, the primary technique used is analysis (of dreams, resistances, transferences, and free associations).

Stage	Age	Sources of pleasure	Result of fixation
Oral	Birth to roughly 12 months	Activities involving the mouth, such as sucking, biting, and chewing	Excessive smoking, overeating, or dependence on others
Anal	Age 2, when the child is being toilet trained	Bowel movements	An overly controlling (anal-retentive) personality or an easily angered (anal-expulsive) personality
Phallic	Age 3-5	Genitals	Guilt or anxiety about sex
Latency	Age 5 to puberty	Sexuality is latent, or dormant, during this period	No fixations at this stage
Genital	Begins at puberty	The genitals; sexual urges return	No fixations at this stage

Individual Psychology

Alfred Adler, a follower of Freud and a member of his inner circle, eventually broke away from Freud and developed his own school of thought, which he called individual psychology. Adler believed that the **main motivations for human behavior are not sexual or aggressive urges, but striving for perfection**. He pointed out that children naturally feel weak and inadequate in comparison to adults. This normal feeling of inferiority drives them to adapt, develop skills, and master challenges. Adler used the term **compensation** to refer to the attempt to shed normal feelings of inferiority.

However, some people suffer from an exaggerated sense of **inferiority**. Such people overcompensate, which means that, rather than try to master challenges, they try to cover up their sense of inferiority by focusing on outward signs of superiority such as status, wealth, and power.

Healthy individuals have a broad social concern and want to contribute to the welfare of others. Unhealthy people are those who are overwhelmed by feelings of inferiority.

The aim of therapy is to develop a more adaptive lifestyle by overcoming feelings of inferiority and self-centeredness and to contribute more toward the welfare of others.

Self Psychology

This approach defines the self as the central organizing and motivating force in personality. As a result of receiving empathic responses from early caretakers (self-objects), a child's needs are met and the child develops a strong sense of selfhood. "Empathic failures" by caretakers result in a lack of self-cohesion.

The objective of self psychology is to help a client develop a greater sense of self-cohesion. Through therapeutic regression, a client reexperiences frustrated self-object needs.

Three self-object needs are:

- **Mirroring:** behavior validates the child's sense of a perfect self
- **Idealization:** child borrows strength from others and identifies with someone more capable
- **Twinship/Twinning:** child needs an alter ego for a sense of belonging

Ego Psychology

Ego psychology focuses on the rational, conscious processes of the ego. Ego psychology is based on an assessment of a client as presented in the present (here and now). Treatment focuses on the ego functioning of a client, because healthy behavior is under the control of the ego. It addresses:

- Behavior is varying situations
- Reality testing: perception of a situation
- Coping abilities: ego strengths
- Capacity for relating to others

The goal is to maintain and enhance the ego's control and management of stress and its effects.

Object Relations Theory

Object relations theory, which was a focus of Margaret Mahler's work, is centered on relationships with others. According to this theory, lifelong relationship skills are strongly rooted in early attachments with parents, especially mothers. Objects refer to people, parts of people, or physical items that symbolically represent either a person or part of a person. Object relations, then, are relationships to those people or items.

Age	Phase	Subphase	Characteristics
0–1 month	**Normal autism**		First few weeks of life. The infant is detached and self-absorbed. Spends most of his or her time sleeping. Mahler later abandoned this phase, based on new findings from her infant research.
1–5 months	**Normal symbiotic**		The child is now aware of his or her mother, but there is not a sense of individuality. The infant and the mother are one, and there is a barrier between them and the rest of the world.
5–9 months	**Separation/ Individuation**	Differentiation/ Hatching	The infant ceases to be ignorant of the differentiation between him or her and the mother. Increased alertness and interest for the outside world. Using the mother as a point of orientation.
9–15 months		Practicing	Brought about by the infant's ability to crawl and then walk freely, the infant begins to explore actively and becomes more distant from the mother. The child experiences himself or herself as one with his or her mother.
15–24 months		Rapprochement	The infant once again becomes close to the mother. The child realizes that his or her physical mobility demonstrates psychic separateness from his or her mother. The toddler may become tentative, wanting the mother to be in sight so that, through eye contact and action, he or she can explore his or her world. The risk is that the mother will misread this need

(*continued*)

Age	Phase	Subphase	Characteristics
			and respond with impatience or unavailability. This can lead to an anxious fear of abandonment in the toddler.
24–38 months	Object Constancy		Describes the phase when the child understands that the mother has a separate identity and is truly a separate individual. Provides the child with an image that helps supply him or her with an unconscious level of guiding support and comfort. Deficiencies in positive internalization could possibly lead to a sense of insecurity and low self-esteem issues in adulthood.

INDICATORS AND DYNAMICS OF ABUSE AND NEGLECT THROUGHOUT THE LIFESPAN

There are various forms of abuse and neglect: **physical abuse** (infliction of physical injury); **sexual abuse** (inappropriate exposure or sexual contact, activity, or behavior without consent); **psychological abuse** (emotional/verbal/mental injury); and **neglect** (failing to meet physical, emotional, or other needs).

Different forms of abuse occur separately, but are often seen in combinations. Psychological abuse almost always accompanies other forms of abuse.

Indicators and Dynamics of Sexual Abuse

Physical or anatomical signs/injuries associated with the genital and rectal areas are signs of physical or sexual abuse. Behavioral signs include any extreme changes in behavior, including regression, fears and anxieties, withdrawal, sleep disturbances, and/or recurrent nightmares. If the victim is a child, he or she may also show an unusual interest in sexual matters or know sexual information inappropriate for his or her age group. Sexual promiscuity, sexual victimization, and prostitution can also be signs.

Some factors influencing the effect of sexual abuse include:

- Age of the victim (at time of abuse and time of assessment)
- Extent and duration of sexual abuse

- Relationship of offender to victim
- Reaction of others to the abuse
- Other life experiences

Immediately after disclosing the abuse, an individual is at risk for:

- Disbelief by others (especially if victim is a child or perpetrator is a spouse/partner of an adult)
- Being rejected by others
- Being blamed for the abuse and the consequences of disclosing the sexual abuse

For a child, one of the most significant factors contributing to adjustment after sexual abuse is the level of parental support.

Some of the effects of sexual abuse can be:

- Aversive feelings about sex, overvaluing sex, sexual identity problems, and/or hypersexual behaviors
- Feelings of shame and guilt or feeling responsible for the abuse, which are reflected in self-destructive behaviors (such as substance abuse, self-mutilation, suicidal ideation and gestures, and acts that aim to provoke punishment)
- Lack of trust, unwillingness to invest in others; involvement in exploitive relationships; angry and acting-out behaviors
- Perceived vulnerability and victimization, phobias, sleep, and eating problems

Indicators and Dynamics of Psychological Abuse and Neglect

Psychological abuse/neglect is sustained, repetitive, and inappropriate behavior aimed at threatening, isolating, discrediting, belittling, teasing, humiliating, bullying, confusing, and/or ignoring. Psychological abuse/neglect can be seen in constant criticism, belittling, teasing, ignoring or withholding of praise or affection, and placing excessive or unreasonable demands, including expectations above what is appropriate.

It can impact intelligence, memory, recognition, perception, attention, imagination, and moral development. Individuals who have been psychologically abused are likely to be fearful, withdrawn, and/or resentful, distressed, and despairing. They are likely to feel unloved, worthless, and unwanted, or only valued in meeting another's needs.

Those who are victims of psychological abuse and neglect often:

- Avoid eye contact and experience deep loneliness, anxiety, and/or despair
- Have a flat and superficial way of relating, with little empathy toward others
- Have a lowered capacity to engage appropriately with others
- Engage in bullying, disruptive, or aggressive behaviors toward others
- Engage in self-harming and/or self-destructive behaviors (i.e., cutting, physical aggression, reckless behavior showing a disregard for self and safety, drug taking)

Indicators and Dynamics of Physical Abuse and Neglect

Most physical abuse and neglect occur within the family by those who are known to the victim. Physical abuse and neglect are also more common in families living in poverty and/or those with drug or alcohol problems.

Neglect can include physical neglect (failing to provide food, clothing, shelter, or other physical necessities), emotional neglect (failing to provide love, comfort, or affection), and/or medical neglect (failing to provide needed medical care).

The major reasons for physical abuse and neglect are feelings of isolation, stress, and frustration by the perpetrator. There is often a lack of coping skills to address feelings of frustration and anger. Support groups and social work services are helpful first steps to diminish the isolation or frustration that fuel physical abuse and neglect. As many perpetrators were themselves victims of physical abuse and neglect as children, they are in need of support to confront, address, and heal wounds in order to ensure that the cycle of abuse and neglect is not perpetuated.

Physical abuse is defined as nonaccidental trauma or physical injury caused by punching, beating, kicking, biting, or burning. It is the most visible form of abuse because there are usually physical signs.

With a child, physical abuse can result from inappropriate or excessive physical discipline.

Indicators of physical abuse include:

- Unexplained bruises or welts on the face, lips, mouth, torso, back, buttocks, or thighs, sometimes reflecting the shape of the article used to inflict them (electric cord, belt buckle, etc.)

- Unexplained burns from a cigar or cigarette, especially on soles, palms, back, or buttocks—sometimes patterned like an electric burner, iron, or similar
- Unexplained fractures to the skull, nose, or facial structure
- Unexplained lacerations or abrasions to the mouth, lips, gums, eyes, and/or external genitalia

Behavioral indicators include being wary of individuals (parent or caretaker if a child is being abused) and behavioral extremes (aggressiveness or withdrawal), as well as fear related to reporting injury.

Functioning of Various Systems

2

THE FAMILY LIFE CYCLE

The emotional and intellectual stages from childhood to retirement as a member of a family are called the family life cycle. In each stage, clients face challenges in family life that allow the building or gaining of new skills.

Not everyone passes through these stages smoothly. Situations such as severe illness, financial problems, or the death of a loved one can have an effect. If skills are not learned in one stage, they can be learned in later stages.

Stage 1: **Family of origin experiences**
Main tasks
- Maintaining relationships with parents, siblings, and peers
- Completing education
- Developing the foundations of a family life

Stage 2: **Leaving home**
Main tasks
- Differentiating self from family of origin and parents and developing adult-to-adult relationships with parents
- Developing intimate peer relationships
- Beginning work, developing work identity, and financial independence

Stage 3: **Premarriage stage**
Main tasks
- Selecting partners
- Developing a relationship
- Deciding to establish own home with someone

Stage 4: **Childless couple stage**

Main tasks

- Developing a way to live together both practically and emotionally
- Adjusting relationships with families of origin and peers to include partner

Stage 5: **Family with young children**

Main tasks

- Realigning family system to make space for children
- Adopting and developing parenting roles
- Realigning relationships with families of origin to include parenting and grandparenting roles
- Facilitating children to develop peer relationships

Stage 6: **Family with adolescents**

Main tasks

- Adjusting parent–child relationships to allow adolescents more autonomy
- Adjusting family relationships to focus on midlife relationship and career issues
- Taking on responsibility of caring for families of origin

Stage 7: **Launching children**

Main tasks

- Resolving midlife issues
- Negotiating adult-to-adult relationships with children
- Adjusting to living as a couple again
- Adjusting to including in-laws and grandchildren within the family circle
- Dealing with disabilities and death in the family of origin

Stage 8: **Later family life**

Main tasks

- Coping with physiological decline in self and others
- Adjusting to children taking a more central role in family maintenance
- Valuing the wisdom and experience of the elderly
- Dealing with loss of spouse and peers
- Preparing for death, life review, and reminiscence

Mastering the skills and milestones of each stage allows successful movement from one stage of development to the next. If not mastered, clients are more likely to have difficulty with relationships and future transitions. Family life cycle theory suggests that successful transitioning may also help to prevent disease and emotional or stress-related disorders.

The stress of daily living, coping with a chronic medical condition, or other life crises can disrupt the normal life cycle. Ongoing stress or a crisis can delay the transition to the next phase of life.

FAMILY DYNAMICS AND FUNCTIONING AND THE EFFECTS ON INDIVIDUALS, FAMILIES, GROUPS, ORGANIZATIONS, AND COMMUNITIES

Family dynamics are the patterns of relating or interactions between family members. Each family system and its dynamics are unique, although there are some common patterns. All families have some helpful and some unhelpful dynamics.

Even where there is little or no present contact with family, there is almost always an influence on a client by dynamics in previous years. Family dynamics often have a strong influence on the way individuals see themselves, others, and the world, and influence their relationships, their behaviors, and their well-being.

An understanding of the impact of family dynamics on a client's self-perception may help social workers pinpoint and respond to the driving forces behind her or his current needs.

Healthy functioning is characterized by:

- Treating each family member as an individual
- Having regular routines and structure
- Being connected to extended family, friends, and the community
- Having realistic expectations
- Spending quality time, which is characterized by fun, relaxed, and conflict-free interactions
- Ensuring that members take care of their own needs and not just the family needs
- Helping one another through example and direct assistance

Family dynamics significantly impact on a client's biological, psychological, and social functioning in both positive and negative ways. Having a close-knit and supportive family provides emotional support, ensures economic well-being, and increases overall health. However, the opposite is also true. When family life is characterized by stress and conflict, well-being can be poor.

Social support is one of the main ways that family positively impacts well-being. Social relationships, such as those found in close families, have been demonstrated to decrease the likelihood of negative outcomes, such as chronic disease, disability, mental illness, and death.

Though good familial relations and social support serve as protective factors and improve overall well-being and health, studies have shown that not all familial relations positively impact these areas. Problematic and nonsupportive familial interactions have a negative impact. For example, growing up in an unsupported, neglectful, or violent home is associated with poor physical health and development.

MODELS OF FAMILY LIFE EDUCATION IN SOCIAL WORK PRACTICE

Family life education aims to strengthen individual and family life through a family perspective. Social workers are well suited to work with a client within the family context, which is essential for such a model.

Much of family life education is delivered through parenting classes, premarriage education, marriage enrichment programs, and/or family financial planning courses. All of these activities focus on improving a client's quality of life individually and, equally as important, within his or her family unit.

Social workers use a strengths perspective, as well as their knowledge of human development, systems and social role theories, and ecological or "PIE" influences, when engaging in family life education.

When conducting family life education, a social worker must be aware of his or her own cultural values and norms with regard to material covered and not impose these beliefs on others or be judgmental.

THEORIES OF COUPLES DEVELOPMENT

Although relationships vary significantly, there are some predictable stages that characterize intimate relationships. Couples interactions follow a developmental model, much like those that explain individual growth throughout the life course.

Stage 1: Romance

The first stage of couples development begins when individuals are introduced and learn that they have common interests and are attracted to one another. Much of this stage consists of conversations and dates to learn more about the other partner. The focus of this stage is attachment. Like early stages of child development, the infancy of couples development is filled with passion, nurturing, and selfless attention to the needs of others. Differences are minimized and partners place few demands on each other. This romantic bond is the foundation that is critical to the health of the relationship in the future.

In this first stage, members engage in *symbiotic or mutualistic relationships*—often putting the needs of others before their own. Individuals who are coupling do not see themselves as unique—much like babies identifying themselves as part of their mothers or caregivers. Differentiation and learning to balance and support the separate needs of others happens in later stages but is not present initially.

Stage 2: Power Struggle

Soon individuals who are engaged in intimate relationships see that they have differences from their mates. These unique qualities result in unique needs that require an ongoing process of defining oneself and managing conflict, which threatens intimacy. As the coupled individuals begin to notice differences and annoyances that were once overlooked, there can be greater separation and loss of romance resulting from self-expression. This stage differs as individuals focus on differences rather than similarities, which was the hallmark of the initial romantic stage.

Time away from each other is often needed for the partners, and the bliss associated with the initial stage of couples development dissolves. *Differentiation*, or seeing oneself as distinct within a relationship, must be managed so that these new feelings do not result in breakups as the illusion of "being one" fades. Critical effort must be made to balance the desire for self-discovery with the desire for intimacy. To "survive" this stage, individuals must acknowledge differences, learn to share power, forfeit fantasies of complete harmony, and accept partners without the need to change them.

Stage 3: Stability

This stage in couples development is characterized by the redirection of personal attention, time, and activities away from partners and toward one's self. Individuals focus on personal needs in a manner that is respectful of others. Autonomy and individuality are key. Relationships are seen as more mature as disagreements can occur with both parties "winning." There is acceptance that partners are different from one another, and power struggles to minimize these differences are avoided.

Margaret Mahler described *practicing* as a subphase of separation-individuation in infant development. Practicing occurs when toddlers begin to explore on their own but still see themselves as part of their mothers/caregivers. The stability stage of couples development mirrors this subphase as partners learn to live independent lives while still identifying as and seeing the value of being part of an intimate relationship.

Another subphase of separation-individuation identified by Mahler, "*rapprochement*," also relates to the stability stage of couples development. Often, partners who have been successful in achieving a well-defined sense of self in relationships will have crises that will threaten their identities or separateness. They may rely more heavily on companionship and intimacy, seeking more comfort and support from each other. Thus, the stability stage is a time when there is still some back and forth between intimacy and independence with the ultimate goal being intimacy that does not sacrifice separateness.

Stage 4: Commitment

While the commitment stage of couples development is when marriage is ideal, it often occurs earlier in the romance stage, perhaps explaining the high rates of divorce caused by the inability to resolve power struggles. Individuals who have stabilized are able to embrace the reality that both partners are human, resulting in shortcomings in all relationships. Partners acknowledge that they want to be with each other and that the good outweighs the bad. Although much work has been done in building relationships, there is still more needed to effectively function in the next and last stage of couplehood.

Stage 5: Co-Creation

Constancy is the hallmark of this last stage. Just like children who are able to internalize and maintain images of their mothers/caregivers and use them to soothe in stressful moments, couples in this stage are able to do something similar. Each partner is able to value and respect the separateness of the other. The foundation of the relationship is no longer personal need, but the appreciation and love of the other and the support and respect for *mutual growth*.

Often, couples in this stage work on projects together, such as businesses, charities, and/or families. This stage aims to make a contribution beyond the relationship itself. Like Erik Erikson's stage of psychosocial functioning in middle adulthood, which focuses on the crisis of generativity versus stagnation, this stage of couples development aims to create or nurture things that are enduring, often by creating positive change that benefits other people. Success leads to feelings of usefulness and accomplishment.

As with Erikson's and other theories of development, stages are not linear. Lessons learned help couples move forward, but couples can revert back to prior stages, especially those including power struggles.

Homo sexual couples also go through these developmental stages but have unique challenges that impact relationship formation. For example, heterosexual couples have a much wider variety of public role models for their partnerships than their homosexual peers. In addition, there may be heightened concerns by partners about acceptance of their mates or even the very existence of their intimate relationships by their respective families.

THEORIES OF GROUP DEVELOPMENT AND FUNCTIONING

Humans are small group beings. Group work is a method of social work that helps individuals to enhance their social functioning through purposeful group experiences, as well as to cope more effectively with their personal, group, or community problems. In group work, **individuals help each other** in order to influence and change personal, group, organizational, and community problems.

A social worker focuses on helping each member change his or her environment or behavior through interpersonal experience. Members help each other change or learn social roles in the particular positions held or desired in the social environment.

A therapeutic group provides a unique microcosm in which members, through the process of interacting with each other, gain more knowledge and insight into themselves for the purpose of making changes in their lives. The goal of the group may be a major or minor change in personality structure or changing a specific emotional or behavioral problem.

A social worker helps members come to agreement regarding the purpose, function, and structure of a group. A group is the major helping agent.

Individual self-actualization occurs through:

- Release of feelings that block social performance
- Support from others (not being alone)
- Orientation to reality and check out own reality with others
- Reappraisal of self

Some types of groups include:

- Groups centered on a shared problem
- Counseling groups
- Activity groups
- Action groups
- Self-help groups
- Natural groups
- Closed versus open groups
- Structured groups
- Crisis groups
- Reference groups (similar values)

Psychodrama is a treatment approach in which roles are enacted in a group context. Members of the group re-create their problems and devote themselves to the role dilemmas of each member.

Despite the differences in goals or purposes, all groups have common characteristics and processes.

The stages of group development are:

1. Preaffiliation—development of trust (known as forming)
2. Power and control—struggles for individual autonomy and group identification (known as storming)
3. Intimacy—utilizing self in service of the group (known as norming)
4. Differentiation—acceptance of each other as distinct individuals (known as performing)
5. Separation/termination—independence (known as adjourning)

Groups help through:

■ Instillation of hope
■ Universality
■ Altruism
■ Interpersonal learning
■ Self-understanding and insight

Factors affecting group cohesion include:

■ Group size
■ Homogeneity: similarity of group members
■ Participation in goal and norm setting for group
■ Interdependence: dependent on one another for achievement of common goals
■ Member stability: frequent change in membership results in less cohesiveness

There are some advantages to participation in group therapy that individual treatment does not provide. The group process serves as a support network and a sounding board for clients. Through the group process, clients hear specific ideas for improving difficult situations or circumstances from others who are going through similar challenges. Group members' opinions are often highly respected as they come with the credibility of having experienced similar issues.

Regularly talking and listening to others also helps clients put their own problems in perspective. Clients may feel that they are the only ones struggling, but they learn, through the group process, that they are not. The ability to see and hear others like themselves indicates to clients that they are not alone and, thereby, reduces stigma and isolation.

Diversity is another important benefit of group therapy. Clients have different personalities and backgrounds and look at situations in different ways.

By seeing how others address problems, clients are afforded new strategies for facing their own concerns.

Observing maladaptive behavior in others also may help clients see the effects of their own similar behavior. Discussing problems in a group may make it easier for clients to discuss their feelings with others, such as friends and family members, outside of the group. Group interaction helps develop healthy social interaction skills. Members can observe the social and coping skills of others who may serve as positive role models. Role playing is also feasible in the group context.

Key Concepts

Groupthink is when a group makes faulty decisions because of group pressures. Groups affected by groupthink ignore alternatives and tend to take irrational actions that dehumanize other groups. A group is especially vulnerable to groupthink when its members are similar in background, when the group is insulated from outside opinions, and when there are no clear rules for decision making.

There are eight causes of groupthink:

1. Illusion of invulnerability—excessive optimism is created that encourages taking extreme risks.

2. Collective rationalization—members discount warnings and do not reconsider their assumptions.

3. Belief in inherent morality—members believe in the rightness of their cause and ignore the ethical or moral consequences of their decisions.

4. Stereotyped views of those "on the out"—negative views of the "enemy" make conflict seem unnecessary.

5. Direct pressure on dissenters—members are under pressure not to express arguments against any of the group's views.

6. Self-censorship—doubts and deviations from the perceived group consensus are not expressed.

7. Illusion of unanimity—the majority view and judgments are assumed to be unanimous.

8. Self-appointed "mindguards"—members protect the group and the leader from information that is problematic or contradictory to the group's cohesiveness, views, and/or decisions.

Group polarization occurs during group decision making when discussion strengthens a dominant point of view and results in a shift to a more extreme position than any of the members would adopt on their own. These more extreme decisions are toward greater risk if individuals' initial tendencies are to be risky and toward greater caution if individuals' initial tendencies are to be cautious.

Effects of the Environment on Systems' Behavior

3

PERSON-IN-ENVIRONMENT (PIE) THEORY

Social psychology focuses on the way in which social interaction influences the behavior of others. Ecological perspectives emphasize the nature of clients' interactions within their physical and sociocultural surroundings. Social ecology attempts to understand the interactions within the social, institutional, and cultural contexts of people–environment relationships. This approach adopts a systemic approach in focusing on the interdependencies of social systems.

All of these fields of study and perspectives recognize the importance of social context on behavior. Humans are social beings. Life depends on others. Infants are unable to care for themselves. Their survival depends on others. Clients develop and learn about the world through the filter of other people. Social interaction is essential to both survival and happiness.

Social workers must understand a systems perspective and the interplay between biological, psychological, and social processes. They must also understand contexts and conditions that inhibit and promote certain human behaviors and/or behavioral change.

The PIE perspective highlights the importance of understanding individual behavior in light of the environmental contexts in which a client lives and acts. The perspective has historical roots in the social work profession.

The PIE classification system was developed as an alternative to the commonly used disease and moral models (i.e., *DSM*, *International Statistical Classification of Diseases and Related Health Problems* [*ICD*], civil or penal codes) to implement social work philosophy and area of expertise. PIE is client-centered, rather than agency-centered.

The PIE system is field-tested and examines social role functioning, the environment, mental health, and physical health.

THE INTERPLAY OF BIOLOGICAL, PSYCHOLOGICAL, SOCIAL, AND SPIRITUAL FACTORS

Human development is a lifelong process beginning before birth and extending to death. At each moment in life, every human being is in a state of personal evolution. Physical changes largely drive the process, as our cognitive abilities advance and decline in response to the brain's growth in childhood and reduced functioning in old age. Psychosocial–spiritual development is also significantly influenced by physical growth, as changing body and brain, together with environment, shape a client's identity and relationships with other people.

Thus, development is the product of the elaborate interplay of biological, psychological, social, and spiritual influences. As children develop physically, gaining greater psychomotor control and increased brain function, they become more sophisticated cognitively—that is, more adept at thinking about and acting upon their environment. These physical and cognitive changes, in turn, allow them to develop psychosocially and spiritually, forming individual identities and relating effectively and appropriately with other people.

THE DYNAMICS OF INTERPERSONAL RELATIONSHIPS

Family theory provides a theoretical and therapeutic base for dealing with family-related situations; it is also useful in understanding and managing individual problems by determining the extent to which such problems are related to family issues. A family systems approach argues that in order to understand a family system, a social worker must look at the family as a whole, rather than focusing on its members.

People do not exist in a vacuum. They live, play, go to school, and work with other people. Most anthropologists agree that, next to their peculiar tendency to think and use tools, one of the distinguishing characteristics of human beings is that they are social creatures. The social group that seems to be most universal and pervasive in the way it shapes human behavior is the family. For social workers, the growing awareness of the crucial impact of families on clients has led to the development of family systems theory.

Family systems theory searches for the causes of behavior, not in the individual alone, but in the interactions among the members of a group. The basic rationale is that all parts of the family are interrelated. Further, the family has properties of its own that can be known only by looking at the relationships and interactions among all members.

The family systems approach is based on several basic assumptions:

- Each family is more than a sum of its members.

- Each family is unique, due to the infinite variations in personal characteristics and cultural and ideological styles.

- A healthy family has flexibility, consistent structure, and effective exchange of information.

- The family is an interactional system whose component parts have constantly shifting boundaries and varying degrees of resistance to change.

- Families must fulfill a variety of functions for each member, both collectively and individually, if each member is to grow and develop.

- Families strive for a sense of balance or **homeostasis.**

- Negative feedback loops are those patterns of interaction that maintain stability or constancy while minimizing change. Negative feedback loops help to maintain homeostasis. Positive feedback loops, in contrast, are patterns of interaction that facilitate change or movement toward either growth or dissolution.

- Families are seen as being goal oriented. The concept of **equifinality** refers to the ability of the family system to accomplish the same goals through different routes.

- The concept of hierarchies describes how families organize themselves into various smaller units or **subsystems** that are comprised by the larger family system. When the members or tasks associated with each subsystem become blurred with those of other subsystems, families have been viewed as having difficulties. For example, when a child becomes involved in marital issues, difficulties often emerge that require intervention.

- Boundaries occur at every level of the system and between subsystems. Boundaries influence the movement of people and the flow of information into and out of the system. Some families have very open boundaries where members and others are allowed to freely come and go without much restriction; in other families, there are tight restrictions on where family members can go and who may be brought into the family system. Boundaries also regulate the flow of information in a family. In more closed families, the rules strictly regulate what information may be discussed and with whom. In contrast, information may flow more freely in families that have more permeable boundaries.

■ The concept of interdependence is critical in the study of family systems. Individual family members and the subsystems comprised by the family system are mutually influenced by and are mutually dependent upon one another. What happens to one family member, or what one family member does, influences other family members.

Genograms are diagrams of family relationships beyond a family tree allowing a social worker and client to visualize hereditary patterns and psychological factors. They include annotations about the medical history and major personality traits of each family member. Genograms help uncover intergenerational patterns of behavior, marriage choices, family alliances and conflicts, the existence of family secrets, and other information that will shed light on a family's present situation.

PSYCHOLOGICAL DEFENSE MECHANISMS AND THEIR EFFECTS ON BEHAVIOR AND RELATIONSHIPS

To manage internal conflicts, people use defense mechanisms. **Defense mechanisms** are behaviors that protect people from anxiety. Defense mechanisms are automatic, involuntary, and usually unconscious psychological activities to exclude unacceptable thoughts, urges, threats, and impulses from awareness for fear of disapproval, punishment, or other negative outcomes. Defense mechanisms are sometimes confused with coping strategies, which are voluntary.

The following are some defense mechanisms (the list of defense mechanisms is huge, and there is no theoretical consensus on the exact number).

1. **Acting Out**—emotional conflict is dealt with through actions rather than feelings (i.e., instead of talking about feeling neglected, a person will get into trouble to get attention).

2. **Compensation**—enables one to make up for real or fancied deficiencies (i.e., a person who stutters becomes a very expressive writer; a short man assumes a cocky, overbearing manner).

3. **Conversion**—repressed urge is expressed disguised as a disturbance of body function, usually of the sensory, voluntary nervous system (as pain, deafness, blindness, paralysis, convulsions, tics).

4. **Decompensation**—deterioration of existing defenses.

5. **Denial**—primitive defense; inability to acknowledge true significance of thoughts, feelings, wishes, behavior, or external reality factors that are consciously intolerable.

6. **Devaluation**—a defense mechanism frequently used by persons with borderline personality organization in which a person attributes exaggerated negative qualities to self or another. It is the split of primitive idealization.

7. **Dissociation**—a process that enables a person to split mental functions in a manner that allows him or her to express forbidden or unconscious impulses without taking responsibility for the action, either because he or she is unable to remember the disowned behavior, or because it is not experienced as his or her own (i.e., pathologically expressed as fugue states, amnesia, or dissociative neurosis, or normally expressed as daydreaming).

8. **Displacement**—directing an impulse, wish, or feeling toward a person or situation that is not its real object, thus permitting expression in a less threatening situation (i.e., a man angry at his boss kicks his dog).

9. **Idealization**—overestimation of an admired aspect or attribute of another.

10. **Identification**—universal mechanism whereby a person patterns himself or herself after a significant other. Plays a major role in personality development, especially superego development.

11. **Identification With the Aggressor**—mastering anxiety by identifying with a powerful aggressor (such as an abusing parent) to counteract feelings of helplessness and to feel powerful oneself. Usually involves behaving like the aggressor (i.e., abusing others after one has been abused oneself).

12. **Incorporation**—primitive mechanism in which psychic representation of a person is (or parts of a person are) figuratively ingested.

13. **Inhibition**—loss of motivation to engage in (usually pleasurable) activity avoided because it might stir up conflict over forbidden impulses (i.e., writing, learning, or work blocks or social shyness).

14. **Introjection**—loved or hated external objects are symbolically absorbed within self (converse of projection; i.e., in severe depression, unconscious unacceptable hatred is turned toward self).

15. **Intellectualization**—where the person avoids uncomfortable emotions by focusing on facts and logic. Emotional aspects are completely ignored as being irrelevant. Jargon is often used as a device of intellectualization. By using complex terminology, the focus is placed on the words rather than the emotions.

16. **Isolation of Affect**—unacceptable impulse, idea, or act is separated from its original memory source, thereby removing the original emotional charge associated with it.

17. **Projection**—primitive defense; attributing one's disowned attitudes, wishes, feelings, and urges to some external object or person.

18. **Projective Identification**—a form of projection utilized by persons with Borderline Personality Disorder—unconsciously perceiving others' behavior as a reflection of one's own identity.

19. **Rationalization**—third line of defense; not unconscious. Giving believable explanation for irrational behavior; motivated by unacceptable unconscious wishes or by defenses used to cope with such wishes.

20. **Reaction Formation**—person adopts affects, ideas, attitudes, or behaviors that are opposites of those he or she harbors consciously or unconsciously (i.e., excessive moral zeal masking strong, but repressed asocial impulses or being excessively sweet to mask unconscious anger).

21. **Regression**—partial or symbolic return to more infantile patterns of reacting or thinking. Can be in service to ego (i.e., as dependency during illness).

22. **Repression**—key mechanism; expressed clinically by amnesia or symptomatic forgetting serving to banish unacceptable ideas, fantasies, affects, or impulses from consciousness.

23. **Splitting**—defensive mechanism associated with Borderline Personality Disorder in which a person perceives self and others as "all good" or "all bad." Splitting serves to protect the good objects. A person cannot integrate the good and bad in people.

24. **Sublimation**—potentially maladaptive feelings or behaviors are diverted into socially acceptable, adaptive channels (i.e., a person who has angry feelings channels them into athletics).

25. **Substitution**—unattainable or unacceptable goal, emotion, or object is replaced by one more attainable or acceptable.

26. **Symbolization**—a mental representation stands for some other thing, class of things, or attribute. This mechanism underlies dream formation and some other symptoms (such as conversion reactions, obsessions, compulsions) with a link between the latent meaning of the symptom and the symbol; usually unconscious.

27. **Turning Against Self**—defense to deflect hostile aggression or other unacceptable impulses from another to self.

28. **Undoing**—a person uses words or actions to symbolically reverse or negate unacceptable thoughts, feelings, or actions (i.e., a person compulsively washing hands to deal with obsessive thoughts).

THE INDICATORS OF PSYCHOSOCIAL STRESS

Psychosocial stress results when there is a perceived threat (real or imagined). Examples of psychosocial stress include threats to social status, social esteem, respect, and/or acceptance within a group; threats to self-worth; or threats that are perceived as uncontrollable.

Psychosocial stress can be caused by upsetting events, such as natural disasters, sudden health problems or death, and/or breakups or divorce.

Although current upsetting events certainly create stress, events from the past can also still affect clients. Social workers should assess the impacts of events such as childhood abuse, bullying, discrimination, violence, and/or trauma.

Often, psychosocial stress is not caused by single events, but by ongoing problems such as caring for a parent or child with disabilities.

Stress may manifest itself in many different ways, such as high blood pressure, sweating, rapid heart rate, dizziness, and/or feelings of irritability or sadness.

When psychosocial stress triggers a stress response, the body releases a group of stress hormones that lead to a burst of energy, as well as other changes in the body. The changes brought about by stress hormones can be helpful in the short-term, but can be damaging in the long run.

It is essential that clients learn to manage psychosocial stress so that the stress response is only triggered when necessary and not for prolonged states of chronic stress.

THE EFFECT OF POVERTY ON INDIVIDUALS, FAMILIES, GROUPS, ORGANIZATIONS, AND COMMUNITIES

Clients who are poor often do not have resources to meet their basic needs. There are many social problems that contribute to and result from poverty, including, but not limited to, little or no education, poor basic nutrition and hygiene, disability or illness, unemployment, substance abuse, and homelessness.

Family income has selective but, in some instances, quite substantial impacts on child and adolescent well-being. Family income appears to be more strongly related to children's ability and achievement than to their emotional outcomes.

Children who live in extreme poverty or who live below the poverty line for multiple years appear, all other things being equal, to suffer the worst outcomes. The timing of poverty also seems to be important for certain outcomes. Children who experience poverty during their preschool and early school years have lower rates of school completion than children and adolescents who experience poverty only in later years. Although more research is needed, findings to date suggest that interventions during early childhood may be most important in reducing poverty's impact on children.

Social workers must also consider the implications on the biopsychosocial–spiritual–cultural aspects of well-being. Medical care may be neglected in order to meet other needs. Coping skills are needed when there are dramatic changes in income and opportunities to adapt and return to economic stability are critical.

Wealth is often poorly distributed. A small minority has all the money, causing major societal tensions and divisions. There are the "haves" and the "have nots." Communities are often homogeneous—with those comprised of poor people being segregated from those living above the poverty line. Communities comprised of the poor have fewer opportunities and resources to assist their members, leading to a greater likelihood that they will not be able to break out of the cycle that originally resulted in their economic insecurity. Thus, those born into poverty often remain there throughout their life course.

THE IMPACT OF THE ENVIRONMENT (E.G., SOCIAL, PHYSICAL, CULTURAL, POLITICAL, ECONOMIC) ON INDIVIDUALS, FAMILIES, GROUPS, ORGANIZATIONS, AND COMMUNITIES

Social workers must be knowledgeable about human behavior across the life course, the range of social systems in which people live, and the ways social systems promote or deter people in maintaining or achieving health and well-being. Social workers should apply theories and knowledge to understand biological, social, cultural, psychological, and spiritual development.

The ecological perspective is rooted in systems theory, which views coping as a transactional process that reflects the "PIE" relationship. Using this perspective, the focus of intervention is the interface between a client (person, family, group, etc.) and a client's environment. The ecological perspective is also concerned with the issues of power and privilege and how they are withheld from some groups, imposing enormous stress on affected individuals.

Environmental factors can have strong positive or negative impacts on development.

ROLE THEORIES

A role is defined as the collection of expectations that accompany a particular social position. Clients have multiple roles in their lives; in different contexts or with different people, such as being students, friends, employees, spouses, or parents.

Each of these roles carries its own expectations about appropriate behavior, speech, attire, and so on. What might be rewarded in one role would be unacceptable for another (e.g., competitive behavior is rewarded for an athlete but not a preschool teacher). Roles range from specific, in that they only apply to a certain setting, to diffuse, in that they apply across a range of situations. For example, gender roles influence behavior across many different contexts. Role theory examines how these roles influence a wide array of psychological outcomes, including behavior, attitudes, cognitions, and social interaction.

There are some important terms used in role theory.

- *Role ambiguity*: lack of clarity of role
- *Role complementarity*: the role is carried out in an expected way (i.e., parent–child; social worker–client)
- *Role discomplementarity*: the role expectations of others differ from one's own
- *Role reversal*: when two or more individuals switch roles
- *Role conflict*: incompatible or conflicting expectations

When assessing, social workers view problems as differences between clients' behaviors and the expectations of others with regard to roles.

SOCIAL AND ECONOMIC JUSTICE

Social work is a profession aimed at helping people address their problems and match them with the resources they need to lead healthy and productive lives. One of the most important values of the social work profession is social and economic justice. Social justice is the view that everyone deserves equal economic, political, and social rights and opportunities.

Economic justice is a component of social justice. It is a set of moral principles for building economic institutions, the ultimate goal of which is to create an opportunity for each person to create a sufficient material foundation upon which to have a dignified, productive, and creative life.

Social workers promote social justice and social change with and on behalf of clients who are individuals, families, groups, organizations, and/or communities.

Social workers aim to open the doors of access and opportunity for all, particularly those in greatest need.

Social workers also apply social justice principles to structural problems in the social service agencies in which they work. Armed with the long-term goal of empowering clients, they use knowledge of existing legal principles and organizational structure to suggest changes to protect clients, who are often powerless and underserved.

THE IMPACT OF GLOBALIZATION ON CLIENTS/CLIENT SYSTEMS (E.G., INTERRELATEDNESS OF SYSTEMS, INTERNATIONAL INTEGRATION, TECHNOLOGY, ENVIRONMENTAL OR FINANCIAL CRISES, EPIDEMICS)

Globalization has had a profound effect on social work practice, changing service delivery; creating new social problems for practitioners to address, such as human trafficking and environmental issues; and producing demands for indigenization, or the development of locality specific forms of theory and practice. *Globalization* refers to an interconnectedness of persons across the world.

The current globalization of the economy requires that social workers broaden their horizons and view many domestic social justice issues within a global framework. Social workers can benefit from knowing how the issues in their town or nation are played out in other towns and nations. There is so much to learn of innovative practices and of possible solutions to social problems that never would have been imagined without an international exchange of information. Globalization has the potential to transport traditional social policy analysis into an ever-widening international arena. Social workers must help people to influence their own governments to consider human rights issues in foreign relations. Contained in the *Universal Declaration of Human Rights* are principles germane to the alleviation of oppression and injustice. Social workers recognize the benefits and disadvantages of globalization for the most vulnerable people in the world, focusing especially on how the economic and environmental consequences affect social relationships and individual opportunity.

Diversity, Discrimination, and Stereotypes

4

THE EFFECT OF DISABILITY ON BIOPSYCHOSOCIAL FUNCTIONING THROUGHOUT THE LIFESPAN

With increased age comes increased likelihood of disability as people live longer and do not encounter fatal diseases. Unfortunately, this positive association between age and disability sometimes leads to a negative image of aging. Given that the aging process often results in some type of disability, examinations of differences in aging outcomes have not centered around whether disabilities will occur, but rather when they will happen, how many will occur, and how severe they will be.

Disability occurs when physical or mental health declines associated with aging, illness, or injury restrict ability to perform activities of daily living (ADLs). Mobility impairment is often tied to disability because being able to ambulate and/or use one's upper extremities are critical to engaging in many activities that allow independence.

The most common causes of disability among older adults are chronic diseases, injuries, mental impairment, and/or malnutrition. Major chronic conditions related to disability include cardiovascular diseases, hypertension, stroke, diabetes, cancer, chronic obstructive pulmonary disease, musculoskeletal conditions including arthritis and osteoporosis, mental health conditions such as dementia and depression, and blindness and visual impairment. Injuries can be due to accidents and/or falls.

There is a relationship between disability and poverty. Poverty can lead to malnutrition, poor or no health services, and/or unsafe living conditions that can result in increased risk for disability. Disability can also result in loss of income and, thus, a greater likelihood of living in poverty.

Interestingly, happiness and well-being tend to be high among older adults overall despite declines in physical and mental health and the onset of disability for some. This discrepancy is due to the fact that not all disability leads to dependence. If the consequences of disability can be reduced or eliminated altogether, its negative effects on quality of life can be minimized.

The environment and improvements in lifestyle are critical. The environment plays an important role in the impact of disability on the lives of older adults, with those remaining outside of institutional settings—such as nursing homes—being more productive and satisfied. In addition, environments based on accessible design promote independent living, which can result in good quality of life for those who are older and/or have disabilities.

Improvements in lifestyle and health behaviors include better nutrition, quitting or reducing smoking, less obesity, and greater physical activity. Benefits from exercise, even when begun later in life, can postpone and/or minimize disability.

THE EFFECT OF CULTURE, RACE, AND ETHNICITY ON BEHAVIORS, ATTITUDES, AND IDENTITY

The United States has a racially and ethnically diverse population. The Census officially recognizes six ethnic and racial categories: White American; American Indian and Alaska Native; Asian; African American; Native Hawaiian and Other Pacific Islander; and people of two or more races. The U.S. Census Bureau also classifies Americans as "Hispanic or Latino" and "Not Hispanic or Latino," which identifies Hispanic and Latino Americans as a racially diverse ethnicity that comprises the largest minority group in the nation.

A social worker must remember that there is tremendous intragroup diversity. In fact, the differences between racial and ethnic groups (intergroup) are often less profound than those found within these groups (intragroup). It is important to view a client as the expert and to not stereotype or make assumptions about values, behaviors, or attitudes based on a client's racial or ethnic group.

The following is an overview of some characteristics recognized as being more prevalent within each of the Census categories/classifications:

White American

- Family: parents with young children; divorce common; personal desires put over family; parents try to be friends with their children; avoid physical punishment

- Communication: language—American Standard English; communication can be long-winded and impersonal
- Spirituality: religion is a private affair, but mainly Protestant and Bible based
- Values: capitalism (i.e., the future is what you make it); poverty is a moral failing and wealth is held in high esteem; physical beauty is valued with white skin, blond hair, and thin body being the ideal; sports are an important part of life (baseball, American football, basketball); democracy and freedom; individual rights

American Indian/Alaska Native

- Family: complex family organizations that include relatives without blood ties; strong kinship bonds (multigenerational, extended families); group valued over individual; husband and wife show a tendency to communicate more with their gender group than with each other; harmony within the group is very important; common sharing of material goods; group decision making
- Communication: indirectness; being still and quiet; comfortable with silence; value listening and nonverbal communication; may avoid making direct eye contact as a show of respect when talking to a higher status person
- Spirituality: fundamental part of life; interconnectedness of all living things; sacredness of all creation; use of traditional and Western healing practices; medicine man, shaman, or spiritual leaders are traditional healers
- Values: holistic; interconnectedness of mind, body, spirit, and heart; time is viewed as a circular flow that is always with us; follow nature's rhythms rather than linear time

Asian

- Family: patriarchal system in which a wife has lower status and is subservient to her father, husband, and oldest son; obligation to parents and respect for elders; hierarchical family structure with strictly prescribed roles and rules of behavior and conduct
- Communication: often indirect in order to avoid direct confrontation and maintain highly valued harmonious relationships; less emotional expressiveness (reserved) and demonstration of affection
- Spirituality: cultures influenced by Confucian and Buddhist philosophies
- Values: shaming and obligation to others are mechanisms for reinforcing cultural norms; adhering to rules of conduct reflects not

only on the individual, but also on the family and extended kinship network, including past and future generations; usually seek help from the family or cultural community

Asian clients may respond to psychotropic drugs differently than clients from other ethnic groups. They typically require lower doses of medications and may experience more severe side effects from the same doses given to other clients. It is sometimes recommended to start Asian clients on less than the normally prescribed dosage. They are also sometimes resistant and view treatment of symptoms via homeopathic methods as more acceptable.

African American

- Family: multigenerational family systems; strong kinship bonds, including extended families and relatives without blood ties; informal adoption of children by extended family members; flexible family roles; women are often viewed as being "all sacrificing" and the "strength of the family"

- Communication: animated; individuals try to get their opinions heard; often includes physical touch; direct; show respect at all times; history of racism; and sense of powerlessness impacts interactions

- Spirituality: turn to community and/or religious leaders if assistance is needed; church is seen as a central part of community life

- Values: strong kinship bonds; strong work orientation; strong religious orientation; use informal support network—church or community; distrust of government; and social services—feel "big brother" doesn't care; don't like to admit they need help—strong sense of pride

Native Hawaiian and Other Pacific Islander

- Family: Western concept of "immediate family" is completely alien to indigenous Hawaiians; family is not restricted to those related by blood; "we are all related"; ties that bind cannot be broken, even by death; cherish their ancestors, with generation upon generation of lineage committed to memory and beautiful chants composed to herald their ancestors' abilities

- Communication: many Native Hawaiian and Pacific Islander subgroups, representing different languages and customs; ability to speak English has a tremendous impact on access to health information, public services; Hawaii is the only state in the United States that has designated a native language, Hawaiian, as one of its two official state languages

■ Spirituality: polytheistic, believing in many deities; belief that spirits are found in nonhuman beings and objects such as animals, waves, and the sky

■ Values: importance of culture and welfare of all living in a community; focus on ensuring the health of the community as a whole; everyone has a responsibility to use his or her talents to the benefit of the whole; sharing is central

Hispanic/Latino

■ Family: extended family system incorporates godparents and informally adopted children; deep sense of commitment and obligation to family; family unity, welfare, and honor are important; emphasis on group rather than individual; male has greater power and authority

■ Communication: often speak Spanish (but do not assume that they wish to receive services in native language); display varied emotional expressiveness depending on language being spoken; when speaking Spanish, client may be very expansive/expressive, friendly, playful, but in switching to English, speech may be more businesslike and guarded

■ Spirituality: most are Roman Catholic; emphasis on spiritual values; strong church and community orientation/interdependence

■ Values: wish to improve their life circumstances; belief in the innate worth of all individuals and that people are born into their lot in life; respect for dignity of self and others; respect for elders; respect for authority; very proud of heritage—never forget where they came from

THE EFFECTS OF DISCRIMINATION AND STEREOTYPES ON BEHAVIORS, ATTITUDES, AND IDENTITY

The negative impacts of discrimination can be seen on both the micro and macro levels. Exposure to discrimination is linked to anxiety and depression as well as other mental health and behavioral problems. In addition, there may be physical effects such as diabetes, obesity, and high blood pressure. These health problems may be caused by not maintaining healthy behaviors (such as physical activity) or engaging in unhealthy ones (such as smoking and alcohol or drug abuse).

These impacts can be long term or short term, including having:

■ Low self-esteem
■ Depression
■ Fear of rejection
■ Stress
■ Low self-worth
■ Feelings of being withdrawn from society
■ Humiliation
■ Fear
■ Anger

These impacts can result in long-term effects, including:

■ Loss of motivation
■ Restricted opportunities
■ Limited access to services
■ Long-term depression
■ Increased behavior problems
■ Difficulty communicating
■ Lack of education and achievement

Those who have been discriminated against based on culture, race, and/or ethnicity can become isolated from society and feel embarrassed about the shame imposed on them and/or their family. Internalized racism can occur in which negative discriminatory attitudes based on culture, race, and/or ethnicity can result, with those in minority groups applying stereotypes toward their own cultural, racial, and/or ethnic groups.

Those who discriminate against others often do so because they have been discriminated against themselves. They may be unhappy or have watched people close to them discriminate against others and/or are copying and responding to their actions.

On a macro level, discrimination also restricts access to the resources and systems needed for good health, education, employment, social support, and participation in sports, cultural, and civic activities. Discrimination and intolerance can also create a climate of despondence, apprehension, and fear within a community. The social and economic effects of discrimination on one generation may flow on to affect future generations, which can lead to cycles of poverty and disadvantage through those generations.

THE INFLUENCE OF SEXUAL ORIENTATION ON BEHAVIORS, ATTITUDES, AND IDENTITY

Sexuality is a crucial part of who we are. Sexual orientation, sexual behavior, and sexual identity are three parts of sexuality that can help to understand the term better.

Sexual orientation refers to an individual's pattern of physical and emotional arousal toward other persons. People do not choose their sexual orientation—it is simply part of who they are.

Sexual behavior refers to sexual contacts or actions. It is important to realize that people's sexual orientation may not fit perfectly with their sexual behavior (what they do sexually). There are many factors that shape or determine sexual behavior and sexual orientation is only one of those factors. Sexual behavior can be influenced by peer pressure, family expectations, cultural expectations, religious beliefs, and so on.

Sexual identity also may be very different from an individual's sexual orientation. Sexual identity is about the way people present their sexual preferences. People may have private sexual identities which may be different from their public identities. Even private sexual identities can differ from sexual orientation or attractions. Many people who experience same-sex attraction and/or have sexual contact with others of the same sex do not see themselves as homosexual or bisexual.

Sexual orientation often does not fit "neatly" into a label or category. People's attractions can be complicated and often are not clear. Clients may be struggling to determine what feels right for them.

Sexual orientation can be fluid with attractions changing over time. Some people take a while to figure out these attractions. That does not mean people "grow out of" their sexual attractions or that one set of feelings was a stage, it just means people change. *It is important to not use labels and let individuals define their own sexual orientation.*

THE IMPACT OF TRANSGENDER AND TRANSITIONING PROCESS ON BEHAVIORS, ATTITUDES, IDENTITY, AND RELATIONSHIPS

"Transgender" is a term for people whose gender identity, expression, or behavior is different from those typically associated with their assigned sex at birth. "Trans" is sometimes used as shorthand for "transgender."

People might realize they are trans (that their gender identity does not align with their birth sex designation) at any point in their lives. Some people may first experience an internal sense of identity that does not match their external characteristics in early childhood. Others report realizing this in puberty or later. Societal gender norms and expectations may contribute to realization of their true gender identity. These assumptions can also contribute to dysphoria, as people might first attempt to conform to societal expectations by expressing gender identities they do not have. Feelings of distress frequently arise, during which people realize that they cannot meet these gender norms as they do not match their identities.

Transition is a time when individuals begin living as the gender with which they identify rather than the gender they were assigned at birth, which often includes changing one's first name and dressing and grooming differently. Transitioning may or may not also include medical and legal aspects, including taking hormones, having surgery, or changing identity documents (e.g., driver's license, Social Security record) to reflect one's gender identity. Medical and legal steps are costly and, therefore, unaffordable.

Transition, whether social, through hormone therapy, through surgery, or through some combination, often improves feelings of dysphoria, though it may not relieve them completely. The goal of many is for their gender to be perceived correctly by others, which is often referred to as "passing." Typically, people transition to align their physical appearance and characteristics with their gender identities. Many people begin the process after years of dysphoria and distress, and transitioning may help them feel as if they are finally able to be their true selves.

Transitioning can have significant psychological, social, and physical benefits. Anxiety and depression caused by gender dysphoria may diminish as dysphoria improves. Individuals who no longer have to make uncomfortable adjustments—such as hiding unwanted physical characteristics—may not only feel better physically but may have greater confidence and self-esteem.

People's reasons for choosing to transition, and the goals they have regarding transition, are personal and unique. Some individuals may not pursue certain aspects of transition, whether through personal choice, lack of resources, or lack of access. There is no single "right" way to transition. Gender identity does not depend on whether they have had surgery or if they are taking hormones.

Friends and family members who may have little to no understanding of gender transition or of what it means to be trans may ask invasive questions or say things that are invalidating or hurtful, regardless of intention. They may also find people's true genders difficult to accept. "You'll always be ____ to me," a mother might say, without the intention of harm. But this type of remark may be invalidating and cause distress.

Social work services can help individuals who are transgender as they consider and move through the transitioning process. They can also help family members by creating safe spaces where they can ask questions, develop a better understanding of what it means to be transgender, and learn more about what transition entails.

SYSTEMIC (INSTITUTIONALIZED) DISCRIMINATION (E.G., RACISM, SEXISM, AGEISM)

Social workers should not practice, condone, facilitate, or collaborate with any form of discrimination on the basis of race, ethnicity, national origin, color, sex, sexual orientation, gender identity or expression, age, marital status, political belief, religion, immigration status, or mental or physical disability (*NASW Code of Ethics, 2008—4.02 Discrimination*).

Discrimination can occur at the individual or institutional level. Individual discrimination is when an individual is treated differently whereas institutionalized discrimination refers to policies or practices that discriminate against a group of people based on these characteristics (achievement gaps in education, residential segregation, etc.).

THE PRINCIPLES OF CULTURALLY COMPETENT SOCIAL WORK PRACTICE

Cultural competence involves working in conjunction with natural, informal support and helping networks within the minority community (neighborhoods, churches, spiritual leaders, healers, etc.). It extends the concept of self-determination to the community. Only when a community recognizes and owns a problem does it take responsibility for creating solutions that fit the context of the culture.

Social workers should promote conditions that encourage respect for cultural and social diversity and promote policies and practices that demonstrate respect for difference, support the expansion of cultural knowledge and resources, advocate for programs and institutions that demonstrate cultural competence, and promote policies that safeguard the rights of all people.

Social workers should act to prevent and eliminate domination of, exploitation of, and discrimination against any person, group, or class on the basis of race, ethnicity, national origin, color, sex, sexual orientation, gender identity or expression, age, marital status, political belief, religion, immigration status, and mental or physical disability.

Since every client's cultural experiences are different, services must be delivered using a flexible and individualized approach. Social workers should be aware of the standards on cultural competence and social diversity (*NASW Code of Ethics, 2008*).

1. Social workers should understand culture and its function in human behavior and society, recognizing the strengths that exist in all cultures.

2. Social workers should have a knowledge base of their clients' cultures and be able to demonstrate competence in the provision of services that are sensitive to clients' cultures and to differences among people and cultural groups. *When social workers are from different racial or cultural backgrounds than their clients, they must clearly understand how these differences impact the problem-solving process.*

3. Social workers should obtain education about and seek to understand the nature of social diversity and oppression with respect to race, ethnicity, national origin, color, sex, sexual orientation, gender identity or expression, age, marital status, political belief, religion, immigration status, and mental or physical disability.

4. Social workers should also not use derogatory language in their written or verbal communications to or about clients. Social workers should use accurate and respectful language in all communications to and about clients (*NASW Code of Ethics, 2008—1.12 Derogatory Language*).

Social workers should be aware of terminology related to cultural barriers and goals.

Ethnocentrism: an orientation that holds one's own culture, ethnic, or racial group as superior to others

Stratification: structured inequality of entire categories of people who have unequal access to social rewards (e.g., ethnic stratification, social stratification)

Pluralism: a society in which diverse members maintain their own traditions while cooperatively working together and seeing others' traits as valuable (cultural pluralism—respecting and encouraging cultural difference)

Social workers must possess specific knowledge about the cultural groups with whom they work, including diverse historical experiences, adjustment styles, socioeconomic backgrounds, learning styles, cognitive skills, and/or specific cultural customs. This knowledge must include theories and principles concerning human behavior development, psychopathology, therapy, rehabilitation, and community functioning because they relate to cultural group members. Institutions, class, culture, and language barriers that prevent ethnic group members from accessing or using services must be identified and addressed.

Some approaches within organizations to promote cultural competency include recruiting multiethnic staff, including cultural competence requirements in job descriptions and performance/promotion measures, reviewing demographic trends for the geographic area served to determine service needs, creating service delivery systems that are more appropriate to the diversity of the target population, and advocating for clients as major stakeholders in the development of service delivery systems to ensure they are reflective of their cultural heritage.

SEXUAL ORIENTATION CONCEPTS

"Sexual orientation" is a term used to describe patterns of emotional, romantic, and sexual attraction—and a sense of personal and social identity based on those attractions. Sexual orientation exists along a continuum, with exclusive attraction to the opposite sex on one end of the continuum and exclusive attraction to the same sex on the other.

There are a bunch of identities associated with sexual orientation:

- People who are attracted to a different gender (e.g., women who are attracted to men or men who are attracted to women) often call themselves straight or heterosexual.
- People who are attracted to people of the same gender often call themselves gay or homosexual. Gay women may prefer the term "lesbian."
- People who are attracted to both men and women often call themselves bisexual.
- People whose attractions span across many different gender identities (male, female, transgender, genderqueer, intersex, etc.) may call themselves pansexual or queer.
- People who are unsure about their sexual orientation may call themselves questioning or curious.
- People who do not experience sexual attraction often call themselves asexual.

It is also important to note that some people don't think any of these labels describe them accurately. Some people don't like the idea of labels at all. Other people feel comfortable with certain labels and not others.

Social workers must let clients identify and use their own labels to describe their own sexual orientations.

GENDER AND GENDER IDENTITY CONCEPTS

A gender role is a theoretical construct that refers to a set of social and behavioral norms that, within a specific culture, are widely considered to be socially appropriate for individuals of a specific sex. Socially accepted gender roles differ widely between different cultures. Gender role theory asserts that observed gender differences in behavior and personality characteristics are, at least in part, socially constructed, and therefore the product of socialization experiences; this contrasts with other models of gender, which assert that gender differences are "essential" to biological sex. Thus, there is a debate over the environmental or biological causes for the development of gender roles.

Gender role theory posits that boys and girls learn to perform one's biologically assigned gender through particular behaviors and attitudes. Gender role theory emphasizes the environmental causes of gender roles and the impact of socialization, or the process of transferring norms, values, beliefs, and behaviors to group members, in learning how to behave as a male or a female. Social role theory proposes that the social structure is the underlying force in distinguishing genders and that sex-differentiated behavior is driven by the division of labor between two sexes within a society. The division of labor creates gender roles, which, in turn, lead to gendered social behavior.

Gender has several definitions. It usually refers to a set of characteristics that are either seen to distinguish between male and female, one's biological sex, or one's gender identity. Gender identity is the gender(s), or lack thereof, a person self-identifies as; it is not based on biological sex, either real or perceived, nor is it always based on sexual orientation. There are two main genders, masculine (male) and feminine (female), although in some cultures there are more genders. Gender roles refer to the set of attitudes and behaviors socially expected from those with a particular gender identity.

Gender identity usually conforms to anatomic sex in both heterosexual and homosexual individuals. However, individuals who identify as transgender feel themselves to be of a gender different from their biological sex; their gender identity does not match their anatomic or chromosomal sex.

Sexual orientation and gender identity are distinct with those who are transgender exhibiting the same full range of possible sexual orientations and interests of those who are not transgender.

It is important to let individuals define their own gender identity. For some, gender is not just about being male or female; in fact, identity can change every day or even every few hours. **Gender fluidity**, when gender expression, shifts between masculine and feminine, can be displayed in dress, expression and self-description.

There are lots of misconceptions about gender fluidity. Gender fluidity is also not the equivalent of transgender, in which a person's gender identity is different from the one assigned at birth.

It is the belief that gender exists on a spectrum and is not binary with the ability to change at any time. Some individuals who are gender fluid prefer the pronoun "they."

Unit II

Intervention Processes and Techniques for Use Across Systems (32%)

Biopsychosocial History and Collateral Data

5

THE COMPONENTS OF A BIOPSYCHOSOCIAL ASSESSMENT

Social workers use an ecological perspective. They understand that, regardless of origin, all problems are systemic and are maintained by an imbalance within and between systems. All client problems are examined through a biopsychosocial–spiritual–cultural lens to understand the interplay between and among these elements.

The *biological* dimension refers to the role of biological systems within the body (i.e., genetic predispositions) and outside (i.e., airborne pathogens that impact functioning).

The *psychological* dimension refers to the role of thoughts, emotion, and behavior on individual, group, or community functioning. Inclusion of this dimension also acknowledges the mind–body connection in the assessment of problems.

The *social* dimension refers to how a client relates to various groups and institutions in society, as well as how groups and institutions relate to him or her. Social workers assist not only individual clients, but all others who might be similarly affected by an issue.

The *spiritual* dimension refers to the role of religious or spiritual belief on well-being, whereas the *cultural* dimension acknowledges the importance of considering traditions, customs, rituals, values, and communications that may be part of a client's cultural heritage.

Systems theory indicates that biopsychosocial–spiritual–cultural dimensions of a client are interrelated and work together. Thus, when one dimension changes within a system, the whole system or a client's well-being is affected.

The biopsychosocial–spiritual–cultural history is a tool that provides information on the current/presenting issue or issues; a client's past and present physical health, including developmental milestones; a client's emotional functioning; educational or vocational background; cultural issues; spiritual and religious beliefs; environmental issues; and social functioning. Each issue may be reviewed for its relationship and/or impact with the presenting issue.

The *biological section* assesses a client's medical history, developmental history, current medications, substance abuse history, and family history of medical illnesses. Issues related to medical problems should be explored because mental health symptoms can exacerbate them. Referrals should be made to address medical concerns that are not being treated. Clients who are on medications should have care coordinated with the treating provider, and more should be known about the medications because side effects can also mask or exacerbate psychiatric symptoms or illnesses.

The *psychological section* assesses a client's present psychiatric illness or symptoms, history of the current psychiatric illness or symptoms, past or current psychosocial stressors, and mental status. Exploration of how the problem has been treated in the past, past or present psychiatric medications, and the family history of psychiatric and substance-related issues is also included.

The *social section* focuses on client systems and unique client context, and may identify strengths and/or resources available for treatment planning. Included are sexual identity issues or concerns, personal history, family of origin history, support system, abuse history, education, legal history, marital/relationship status and concerns, work history, and risks.

The assessment should also include information about a client's spiritual beliefs, as well as his or her cultural traditions.

THE COMPONENTS AND FUNCTION OF THE MENTAL STATUS EXAMINATION

A mental status examination is a structured way of observing and describing a client's current state of mind under the domains of appearance, attitude, behavior, mood and affect, speech, thought process, thought content, perception, cognition, insight, and judgment. A mental status examination is a necessary part of any client assessment no matter what the presenting problem. It should be documented in the record either in list form or in narrative form. The following client functions should be included:

1. *Appearance*—facial expression, grooming, dress, gait, and so on

2. *Orientation*—awareness of time and place, events, and so on

3. *Speech pattern*—slurred, pressured, slow, flat tone, calm, and so on

4. *Affect/mood*—mood as evidenced in both behavior and client's statements (sad, jittery, manic, placid, etc.)

5. *Impulsive/potential for harm*—impulse control with special attention to potential suicidality and/or harm to others

6. *Judgment/insight*—ability to predict the consequences of her or his behavior, to make "sensible" decisions, to recognize her or his contribution to her or his problem

7. *Thought processes/reality testing*—thinking style and ability to know reality, including the difference between stimuli that are coming from inside herself or himself and those that are coming from outside herself or himself (statements about delusions, hallucinations, and conclusions about whether or not a client is psychotic would appear here)

8. *Intellectual functioning/memory*—level of intelligence and of recent and remote memory functions

A paragraph about mental status in the record might read as follows:

> "Client is a 43-year-old woman who looks older than her stated age. She is well groomed and appropriately dressed for a professional interview. She is well oriented. Her speech is slow as if it is painful to talk. She has had occasional thoughts of 'ending it all,' but has not made any suicidal plans or preparations. She talks about future events with expectation to be alive. She is aware that she is 'depressed' and recognizes that the source of some of the feeling comes from 'inside moods' although she often refers to the difficulties of her situation. Her thoughts are organized. She is not psychotic."

BIOPSYCHOSOCIAL RESPONSES TO ILLNESS AND DISABILITY

The ways in which clients experience chronic illness or disability are influenced by numerous factors including:

- Personal characteristics (such as gender, race, age, coping style, past experience)
- Social and family supports
- Socioeconomic status
- Culture
- Environment (physical, social, and political)
- Activities (restrictions on those related to daily living, work, school, social)
- Personal goals

The responses to illness or disability are dependent on the interplay between these factors. Limitations faced may not be due to the illness or disability, but instead the environment. In addition, societal attitudes may influence their responses with norms focused more on the limitations than on actual functioning.

Clients also vary in terms of their personal resources such as tolerance of symptoms, functional capabilities, coping strategies, and social supports. Consequently, social workers must assess biopsychosocial responses individually. The health condition or disability is only one factor that determines clients' abilities to function effectively.

BIOPSYCHOSOCIAL FACTORS RELATED TO MENTAL HEALTH

When a client has a mental health problem or illness, it impacts on all aspects of his or her life, including health, psychological functioning, and socialization. In addition, there are biological, psychological, and social risk factors related to mental health and illness.

It is not possible to understand mental health and the onset or course of mental disorders without knowing about biological, psychological, and social factors and how they interact across the lifespan.

Biological Factors

There is clear evidence to support the role that genes play as a factor in the development of psychiatric disorders. New information also keeps emerging about how brain structure and functioning relate to the existence of mental disorders. It is thought that brain growth in utero or early life can be affected by exposure to adverse factors, leading to changes in brain structure that increase the risk of development of particular mental disorders.

For example, some mental illnesses have been linked to *biological* factors, such as abnormal brain functioning, and medication/procedures can assist in improving the brain to operate more efficiently. Injury and/or abnormal development to certain areas of the brain have also been linked to some mental conditions.

Mental illnesses can also be present in families, suggesting that those who have family members with them may be somewhat more susceptible to their development. Such susceptibility does not mean that mental illnesses will occur, only that there is a greater likelihood. Lastly, certain infections have been linked to brain damage and the development of mental illness or the worsening of its symptoms. Poor nutrition and exposure to toxins may also exacerbate symptoms and/or be related to the development of mental health problems.

Psychological Factors

Personality, relating to others and reacting to the world, includes a wide range of psychological responses to cope with different situations. Psychoanalytic, cognitive, and behavioral theories have all had an influence on how personality is understood, its impact on mental disorders, and how it can be influenced in treatment.

Psychological trauma suffered as a child, such as emotional, physical, or sexual abuse; loss of a caregiver; neglect; or poor ability to relate to others, also adversely impacts mental health and can place individuals at risk, especially those with a biological predisposition.

Social Factors

Social factors can influence mental health in dramatic ways and it is necessary to investigate social factors thoroughly to fully understand mental health and disorder. Factors such as socio-economic situation, age, gender, social networks, level of support, life events, migration, and culture can all play a role in influencing the onset and course of mental illnesses.

Certain *social* stressors can also trigger mental health problems or the development of mental illness in those who are susceptible to it. These stressors include death, divorce, dysfunctional family life, feelings of inadequacy, low self-esteem, anxiety, anger, loneliness, change in life circumstance, social or cultural expectations, and/or substance use/abuse.

A social worker must use a systems approach in assessment of client mental health. A change in one aspect of a client's life—such as loss of a job, diagnosis of a physical illness, and so on—can affect his or her mental health. Conversely, mental health problems can have a dramatic impact on earnings, role fulfillment, friendships and social relationships, and even physical health.

BASIC MEDICAL TERMINOLOGY

Social workers must recognize the relationship between physical well-being and mental status. Social workers should always rule out medical etiology before making psychiatric diagnoses. A **differential diagnosis** is a systematic diagnostic method used to identify the presence of an entity where multiple alternatives are possible.

Social workers must know the major body systems and medical conditions associated with them that can affect psychological functioning and mood.

1. *Circulatory System*

   The circulatory system is the body's transport system. It is made up of a group of organs that transport blood throughout the body. The heart pumps the blood and the arteries and veins transport it.

2. *Digestive System*

The digestive system is made up of organs that break down food into protein, vitamins, minerals, carbohydrates, and fats, which the body needs for energy, growth, and repair.

3. *Endocrine System*

The endocrine system is made up of a group of glands that produce the body's long-distance messengers, or hormones. Hormones are chemicals that control body functions, such as metabolism, growth, and sexual development.

4. *Immune System*

The immune system is a body's defense system against infections and diseases. Organs, tissues, cells, and cell products work together to respond to dangerous organisms (like viruses or bacteria) and substances that may enter the body from the environment.

5. *Lymphatic System*

The lymphatic system is also a defense system for the body. It filters out organisms that cause disease, produces white blood cells, and generates disease-fighting antibodies. It also distributes fluids and nutrients in the body and drains excess fluids and protein so that tissues do not swell.

6. *Muscular System*

The muscular system is made up of tissues that work with the skeletal system to control movement of the body. Some muscles—like those in arms and legs—are voluntary, meaning that an individual decides when to move them. Other muscles, like the ones in the stomach, heart, intestines, and other organs, are involuntary. This means that they are controlled automatically by the nervous system and hormones—one often does not realize they are at work.

7. *Nervous System*

The nervous system is made up of the brain, the spinal cord, and nerves. One of the most important systems in the body, the nervous system is the body's control system. It sends, receives, and processes nerve impulses throughout the body. These nerve impulses tell muscles and organs what to do and how to respond to the environment.

8. *Reproductive System*

The reproductive system allows humans to produce children. Sperm from the male fertilizes the female's egg, or ovum, in the fallopian tube. The fertilized egg travels from the fallopian tube to the uterus, where the fetus develops over a period of 9 months.

9. *Respiratory System*

The respiratory system brings air into the body and removes carbon dioxide. It includes the nose, trachea, and lungs.

10. *Skeletal System*

The skeletal system is made up of bones, ligaments, and tendons. It shapes the body and protects organs. The skeletal system works with the muscular system to help the body move.

11. *Urinary System*

The urinary system eliminates waste from the body in the form of urine. The kidneys remove waste from the blood. The waste combines with water to form urine.

THE INDICATORS OF MENTAL AND EMOTIONAL ILLNESS THROUGHOUT THE LIFESPAN

Psychopathology refers to either the study of mental illness or the manifestation of behaviors that may be indicative of mental illness or psychological impairment.

In the 16th and 17th centuries, bizarre behavior associated with mental illness was believed to be acts of evil spirits, demons, or the devil. To remedy this, many individuals suffering from mental illness were tortured in an attempt to drive out demons. When the torturous methods failed to return individuals to sanity, they were typically deemed eternally possessed and were executed.

By the 18th century, mental illness was viewed differently. It was during this time period that "madness" began to be seen as an illness beyond the control of an individual rather than the act of a demon. Because of this, thousands of people were confined to asylums where medical forms of treatment began to be investigated.

Today, the medical model is a driving force in the diagnosing and treatment of psychopathology.

There is a general consensus that psychopathology is influenced by the milieus in which clients are socialized and the cultural experiences to which they have been exposed. The magnitude of cultural influences on psychopathology is not fully known. Certainly definitions of aberrant behavior vary between cultural groups.

Many different professions, including social work, are involved in studying and/or treating mental illness or psychopathology.

Although the *Diagnostic and Statistical Manual of Mental Disorders (DSM)* provides a framework and criteria for applying uniform labels to psychiatric dysfunction, the process of social work assessment and diagnosis is much broader.

Diagnosis refers to the process of identifying problems, with their underlying causes and practical solutions.

A diagnosis is generally obtained after a social worker utilizes information gained through the assessment. Diagnosing includes drawing inferences and reaching conclusions based on the data available. A social worker should not diagnose if adequate information or data is not available.

A social worker must consider biological, psychological, and social factors when identifying the root causes of client problems.

Diagnostic information should always be shared with clients and used to facilitate the establishment of intervention plans.

Assessment and diagnosis must be a continual part of the problem-solving process.

The assessment process must focus on client strengths and resources for addressing problems.

There are some terms and concepts that a social worker should be familiar with when making assessments and/or diagnosing.

1. *Comorbid*: existing with or at the same time; for instance, having two different illnesses at the same time

2. *Contraindicated*: not recommended or safe to use (a medication or treatment that is contraindicated would not be prescribed because it could have serious consequences)

3. *Delusion*: false, fixed belief despite evidence to the contrary (believing something that is not true)

4. *Disorientation*: confusion with regard to person, time, or place

5. *Dissociation*: disturbance or change in the usually integrative functions of memory, identity, perception, or consciousness (often seen in clients with a history of trauma)

6. *Endogenous depression*: depression caused by a ~~biochemical imbalance~~ *internal stressor* rather than a psychosocial stressor or external factors

7. *Exogenous depression*: depression caused by external events or psychosocial stressors

8. *Folie à deux*: shared delusion

9. *Hallucinations*: hearing, seeing, smelling, or feeling something that is not real (auditory most common)

10. *Hypomanic*: elevated, expansive, or irritable mood that is less severe than full-blown manic symptoms (not severe enough to interfere with functioning and not accompanied by psychotic symptoms)

11. *Postmorbid*: subsequent to the onset of an illness

12. *Premorbid*: prior to the onset of an illness

13. *Psychotic*: experiencing delusions or hallucinations

CO-OCCURRING DISORDERS AND CONDITIONS

Co-occurring disorders and conditions are present when there are two or more disorders occurring at the same time. For example, clients may have one or more disorders relating to the use of alcohol and/or other drugs, as well as one or more mental disorders. In order for a disorder or condition to be co-occurring, it must be independent and not symptomatology resulting from the other disorder(s)/condition(s).

Co-occurring disorders used to be called dual diagnoses or dual disorders. Just as the field of treatment for substance use and mental disorders has evolved to become more precise, so too has the terminology used to describe clients with both substance use and mental disorders. Many clients with severe mental illness are further impaired by Substance Use Disorders. However, co-occurring can also be used to describe clients with other conditions, such as those with physical and/or intellectual disabilities.

Though co-occurring, disorders and conditions may not be equivalent in severity, chronicity, and/or degree of impairment in functioning. For example, disorders or conditions may each be severe or mild, or one may be more severe than the other. The severity of both disorders or conditions may also change over time.

Compared with clients who have a single disorder or condition, clients with co-occurring disorders or conditions often require longer treatment, have more crises, and progress more gradually in treatment. Integrated treatment or treatment that considers the presence of all the disorders or conditions at the same time is associated with lower costs and better outcomes.

SYMPTOMS OF NEUROLOGIC AND ORGANIC DISORDERS

Neurologic and organic symptoms are those that are caused by disorders that affect part or all of the nervous system or are biologically based. These symptoms can vary greatly. For example, the nervous system controls many different body functions. Symptoms can, but do not have to, be associated with pain, including headache and back pain. Neurologic symptoms can also include muscle weakness or lack of coordination, abnormal sensations in the skin, and disturbances of vision, taste, smell, and hearing.

They may be minor (such as a foot that has fallen asleep) or life threatening (such as coma due to stroke).

Some Common Neurologic Symptoms

Pain

- Back pain
- Neck pain

- Headache
- Pain along a nerve pathway (as sciatica)

Muscle malfunction

- Weakness
- Tremor (rhythmic shaking of a body part)
- Paralysis
- Involuntary (unintended) movements (such as tics)
- Clumsiness or poor coordination
- Muscle spasms

Changes in sensation

- Numbness of the skin
- Tingling or a "pins-and-needles" sensation
- Hypersensitivity to light touch
- Loss of sensation for touch, cold, heat, or pain

Other symptoms

- Vertigo
- Loss of balance
- Slurred speech (dysarthria)

Changes in consciousness

- Fainting
- Confusion or delirium
- Seizures (ranging from brief lapses in consciousness to severe muscle contractions and jerking throughout the body)

Changes in cognition (mental ability)

- Difficulty understanding language or using language to speak or write (aphasia)
- Poor memory
- Inability to recognize familiar objects (agnosia) or familiar faces (prosopagnosia)
- Inability to do simple arithmetic (acalculia)

Changes in the senses

- Disturbances of smell and taste
- Partial or complete loss of vision

- Double vision
- Deafness
- Ringing or other sounds originating in the ears (tinnitus)

Organic brain syndrome is a term used to describe physical disorders that impair mental function. The most common symptoms are confusion; impairment of memory, judgment, and intellectual function; and agitation. Disorders that cause injury or damage to the brain and contribute to organic brain syndrome include, but are not limited to, alcoholism, Alzheimer's disease, Fetal Alcohol Spectrum Disorders (FASDs), Parkinson's disease, and stroke.

Elderly clients are at high risk for depression, as well as cognitive disorders, the latter of which can be chronic (as in dementia) or acute (as in delirium). Some patients have both affective (mood) and cognitive disorders. Clarifying the diagnosis is the first step to effective treatment, but this can be particularly difficult because elderly clients often have medical comorbidities that can contribute to cognitive and affective changes.

	Delirium	Dementia	Depression
Alertness	Altered level of consciousness; alertness may fluctuate	May vary	May vary
Motor behavior	Fluctuates; lethargy or hyperactivity	May vary	Psychomotor behavior may be agitated or unaffected
Attention	Impaired and fluctuates	Usually normal	Usually normal, but may be distractible
Awareness	Impaired, reduced	Clear	Clear
Course	Acute; responds to treatment	Chronic, with deterioration over time	Chronic; responds to treatment
Progression	Abrupt	Slow but stable	Varies
Orientation	Fluctuates in severity; usually impaired	May be impaired	May be selective disorientation
Memory	Recent and immediate impaired	Recent and remote impaired	Selective or patchy impairment

(continued)

	Delirium	Dementia	Depression
Thinking	Disorganized, distorted, incoherent; slow or accelerated	Difficulty with abstraction; thoughts impoverished; difficulty finding words; poor judgment	Intact, but may voice hopelessness and self-deprecation
Instrumental activities of daily living (IADLs)	May be intact or impaired	May be intact early; impaired ADLs as disease progresses	May be intact or impaired
Stability	Variable, hour-to-hour	Fairly stable	Some variability
Emotions	Irritable, aggressive, fearful	Labile, apathetic, irritable	Flat, unresponsive, or sad; may be irritable
Activities of daily living (ADLs)	May be intact or impaired	May be intact early, impaired as disease progresses	May neglect basic self-care

THE TYPES OF INFORMATION AVAILABLE FROM OTHER SOURCES (E.G., AGENCY, EMPLOYMENT, MEDICAL, PSYCHOLOGICAL, LEGAL, OR SCHOOL RECORDS)

Assessment is ongoing within the problem-solving process. In order to ensure that all relevant information is considered, social workers often rely on information available from clients' existing records in addition to the data that they collect directly.

In order to access this information, it is critical that social workers are aware of laws governing the release of such information and get the informed consent of clients prior to requesting these documents. The consent process must make clients aware of the reasons for such requests and the benefits and risks of social workers obtaining this information.

When information is obtained, it becomes part of the client record. Though protected by the Health Insurance Portability and Accountability Act (HIPAA), these client records can be subject to subpoenas and/or court orders. Thus, inclusion of this information in their records can have some additional risks associated with the legal duty to release them if court ordered to do so.

Despite this risk, using existing employment, medical, psychological, psychiatric, and educational records can be very helpful when completing a biopsychosocial–spiritual–cultural history.

Employment records may help social workers construct clients' work histories and obtain data about income earned from their jobs. These records may be essential if clients need assistance with applying for Unemployment Insurance or other public benefits (Temporary Assistance for Needy Families [TANF], Supplemental Nutrition Assistance Program [SNAP], and so on).

Medical records are essential to ensure that client problems are not a result of health issues and to better understand the impact of past or current medical problems on client functioning.

Psychological records can be helpful as they can contain the results of any psychological testing that has been completed and whether any mental health diagnoses have been assigned. Whether or not a client has been prescribed psychotropic medications and/or received any subsequent treatment for behavioral health concerns would also be contained in psychiatric records.

When working with children, educational records are often consulted to determine performance in school and whether any problems experienced at home or elsewhere are being manifested in this setting as well. When working with adults, educational records can provide clues as to the age at which problems or difficulties began. Historical educational records are often used to diagnose adults with intellectual or developmental disabilities if they were not appropriately identified while in school.

THE IMPACT OF CAREGIVING ON FAMILIES

Although caregiving is at the heart of family functioning, the dynamics of families can be greatly altered when family members experience physical illness or disability. For example, when a primary family caregiver becomes ill or disabled, family roles must shift to redistribute the tasks he or she is unable to perform. This redistribution includes both instrumental and emotional tasks, as the family may face a loss of both financial and emotional support that was provided by the primary family caregiver.

When a child is ill or disabled, parents can be overwhelmed by the added responsibilities to typical childrearing. In addition, healthy siblings may also feel the strain and may feel that they should not "burden" parents any further, so they ignore their own emotional and/or physical needs.

The stage when physical illness or disability occurs within the life course can also have differential impacts. For example, parents of children born ill or disabled may be more accepting of the situation than those who are faced with the illness or disability of children that occurs later. At any time, it is a major challenge for a family to tend to its members' individual developmental needs and meet the caregiving demands of a serious illness or disability. Some families may be paralyzed at the time of the illness or onset of the disability. Crisis intervention may be needed to stabilize the situation and develop coping skills.

Addressing the grief or loss that can accompany chronic illness or disability may also be needed. In addition, families may seek help from social workers to identify critical resources because they are not able to meet family members' needs and/or their own without them. Lastly, illness and disability can be isolating for an individual, as well as his or her family.

THE DYNAMICS AND EFFECTS OF LOSS, SEPARATION, AND GRIEF

Elisabeth Kübler-Ross outlined what has been the traditional five stages of grief. She originally developed this model based on her observations of people suffering from terminal illness. She later expanded her theory to apply to any form of personal loss, such as the death of a loved one, the loss of a job or income, major rejection, the end of a relationship or divorce, drug addiction, incarceration, the onset of a disease or chronic illness, and/or an infertility diagnosis, as well as many tragedies and disasters (and even minor losses).

> **Denial and isolation:** Shock is replaced with the feeling of "this can't be happening to me."
>
> **Anger:** The emotional confusion that results from this loss may lead to anger and finding someone or something to blame—"why me?"
>
> **Bargaining:** The next stage may result in trying to negotiate with one's self (or a higher power) to attempt to change what has occurred.
>
> **Depression:** A period of sadness and loneliness will then occur, in which a person reflects on his or her grief and loss.
>
> **Acceptance:** After time feeling depressed about the loss, a person will eventually be at peace with what happened.
>
> Hope is not a separate stage, but is possible at any stage.

THE IMPACT OF PHYSICAL AND MENTAL ILLNESS ON FAMILY DYNAMICS

Physical illness and/or disability places a set of extra demands on the family system. An illness and/or disability can consume a lot of a family's resources of time, energy, and money, so that other individual and family needs may go unmet.

Day-to-day assistance may lead to exhaustion and fatigue, taxing the physical and emotional energy of family members. There can be emotional strain, including worry, guilt, anxiety, anger, and uncertainty about the cause or prognosis of the disability, about the future, about the needs of other family members, and about whether the individual is getting enough assistance.

There can be a financial burden associated with getting health, education, and social services; buying or renting equipment and devices; making accommodations to the home; transportation; and acquiring medications and/or special food. The person or family may be eligible for payment or reimbursement from an insurance company and/or a publicly funded program such as Medicaid or Supplemental Security Income. However, knowing about services and programs and then working to become eligible is another major challenge faced by families.

Working through eligibility issues and coordinating among different providers is a challenge faced by families for which they may want a social worker to assist.

Many communities still lack programs, facilities, and resources that allow for the full inclusion of persons with disabilities. Families often report that one burden comes from dealing with people in the community whose attitudes and behaviors are judgmental, stigmatizing, and rejecting.

There are differential impacts on families. The degree to which a physical illness and/or disability limits activities or functions of daily living or the ages of individuals or parents when an illness/disability emerges are important factors that may impact on adjustment.

The impact of mental illness on family dynamics also can be profound. Mental illness of a family member affects all aspects of family functioning, including physical, financial, and emotional well-being. These impacts often depend upon the relationship of family members to a person with a mental illness. For those closest, there can be considerable time spent addressing some of the practical impacts of mental illness, such as financial problems and disruptions to daily life. This time commitment can result in family members giving up things they care about or missing appointments needed for their own health or well-being.

When mental illness is first diagnosed, family members may deny that there is a continuing illness. If there is a crisis, family members may be upset about what is happening, but the desire to put the incident "behind them" often emerges once the episode is over. Thus, family members may believe that the symptomatic behavior of the mental illness will never return. Some family members often do understand the reality of the illness, whereas others do not. This can cause problems and tension within the family, as well as isolation and loss of meaningful relationships with those who are not supportive of the illness.

Due to the stigma sometimes associated with mental illness, family members may often be reluctant to discuss it with others because they do not know how other people will react. Isolation can also occur because family members may be reluctant to invite anyone to the home for fear of the presence of unpredictable behavior and/or the fear that the activity may be a stressor, triggering behavior related to the illness. This isolation causes families to withdraw from previous relationships to protect both themselves and their loved ones.

Families may have little knowledge about mental illness. They may inappropriately believe that it is a condition that is totally disabling. Without correct information, families may become very pessimistic about the future. They may need assistance from social workers in learning how to manage the illness and to plan for the future.

It is difficult for anyone to deal with strange thinking and bizarre and unpredictable behavior. Family members may be bewildered, frightened, and exhausted. Even when stabilized, those with mental illness may have apathy and lack of motivation that can be frustrating to family members. Family members may become angry and frustrated as they struggle to get back to a routine that previously they took for granted. If the illness is not stable, families go from crisis to crisis, feeling that they have no control over what is happening. Family life can be unsettled and unpredictable. It becomes very difficult, often impossible, to plan for family outings or vacations. The needs of those with mental illness take over the attention of families and siblings can feel that their needs are put off or ignored.

THE INDICATORS OF BEHAVIORAL DYSFUNCTION

"Normal" and "abnormal" depend on the person, place, and situation, and are largely shaped by social standards. Definitions of "normal" change with societal standards and norms. Normality is often viewed as good, whereas abnormality is seen as bad. When people do not conform to what is perceived as "normal," they are often given a number of negative labels, including unusual, sick, or disabled. These labels can lead to that individual being marginalized, or stigmatized.

The most comprehensive attempt to distinguish normality from abnormality is the *DSM*. The *DSM* shows how normality has changed throughout history and how it often involves value judgments. The *DSM* explicitly distinguishes mental disorders and nondisordered conditions.

THE INDICATORS OF FEIGNING ILLNESS

Malingering is not considered a mental illness. In the *DSM-5*, malingering receives a V code as one of the other conditions that may be a focus of clinical attention. The *DSM-5* defines malingering as intentionally falsely or grossly exaggerating physical or psychological problems. Motivation for malingering is usually external, such as avoiding work/military, obtaining reward (financial resources, medications, etc.), avoiding legal action, and so on. On the other hand, malingering also may be an adaptive response such as an inmate with mental illness trying to obtain relatively sparse and difficult-to-obtain mental health resources in prison.

Malingering varies in intensity, from all symptoms being falsified to some symptoms being falsified or symptoms being exaggerated. Malingering is not easy to diagnose because of the difficulty in gathering external evidence.

Prolonged direct observation can reveal evidence of malingering because it is difficult for a client who is malingering to maintain consistency with the false or exaggerated claims for extended periods. Malingering can be detected by discrepancies between the claimed distress and the objective findings or lack of cooperation during evaluation and in complying with prescribed treatment. Clues may be reports of rare or improbable symptoms. Rare symptoms—by definition—occur very infrequently, and clients almost never report improbable symptoms. In addition, social workers should watch closely for internal or external inconsistent presentation of symptoms. Often diagnosis comes as a result of the use of collateral data beyond the social work interview.

Malingering is different from Factitious Disorder (in which the motive is the desire to occupy a sick role, rather than some form of material gain) and Somatic Symptom and Related Disorders (in which symptoms are not produced willfully).

Three categories of malingering are:

- Pure malingering (feigning a nonexistent disorder)
- Partial malingering (consciously exaggerating real symptoms)
- False imputation (ascribing real symptoms to a cause a client knows is unrelated to the symptoms)

THE INDICATORS OF SOMATIZATION

Somatization is the unconscious process by which psychological distress is expressed as physical symptoms. Somatic symptoms often occur as reactions to stressful situations and are not considered abnormal if they occur sporadically. However, some clients experience continuing somatic symptoms and even seek medical care for them.

Persistent somatization is associated with considerable distress and disability. Somatization may lead to overutilization of medical care, including unnecessary medical tests, and even increased hospitalization rates.

Not all somatizing clients are motivated by an unconscious wish to adopt the sick role, as is observed in clients with Factitious Disorder. Clients may vary in their degree of conviction that their symptoms are caused by a physical illness or disease. Clients may also present in multiple ways, including having multiple unexplained somatic symptoms, exhibiting predominantly illness worry or hypochondriacal beliefs, and/or displaying somatization as a manifestation of a variety of mental disorders.

BODY IMAGE AND ITS IMPACT (E.G., IDENTITY, SELF-ESTEEM, RELATIONSHIPS, HABITS)

Body image is the way one perceives and relates to his or her body, and how one thinks he or she is seen.

Body image affects nearly everyone from time to time. Body image is not only influenced by the perceptions of others, but by the media and cultural forces as well. Senses are bombarded by an onslaught of mixed messages about how one "should" look or think about his or her body.

Having a healthy body image is a key to well-being, both mentally and physically. A positive body image means that, most of the time, a client has a realistic perception of, and feels comfortable with, his or her looks.

Factors associated with positive body image:

- Acceptance and appreciation of natural body shape and body differences
- Self-worth not tied to appearance
- Confidence in and comfort with body
- An unreasonable amount of time is not spent worrying about food, weight, or calories
- Judgment of others is not made related to their body weight, shape, and/or eating or exercise habits
- Knowing physical appearance says very little about character and value as a person

Factors of negative body image:

- Distorted perception of shape or body parts, unlike what they really are
- Believing only other people are attractive and that body size or shape is a sign of personal failure
- Feeling body doesn't measure up to family, social, or media ideals
- Ashamed, self-conscious, and anxious about body
- Uncomfortable and awkward in body
- Constant negative thoughts about body and comparisons to others

Some possible effects of a negative body image:

- Emotional distress
- Low self-esteem
- Unhealthy dieting habits
- Anxiety

- Depression
- Eating disorders
- Social withdrawal or isolation

THE INDICATORS OF TRAUMATIC STRESS AND VIOLENCE

Stress is a typical response to feeling overwhelmed or threatened. Fight, flight, and freeze are survival responses to protect individuals from danger. Individuals react and respond to stress in different ways. There are many disadvantages to a stressful lifestyle that creates constant feelings of being overwhelmed, as well as physiological stimulation. Interventions aimed at social and lifestyle changes can usually restore physiological and psychological balance in order to address stress.

This is not the case when traumatization occurs. Traumatization is when a client experiences neurological distress that does not go away or when he or she is not able to return to a state of equilibrium. Traumatization can lead to mental, social, emotional, and physical disability. Like stress, trauma is also experienced differently by different individuals.

There are many indicators of traumatic stress and violence, including:

1. Addictive behaviors related to drugs, alcohol, sex, shopping, and gambling
2. An inability to tolerate conflicts with others or intense feelings
3. A belief of being bad, worthless, without value or importance
4. Dichotomous "all or nothing" thinking
5. Chronic and repeated suicidal thoughts/feelings
6. Poor attachment
7. Dissociation
8. Eating disorders—anorexia, bulimia, and obesity
9. Self-blame
10. Intense anxiety and repeated panic attacks
11. Depression
12. Self-harm, self-mutilation, self-injury, or self-destruction
13. Unexplained, but intense, fears of people, places, or things

When trauma or violence occurs during childhood, children may have problems regulating their behaviors and emotions. They may be clingy and fearful of new situations, easily frightened, difficult to console, aggressive, impulsive, sleepless, delayed in developmental milestones, and/or regressing in functioning and behavior.

In order to practice competently in this area, social workers must:

1. Realize the widespread impact of trauma and understand potential paths for recovery

2. Recognize the signs and symptoms of trauma in clients, families, staff, and other systems

3. Respond by fully integrating knowledge about trauma into social work policies, procedures, and practices

4. Seek to actively resist retraumatization

THE EFFECTS OF LIFE EVENTS, STRESSORS, AND CRISES ON INDIVIDUALS, FAMILIES, GROUPS, ORGANIZATIONS, AND COMMUNITIES

Crisis is an essential component in the understanding of human growth and development. It has important implications for quality of life and subjective well-being. Crisis situations are viewed as unusual, mostly negative events that tend to disrupt the normal life of a person.

A crisis is an upset to a steady state. When a stressful event becomes a crisis, the individual or family is vulnerable and feels mounting anxiety, tension, and disequilibrium. A precipitating cause of a crisis does not have to be a major event. It may be the "last straw" in a series of events that exceed a client's ability to cope.

An individual or family, at this point, may be emotionally overtaxed, hopeless, and incapable of effective functioning or making good choices and decisions. The person or family is at a "critical turning point" of coping effectively or not effectively.

The way in which life crises are addressed—whether surviving trauma, parental divorce, or a personal loss—has a very significant role to play in determining quality of life. When crises are understood, dealt with, and overcome, clients emerge as healthier and happier.

Crisis situations are viewed as unusual, mostly negative life events that tend to disrupt typical functioning. The concept of crises is an essential component in the understanding of human growth and development. Erickson's theory of psychosocial development suggests that crises and major life transitions are similar in their components, though they vary in their degree and intensity.

It is difficult to avoid crises and the ways in which they are handled is significant in determining subsequent quality of life. The same life events can strengthen the mutual ties of one family and leave another ready to collapse.

Crises can result from family problems, domestic violence, separation and divorce, addictions, financial distress, illness, and/or death. According to systems theory, a life event or stress-producing situation for a client will result in impacts to his or her family as well.

Family crises are disruptions in families' usual patterns of functioning. Families in crisis find that their usual ways of coping or problem solving do not work; as a result, they feel vulnerable, anxious, and overwhelmed. Family members may have difficulty thinking clearly, dwell on meaningless activities, express hostility or numbness, be impulsive or dependent, and/or feel incompetent.

Families are thrust into crises when more than one of the following occurs:

- They experience a stress-producing situation
- They have difficulty coping
- They show chronic difficulty meeting basic family responsibilities
- They lack sources of support

These negative life events are not always the causes of crises. Positive events, such as marriages or job promotions, can also trigger crises as individuals may move out of their family homes or have increased employment demands that impact the functioning of their family units.

Crises are time-limited and can be characterized by the following phases that are not necessarily sequential or discrete.

1. Life event occurs
2. Life event is seen as threatening
3. Family responds in a disorganized manner
4. Family searches for a solution
5. Family adopts new coping strategies

Crises present opportunities for positive change, and social workers should work with families toward such change. Crises help families discover and strengthen problem-solving skills. During a period of intense crisis, when usual methods of coping fail, families may be open to learning new problem-solving approaches. The goal is to resolve crises constructively and better prepare families for their next challenges. Quick, highly active responses by social workers are essential during crises to mitigate negative effects.

THE IMPACT OF OUT-OF-HOME PLACEMENT (E.G., HOSPITALIZATION, FOSTER CARE, RESIDENTIAL CARE, CRIMINAL JUSTICE SYSTEM) ON CLIENTS/CLIENT SYSTEMS

The use of out-of-home placement is generally viewed as an intervention that only occurs when there is a health or safety risk in the home. This risk can be due to the individual who is being removed (caused by a medical or behavioral health issue of the individual being removed) or his or her family members (caused by child abuse or neglect, medical or behavioral health issues of a family member, etc.). Often, out-of-home placement occurs after in-home interventions have been tried and failed.

Individuals who are placed outside of their homes often experience significant life problems. Determining whether these issues are directly caused by the removal is difficult as these individuals are likely to be at-risk for such problems prior to the placements.

For example, children who are removed from their homes due to abuse and/or neglect typically use mental health or other social services more than before they were placed away from their parents. These children often report a high level of stress, which may manifest in substance abuse, chronic aggressive or destructive behavior, suicidal ideation or acting out, and/or patterns of runaway behavior. Academic problems are also common among these children.

For all those leaving their homes, regardless of age, there is a disruption of emotional bonds with other family members, which is often accompanied by rage, grief, sadness, and/or despair.

THE IMPACT OF OUT-OF-HOME DISPLACEMENT (E.G., NATURAL DISASTER, HOMELESSNESS, IMMIGRATION) ON CLIENTS/CLIENT SYSTEMS

The homes in which clients live are part of their self-definition. They are decorated to reflect likes or dislikes, telling others about their occupants and accommodating interests such as gardening, cooking, and others. Homes are seen as extensions of their residents and distinguish people from each other.

Behavior is also cued by the physical environment. Homes remind inhabitants of experiences which took place in the past, as well as what to do in the future. Homes are familiar and are often viewed as safe havens where clients can behave without being judged.

Thus, involuntary displacement outside the home due to hospitalization, incarceration, needed safety, or long-term care needs can be traumatic for many reasons. First, such movement may be associated with losses such as those due to health issues, financial concerns, or safety problems. These losses alone can cause depression, anxiety, confusion, and/or other emotional reactions, which are compounded from having to move from the communities or homes in which clients live.

In out-of-home placements, clients may have changes in roles, causing them to develop poor self-image. For example, the roles of neighbor, community leader, gardener, and so on, which provided fulfillment and recognition, may be lost and no longer possible. Since there is status attached to these roles, their loss can negatively affect self-image.

There also may be a loss of possessions associated with displacement. Precious items that represent a lifetime of memories may have been destroyed, such as by a natural disaster, or sold/given away as there may be no room to keep them in the new settings—especially if they are shared with others.

There also may be a cost associated with involuntary displacement. For example, long-term care can drain client assets and make clients feel guilty about spending money on themselves or fearful about running out of funds for sustained care and housing.

Out-of-home displacement also often accompanies loss of relationships. Relatives and friends who interfaced with clients in their homes may find it inconvenient or impossible to see them in the new settings. Sometimes the lack of private space in which to visit puts up barriers. Visitors may also be intimidated by the sights and sounds of hospitals, jails, or nursing homes.

Clients frequently do not have the same freedom or control that they had when they were at home. In congregate settings, meals, activities, room cleaning, and bathing may be overseen and scheduled for the sake of organization and efficiency, and there are usually numerous rules, policies, and procedures to follow with less individual autonomy and choice.

THE INDICATORS AND RISK FACTORS OF THE CLIENT'S/CLIENT SYSTEM'S DANGER TO SELF AND OTHERS

There are risk factors that must be considered in any assessment, because they are linked to a risk of suicide or violence.

Danger to Self: Suicide

Risk Factors

- History of previous suicide attempt (best predictor of future attempt; medical seriousness of attempt is also significant)
- Lives alone; lack of social supports
- Presence of psychiatric disorder—depression (feeling hopeless), Anxiety Disorder, Personality Disorder (*A client is also at greater risk after*

being discharged from the hospital or after being started on antidepressants as he or she may now have the energy to implement a suicide plan.)

- Substance abuse
- Family history of suicide
- Exposure to suicidal behavior of others through media or peers
- Losses—relationship, job, financial, social
- Presence of firearm or easy access to other lethal methods

Some Protective Factors

- Effective and appropriate clinical care for mental, physical, and Substance Use Disorders
- Easy access to a variety of clinical interventions and support (i.e., medical and mental health care)
- Restricted access to highly lethal methods
- Family and community support
- Learned coping and stress-reduction skills
- Cultural and religious beliefs that discourage suicide and support self-preservation

Some Behavioral Warning Signs

- Change in eating and sleeping habits
- Drug and alcohol use
- Unusual neglect of personal appearance
- Marked personality change
- Loss of interest in pleasurable activities
- Not tolerating praise or rewards
- Giving away belongings
- Isolation from others
- Taking care of legal and other issues
- Dramatic increase in mood (might indicate a client has made a decision to end his or her life)
- Verbalizes threats to commit suicide or feelings of despair and hopelessness
  - "I'm going to kill myself."
  - "I wish I were dead."
  - "My family would be better off without me."
  - "The only way out for me is to die."

■ "It's just too much for me to put up with."

■ "Nobody needs me anymore."

Danger to Others: Violence

Risk Factors

■ Youth who become violent before age 13 generally commit more crimes, and more serious crimes, for a longer time; these youth exhibit a pattern of escalating violence throughout childhood, sometimes continuing into adulthood

■ Most highly aggressive children or children with behavioral disorders do not become serious violent offenders

■ Serious violence is associated with drugs, guns, and other risky behaviors

■ Involvement with delinquent peers and gang membership are two of the most powerful predictors of violence

Some Protective Factors

■ Effective programs combine components that address both individual risks and environmental conditions; building individual skills and competencies; changes in peer groups

■ Interventions that target change in social context appear to be more effective, on average, than those that attempt to change individual attitudes, skills, and risk behaviors

■ Effective and appropriate clinical care for mental, physical, and substance abuse disorders

■ Easy access to a variety of clinical interventions and support (i.e., medical and mental health care)

■ Restricted access to highly lethal methods

■ Family and community support

■ Learned coping and stress reduction skills

Some Behavioral Warning Signs

■ Drug and alcohol use

■ Marked personality changes

■ Angry outbursts

■ Preoccupation with killing, war, violence, weapons, and so on

- Isolation from others
- Obtaining guns or other lethal methods

THE IMPACT OF STRESS, TRAUMA, AND VIOLENCE

Emotional and psychological trauma is the result of extraordinarily stressful events that destroy a sense of security, making a client feel helpless and vulnerable in a dangerous world.

Traumatic experiences often involve a threat to life or safety, but **any situation that leaves a client feeling overwhelmed and alone can be traumatic, even if it does not involve physical harm.** It is not the objective facts that determine whether an event is traumatic, but a subjective emotional experience of the event.

An event will most likely lead to emotional or psychological trauma if:

- It happened unexpectedly
- There was not preparation for it
- There is a feeling of having been powerless to prevent it

- It happens repeatedly
- Someone was intentionally cruel
- It happened in childhood

Emotional and psychological trauma can be caused by one-time events or ongoing, relentless stress.

Not all potentially traumatic events lead to lasting emotional and psychological damage. Some clients rebound quickly from even the most tragic and shocking experiences. Others are devastated by experiences that, on the surface, appear to be less upsetting.

A number of risk factors make clients susceptible to emotional and psychological trauma. Clients are more likely to be traumatized by a stressful experience if they are already under a heavy stress load or have recently suffered a series of losses.

Clients are also more likely to be traumatized by a new situation if they have been traumatized before—especially if the earlier trauma occurred in childhood. Experiencing trauma in childhood can have a severe and long-lasting effect. Children who have been traumatized see the world as a frightening and dangerous place. When childhood trauma is not resolved, this fundamental sense of fear and helplessness carries over into adulthood, setting the stage for further trauma.

THE EFFECTS OF PHYSICAL, SEXUAL, AND PSYCHOLOGICAL ABUSE ON INDIVIDUALS, FAMILIES, GROUPS, ORGANIZATIONS, AND COMMUNITIES

Abuse and neglect have both immediate and long-term consequences. The impacts are often influenced by various factors including the extent and type of abuse or neglect, whether it was continual or infrequent, the age at which it occurred, the relationship to the perpetrator (if abuse), and how the abuse or neglect was discovered and addressed upon disclosure. Client personality traits, inner strength, and support systems also influence the effects.

For many, the impacts of abuse and neglect will not be immediately evident. Physical injuries, if there are any, are usually temporary. The more damaging and lasting impacts are those that result from impaired language, cognitive, and physical development due to the abuse and neglect. Children who have been abused and neglected are at risk of academic problems and school failure due to difficulty following rules, being respectful, staying in their seats and keeping on-task, temper tantrums, and/or difficult peer relationships.

In addition, social and emotional problems, poor relationships, substance use and dependency, risky or violent behaviors, and delinquency are manifestations of abuse and neglect. The psychological consequences of abuse and neglect include isolation, fear, inability to trust, low self-esteem, anxiety, depression, and hopelessness. These difficulties can lead to relationship problems and the possibility of antisocial behavioral traits.

It is important to note that not all those who have been abused and neglected will experience physical, behavioral, and/or psychological problems—though they are more likely. Thus, a lack of these problems should not be used as evidence that abuse or neglect did not occur.

THE INDICATORS, DYNAMICS, AND IMPACT OF EXPLOITATION ACROSS THE LIFESPAN (E.G., FINANCIAL, IMMIGRATION STATUS, SEXUAL TRAFFICKING)

Exploitation is treating someone badly in order to benefit from his or her resources or work. It is when someone uses a situation to gain unfair advantage for himself or herself. Exploitation is more common when there is a power differential between parties due to social status, abilities, income, education, job position, and so on.

Social workers have ethical mandates not to exploit clients, supervisees, students, and others who they come in contact with in their work.

They also may be asked to assess exploitation of clients by others and intervene when needed. For example, a form of maltreatment sometimes seen with older adults is financial/material exploitation or unauthorized use of an older person's resources. Individuals may befriend an older person to gain his or her trust so that the older adult's money or items of value can be inappropriately used for the individual's wants or needs and not the care of the older adult.

On a macro level, it is also important to see the relationship between discrimination and exploitation of individuals. When individuals are not provided the same access to social rewards, they are inherently exploited. Most social problems are aggravated by the status of particular groups in the society, including that:

- There is a greater prevalence of poverty among people of color and female household heads.
- Poverty decreases the opportunities for employment, education, goods, and so on.
- Poverty creates greater stresses that lead to physical and mental illnesses, family breakdown, inability to work, and other problems.
- Discrimination creates deficits in social power.

THE CHARACTERISTICS OF PERPETRATORS OF ABUSE, NEGLECT, AND EXPLOITATION

Many individuals with these characteristics do not commit acts of abuse. However, some factors are more likely to be present in those who commit abusive acts. Thus, having one of these risk factors does not mean that an individual will become an abuser, but an abuser is likely to have one or more of these risk factors.

A past history of violent behavior is the best predictor of future violence. Each prior act of violence increases the chance of future episodes of violence. In addition, those who suffered some form of abuse as children are more likely to be perpetrators of abuse as adults.

Risk factors include:

1. History of owning weapons and using them against others

2. Criminal history; repetitive antisocial behavior

3. Drug and alcohol use (substance use is associated with the most violent crimes)

4. Psychiatric disorder with coexisting substance abuse

5. Certain psychiatric symptoms such as psychosis, intense suspiciousness, anger, and/or unhappiness

6. Personality Disorders (Borderline and Antisocial Personality Disorders)

7. History of impulsivity; low frustration tolerance; recklessness; inability to tolerate criticism; entitlement

8. Angry affect without empathy for others—high anger scores associated with increased chance of violence

9. Environmental stressors: lower socioeconomic status or poverty; job termination

A social worker should take all reports of abuse and all threats for harm seriously.

A social worker can distinguish between static and dynamic risk factors.

Static risk factors: factors that cannot be changed by interventions such as past history of violent behavior or demographic information.

Dynamic risk factors: factors that can be changed by interventions such as change in living situation, treatment of psychiatric symptoms, abstaining from drug and alcohol use, access to weapons, and so on. Each client presents with a unique set of risk factors that require an individualized plan.

Some of the risk factors include the following:

- *Stressors*: history of abuse; isolated with lack of social supports; low sense of self-competence and self-esteem; financial problems
- *Poor skills*: rigid, authoritarian; low intelligence quotient (IQ); poor self-control; poor communication, problem-solving, and interpersonal skills
- *Family issues*: marital discord, imbalanced relationship with marital partner (dominant or noninvolved); domestic violence; substance abuse

The victim is often blamed for the abuse by the perpetrator.

Interventions to reduce dynamic risk factors include:

- Pharmacological interventions
- Substance use treatment
- Psychosocial interventions
- Removal of weapons
- Increased level of supervision

THE INDICATORS OF ADDICTION AND SUBSTANCE ABUSE

Some people are able to engage in behaviors or use substances without abusing them and/or becoming addicted.

There are signs when clients are addicted to behaviors and/or substances are being abused. These include, but are not limited to, indications that the behavior or substance use is:

- Causing problems at work, home, school, and in relationships
- Resulting in neglected responsibilities at school, work, or home (i.e., flunking classes, skipping work, neglecting children)
- Dangerous (i.e., driving while on drugs, using dirty needles, having unprotected sex, binging/purging despite medical conditions)
- Causing financial and/or legal trouble (i.e., arrests, stealing to support shopping, gambling, or drug habit)
- Causing problems in relationships, such as fights with partner or family members or loss of old friends
- Creating tolerance (more of the behavior or substance is needed to produce the same impact)
- Out of control or causing a feeling of being powerless
- Life-consuming, resulting in abandoned activities that used to be enjoyed
- Resulting in psychological issues such as mood swings, attitude changes, depression, and/or paranoia

Signs of Drug Use

- Marijuana: glassy, red eyes; loud talking, inappropriate laughter followed by sleepiness; loss of interest, motivation; weight gain or loss
- Cocaine: dilated pupils; hyperactivity; euphoria; irritability; anxiety; excessive talking followed by depression or excessive sleeping at odd times; may go long periods of time without eating or sleeping; weight loss; dry mouth and nose
- Heroin: contracted pupils; no response of pupils to light; needle marks; sleeping at unusual times; sweating; vomiting; coughing, sniffling; twitching; loss of appetite

THE EFFECTS OF ADDICTION AND SUBSTANCE ABUSE ON INDIVIDUALS, FAMILIES, GROUPS, ORGANIZATIONS, AND COMMUNITIES

There are biopsychosocial–spiritual–cultural impacts of substance abuse or dependence on clients themselves. Clients who use drugs experience a wide array of physical effects other than those expected. The excitement or high that results from the use of cocaine is followed by a "crash": a period of anxiety, fatigue, depression, and an acute desire for more cocaine to alleviate these continued feelings. Marijuana and alcohol interfere with motor control and are factors in many automobile accidents. Users of hallucinogenic drugs may experience flashbacks, which are unwanted recurrences of the drug's effects weeks or months after use. Sudden abstinence from certain drugs results in withdrawal symptoms. For example, heroin withdrawal can cause vomiting, muscle cramps, convulsions, and delirium. With the continued use of substances that are physically addictive, tolerance develops; that is, constantly increasing amounts of the drug are needed to duplicate the initial effect.

Substance abuse or dependence also impacts mental health because it causes irrational behavior, violence, and lapses in memory. Chronic use of some substances can cause long-lasting changes in the brain, which may lead to paranoia, depression, aggression, and hallucinations.

In addition, because the purity and dosage of illegal drugs are uncontrolled, drug overdose is a constant risk. Many drug users also engage in criminal activity, such as burglary and prostitution, to raise money to buy drugs.

Substance use can disrupt family life and destroy relationships. A client's preoccupation with the substance, plus its impacts on mood and performance, can lead to relationship/marital problems. A client may spend more time on getting and using substances than attending to his or her relationships with others. Drug use can also create destructive patterns of codependency. Codependency occurs when a partner/spouse or members of the family, out of love or fear of consequences, inadvertently enables a client to continue using substances by covering up, supplying money, or denying there is a problem.

In addition, substance abuse or dependence can result in accidental injury, disability, legal involvement, and/or loss of income or employment, which negatively impacts on those who are friends or family members of a client. Neglect of friends and family, as well as anger that can lead to verbal assaults or physical violence, are also seen as a result of substance abuse or dependence.

Clients who are using or dependent on substances may also tend to neglect "old" relationships and find those who also engage in similar behaviors.

Clients with other addictions feel strong cravings or a dependency on whatever they are addicted to and feel afraid or powerless to let it go. Clients may feel ashamed or fear the consequences of their addictions being discovered. They will sometimes lie to conceal engagement in the behaviors or the extent of their problems.

Secrecy and deceit cause breakdowns in trust within relationships. Family members of those who are addicted may question their behavior and feel confused, scared, and angry at changes that they witness. Family members are frightened by unpredictable situations encountered due to those who are addicted experiencing ups and downs. One moment they are happy and positive, but then they can quickly become anxious, irritable, or depressed. Individuals may be preoccupied with their addictions and pay less attention to role responsibilities or the feelings/needs of others. They also may lose interest in family activities and appear withdrawn.

Family members of those who are addicted often take on more responsibility at home to compensate for the unreliability or unpredictability that accompanies addiction. Family members may feel they have to take control of everything as a way of compensating for the feelings of instability or unpredictability. Family members often feel strained as they try to successfully juggle extra responsibilities. Communication in these situations breaks down and relationships become strained or broken. Distance in relationships can result in a loss of interest in sex or intimacy.

Family members may be worried that their behavior will exacerbate the situation or cause clients' addictions to worsen. Children in families with addiction also feel the effects because they are aware of arguments and tension in the home and feel scared and confused. They are also more likely to develop addictive behaviors as ways of coping.

CRIMINAL JUSTICE SYSTEMS

Social work is an essential component of the nation's criminal justice system. For the most part, social work practice as performed in the various criminal (and juvenile) justice systems in the United States is variously referred to as criminal justice social work, correctional social work, or forensic social work.

Criminal justice social workers serve as frontline staff and administrators in criminal justice settings. There are many thousands of social workers employed in criminal justice settings, serving criminal justice populations, or both.

The criminal justice system encompasses a broad spectrum of public and private agencies, and settings including, but not limited to, state and federal correctional facilities; city and county jails; federal, state, and city parole and probation agencies; federal, state, and local court systems (including drug courts and mental health courts); community-based nonprofit agencies; faith-based agencies; and primary health and behavioral health care providers.

Schools of social work prepare their graduates to address the complex psychosocial needs of individuals in the criminal justice system. Social work is adapting to the evolving changes in the country's philosophy on the best ways to balance the sometimes conflicted dichotomy between the need for public safety and the need to address the biopsychosocial needs of offenders. The ethical challenge to social workers is to weigh the needs of the justice system against those of the offender. The social worker should take on the challenge by participating in legislative action to mold social policy to create a balance between the justice system and the offender. Thus, the social worker can help the justice system provide more effective services to the offender, their families, and their communities as professionals by participating in the process of public policy development.

Two competing, dichotomous schools of thought drive the discussion related to crime prevention. One, the pro-punishment school of thought postulates that punishment is the means to preventing; whereas the positivist (pro-treatment) philosophy suggests that some instances of criminal behavior is determined by factors, such as mental illness, that offenders find difficult to control. Therefore, treatment becomes a means of preventing future criminal behaviors. Social work has historically been strongly associated with the positivist school of thought of crime prevention. Social work must recognize its professional obligation both to the offender and to the community (from a public safety perspective) and participate in the process of developing crime reduction policies that reflect social work's commitment to both the offender and the community.

COMMON PSYCHOTROPIC AND NON-PSYCHOTROPIC PRESCRIPTIONS AND OVER-THE-COUNTER MEDICATIONS AND THEIR SIDE EFFECTS

Psychotropic medications affect brain chemicals associated with mood and behavior. Psychotropic drugs are prescribed to treat a variety of mental health problems and typically work by changing the amounts of important chemicals in the brain called neurotransmitters. Psychotropic drugs are usually prescribed by psychiatrists, though other physicians and professionals may be allowed to prescribe them in certain jurisdictions. Psychotropic drugs may be needed to treat disorders such as Schizophrenia or Bipolar Disorder, but are often combined with other supports, such as that from family and friends, therapy, lifestyle changes, and other treatment protocols, to ensure healthy everyday living.

Antipsychotics

Used for the treatment of Schizophrenia and mania

Typical

Haldol (haloperidol)

Haldol Decanoate (long-acting injectable)

Loxitane (loxapine)

Mellaril (thioridazine)

Moban (molindone)

Navane (thiothixene)

Prolixin (fluphenazine)

Serentil (mesoridazine)

Stelazine (trifluoperazine)

Thorazine (chlorpromazine)

Trilafon (perphenazine)

Atypical

Abilify (aripiprazole)

Clozaril (clozapine)

Geodon (ziprasidone)

Risperdal (risperidone)

Seroquel (quetiapine)

Zyprexa (olanzapine)

With Clozaril, there is an increased risk of agranulocytosis that requires blood monitoring.

Some antipsychotics are available in injectable forms; these are useful for clients who are noncompliant with oral medications.

Tardive dyskinesia (abnormal, involuntary movements of the tongue, lips, jaw, and face, as well as twitching and snakelike movement of the extremities and occasionally the trunk) may result from taking high doses of antipsychotic medications over a long period of time. Symptoms may persist indefinitely after discontinuation of these medications. Thus, antipsychotic use should be closely monitored and prescribed at low doses if possible.

Antimanic Agents (Mood Stabilizers)

Used for the treatment of Bipolar Disorder

Depakene (valproic acid, sodium divalproex), Depakote sprinkles

Lamictal (lamotrigine)

Lithium (lithium carbonate), Eskalith, Lithobid

Tegretol (carbamazepine), Carbotrol

Topamax (topiramate)

There is a small difference between toxic and therapeutic levels (narrow therapeutic index) that necessitates periodic checks of blood levels of lithium. Also, there is a need for periodic checks of thyroid and kidney functions, because lithium can affect the functioning of these organs.

Antidepressants

Used for the treatment of Depressive Disorders

Selective Serotonin Reuptake Inhibitors (SSRIs)

Celexa (citalopram)

Lexapro (escitalopram)

Luvox (fluvoxamine)

Paxil (paroxetine)

Prozac (fluoxetine)

Zoloft (sertraline)

Tricyclics

Anafranil (clomipramine)

Asendin (amoxapine)

Elavil (amitriptyline)

Norpramin (desipramine)

Pamelor (nortriptyline)

Aventyl Sinequan (doxepin)

Surmontil (trimipramine)

Tofranil (imipramine)

Vivactil (protriptyline)

Monoamine Oxidase Inhibitors (MAOIs)

Nardil (phenelzine)

Parnate (tranylcypromine)

There are dietary restrictions of foods that contain high levels of tyramine (generally food that has been aged). Foods to avoid may include beer, ale, wine (particularly Chianti), cheese (except cottage and cream cheese), smoked or pickled fish (herring), beef or chicken liver, summer (dry) sausage, fava or broad bean pods (Italian green beans), and yeast vitamin supplements (brewer's yeast).

Others

Desyrel (trazodone)

Effexor (venlafaxine)

Remeron (mirtazapine)

Serzone (nefazodone)

Wellbutrin (bupropion), Zyban

Antianxiety Drugs

Used for the treatment of Anxiety Disorders

Benzodiazepines are a class of drugs primarily used for treating anxiety, but they also are effective in treating several other conditions.

Ativan (lorazepam)

Buspar (buspirone)

Klonopin (clonazepam)

Valium (diazepam)

Xanax (alprazolam)

There is a high abuse potential of these drugs and they can be dangerous when combined with alcohol or illicit substances. It is critical to look for signs of impaired motor or other functioning.

Stimulants

Used for the treatment of Attention-Deficit/Hyperactivity Disorder

Adderall (amphetamine, mixed salts)

Concerta (methylphenidate, long acting)

Dexedrine (dextroamphetamine), Dextrostat

Dexedrine Spansules (dextroamphetamine, long acting)

Metadate (methylphenidate, long acting), Ritalin SR

Ritalin (methylphenidate), Methylin

Common Prescription Medications

The vast majority of Americans take at least one prescription medication, with more than half of Americans taking two or more. The most commonly prescribed include the following medications.

Advair Diskus is a prescription used to treat asthma and chronic obstructive pulmonary disease (COPD).

Crestor is a lipid-lowering agent taken orally.

Cymbalta is a selective serotonin and norepinephrine reuptake inhibitor (SSNRI) for oral administration.

Diovan is used to treat heart disease or heart failure.

Hydrocodone/acetaminophen is the most popular painkiller used to treat moderate to severe pain. Hydrocodone, a narcotic analgesic, relieves pain through the central nervous system, and it also is used to stop or prevent coughing. This drug can become habit-forming when used over an extended period of time.

Levothyroxine sodium is used to treat hypothyroidism, a condition where the thyroid gland does not produce enough of the thyroid hormone. This drug also is used to treat thyroid cancer and to help shrink an enlarged thyroid gland.

Lantus is a sterile solution of insulin glargine for use as a subcutaneous injection for diabetes.

Lisinopril (which used to be sold under the brand names Zestril and Prinivil) is a high blood pressure medication. Its main function is to block chemicals in the body that trigger the tightening of blood vessels. Lisinopril also is used to help treat heart failure.

Lyrica is used to control seizures, as well as treat nerve pain and fibromyalgia.

Metoprolol, the generic version of Lopressor, is used to treat high blood pressure and also helps reduce the risk of repeated heart attacks. Metoprolol also treats heart failure and heart pain or angina.

Nexium is used to treat symptoms of gastroesophageal reflux disease (GERD) and other conditions involving excessive stomach acid.

Simvastatin (generic Zocor) is prescribed to treat high cholesterol and is typically recommended in conjunction with diet changes. This drug is believed to have a variety of benefits including helping to prevent heart attacks and strokes.

Synthroid is a prescription, man-made thyroid hormone that is used to treat hypothyroidism.

Ventolin solution is used in inhalers for asthma.

Vyvanse is used to treat hyperactivity and impulse control disorders.

Assessment Methods and Techniques

6

THE FACTORS AND PROCESSES USED IN PROBLEM FORMULATION

In both micro and macro practice, social workers must work with clients to identify the problem(s) to be addressed. Problem identification concerns determining the problem targeted for intervention. Although this seems straightforward, it is often difficult to isolate the issue that, when addressed, will result in a change in the symptomology of a client and/or client system.

Part of problem identification is determining the issue in exact definable terms, when it occurs, and its magnitude. When doing macro practice, a social worker may often need to get consensus from the group regarding whether there is agreement as to the nature of the problem and its occurrence and magnitude.

It is often useful in problem identification to determine that which is not the problem. Such a technique will ensure that these elements are not grouped in with those that are targeted and will assist in narrowing down the focus.

The problem should always be considered within the person-in-environment perspective and using a strengths-based approach. It should not blame a client and/or client system for its existence.

METHODS OF INVOLVING CLIENTS/CLIENT SYSTEMS IN PROBLEM IDENTIFICATION (E.G., GATHERING COLLATERAL INFORMATION)

Social workers focus on assisting clients to identify problems and areas of strength, as well as increasing problem-solving strategies.

It is essential that, throughout the problem-solving process, social workers view clients as experts in their lives.

Clients should be asked about what they would like to see changed in their lives and clients' definitions of problems should be accepted.

Clients should be asked about what will be different in their lives when their problems are solved. Social workers should listen carefully for, and work hard to respect, the directions in which clients want to go with their lives (their goals) and the words they use to express these directions.

Clients should be asked about the paths that they would like to take to make desired changes. Clients' perceptions should be respected and clients' inner resources (strengths) should be maximized as part of treatment.

Use of Collateral Sources

Social workers often use collateral sources—family, friends, other agencies, physicians, and so on—as informants when collecting information to effectively treat clients. These sources can provide vital information because other professionals or agencies may have treated clients in the past. Family members and friends may also provide important information about the length or severity of issues or problems.

Collateral information is often used when the credibility and validity of information obtained from a client or others is questionable. For example, child custody cases are inherently characterized by biased data within an adversarial process. Thus, it is often necessary to evaluate the integrity of information gathered through use of collateral information.

However, social workers should always assess the credibility of collateral informants, because data from more neutral parties has higher integrity. In addition, informants who have greater access to key information may produce more valid data.

When an account by a collateral informant agrees with information gathered from a client, it enhances the trustworthiness of the data collected.

Using multiple information sources (or triangulation) is an excellent method for social workers to have accurate accounts upon which to make assessments or base interventions.

It is essential that a social worker get a client's informed consent prior to reaching out to collateral sources. However, they can be a valuable source of data to supplement that obtained directly from a client, as well as provide contextual or background information that a client may not know.

TECHNIQUES AND INSTRUMENTS USED TO ASSESS CLIENTS/ CLIENT SYSTEMS

There are many psychological tests in existence for assessment and diagnostic purposes. The following are a few of the most well known.

Beck Depression Inventory

The Beck Depression Inventory (BDI) is a 21-item test, presented in multiple-choice format, that assesses the presence and degree of depression in adolescents and adults.

The Minnesota Multiphasic Personality Inventory

The Minnesota Multiphasic Personality Inventory (MMPI) is an objective verbal inventory designed as a personality test for the assessment of psychopathology consisting of 550 statements, 16 of which are repeated.

Myers–Briggs Type Indicator

The Myers–Briggs Type Indicator (MBTI) is a forced-choice, self-report inventory that attempts to classify individuals along four theoretically independent dimensions. The first dimension is a general attitude toward the world, either extraverted (E) or introverted (I). The second dimension, perception, is divided between sensation (S) and intuition (N). The third dimension is that of processing. Once information is received, it is processed in either a thinking (T) or feeling (F) style. The final dimension is judging (J) versus perceiving (P).

Rorschach Inkblot Test

Client responses to inkblots are used to assess perceptual reactions and other psychological functioning. It is one of the most widely used projective tests.

Stanford–Binet Intelligence Scale

The Stanford–Binet Intelligence Scale is designed for the testing of cognitive abilities. It provides verbal, performance, and full scale scores for children and adults.

Thematic Apperception Test

The Thematic Apperception Test (TAT) is another widely used projective test. It consists of a series of pictures of ambiguous scenes. Clients are asked to make up stories or fantasies concerning what is happening, has happened, and is going to happen in the scenes, along with a description of their thoughts and feelings. The TAT provides information on a client's perceptions and imagination for use in the understanding of a client's current needs, motives, emotions, and conflicts, both conscious and unconscious. Its use in clinical assessment is generally part of a larger battery of tests and interview data.

Wechsler Intelligence Scale

The Wechsler Intelligence Scale (WISC) is designed as a measure of a child's intellectual and cognitive ability. It has four index scales and a full scale score.

METHODS TO INCORPORATE THE RESULTS OF PSYCHOLOGICAL AND EDUCATIONAL TESTS INTO ASSESSMENT

Social workers use both tests and assessments to help formulate diagnoses and to guide treatment for their clients.

Psychological tests are instruments used to measure an assortment of mental abilities and characteristics, such as personality, achievement, intelligence, and neurological functioning. They often take the form of questionnaires. They may be written, verbal, or pictorial tests (like the famous Rorschach test that uses inkblot images). The tests may also be referred to as scales, surveys, screens, checklists, assessments, measures, inventories, and so on.

Educational tests measure cognitive (thinking) abilities and academic achievement. These measurements provide a profile of strengths and weaknesses that accurately identify areas for academic remediation and insight into the best learning strategies. They provide details into the learning process that will provide clients, family members, and school staff the best learning strategies. Educational assessments provide the necessary documentation for the legal purposes of establishing the presence of disabilities, but they do not guarantee that their findings will be accepted by schools and/or accommodations provided. Reaching decisions to have educational testing is often arrived at after a period of struggle, distress, and different efforts at improving the educational process with limited success.

Social work assessment is a more comprehensive process that may utilize the results from educational and psychological tests, but can also involve interviewing a client and/or family, reviewing a client's history, checking existing records, and consulting with previous or concurrent providers.

Some common tests are:

- *Achievement/Aptitude tests*: typically used in education, measure how much clients know (have *achieved*) in a certain subject or subjects, or have ability (*aptitude*) to learn
- *Intelligence tests*: measure intelligence (IQ)
- *Job/Occupational tests*: match interests with careers
- *Personality tests*: measure basic personality traits/characteristics
- *Neuropsychological tests*: assess and measure cognitive functioning (e.g., how a particular problem with the brain affects recall, concentration, etc.)
- *Specialized clinical tests*: investigates areas of clinical interest, such as anxiety, depression, Posttraumatic Stress Disorder (PTSD), and so on.

METHODS TO ASSESS EGO STRENGTHS

Ego strength is the ability of the ego to effectively deal with the demands of the id, the superego, and reality. It is a basis for resilience and helps maintain emotional stability by coping with internal and external stress.

Traits usually considered to be indicators of positive ego strengths include tolerance of pain associated with loss, disappointment, shame, or guilt; forgiveness of others, with feelings of compassion rather than anger; persistence and perseverance in the pursuit of goals; and/or openness, flexibility, and creativity in learning to adapt. Those with positive ego strength are less likely to have psychiatric crises.

Other indicators of positive ego strength include clients:

- Acknowledging their feelings—including grief, insecurity, loneliness, and anxiety
- Not getting overwhelmed by their moods
- Pushing forward after loss and not being paralyzed by self-pity or resentment
- Using painful events to strengthen themselves
- Knowing that painful feelings will eventually fade
- Empathizing with others without trying to reduce or eliminate their pain
- Being self-disciplined and fighting addictive urges
- Taking responsibility for actions
- Holding themselves accountable

- Not blaming others
- Accepting themselves with their limitations
- Setting firm limits even if it means disappointing others or risking rejection
- Avoiding people who drain them physically and/or emotionally

METHODS TO ASSESS ORGANIZATIONAL FUNCTIONING (E.G., AGENCY ASSESSMENTS)

There are many ways to measure the functioning and effectiveness of organizations. For example, the functioning can be analyzed related to productivity, turnover, stability, cohesion, and so on. Usually, functioning is assessed as it relates to organizational structures, processes, and outcomes.

Structural indicators influence the capacity of the organization for effective performance. Assessments aimed at organizational structure evaluate organizational features, such as training, equipment, and office space, or worker characteristics including degrees attained and licenses held. Structural characteristics form the basis for accreditation reviews and licensing. When an organization is not operating efficiently or effectively, a review of the available structural resources is often completed to determine the extent to which they may be responsible for the problems.

Evaluations of organizational processes assess effort rather than effect. Formative evaluations look at how the work gets done in organizations and the satisfaction of those doing the work, rather than the ultimate outcomes or performance. Given that the majority of social work services are delivered in organizations with complex structures, it is essential to determine the extent to which processes inhibit or promote quality outcomes.

Outcome assessments determine the extent to which tangible, defined differences have been made. Though essential, these assessments can be difficult to make due to threats to internal validity.

The complexity of organizational assessments varies widely. They can be as simple as asking stakeholders for feedback on how the organization is operating or can involve intensive, structured work plans, information collection and analyses, and reporting. Typically this complexity is driven by financial and time constraints and the degree to which there is concern about the organization's performance and effectiveness.

METHODS TO OBTAIN SENSITIVE INFORMATION (E.G., SUBSTANCE ABUSE, SEXUAL ABUSE)

Clients are often reluctant to reveal sensitive information about themselves and others in their families. However, this information may be vital to understanding client problems and designing interventions that will be effective. While there is no set road map of how to elicit this information, there are some techniques that may assist.

- A social worker should start off with some open-ended and nonthreatening questions to gather needed background and get a client used to talking about his or her situation before having to disclose more sensitive material. This initial questioning will also give a client time to "test the waters" with a social worker and gauge his or her reaction as more sensitive information is provided. Trust is often needed in a therapeutic relationship before a client can be completely honest about his or her situation.

- A social worker should be aware of verbal and nonverbal clues when speaking with a client. A client may avoid eye contact, fail to completely answer a question, look down when speaking, or laugh nervously when feeling anxious about a topic. A social worker may want to repeat a question or probe further into this area to see if there is something undisclosed which is causing this behavior.

- A client who is engaged in couples, family, or group treatment may worry about the confidentiality of revealing sensitive information, as well as the reactions of others to such disclosure. In these instances, a social worker may want to explore with a client whether individual treatment in lieu of or in conjunction with couples, family, or group treatment may be appropriate.

- A social worker may want to review with a client the professional mandate for confidentiality and what information will be stored in a client file.

- A client may be reluctant to reveal sensitive information if he or she thinks there could be negative repercussions as a result of the information being disclosed to others verbally or lack of security related to the file.

- A client is much more likely to disclose sensitive information if a social worker reacts to such disclosures with acceptance and a neutral stance, being neither judgmental nor confrontational and not interrupting when information is being gathered.

COMMUNICATION THEORIES AND STYLES

Communication theory involves the ways in which information is transmitted; the effects of information on human systems; how people receive information from their own feelings, thoughts, memories, physical sensations, and environments; how they evaluate this information; and how they subsequently act in response to the information.

Effective communication skills are one of the most crucial components of a social worker's job. Every day, social workers must communicate with clients to gain information, convey critical information, and make important decisions. Without effective communication skills, a social worker may not be able to obtain or convey that information, thereby causing detrimental effects on clients.

One cannot not communicate. Even when one is silent one is communicating, and another person is reacting to the silence. **Silence** is very effective when faced with a client who is experiencing a high degree of emotion, because the silence indicates acceptance of these feelings. On the other hand, silence on the part of a client can indicate a reluctance to discuss a subject. A social worker should probe further with a client who is silent for an unusually long period of time. If persons do not communicate clearly, mutual understanding, acceptance, or rejection of the communication will not occur, and relationship problems can arise.

Some communication styles can serve to inhibit effective communication with clients.

1. Using "shoulds" and "oughts" may be perceived as moralizing or sermonizing by a client and elicit feelings of resentment, guilt, or obligation. In reaction to feeling judged, a client may oppose a social worker's pressure to change.

2. Offering advice or solutions prematurely, before thorough exploration of the problem, may cause resistance because a client is not ready to solve the problem.

3. Using logical arguments, lecturing, or arguing to convince a client to take another viewpoint may result in a power struggle with a client. A better way of helping a client is to assist him or her in exploring options in order to make an informed decision.

4. Judging, criticizing, and blaming are detrimental to a client, as well as to the therapeutic relationship. A client could respond by becoming defensive or, worse yet, internalizing the negative reflections about himself or herself.

5. Talking to a client in professional jargon and defining a client in terms of his or her diagnosis may result in a client viewing himself or herself in the same way (as "sick").

6. Providing reassurance prematurely or without a genuine basis is often for a social worker's benefit rather than a client's. It is a social worker's responsibility to explore and acknowledge a client's feelings, no matter how painful they are. A client may also feel that a social worker does not understand his or her situation.

7. Ill-timed or frequent interruptions disrupt the interview process and can annoy clients. Interruptions should be purposive, well-timed, and done in such a way that they do not disrupt the flow of communication.

8. It is counterproductive to permit excessive social interactions rather than therapeutic interactions. In order for a client to benefit from the helping relationship, he or she has to self-disclose about problematic issues.

9. Social workers must provide structure and direction to the therapeutic process on a moment-to-moment basis in order to maximize the helping process. Passive or inactive social workers may miss fruitful moments that could be used for client benefit. Clients may lose confidence in social workers who are not actively involved in the helping process.

The following are some communication concepts that are critical to social work practice.

Acceptance
An acknowledgment of "what is." Acceptance does not pass judgment on a circumstance and allows clients to let go of frustration and disappointment, stress and anxiety, regret and false hopes. Acceptance is the practice of recognizing the limits of one's control. Acceptance is not giving up or excusing other people's behavior and allowing it to continue. Acceptance is not about giving in to circumstances that are unhealthy or uncomfortable. The main thing that gets in the way of acceptance is wanting to be in control.

Cognitive dissonance
Arises when a person has to choose between two contradictory attitudes and beliefs. The most dissonance arises when two options are equally attractive. Three ways to reduce dissonance are to (a) reduce the importance of conflicting beliefs, (b) acquire new beliefs that change the balance, or (c) remove the conflicting attitude or behavior. This theory is relevant when making decisions or solving problems.

Context
The circumstances surrounding human exchanges of information.

Double bind
Offering two contradictory messages and prohibiting the recipient from noticing the contradiction.

Echolalia

Repeating noises and phrases. It is associated with Catatonia, Autism Spectrum Disorder, Schizophrenia, and other disorders.

Information

Anything people perceive from their environments or from within themselves. People act in response to information.

Information processing

Responses to information that are mediated through one's perception and evaluation of knowledge received.

Information processing block

Failure to perceive and evaluate potentially useful new information.

Metacommunication

The context within which to interpret the content of the message (i.e., nonverbal communication, body language, vocalizations).

Nonverbal communications

Facial expression, body language, and posture can be potent forms of communication.

In communication, there are two types of content: manifest and latent. Manifest content is the concrete words or terms contained in a communication, whereas latent content is that which is not visible, the underlying meaning of words or terms.

Relying just on the manifest content to understand client experiences or problems may result in not really understanding their meaning to individuals.

There are social work techniques such as clarifying, paraphrasing, confronting, and interpreting that can assist social workers in developing a better understanding of the meaning of clients' communication.

In addition, therapeutic techniques, such as psychoanalysis, focus on the hidden meaning of fantasies or dreams.

RISK ASSESSMENT METHODS

Social workers are often called upon to assess risks of clients to themselves and others. Such assessments are not easy, because there are no indicators that definitively predict whether a client will act on his or her feelings or desires to hurt himself or herself. A social worker must review all assessment data in order to determine the appropriate level of care and a treatment plan. Such an assessment must include examining risk and protective factors, as well as the presence of behavioral warning signs. Such an assessment may include examining:

■ Frequency, intensity, and duration of suicidal or violent thoughts
■ Access to or availability of method(s)

- Ability or inability to control suicidal/violent thoughts
- Ability not to act on thoughts
- Factors making a client feel better or worse
- Consequences of actions
- Deterrents to acting on thoughts
- Whether client has been using drugs or alcohol to cope
- Measures a client requires to maintain safety

In situations where a client is seen to be a danger to self or others, a social worker may limit a client's right to self-determination and seek involuntary treatment such as commitment to an inpatient setting. If a client is deemed to be a danger to an identifiable third party, a social worker should consider this as a "duty to warn" situation (under the Tarasoff decision), as well as the party in danger.

METHODS TO ASSESS THE CLIENT'S/CLIENT SYSTEM'S STRENGTHS, RESOURCES, AND CHALLENGES (E.G., INDIVIDUAL, FAMILY, GROUP, ORGANIZATION, COMMUNITY)

Clients typically seek social work services for help with problems or difficulties. As a result, the assessment generally focuses on the problems. This focus can lead to an overemphasis on client pathology and dysfunction without the same attention to client strengths, capabilities, and achievements. Information on both strengths and challenges are needed to get a full understanding of the client situation.

Social workers must be sensitive to client strengths and skillful in using them to achieve service goals. Social workers who do not attend to client strengths will not be able to determine clients' potential for growth and the steps needed to get there. Often clients are experiencing self-doubt or poor self-esteem. To assist with helping clients view themselves more positively, social workers must be able to emphasize their strengths.

Strengths which may be overlooked include clients:

- Facing problems by seeking help—rather than denying them;
- Taking risks by sharing problems with social workers;
- Persevering under difficult situations;
- Being resourceful;
- Meeting family and financial obligations;
- Seeking to understand the actions of others;
- Functioning in stressful situations; and/or
- Considering alternative courses of action.

Methods to identify more about client strengths, resources, and challenges can be obtained by:

- Seeking exceptions—determining when the problem does not exist or occur (locations, times, and contexts);
- Scaling the problem—identifying the severity of the problem on a scale from 1 to 10 according to the client;
- Scaling motivation—estimating the degree to which client feels hopeful about resolution; and/or
- Miracle question—having the client determine what would be different if problem did not exist.

When conducting community assessments, it is essential for social workers to identify strengths and challenges. Strengths are positive features of the community that can be leveraged to develop solutions to problems. Strengths can include organizations, people, partnerships, facilities, funding, policies, regulations, and culture.

A social worker should consider the current assets that are already in existence to promote the quality of life of community members. For example, organizations that provide after-school programs that help youth graduate on time would be included in a community assessment focused on keeping kids in school. In some instances, a social worker may want to look at experiences of other communities with similar demographics that have successfully addressed similar problems. Examining the presence and utilization of strengths in these communities can assist a social worker in determining if similar assets can be found in its target community.

A social worker must also develop an informed understanding of the gaps or needs that exist within a community. These needs serve as challenges that can affect a large or small number of community members. If community needs affect a large number of community members, there may be more support for addressing them. Collaboration and community building are essential in addressing community challenges.

There are a number of methods for data collection related to community strengths and challenges including interviews, observation, and surveys. Ensuring that the data collection procedures are robust is essential in conducting a complete and accurate community assessment.

THE INDICATORS OF MOTIVATION, RESISTANCE, AND READINESS TO CHANGE

Social workers should not assume that clients are ready or have the skills needed to make changes in their lives. Clients may be oppositional, reactionary, noncompliant, and/or unmotivated. These attitudes or behaviors are often referred to as resistance.

There are indicators that a social worker should use as evidence that a client may be resistant or not ready/able to fully participate in services. These indicators include:

- Limiting the amount of information communicated to a social worker
- Silence/minimal talking during sessions
- Engaging in small talk with a social worker about irrelevant topics
- Engaging in intellectual talk by using technical terms/abstract concepts or asking questions of a social worker that are not related to client issues or problems
- Being preoccupied with past events, instead of current issues
- Discounting, censoring, or editing thoughts when asked about them by a social worker
- False promising
- Flattering a social worker in an attempt to "soften" him or her so client will not be pushed to act
- Not keeping appointments
- Payment delays or refusals

It is essential to determine the extent to which this resistance or these inabilities are caused by a client, a social worker, and/or the conditions present.

A client may be resistant due to feelings of guilt or shame and may not be ready to recognize or address the feelings and behaviors being brought up by a social worker. Clients may be frightened of change and may be getting some benefit from the problems that they are experiencing.

Social workers may experience a lack of readiness, as they have not developed sufficient rapport with clients. There also may not be clear expectations by clients of their role versus those of social workers. Social workers need to use interventions that are appropriate for clients.

Sometimes, a lack of readiness or ability is a result of external factors, such as changes in clients' living situations, physical health problems, lack of social support, and/or financial problems.

Whatever the causes, a social worker must address these barriers as clients will not make changes until they are ready and able.

Behavior change is best understood as a process with different stages of readiness. For most clients, behavior change occurs gradually over time, with a client progressing from being uninterested, unaware, or unwilling to make a change (precontemplation), to considering a change (contemplation), to deciding and preparing to make a change (preparation). This is followed by definitive action, as well as attempts to maintain the new behavior over time (maintenance). Clients can progress in both directions in the stages of change.

Often a client comes to a social worker in the *precontemplation* stage, in which he or she is not even considering changing or is in denial about the need to change. *Contemplation* is the first time that there is some movement toward change because a client, while ambivalent about changing, may weigh the benefits versus costs (i.e., time, expense, effort) of change. In *preparation*, a client may indicate a willingness to experiment with small changes, whereas the *action* stage is characterized by definitive change behaviors.

The goal is to move a client along the continuum toward making a positive change. Patience is needed as it is unrealistic to expect that change will occur with a single intervention.

Techniques that a social worker can use to determine a client's readiness to change include asking him or her:

- What would your life be like . . . (describe behavior needing change)?
- Is that a life that you would like?
- What would be a good result of changing?
- How will you know when it is time to think about changing?
- What signals will tell you to think about making a change?
- How ready are you on a scale from 1 to 10 to make a change?
- What are the good things about the way you are currently trying to change?
- What are the things that are not so good?
- What are the barriers to changing?
- What are some things that could help you overcome this barrier?

Participating in the problem-solving process and showing up for appointments on time are good indicators that a client is engaged and willing to work toward change. Small considerations toward making change or a willingness to discuss behavioral alternatives should be built upon as they are strong indicators that real action steps toward change can occur next.

METHODS TO ASSESS MOTIVATION, RESISTANCE, AND READINESS TO CHANGE

Motivation and resistance exist along a continuum of readiness. When assessing motivation and resistance of a client, it is important to determine what stage of change a client is in. This will provide a social worker with appropriate clinical strategies to use to address these issues. If social workers push clients at a faster pace than they are ready to take, the therapeutic alliance may break down.

A lack of motivation and resistance are often found in *precontemplation* and *contemplation* before making the decision to change. There can also be motivational challenges during preparation, action, and maintenance, but they are more easily addressed. When resistance occurs in these latter stages of change, a social worker should reassess the problem and appropriateness of the intervention to ensure that there have not been new developments in a client's life that need to be considered. They may be distracting a client from making progress or serving as barriers to making real change.

In precontemplation, a client is unaware, unable, and/or unwilling to change. In this stage, there is the greatest resistance and lack of motivation. It can be characterized by arguing, interrupting, denial, ignoring the problem, and/or avoiding talking or thinking about it. A client may not even show up for appointments and does not agree that change is needed.

A social worker can best deal with lack of motivation and resistance in this stage by establishing a rapport, acknowledging resistance or ambivalence, keeping conversation informal, trying to engage a client, and recognizing a client's thoughts, feelings, fears, and concerns.

In contemplation, a client is ambivalent or uncertain regarding behavior change; thus, his or her behaviors are unpredictable. In this stage, a client may be willing to look at the pros and cons of behavior change, but is not committed to working toward it.

A social worker can best deal with lack of motivation and resistance in this stage by emphasizing a client's free choice and responsibility, as well as discussing the pros and cons of changing. It is also useful to discuss how change will assist a client in achieving his or her goals in life. Fear can be reduced by producing examples of change and clarifying what change is and is not.

There are many *self-motivating techniques* that a client can use to assist in reaching a goal. A social worker can assist a client in identifying which of these techniques may be useful, as well as creating others that may be helpful. Some common self-motivating techniques include a client:

- Visualizing his or her goals, including using visual images on the refrigerator or in a place that will remind a client of the desired aim
- Reminding himself or herself of why change is needed
- Making up a contract with himself or herself of steps that will be taken toward reaching the desired end result
- Rewarding himself or herself when progress is made on the goals
- Taking a break to do something that is liked or be with a friend to stay encouraged

- Being around positive people who will encourage and not create barriers to change
- Educating himself or herself about steps that will assist in the change effort
- Breaking down goals into achievable steps
- Forgiving himself or herself when setbacks in progress occur
- Conceptualizing a new reality or what life will be like when change happens

METHODS TO ASSESS THE CLIENT'S/CLIENT SYSTEM'S COMMUNICATION SKILLS

Social workers must involve clients in every aspect of treatment. In order to do so, social workers must assess clients' communication skills and determine effective methods to gather needed information, as well as to ensure that clients understand data that is presented to them. Thus, the expressive and receptive communication of clients must be considered.

As many clients may have experienced trauma, it is essential that social workers understand how such experiences may impact on clients' communication styles and patterns. Much of communication is also cultural and should be viewed within the context of clients' backgrounds and experiences.

Silence is a form of communication and should be considered by a social worker when used by a client.

Social workers should understand how to communicate with clients who are upset and angry, as well as how some wording choices and tones can be upsetting to clients based on their ethnic backgrounds and/or past experiences, such as victimization.

METHODS TO ASSESS THE CLIENT'S/CLIENT SYSTEM'S COPING ABILITIES

Social workers can learn a lot about clients' difficulties by determining how clients have attempted to cope with their problems in the past. The coping abilities that clients employ give valuable clues about their levels of stress and functioning. Investigation may indicate that clients have few coping abilities, but rely on rigid patterns that are unhelpful or cause further problems. Some clients follow avoidance pattern by immersing themselves in work, withdrawing, or using drugs or alcohol. Others attempt to cope by being aggressive or acting out. Lastly, others become dependent and rely on family members or friends to manage difficulties for them.

Exploring how clients have attempted to cope with problems may reveal that they have struggled with the same or similar problems in the past. As they are no longer able to manage, it is important to find out what has changed ("why now?"). In order to assess coping skills, social workers might want to ask about the extent to which clients:

- Turn to work or other substitute activities to take their minds off things
- Get upset and let their emotions out
- Get advice from others about what to do
- Concentrate on doing something about their problems
- Put their trust in high beings
- Laugh about their situations
- Discuss their feelings with others
- Use alcohol or drugs to make themselves feel better
- Pretend that their problems do not exist
- Seek out others who have similar experiences

THE INDICATORS OF CLIENT'S/CLIENT SYSTEM'S STRENGTHS AND CHALLENGES

Strength is the capacity to cope with difficulties, to maintain functioning under stress, to return to equilibrium in the face of significant trauma, to use external challenges to promote growth, and to be resilient by using social supports.

There is not a single approach to the assessment of strengths. However, social workers can view all of these areas as strengths or protective factors that can assist clients when they experience challenges. These characteristics can also be abilities that need to be bolstered as a focus of treatment.

1. *Cognitive and appraisal skills*

    - Intellectual/cognitive ability
    - Creativity and curiosity
    - Initiative, perseverance, and patience
    - Common sense
    - Ability to anticipate problems
    - Realistic appraisal of demands and capacities
    - Ability to use feedback

2. *Defenses and coping mechanisms*

    - Ability to regulate impulses and affect
    - Self-soothing
    - Flexible; can handle stressors

3. *Temperamental and dispositional factors*

- Belief in trustworthiness of others
- Belief in justice
- Self-esteem and self-worth
- Sense of mastery, confidence, and optimism
- Ability to tolerate ambiguity and uncertainty
- Ability to make sense of negative events
- Sense of humor
- Lack of hostility, anger, and anxiety
- Optimistic and open
- Ability to grieve
- Lack of helplessness
- Responsibility for decisions
- Sense of direction, mission, and purpose

4. *Interpersonal skills and supports*

- Ability to develop/maintain good relationships
- Ability to confide in others
- Problem-solving skills
- Capacity for empathy
- Presence of an intimate relationship
- Sense of security

5. *Other factors*

- Supportive social institutions, such as church
- Good physical health
- Adequate income
- Supportive family and friends

METHODS USED TO ASSESS TRAUMA

Trauma is the response that a client has to an extremely negative event. Although trauma is a normal reaction to a horrible event, the effects can be so severe that they interfere with a client's ability to live life. Thus, a social worker is needed to treat the stress and dysfunction caused by the traumatic event and to restore a client to his or her previous emotional state.

Emotional reactions are the common effects of trauma. Impacts of trauma on clients' self-image include, but are not limited to:

- Anxiety
- Denial
- Agitation
- Irritability or rage

- Flashbacks or intrusive memories
- Feeling disconnected from the world
- Unrest in certain situations
- Being "shut down"
- Being very passive
- Feeling depressed
- Guilt/shame/self-blame
- Unusual fears
- Impatience
- Having a hard time concentrating
- Wanting to hurt oneself
- Being unable to trust anyone
- Feeling unlikable
- Feeling unsafe

Trauma often manifests physically, including both physiological and behavioral symptoms. Behavioral manifestations of trauma include, but are not limited to:

- Insomnia or fatigue
- Using harmful substances
- Keeping to oneself
- Overworking
- Lethargy
- Eating problems
- Drug or alcohol use
- Needing to do certain things over and over
- Always having to have things a certain way
- Doing strange or risky things

Clients may have anxiety or panic attacks and be unable to cope in certain circumstances. Social workers must often work with clients to address the underlying emotional impacts of the trauma in order for clients to make behavioral changes.

Clients who experience trauma often believe that they cannot trust, the world is not safe, and they are powerless to change their circumstances. Beliefs about themselves, others, and the world diminish their sense of competency. Thus, clients view themselves as powerless or "damaged" and have trouble feeling hopeful.

Clients who have experienced trauma may display intense emotions toward others, such as friends or family members. Clients can also emotionally retreat from these individuals, choosing to isolate themselves. Thus, trauma can be difficult for those who are close to clients as well.

PLACEMENT OPTIONS BASED ON ASSESSED LEVEL OF CARE

Social workers must assess the client's needed level of care, with the belief that there should be a continuum of intensity depending upon the level of crisis. Clients should enter treatment at a level appropriate to their needs and then step up to more intense treatment or down to less intense treatment as needed. An effective continuum of care features successful transfer of a client between levels of care.

Levels of care for behavioral health services, for example, vary from early intervention services/outpatient services to intensive outpatient/partial hospitalization to residential/inpatient services.

Early intervention or outpatient services are appropriate unless a client is experiencing crisis or at risk for residential/inpatient services, which may then warrant a step up to intensive outpatient or partial hospitalization. The goal is to serve clients in the least restrictive environment, while ensuring health and safety.

THE USE OF THE DIAGNOSTIC AND STATISTICAL MANUAL OF THE AMERICAN PSYCHIATRIC ASSOCIATION

The *Diagnostic and Statistical Manual of Mental Disorders* (5th ed.; DSM-5®) was published in 2013 and is the current diagnostic framework used by social workers. It has many revisions in content and format from the *DSM-IV-TR*, which was used previously.

The *DSM-5* deleted a separate section for "Disorders Usually First Diagnosed in Infancy, Childhood, or Adolescence" and now lists them in other chapters.

The *DSM-5* replaces the Not Otherwise Specified (NOS) categories with two options: Other Specified Disorder and Unspecified Disorder. The first allows a social worker to specify the reason that the criteria for a specific disorder is not met, whereas the second allows a social worker the option to forgo specification.

The *DSM-5* has discarded the multiaxial system of diagnosis (formerly Axis I, Axis II, and Axis III) and combines the first three axes outlined in past editions of the *DSM* into one axis with all mental and other medical diagnoses.

It has replaced Axis IV with significant psychosocial and contextual features and dropped Axis V (Global Assessment of Functioning, known as GAF).

The *World Health Organization Disability Assessment Schedule 2.0* (*WHODAS 2.0*) is added to Section III, Emerging Measures and Models, under Assessment Measures.

1. *Neurodevelopmental Disorders*

This is a new chapter.

Intellectual Disabilities

* Intellectual Disability (Intellectual Developmental Disorder)

"Mental retardation" is now Intellectual Disability (Intellectual Developmental Disorder).
Intelligent quotient (IQ) scores and adaptive functioning are both used in determining a client's ability.

* Global Developmental Delay

Unspecified Intellectual Disability (Intellectual Developmental Disorder)

Communication Disorders

Language Disorder

Speech Sound Disorder

Previously Phonological Disorder

Childhood-Onset Fluency Disorder (Stuttering)

Social (Pragmatic) Communication Disorder

This is a new condition that has impaired social, verbal, and nonverbal communication.

Unspecified Communication Disorder

Autism Spectrum Disorder

* Autism Spectrum Disorder

Autism Spectrum Disorder incorporates Asperger Disorder, Childhood Disintegrative Disorder, and Pervasive Developmental Disorder Not Otherwise Specified (PDD-NOS).
In DSM-IV, symptoms were divided into three areas (social reciprocity, communicative intent, and restricted and repetitive behaviors). Diagnostic criteria in the *DSM-5* have been rearranged into two areas: (a) social communication/interaction and (b) restricted and repetitive behaviors. Symptoms can be current or historical in these two areas.

Attention-Deficit/Hyperactivity Disorder

Attention-Deficit/Hyperactivity Disorder

Must appear by age 12

Other Specified Attention-Deficit/Hyperactivity Disorder

Unspecified Attention-Deficit/Hyperactivity Disorder

Specific Learning Disorder
Specific Learning Disorder

Motor Disorders
New subcategory

Developmental Coordination Disorder

Stereotypic Movement Disorder

Tic Disorders
Tourette's Disorder
Persistent (Chronic) Motor or Vocal Tic Disorder
Provisional Tic Disorder
Other Specified Tic Disorder
Unspecified Tic Disorder

Other Neurodevelopmental Disorders
Other Specified Neurodevelopmental Disorder

Unspecified Neurodevelopmental Disorder

2. Schizophrenia Spectrum and Other Psychotic Disorders

All subtypes of Schizophrenia were deleted—paranoid, disorganized, catatonic, undifferentiated, and residual.

Schizotypal (Personality) Disorder

Delusional Disorder

Has new criteria and is no longer separate from Shared Delusional Disorder

Brief Psychotic Disorder

Schizophreniform Disorder

✦ Schizophrenia

Is not diagnosed unless a client experiences disturbance (psychotic symptoms) for at least 6 months and has at least 1 month of active symptoms. *DSM-5* raises the symptom threshold, requiring that an individual exhibit at least two of the specified symptoms, instead of one as per the *DSM-IV*.
Schizophrenia is characterized by delusions, hallucinations, disorganized speech and behavior, and other symptoms that cause social or occupational dysfunction. All subtypes of Schizophrenia were deleted (paranoid, disorganized, catatonic, undifferentiated, and residual). Some of the subtypes, such as Catatonia (marked by motor immobility and stupor), are now specifiers to help provide further detail in diagnosis.

✦ Schizoaffective Disorder

Requires a major mood episode,

Substance/Medication-Induced Psychotic Disorder

Psychotic Disorder Due to Another Medical Condition

Catatonia
Requires three of a total of 12 symptoms. Catatonia may be a specifier for Depressive, Bipolar, and Psychotic Disorders; part of another medical condition; or of another specified diagnosis.

Catatonia Associated With Another Mental Disorder
> Catatonia Specifier

Catatonic Disorder Due to Another Medical Condition

Unspecified Catatonia

Other Specified Schizophrenia Spectrum and Other Psychotic Disorders

Unspecified Schizophrenia Spectrum and Other Psychotic Disorder

3. *Bipolar and Related Disorders*

The *DSM-5* makes changes to Bipolar Disorder (previously known as Manic Depression).

Manic symptoms: inflated self-esteem; decreased need for sleep while feeling full of energy; loud and rapid speech that is difficult to interrupt; continuous flow of speech with abrupt changes of topic; distractibility; restlessness; increased sociability; and disorganized, flamboyant, or bizarre activities. There may be rapid shifts of elevated mood to anger or depression.

Depressive symptoms: sadness, loss of interest in usual activities, and sleep and appetite disturbances; feelings of worthlessness and guilt; difficulties in thinking or concentrating; and suicidal thoughts or recurring thoughts of death.

The primary criteria for manic and hypomanic episodes (Criterion A) now includes an emphasis on *changes in activity and energy*—not just mood.

New specifier "with mixed features" can be applied to Bipolar I Disorder, Bipolar II Disorder, Bipolar Disorder NED (not elsewhere defined, previously called "NOS," not otherwise specified).

Anxiety symptoms are a specifier (called "anxious distress") added to Bipolar Disorder and to Depressive Disorders (but are not part of the bipolar diagnostic criteria).

The *DSM-IV* diagnosis of Bipolar I Disorder, Mixed Episode, requiring a client to simultaneously meet full criteria for both mania and major depressive episode, has been removed from the *DSM-5*. Instead, a new specifier, "with mixed features," has been added and can be applied to episodes of mania or hypomania when depressive features are present.

* Bipolar I Disorder

* Bipolar II Disorder

Cyclothymic Disorder

Substance/Medication-Induced Bipolar and Related Disorder

Bipolar and Related Disorder Due to Another Medical Condition

Other Specified Bipolar and Related Disorder

Allowed for particular conditions, including categorization for individuals with a past history of a Major Depressive Disorder who meet all criteria for hypomania except the duration criterion (i.e., at least 4 consecutive days). A second condition constituting a diagnosis of Other Specified Bipolar and Related Disorder is that too few symptoms of hypomania are present to meet criteria for Bipolar II, although the duration is sufficient at 4 or more days.

Unspecified Bipolar and Related Disorder

4. *Depressive Disorders*

The bereavement exclusion was removed.

The *DSM-5* introduces two new disorders: Disruptive Mood Dysregulation Disorder and Premenstrual Dysphoric Disorder.

A new specifier is available for those clients who display suicidality factors and are is depressed. Another new specifier allows for the presence of mixed symptoms across both the Bipolar and the Depressive Disorders, allowing for the possibility of manic features in clients with a diagnosis of depression. The "with anxious distress" specifier also gives a social worker the opportunity to rate the severity of anxious distress in all clients with Bipolar or Depressive Disorders.

* Disruptive Mood Dysregulation Disorder

DMDD; this is a new condition to address symptoms associated with "Childhood Bipolar Disorder" before the *DSM-5*'s publication. This new disorder can be diagnosed in children up to age 18 years who exhibit persistent irritability and frequent episodes of extreme, out-of-control behavior.

* Major Depressive Disorder, Single and Recurrent Episodes

Neither the core criteria, nor the requisite 2-week time period needed before diagnoses, has changed for clinical depression—or, as the *DSM* has long referred to it, Major Depressive Disorder.

* Persistent Depressive Disorder

Previously Dysthymia
The new condition includes both Chronic Major Depressive Disorder and the previous Dysthymic Disorder.

* Premenstrual Dysphoric Disorder

New disorder
Now an official diagnosis. In most menstrual cycles during the past year, five (or more) of the specified symptoms must occur during the final week before the onset of menses, start to improve within a few days after the onset of menses, and be minimal or absent in the week postmenses.

Substance/Medication-Induced Depressive Disorder

Depressive Disorder Due to Another Medical Condition

Other Specified Depressive Disorder

Unspecified Depressive Disorder

5. *Anxiety Disorders*

* Separation Anxiety Disorder

Previously a Disorder of Early Onset

Selective Mutism

Previously a Disorder of Early Onset

* Specific Phobia

* Social Anxiety Disorder (Social Phobia)

Social Phobia in the *DSM-IV* has been renamed Social Anxiety Disorder. This change reflects a broader understanding of the condition. In the past, Social Phobia primarily was diagnosed if an individual felt extreme discomfort or fear when performing in front of others. In the *DSM-5*, Social Anxiety Disorder can be diagnosed because of responses to various social situations. The fear or anxiety is out of proportion—in frequency and/or duration—to the actual situation.

The symptoms must be persistent, lasting 6 months or longer. In *DSM-IV*, the time frame was required only for children; *DSM-5* expands this criterion to include adults as well.

To be diagnosed with Social Anxiety Disorder, a client must suffer significant distress or impairment that interferes with his or her ordinary routine in social settings, at work or school, or during other everyday activities. Unlike in *DSM-IV*, which requires that a client recognize that his or her response is excessive or unreasonable, the *DSM-5* criteria shift that judgment to the social worker.

Several changes were made to expand the criteria to assist with diagnosing Social Anxiety Disorder at young ages.

* Panic Disorder

It is separated from Agoraphobia.

* Panic Attack

  * Specifier; applies to all *DSM-5* diagnoses

* Agoraphobia

* Generalized Anxiety Disorder

Substance/Medication-Induced Anxiety Disorder

Anxiety Disorder Due to Another Medical Condition

Other Specified Anxiety Disorder

Unspecified Anxiety Disorder

6. *Obsessive-Compulsive and Related Disorders*

* Obsessive-Compulsive Disorder

Body Dysmorphic Disorder

New criteria were added that describe repetitive behaviors or mental acts that may arise with perceived defects or flaws in physical appearance.

A specifier was expanded to allow for good or fair insight, poor insight, and "absent insight/delusional" (i.e., complete conviction that Obsessive-Compulsive Disorder beliefs are true).

* Hoarding Disorder

New disorder defined as a persistent difficulty discarding or parting with possessions due to a perceived need to save the items and distress associated with discarding them.

A specifier was expanded to allow for good or fair insight, poor insight, and absent insight/delusional (i.e., complete conviction that Obsessive-Compulsive Disorder beliefs are true).

Trichotillomania (Hair-Pulling Disorder)

Moved from "Impulse-Control Disorders Not Elsewhere Classified."

Excoriation (Skin-Picking) Disorder

New disorder

Substance/Medication-Induced Obsessive-Compulsive and Related Disorder

New disorder

Obsessive-Compulsive and Related Disorder Due to Another Medical Condition

New disorder

Other Specified Obsessive-Compulsive and Related Disorder

New disorder
Includes Body-Focused Repetitive Behavior Disorder (behaviors like nail biting, lip biting, and cheek chewing, other than hair pulling and skin picking) or obsessional jealousy.

Unspecified Obsessive-Compulsive and Related Disorder

New disorder

7. *Trauma- and Stressor-Related Disorders*

Separate criteria were added for children 6 years old or younger.
Beginning with the publication of the *DSM-III-R* in 1987, two subtypes of Reactive Attachment Disorder have been recognized—an emotionally withdrawn, inhibited type and an indiscriminately social/disinhibited type. In the *DSM-5*, "Reactive Attachment Disorder" is now reserved for the emotionally withdrawn/ inhibited type. The indiscriminately social/disinhibited type is now referred to as "Disinhibited Social Engagement Disorder" and considered a separate disorder.

★ Reactive Attachment Disorder

Was previously a subtype, but now a separate disorder

Disinhibited Social Engagement Disorder

Indiscriminately social/disinhibited was previously a subtype, but now a separate disorder.

★ Posttraumatic Stress Disorder

Criteria were modified and now has four clusters.

Acute Stress Disorder

Criteria were modified.

★ Adjustment Disorders

Moved, and now recognized as a stress-response syndrome

Other Specified Trauma- and Stressor-Related Disorder

Unspecified Trauma- and Stressor-Related Disorder

8. *Dissociative Disorders*

Dissociative Identity Disorder

The criteria were expanded to include "possession-form phenomena and functional neurological symptoms."
It is made clear that "transitions in identity may be observable by others or self-reported."
Criterion was modified for clients who experience gaps in recall of everyday events—not only trauma.

Dissociative Amnesia

"Dissociative fugue" became a specifier.

Depersonalization/Derealization Disorder
Previously Depersonalization Disorder

Other Specified Dissociative Disorder

Unspecified Dissociative Disorder

9. *Somatic Symptom and Related Disorders*

Somatoform Disorders are now called Somatic Symptom and Related Disorders." Somatization Disorder, Hypochondriasis, Pain Disorder, and Undifferentiated Somatoform Disorder were deleted. Medically unexplained symptoms are not needed, except in the cases of Conversion Disorder and Pseudocyesis (false pregnancy).
People with chronic pain can now be diagnosed with Somatic Symptom Disorder With Predominant Pain; or Psychological Factors That Affect Other Medical Conditions; or an Adjustment Disorder.

Somatic Symptom Disorder

Somatization Disorder and Undifferentiated Somatoform Disorder were combined to become Somatic Symptom Disorder, a diagnosis that no longer requires a specific number of somatic symptoms. It is characterized by somatic symptoms that are either very distressing or result in significant disruption of functioning, as well as excessive and disproportionate thoughts, feelings, and behaviors regarding those symptoms. To be diagnosed, a client must be persistently symptomatic (typically at least for 6 months).

Illness Anxiety Disorder

Conversion Disorder

Functional Neurological Symptom Disorder; criteria were changed
Conversion Disorder is now called "Conversion Disorder (Functional Neurological Symptom Disorder)." Although this disorder is associated with actual loss of motor function or symptoms and deficits that affect voluntary motor function, the client does not produce or control them voluntarily.

Psychological Factors Affecting Other Medical Conditions
New disorder

Factitious Disorder

In its milder forms, Factitious Disorder may be only a slight exaggeration of physical symptoms. The most extreme and dramatic form is called "Munchausen Syndrome;" it can include the seeking of multiple invasive procedures and operations, sometimes with serious risk to life.
Factitious Disorder should be distinguished from malingering and Somatic Symptom and Related Disorders. Malingering is not considered a mental illness and receives a V code as one of the other conditions that may be a focus of clinical attention. In malingering, there is an external incentive (i.e., avoiding work or obtaining money), whereas Factitious Disorder has no other incentive than to experience the sick role. In malingering and Factitious Disorder, clients provide false information and behave deceptively, but in Somatic Symptom Disorder, Illness Anxiety Disorder, and Conversion Disorder, there is no evidence that clients are deceiving social workers.
Factitious Disorder and malingering occasionally occur together, whereas concurrent Factitious Disorder and Somatic Symptom and Related Disorders are rare.

Other Specified Somatic Symptom and Related Disorder

Unspecified Somatic Symptom and Related Disorder

10. *Feeding and Eating Disorders*

Pica

Criteria now refer to clients of any age.

Rumination Disorder

Criteria now refer to clients of any age.

Avoidant/Restrictive Food Intake Disorder

Previously "Feeding Disorder of Infancy or Early Childhood;" the criteria were expanded.

✶ Anorexia Nervosa

Criteria changed and there is no longer a requirement of amenorrhea.

✶ Bulimia Nervosa

Requirements were changed from "at least twice weekly for 6 months" to "at least once weekly over the last 3 months."

✶ Binge-Eating Disorder

New disorder

Other Specified Feeding or Eating Disorder

Unspecified Feeding or Eating Disorder

11. *Elimination Disorders*

✶ Enuresis

Social worker needs to rule out medical reasons for bedwetting–infection, physiological abnormalities.

✶ Encopresis

Involves repeated passage of feces in inappropriate places, causing embarrassment. Client may avoid situations that lead to embarrassment—camp or sleepovers).

Other Specified Elimination Disorder

Unspecified Elimination Disorder

12. *Sleep–Wake Disorders*

"Sleep Disorders Related to Another Mental Disorder" and "Sleep Disorders Related to a General Medical Condition" were deleted.

Insomnia Disorder

Previously Primary Insomnia

Hypersomnolence Disorder

Narcolepsy

Breathing-Related Sleep Disorders
Obstructive Sleep Apnea Hypopnea

New disorder

Central Sleep Apnea

New disorder

Sleep-Related Hypoventilation

New disorder

Circadian Rhythm Sleep–Wake Disorders

Includes advanced sleep phase syndrome, irregular sleep–wake type, and non–24-hour sleep–wake type. Jet lag was removed.

Parasomnias

Non-Rapid Eye Movement Sleep Arousal Disorders

Sleepwalking

Sleep Terrors

Nightmare Disorder

Rapid Eye Movement Sleep Behavior Disorder

A separate disorder instead of being listed under "Dyssomnia Not Otherwise Specified"

Restless Legs Syndrome

A separate disorder instead of being listed under "Dyssomnia Not Otherwise Specified"

Substance/Medication-Induced Sleep Disorder

Other Specified Insomnia Disorder

Unspecified Insomnia Disorder

Other Specified Hypersomnolence Disorder

Unspecified Hypersomnolence Disorder

Other Specified Sleep–Wake Disorder

Unspecified Sleep–Wake Disorder

13. *Sexual Dysfunctions*

DSM-5 has sex-specific sexual dysfunctions. Sexual Aversion Disorder was deleted. Sexual Dysfunctions (except Substance/Medication-Induced Sexual Dysfunction) now require a duration of approximately 6 months and more exact severity criteria. Subtypes for all disorders include only "lifelong versus acquired" and "generalized versus situational."

Two subtypes were deleted: "Sexual Dysfunction Due to a General Medical Condition" and "Due to Psychological Versus Combined Factors."

Delayed Ejaculation

Erectile Disorder

Female Orgasmic Disorder

Female Sexual Interest/Arousal Disorder

For females, Sexual Desire and Arousal Disorders are combined into this single disorder.

Genito-Pelvic Pain/Penetration Disorder

A new diagnosis combines Vaginismus and Dyspareunia

Male Hypoactive Sexual Desire Disorder

Premature (Early) Ejaculation

Substance/Medication-Induced Sexual Dysfunction

Other Specified Sexual Dysfunction

Unspecified Sexual Dysfunction

14. *Gender Dysphoria*

Now its own category
Separate criteria for children, adolescents, and adults that are appropriate for varying developmental states are added.
Subtypes of Gender Identity Disorder based on sexual orientation were deleted.
Among other wording changes, Criterion A and Criterion B (cross-gender identification, and aversion toward one's gender) were combined.
Gender Dysphoria is a new diagnostic class with revised criteria to better characterize the experiences in children, adolescents, and adults.

Gender Dysphoria

Other Specified Gender Dysphoria

Unspecified Gender Dysphoria

15. *Disruptive, Impulse-Control, and Conduct Disorders*

These disorders are unique in that these problems are manifested in behaviors that violate the rights of others (i.e., aggression, destruction of property) and/or bring a client into significant conflict with societal norms or authority figures. The underlying causes of the problems in the self-control of emotions and behaviors can vary greatly across and within these disorders.

★ Oppositional Defiant Disorder

There are three types: angry/irritable mood, argumentative/defiant behavior, and vindictiveness.
The Conduct Disorder exclusion is deleted.
The criteria were also changed, with a note on frequency requirements and a measure of severity.

Intermittent Explosive Disorders

A specifier was added for people with limited "prosocial emotion," showing callous and unemotional traits.

★ Conduct Disorder

Conduct Disorder is characterized by behavior that violates either the rights of others or major societal norms. These symptoms must be present for at least 3 months with one symptom having been present in the past 6 months. To be diagnosed with Conduct Disorder, the symptoms must cause significant impairment in social, academic, or occupational functioning. The disorder is typically diagnosed *prior to* adulthood.
A specifier was added for clients with limited "prosocial emotion" showing callous and unemotional traits. People with Conduct Disorder who show this specifier display limited empathy and little concern for the feelings, wishes, and well-being of others. Clients with Conduct Disorder who meet criteria for the specifier have a relatively more severe form of the disorder and a different treatment response.

Antisocial Personality Disorder

Pyromania

Kleptomania

Other Specified Disruptive, Impulse-Control, and Conduct Disorder

Oppositional Defiant Disorder, Conduct Disorder, and Disruptive Behavior Disorder Not Otherwise Specified became Other Specified and Unspecified Disruptive, Impulse-Control, and Conduct Disorders.

Unspecified Disruptive, Impulse-Control, and Conduct Disorder

16. *Substance-Related and Addictive Disorders*

Substance Abuse and Substance Dependence have been combined into a single Substance Use Disorders category specific to each substance of abuse.
"Recurrent legal problems" was deleted and "craving or a strong desire or urge to use a substance" was added to the criteria.
The threshold of the number of criteria that must be met was changed. Severity from mild to4severe is based on the number of criteria endorsed.
New specifiers were added for early and sustained remission along with new specifiers for "in a controlled environment" and "on maintenance therapy."

Substance-Related Disorders

* Substance Use Disorders

mild– severe spectrum + general symptoms

* Substance-Induced Disorders

* Substance Intoxication and Withdrawal

* Substance/Medication-Induced Mental Disorders

Alcohol-Related Disorders
Alcohol Use Disorder

Alcohol Intoxication

Alcohol Withdrawal

Other Alcohol-Induced Disorders

Unspecified Alcohol-Related Disorder

Caffeine-Related Disorders
Caffeine Intoxication

Caffeine Withdrawal
New disorder

Other Caffeine-Induced Disorders

Unspecified Caffeine-Related Disorder

Cannabis-Related Disorders
Cannabis Use Disorder

Cannabis Intoxication

Cannabis Withdrawal
New disorder

Other Cannabis-Induced Disorders

Unspecified Cannabis-Related Disorder

Hallucinogen-Related Disorders
Phencyclidine Use Disorder

Other Hallucinogen Use Disorder

Phencyclidine Intoxication

Other Hallucinogen Intoxication

Hallucinogen Persisting Perception Disorder

Other Phencyclidine-Induced Disorders

Other Hallucinogen-Induced Disorders

Unspecified Phencyclidine-Related Disorder

Unspecified Hallucinogen-Related Disorder

Inhalant-Related Disorders
Inhalant Use Disorder

Inhalant Intoxication

Other Inhalant-Induced Disorders

Unspecified Inhalant-Related Disorder

Opioid-Related Disorders
Opioid Use Disorder

Opioid Intoxication

Opioid Withdrawal

Other Opioid-Induced Disorders

Unspecified Opioid-Related Disorder

Sedative-, Hypnotic-, or Anxiolytic-Related Disorders
Sedative, Hypnotic, or Anxiolytic Use Disorder

Sedative, Hypnotic, or Anxiolytic Intoxication

Sedative, Hypnotic, or Anxiolytic Withdrawal

Other Sedative-, Hypnotic-, or Anxiolytic-Induced Disorders

Unspecified Sedative-, Hypnotic-, or Anxiolytic-Related Disorder

Stimulant-Related Disorders
Stimulant Use Disorder

Stimulant Intoxication

Stimulant Withdrawal

Other Stimulant-Induced Disorders

Unspecified Stimulant-Related Disorder

Tobacco-Related Disorders
New category of disorders

Tobacco Use Disorder

Tobacco Withdrawal

Other Tobacco-Induced Disorders

Unspecified Tobacco-Related Disorder

Other (or Unknown) Substance-Related Disorders
Other (or Unknown) Substance Use Disorder

Other (or Unknown) Substance Intoxication

Other (or Unknown) Substance Withdrawal

Other (or Unknown) Substance-Induced Disorders

Unspecified Other (or Unknown) Substance-Related Disorder

Non-Substance-Related Disorders
Gambling Disorder
> New disorder

17. *Neurocognitive Disorders*

✳ Delirium — acute temporary quick onset

Other Specified Delirium

Unspecified Delirium

Major and Mild Neurocognitive Disorders
> Dementia and Amnestic Disorder became Major or Mild Neurocognitive Disorder (Major NCD or Mild NCD). New separate criteria are now presented for Major or Mild NCD due to various conditions.

✳ Major Neurocognitive Disorder → dementia
✳ Mild Neurocognitive Disorder   progressive

Major or Mild Neurocognitive Disorder Due to Alzheimer's Disease

Major or Mild Frontotemporal Neurocognitive Disorder

Major or Mild Neurocognitive Disorder With Lewy Bodies

Major or Mild Vascular Neurocognitive Disorder

Major or Mild Neurocognitive Disorder Due to Traumatic Brain Injury

Substance/Medication-Induced Major or Mild Neurocognitive Disorder
> New disorder

Major or Mild Neurocognitive Disorder Due to HIV Infection

Major or Mild Neurocognitive Disorder Due to Prion Disease

Major or Mild Neurocognitive Disorder Due to Parkinson's Disease

Major or Mild Neurocognitive Disorder Due to Huntington's Disease

Major or Mild Neurocognitive Disorder Due to Another Medical Condition

Major or Mild Neurocognitive Disorder Due to Multiple Etiologies

Unspecified Neurocognitive Disorder

> New disorder

✦ 18. *Personality Disorders*

Personality Disorders are associated with ways of thinking and feeling that significantly and adversely affect how a client functions in many aspects of life. A personality disorder is an enduring pattern of inner experience and behavior that deviates from the expectations of a client's culture. The pattern is manifested in cognition, affect, interpersonal functioning, and/or impulse control. Personality Disorders previously belonged on a different axis than almost all other disorders, but they are now with all mental and other medical diagnoses.

General Personality Disorder

Cluster A: Odd and Eccentric

★ Schizoid Personality Disorder

> Introverted, withdrawn, solitary, emotionally cold, and distant; absorbed with own thoughts and feelings and fearful of closeness and intimacy with others.

Paranoid Personality Disorder

> Interpreting the actions of others as deliberately threatening or demeaning; untrusting, unforgiving, and prone to angry or aggressive outbursts.

Schizotypal Personality Disorder

> A pattern of peculiarities—odd or eccentric manners of speaking or dressing; strange, outlandish, or paranoid beliefs; display signs of "magical thinking."

Cluster B: Dramatic, Emotional, and Erratic

✦ Antisocial Personality Disorder

> Impulsive, irresponsible, and callous; history of legal difficulties; belligerent and irresponsible behavior; aggressive and even violent relationships; no respect for others.

★ Borderline Personality Disorder

> Unstable in interpersonal relationships, behavior, mood, and self-image; abrupt and extreme mood changes; stormy interpersonal relationships; fluctuating self-image; self-destructive actions.

Narcissistic Personality Disorder

> Exaggerated sense of self-importance; absorbed by fantasies of unlimited success; seek constant attention; oversensitive to failure.

Histrionic Personality Disorder

> Behave melodramatically or "over the top," constantly displaying an excessive level of emotionality; attention seeking.

Cluster C: Anxious and Fearful

★ Avoidant Personality Disorder

> Hypersensitive to rejection and unwilling to become involved with others unless sure of being liked; avoidance of social situations or work that involves interpersonal contact.

  ✶ Dependent Personality Disorder

      Pattern of dependent and submissive behavior; relying on others to make personal decisions; require excessive reassurance and advice.

  ✶ Obsessive-Compulsive Personality Disorder

      Conscientious, with high levels of aspiration; strive for perfection; never satisfied with achievements.

  Other Personality Disorders

      Personality Change Due to Another Medical Condition

Other Specified Personality Disorder

Unspecified Personality Disorder

19. *Paraphilic Disorders*

      New specifiers "in a controlled environment" and "in remission" were added to criteria for all Paraphilic Disorders.
      "Disorder" added to names to distinguish between behavior and disorder. Must have both qualitative criteria and negative consequences to have the disorder and be diagnosed.

Voyeuristic Disorder

Exhibitionistic Disorder

Frotteuristic Disorder

Sexual Masochism Disorder

Sexual Sadism Disorder

Pedophilic Disorder

Fetishistic Disorder

Transvestic Disorder

Other Specified Paraphilic Disorder

Unspecified Paraphilic Disorder

20. *Other Mental Disorders*

Other Specified Mental Disorder Due to Another Medical Condition

Unspecified Mental Disorder Due to Another Medical Condition

Other Specified Mental Disorder

Unspecified Mental Disorder

21. *Medication-Induced Movement Disorders and Other Adverse Effects of Medication*

22. *Other Conditions That May Be a Focus of Clinical Attention*

7

Intervention Planning and Implementation

THE PRINCIPLES AND TECHNIQUES OF INTERVIEWING (E.G., SUPPORTING, CLARIFYING, FOCUSING, CONFRONTING, VALIDATING, FEEDBACK, REFLECTING, LANGUAGE DIFFERENCES, USE OF INTERPRETERS, REDIRECTING)

In social work, an interview is always purposeful and involves verbal and nonverbal communication between a social worker and client, during which ideas, attitudes, and feelings are exchanged. The actions of a social worker aim to gather important information and keep a client focused on the achievement of the goal.

A social work interview is designed to serve the interest of a client; therefore, the actions of a social worker during the interview must be planned and focused. Questions in a social work interview should be tailored to the specifics of a client, not generic, "one size fits all" inquiries. The focus is on the uniqueness of a client and his or her unique situation.

The purpose of the social work interview can be informational, diagnostic, or therapeutic. The same interview may serve more than one purpose.

Communication during a social work interview is interactive and interrelational. A social worker's questions will result in specific responses by a client that, in turn, lead to other inquiries. The message is formulated by a client, encoded, transmitted, received, processed, and decoded. The importance of words and messages may be implicit (implied) or explicit (evident). *A social worker should listen, being nonjudgmental, throughout a social work interview.*

There are a number of techniques that a social worker may use during an interview to assist clients.

- *Universalization*—the generalization or normalization of behavior
- *Clarification*—reformulate problem in a client's words to make sure that the social worker is on the same wavelength
- *Confrontation*—calling attention to something
- *Interpretation*—pulling together patterns of behavior to get a new understanding
- *Reframing and relabeling*—stating problem in a different way so a client can see possible solutions

Summarization seeks to bring together the important points of a discussion and to give a client and social worker awareness of the progress made. It can give a client a sense that a social worker understands and/ or brings a sense of closure. It omits irrelevant information and organizes pertinent aspects of the interaction. It allows a social worker and a client to leave an interaction with the same ideas in mind and provides a sense of closure at the completion of a discussion. Summarizing can be done periodically throughout the discussion or only at its close. But no matter who does it or how frequently it occurs, summarization is a valuable intervention technique.

During summarization, a social worker and a client strive to grasp the significance of what has been said, to formulate the meaning of the information, and to achieve new understandings. Summarization is helpful in pulling together what seems to be disorganized or unrelated material.

There are a variety of summarization approaches. A social worker can summarize the content and essential feelings expressed at any point or at the end of an interaction. A social worker can ask a client to review what he/she has accomplished or the status of the presenting problem. Finally, a social worker and a client may jointly look at what has been achieved.

Summarization statements can include a social worker saying, "Have I got this correct...?," "You have said that...," and/or "During the past hour, you and I have discussed...."

Social workers must be proficient in the languages spoken by clients or use qualified interpreters. *It is not appropriate to use family members to interpret or provide services in which social workers are not linguistically competent as valuable information may be missed during social work interviews.* When working with interpreters, social workers should face clients and speak directly to them—not the interpreters. Social workers also should not ask for the opinions of the interpreters or have conversations with them as their focus must be on clients.

METHODS TO INVOLVE CLIENTS/CLIENT SYSTEMS IN INTERVENTION PLANNING

The participation of clients in the process of identifying what is important to them now and in the future, and acting upon these priorities, is paramount. Clients' participation in the process will reduce resistance, increase motivation to change, and ensure sustainability of progress made.

In order to involve clients, social workers must continually listen to, learn about, and facilitate opportunities with clients who they are serving. Client involvement should not just occur during intervention planning, but instead during the entire problem-solving process.

The problem-solving process drives intervention planning.

In *engagement*, a social worker should be actively involved with a client in determining why treatment was sought; what has precipitated the desire to change now; the parameters of the helping relationship, including defining the roles of a social worker and client; and the expectations for treatment (what will occur and when it will happen). Client involvement is essential in determining what is important to a client now and in the future.

In *assessment*, a client is the source of providing essential information upon which to define the problem and solutions, as well as identifying collateral contacts from which gaps in data can be collected.

In *planning*, a client and social worker must develop a common understanding of a client's preferred lifestyle. Goals are developed from this common understanding in order to provide a direction to help a client move toward this lifestyle. Specific action plans are developed and agreed upon in order to specify who will do what, what and how resources will be needed and used, and timelines for implementation and review.

In planning, a social worker and client should be

1. Defining the problem (in a well-defined, clear, and data-driven format)

2. Examining the causes of the problem and how it relates to other positive/negative aspects of a client's life

3. Generating possible solutions that will impact on the problem

4. Identifying the driving and restraining forces related to implementation of each of the possible solutions

5. Rating the driving and restraining forces related to consistency and potency

6. Prioritizing these solutions based on these ratings

7. Developing SMART objectives—Specific, Measurable, Achievable, Relevant, and Time-specific—related to the chosen solutions

8. Creating strategies and activities related to the objectives

In *intervention*, a client must be actively involved in mobilizing his or her support network to realize continued progress and sustainable change. A client must bring to the attention of a social worker issues that arise which may threaten goal attainment. Progress, based upon client reports, must be tracked and plans/timelines adjusted accordingly.

In *evaluation*, subjective reports of a client, in conjunction with objective indicators of progress, should be used to determine when goals or objectives have been met and whether new goals or objectives should be set. Client self-monitoring is a good way to involve a client so he or she can see and track progress himself or herself.

In *termination*, a client should reflect on what has been achieved and anticipate what supports are in place if problems arise again. Although this is the last step in the problem-solving process, it still requires active involvement by both a social worker and client.

CULTURAL CONSIDERATIONS IN THE CREATION OF AN INTERVENTION PLAN

It is essential that a social worker address cultural considerations into treatment or intervention planning. These considerations should include the identification of cross-cultural barriers, which may hinder a client's engagement and/or progress in treatment.

Social workers also have an ethical mandate to take information learned when working with individual clients and adapt agency resources to meet others who may also have similar cultural considerations and/or language assistance needs.

A social worker should understand and validate each client's cultural norms, beliefs, and values. Areas in treatment or intervention planning that can be greatly influenced by cultural factors include identification of client strengths and problems, goals and objectives, and modalities of treatment.

For example, a client's culture can provide him or her with strengths that can be brought to the intervention process. These strengths can include, but are not limited to:

- Supportive family and community relations
- Community and cultural events and activities
- Faith and spiritual or religious beliefs
- Multilingual capabilities

■ Healing practices and beliefs

■ Participation in rituals (religious, cultural, familial, spiritual, community)

■ Dreams and aspirations

A culturally informed intervention plan must be based on a therapeutic relationship in which a client feels safe to explore his or her problems within his or her cultural context.

Intervention will be most effective when it is consistent with a consumer's culture. A social worker should consider the following given their cultural appropriateness:

■ Individual versus group treatment

■ Alternative treatment approaches (yoga, aromatherapy, music, writing)

■ Medication (western, traditional, and/or alternative)

■ Family involvement

■ Location/duration of intervention

The *DSM-5* incorporates a greater cultural sensitivity throughout the manual rather than a simple list of culture-bound syndromes.

Different cultures and communities exhibit or explain symptoms in various ways. Because of this, it is important for social workers to be aware of relevant contextual information stemming from clients' cultures, races, ethnicities, religious affiliations, and/or geographical origins so social workers can more accurately diagnose client problems, as well as more effectively treat them.

In the *DSM-5*, specific diagnostic criteria were changed to better apply across diverse cultures. *The Cultural Formulation Interview Guide* is included to help social workers assess cultural factors influencing clients' perspectives of their symptoms and treatment options. It includes questions about clients' backgrounds in terms of their culture, race, ethnicity, religion, or geographical origin. The Interview provides an opportunity for clients to define their distress in their own words and then relate this distress to how others, who may not share their culture, see their problems.

THE CRITERIA USED IN THE SELECTION OF INTERVENTION/ TREATMENT MODALITIES (E.G., CLIENT/CLIENT SYSTEM ABILITIES, CULTURE, LIFE STAGE)

Social workers are employed in different settings, such as hospitals, mental health centers, child welfare agencies, schools, and correctional facilities.

In addition, clients within these settings have different needs or problems. The types of interventions or treatments used by social workers are strongly influenced by both practice settings and the needs or problems of clients.

Social work interventions/treatments must be selected based upon the biopsychosocial–spiritual–cultural assessments of clients, which include the strengths that they possess, as well as the identification of feasible and desired outcomes within these larger service contexts.

There are diverse intervention or treatment models within gerontology, behavioral health, child welfare, and so forth. Interventions include those at the micro, mezzo, and macro levels. Micro interventions include, but are not limited to, the provision of therapy, case management, education, and/or crisis intervention. Macro interventions include advocacy and organizing.

In all instances, social workers should work in partnership with clients to select and reevaluate choices related to the selection of intervention or treatment approaches. Social workers should also keep abreast of research done on the effectiveness of these strategies and select those that are evidence based.

A social worker develops an intervention plan by consulting the relevant practice research and then flexibly implementing an approach to fit a client's needs and circumstances. The intervention plan is driven by the data collected as part of assessment. Assessment is informed by current human behavior and development research that provides key information about how clients behave and research about risk and resilience factors that affect human functioning. These theories inform social workers about what skills, techniques, and strategies must be used by social workers, clients, and others for the purpose of improving well-being. These techniques and strategies are outlined in an intervention plan.

An intervention plan should be reviewed during the intervention, at termination, and, if possible, following the termination of services to make adjustments, ensure progress, and determine the sustainability of change after treatment.

THE COMPONENTS OF INTERVENTION, TREATMENT, AND SERVICE PLANS

Planning is the bridge between assessment and intervention. It begins with specifying goals that a client hopes to achieve, then identifying what changes need to be made to achieve the goals, the change strategies needed to reach the goals, and the timelines for completing these actions.

Effective planning is the responsibility of both a social worker and a client. A social worker supports a client while structuring the process, and a client evaluates alternative courses of action. Planning should be based on information collected during the assessment phase.

It is important for a social worker and a client to develop a contract (i.e., an agreement that spells out the activities to be conducted by each, along with a timetable for action). **A contract can be a written, oral, or even implied agreement, although the more specific a contract, the more likely it is to prevent misunderstandings. A contract should delineate the problems or concerns to be addressed, goals and objectives of the intervention, activities that a client will undertake, tasks to be performed by a social worker, expected duration of the intervention, schedule of time and place for meetings, and/ or identification of other persons, agencies, or organizations expected to assist with the change process.**

Except in those cases in which contracts are written into court orders, contracts are not viewed as legally binding.

Contracts are also known as service agreements/plans, case plans, treatment plans, intervention plans, or individual/family support plans.

The greater the specificity about who will do what, when, and how, the greater the chances of the plan being fully implemented. Contracting is often reassuring to clients because it provides blueprints for change. It also encourages social workers to rethink assumptions and steps, ensuring that all change efforts are unique to individual client situations.

PSYCHOTHERAPIES

Psychotherapy aims to treat clients with mental disorders or problems by helping them understand their illness or situation. Social workers use verbal techniques to teach clients strategies to deal with stress, unhealthy thoughts, and dysfunctional behaviors. Psychotherapy helps clients manage their symptoms better and function optimally in everyday life.

Sometimes, psychotherapy alone may be the best treatment for a client, depending on the illness and its severity. Other times, psychotherapy is combined with the use of medication or a psychopharmacological approach.

There are many kinds of psychotherapy, so social workers must determine which is best to meet a client's need. A social worker should not use a "one size fits all approach" or a particular type of psychotherapy because it is more familiar or convenient. Some psychotherapies have been scientifically tested more than others for particular disorders.

For example, cognitive behavioral therapy (CBT), a blend of cognitive and behavioral therapy, is used for depression, anxiety, and other disorders. Dialectical behavior therapy (DBT), a form of CBT developed by Marsha Linehan, was developed to treat people with suicidal thoughts and actions. It is now also used to treat people with Borderline Personality Disorder. A social worker assures a client that his or her feelings are valid and understandable, but coaches him or her to understand that they are unhealthy or disruptive and a balance must be achieved. A client understands that it is his or her personal responsibility to change the situation.

Some psychotherapies are effective with children and adolescents and can also be used with families.

THE IMPACT OF IMMIGRATION, REFUGEE, OR UNDOCUMENTED STATUS ON SERVICE DELIVERY

Social workers may have a general concept of immigration requirements, but this area of law is both complex and volatile. Laws and policies affecting the status of immigrants have evolved over time in response to various social, political, and economic pressures. Most recently, immigration policy has had an exclusionary focus that has turned toward conflating criminality and undocumented immigration status. Although immigration laws are within the exclusive purview of the federal government, some states have attempted to address concerns by passing their own measures. This situation creates legal questions and ethical dilemmas for social workers who are employed in programs or areas serving immigrants.

Professional social work standards support immigration and refugee policies that uphold and support equity and human rights, while protecting national security. The social work profession recognizes the challenge of competing claims; however, immigration policies must promote social justice and avoid racism and discrimination or profiling on the basis of race, religion, country of origin, gender, or other grounds. The impact of refugee and immigration policies on families and children have to be closely monitored. Policies that encourage family reunification and ensure that children do not grow up unduly disadvantaged by the immigration status of their parents must be enacted and upheld.

Given the great diversity and myriad needs of the growing immigrant population, it is essential that social workers understand the legal and political, as well as psychological and social, issues surrounding immigration. Undocumented immigrants represent a large and vulnerable population in the United States. When conducting individual practice with undocumented immigrants, social workers must be aware of the laws that impact service provision and the unique psychosocial stressors that are experienced by this population.

Numerous immigrant households are comprised of mixed-status families in which family members hold different legal statuses. Each status carries different benefit entitlements, services, and legal rights.

DISCHARGE, AFTERCARE, AND FOLLOW-UP PLANNING

Discharge may occur for a variety of reasons; for example, a client may have met his or her goals or no longer needs the services; decides not to continue to receive them from a particular social worker or in general; and/or requires a different level of care. In addition, when a social worker leaves an agency, a client may continue to receive the same service from this agency, but from another worker. Although this is not a "discharge" from services, there is careful planning and standards that need to be followed to ensure continuity of care and prevent gaps in service.

The 2008 *NASW Code of Ethics* provides some guidance with regard to discharge or terminations, as well as aftercare and follow-up services.

Social workers should terminate services to clients and professional relationships with them when such services and relationships are no longer required or no longer serve client needs or interests (*NASW Code of Ethics, 2008—1.16 Termination of Services*).

Social workers should take reasonable steps to avoid abandoning clients who are still in need of services. Social workers should withdraw services precipitously only under unusual circumstances, giving careful consideration to all factors in the situation and taking care to minimize possible adverse effects. Social workers should assist in making appropriate arrangements for continuation of services when necessary (*NASW Code of Ethics, 2008—1.16 Termination of Services*).

Social workers in fee-for-service settings may terminate services to clients who are not paying an overdue balance if the financial contractual arrangements have been made clear to a client, if a client does not pose an imminent danger to self or others, and if the clinical and other consequences of the current nonpayment have been addressed and discussed with a client (*NASW Code of Ethics, 2008—1.16 Termination of Services*).

Social workers should not terminate services to pursue a social, financial, or sexual relationship with a client (*NASW Code of Ethics, 2008—1.16 Termination of Services*).

Social workers who anticipate the termination or interruption of services to clients should notify clients promptly and seek the transfer, referral, or continuation of services in relation to client needs and preferences (*NASW Code of Ethics, 2008—1.16 Termination of Services*).

Social workers who are leaving an employment setting should inform clients of appropriate options for the continuation of services and of the benefits and risks of the options (*NASW Code of Ethics, 2008—1.16 Termination of Services*).

It is unethical to continue to treat clients when services are no longer needed or in their best interests.

Another standard that is relevant to termination of services (*NASW Code of Ethics, 2008—1.15 Interruption of Services*) mandates that social workers should make reasonable efforts to ensure continuity of services in the event that services are interrupted by factors such as unavailability, relocation, illness, disability, or death.

Social workers must involve clients and their families (when appropriate) in making their own decisions about follow-up services or aftercare. Involvement must include, at a minimum, discussion of client and family preferences (when appropriate).

Social workers are often responsible for coordination of clients' follow-up services, when needed.

A return of clients to services quickly may suggest either that they did not receive needed follow-up services or that these services were inadequate. Termination may have occurred prematurely.

Clients who are at high risk for developing problems after services have ended should receive regular assessments after discharge to determine whether services are needed or discharge plans are being implemented as planned.

THE PHASES OF INTERVENTION AND TREATMENT

The use of timing in social work interventions is critical. Both verbal expressions and nonverbal communication by a social worker, if timed appropriately, can cause a client to feel joined with a social worker, resulting in a stronger therapeutic alliance that can lead to enhanced outcomes. However, the same expressions or communication at the wrong time can result in a client thinking that a social worker is not aligned or relating to a client's experiences.

Social workers must examine cues provided by clients to determine the appropriateness of communication styles and strategies, as well as when clients are ready to move forward in the problem-solving process. In addition, sometimes a social worker must reassess, with a client, the continued appropriateness of an agreed upon intervention because factors have made it no longer feasible or desirable.

Maslow's hierarchy of needs can help identify which client problems need immediate attention and should be prioritized for intervention first.

Often clients have multiple service needs that must be prioritized. Social workers should consider Maslow's hierarchy of needs when working with clients. Clients will need services that address "deficiency needs" (such as those related to physiological, security, social, and esteem concerns) prior to accessing support to promote their "growth needs" (such as self-actualization).

In addition, making sure that psychological and social issues are not caused, and cannot be subsequently addressed, by medical and/or substance use issues is paramount. Social workers should always address these problems first.

Interventions and services are intended to aid clients in alleviating problems impeding their well-being. The interventions used by social workers and the services available to clients are those that are identified as potentially helpful on the basis of the ongoing assessment of clients.

The selection and prioritization of service needs may be driven by many factors, including client desires and motivation, treatment modality selected, agency setting, available resources, funding and time constraints, and so forth. A social worker should focus on ensuring that service needs chosen are outlined in the intervention or treatment plan and are reevaluated on a regular basis. A social worker should also make sure that the needs are based on an unbiased assessment and client wishes. They should *not* be solely driven by funding and time constraints.

Social workers should *not* recommend only services that are familiar or provided by their employing agencies because this is a "cookie cutter" or "one size fits all" approach.

Social work aims to assist with making change on the micro, mezzo, or macro levels to enhance well-being. Despite the level of intervention, the steps that a social worker takes are similar.

Step 1: Engagement with client, group, or community
In *engagement*, a social worker should be actively involved in determining why change is sought, what has precipitated the desire to change now, and the parameters of the helping relationship, including defining the roles of a social worker and the expectations for treatment (what will occur and when it will happen).

Step 2: Assessment of strengths and needs
In *assessment*, essential information is collected upon which to define the problem and solutions, as well as identify collateral contacts from which gaps in data can be collected.

Step 3: Planning or design of intervention
In *planning*, an understanding of the problem is developed. Goals are developed from this understanding in order to provide a direction to help or assist. Specific action plans are developed and agreed upon in order to specify who will do what, what resources will be needed and how they will be used, and timelines for implementation and review.

Step 4: Intervention aimed at making change
In *intervention*, there is active involvement to realize continued progress and sustainable change. Issues that may threaten goal attainment must be addressed. Progress must be tracked and plans and timelines adjusted accordingly.

Step 5: Evaluation of efforts
In *evaluation*, subjective reports, in conjunction with objective indicators of progress, should be used to determine when goals and objectives have been met and whether new goals or objectives should be set.

Step 6: Termination and anticipation of future needs
In *termination*, progress that has been achieved should be reviewed and supports anticipated to be needed in the future should be identified.

Usually change does not occur easily and there are stages of change that occur. Understanding these stages can help achieve goals.

Precontemplation	Denial, ignorance of the problem
Contemplation	Ambivalence, conflicted emotion
Preparation	Experimenting with small changes, collecting information about change
Action	Taking direct action toward achieving a goal
Maintenance	Maintaining a new behavior, avoiding temptation
Relapse	Feelings of frustration and failure

In order for real change to occur, all intervention steps must occur and change must be understood in these sequential stages.

To achieve this goal, social workers must engage in interactions at three levels of intervention—micro, mezzo, and macro.

Micro

At the micro level of intervention, social workers concentrate on helping clients solve their problems. These problems may relate to difficulties with partners/spouses, children, other family members, coworkers, and/or neighbors. At the micro level, social workers help clients to access needed services from other agencies, as well as provide direct support and counseling. This type of social work intervention is often the focus of clinical practice in social work and clients can include individuals, couples, and/or families.

Mezzo

The second level of intervention for social workers is mezzo (also known as meso). Mezzo interventions apply to larger groups or communities. At the mezzo intervention level, social workers attempt to make connections between the micro and macro levels.

Macro

The third level of intervention for social workers is macro. This level stresses the importance of economic, historical, sociopolitical, and environmental influences on client well-being and functioning. Social workers determine how these factors can facilitate growth and/or create problems for clients.

Social workers are charged with making systems-level changes that can lead to opportunities and/or reduce barriers. Macro interventions can include creating or changing policies, procedures, regulations, and laws. They are aimed at not only assisting individual clients, but others who are experiencing the same difficulties. The focus of social work to engage in broader macro-level changes is what distinguishes it from other allied professions.

THE CLIENT'S/CLIENT SYSTEM'S ROLE IN THE PROBLEM-SOLVING PROCESS

Clients often tend to think of themselves and their problems as unique. A client may think his or her difficulties are so different from those of others that no one else could ever understand them. He or she may even enjoy this feeling of uniqueness. It may be a defense against the discomfort of exploring his or her fears of being like others. At this point, a client may not be ready to look at the problem. It is hard to admit difficulties, even to oneself.

There may also be concerns as to whether social workers can really be trusted. Some people, because of unfortunate experiences in their childhoods, grow up with distrust of others. Furthermore, people are generally afraid of what others will think of them.

A client may only be looking for sympathy, support, and/or empathy, rather than searching for a new way to solve his or her difficulties. A client may not see that change must occur. When a social worker points out some of the ways in which a client is contributing to his or her own problems, he or she stops listening. Solving the problem often requires a client to uncover some aspects of himself or herself that he or she has avoided thinking about in the past and wants to avoid thinking about in the future.

A client may have struggled very hard to make himself or herself an independent person. The thought of depending on or receiving help from another individual seems to violate something. A client must constantly defend against a sense of weakness and may have difficulty listening to and using the assistance of another person.

There are also many clients who have strong needs to lean on others. Some spend much of their lives looking for others on whom they can be dependent. In the helping situation, they may constantly and inappropriately seek to repeat this pattern.

PROBLEM-SOLVING MODELS AND APPROACHES (E.G., BRIEF, SOLUTION-FOCUSED METHODS OR TECHNIQUES)

The problem-solving approach is based on the belief that an inability to cope with a problem is due to some lack of motivation, capacity, or opportunity to solve problems in an appropriate way. Clients' problem-solving capacities or resources are maladaptive or impaired.

The goal of the problem-solving process is to enhance client mental, emotional, and action capacities for coping with problems and/or making accessible the opportunities and resources necessary to generate solutions to problems.

A social worker engages in the problem-solving process via the following steps:

1. Engaging

2. Assessing (includes a focus on client strengths and not just weaknesses)

3. Planning

4. Intervening

5. Evaluating

6. Terminating

Short-Term Interventions

The growing need for time-limited treatment, fueled by the widening influence of managed care in the behavioral health field, has produced a renewed focus on short-term therapy. Short-term interventions vary greatly in their duration.

Research has suggested that a social worker's and client's views on the time of treatment are more important than the duration of treatment itself. Sometimes these approaches are used because of organizational or financial constraints. In other instances, clients are choosing them over open-ended approaches. Although some have been wary of the effectiveness of these techniques to instill long-lasting change, they are being used more broadly than ever before. Some short-term interventions include a crisis intervention model and a cognitive behavioral model.

Although psychoanalysis is often thought of as long term, this was not the case with Freud's early work, and psychoanalysis did not start out this way. A number of short-term psychodynamic approaches focus on the belief that childhood experiences are the root of adult dysfunction.

METHODS TO ENGAGE AND MOTIVATE CLIENTS/ CLIENT SYSTEMS

A motivational approach aims to help clients realize what needs to change and to get them to talk about their daily lives, as well as their satisfaction with current situations. Social workers want to create doubt that everything is "OK" and help clients recognize consequences of current behaviors or conditions that contribute to dissatisfaction.

It is much easier if clients believe goals can be achieved and life can be different. Sometimes clients are incapacitated by conditions that need to be addressed first (i.e., depression). Social workers can help clients think of a time when things were better or create a picture of what their lives could look like with fewer stresses.

The role of a social worker is to create an atmosphere that is conducive to change and to increase a client's intrinsic motivation, so that change arises from within rather than being imposed from without.

Motivation is a state of readiness or eagerness to change, which may fluctuate from one time or situation to another.

Some additional techniques include:

- Clearly identifying the problem or risk area
- Explaining why change is important
- Advocating for specific change
- Identifying barriers and working to remove them
- Finding the best course of action
- Setting goals
- Taking steps toward change
- Preventing relapse

Empathy is a factor that increases motivation, lowers resistance, and fosters greater long-term behavioral change.

METHODS TO ENGAGE AND WORK WITH INVOLUNTARY CLIENTS/CLIENT SYSTEMS

Social workers often find themselves providing services to those who did not choose to receive them, but instead have to do so as mandated by law, including families in the child protection system, people in the criminal justice system, and so on. Working with involuntary clients can be challenging because they may want to have no contact or may only participate because they feel that they have no other choice.

Often these situations require social workers to receive peer support or supervision to process struggles encountered, as well as reassert their professionalism, because clients may try to test and exhibit anger at social workers, who represent the mandates placed upon them.

Some methods that can be helpful in working with involuntary clients include:

- Acknowledging clients' circumstances and understanding how they came about given clients' histories

- Listening to clients' experiences in order to try to understand how they feel about intervention

- Engaging in clear communication because involuntary clients struggle to understand what is happening to them

- Making clear what the purpose of the intervention is, what clients have control over and what they do not, what is going to happen next, and what the likely consequences will be if they do not participate

- Assisting at an appropriate pace as progress may be slow

- Building trust, even on the smallest scale, by consistently being honest and up-front about the situation and why a social worker is involved

- Giving clients practical assistance when needed to help them fight for their rights

- Paying attention to what is positive in clients' behavior and celebrating achievements

- Showing empathy and viewing clients as more than the problems that brought them into services

METHODS TO OBTAIN AND PROVIDE FEEDBACK

Social workers interface with professionals and others in order to achieve the best possible outcomes for clients. Feedback is essential in order to learn what works and what can be done better.

There is no single method for social workers to seek feedback. Many factors may impact on how such feedback is solicited and incorporated into practice. However, there are some important principles that social workers should adhere to when obtaining or providing feedback.

1. Feedback may be either verbal or nonverbal, so social workers must make efforts to see what clients are trying to convey verbally or via their behavior and nonverbal cues in order to see whether interventions should be altered.

2. When social workers involve consultants or others in the feedback process related to client care, clients should provide consent.

3. Social workers should ask for feedback in difficult circumstances—not just when circumstances appear neutral or positive. It can be tempting only to ask for feedback from people who will say something positive. Sometimes the best learning can be from those who will be critical. Talking through difficult feedback in supervision is important.

4. Feedback is especially critical at key decision points (such as when transferring or closing cases).

5. It is important to guard against influencing people to respond in a particular way; this influence may be unintentional, because a social worker may have more influence or power than the individual from whom feedback is sought.

6. Confidentiality should be respected if the informant wants it.

7. Always be clear about why feedback is needed and what will be done with the information.

8. Documentation of feedback is essential.

9. Be aware that the feedback may be very different depending upon when it is solicited. It is critical to realize how recent events may have influenced information received. Getting feedback repeatedly at several different times may be needed to see if responses differ.

10. A social worker must make sure that the communication method is appropriate. For a younger person, texting, email, or an online questionnaire may work, whereas a face-to-face conversation may be needed for others. The language should be jargon free and issues such as language, culture, and disability may affect the ways in which people both understand and react to requests for feedback. A social worker may want to use closed-ended questions and/or open ones to capture needed data.

There are varied methods for feedback. It can be formal or informal, mutual or one-way, written or verbal, personal or impersonal, and/or requested or unsolicited. Feedback can even be anonymous.

The following are some common feedback methods.

One-on-One Feedback

An individual delivering feedback to another, face-to-face, is probably the most common form. Such feedback needs to be delivered sensitively and according to the principles of the profession.

Intragroup Feedback

Individuals in a group provide feedback to the group and/or to one or more individuals within the group. If the feedback is directed to the performance of the group, it can be particularly effective.

Group-to-Group Feedback

This might take place between two groups that are working together. The feedback may go in one direction or both. The feedback might be directed at particular individuals or at the group as a whole.

Consultative Feedback

An individual or group serves as a formal or informal consultant to another (usually to a group, but occasionally to an individual). The individual or group receiving the feedback may be more apt to accept and consider the feedback, given the expertise of the consultative entity, but has no obligation to do so.

360° Feedback

This method involves feedback from all directions—supervisors, peers, subordinates, the community, and so forth. The idea is that the feedback reflects multiple viewpoints and gives a complete picture.

All models of feedback in social work practice should be supportive, use a strengths perspective (emphasizing the positives), and not "attack," rather than focusing on actions needed for change.

THE PRINCIPLES OF ACTIVE LISTENING AND OBSERVATION

Active listening skills are an essential part of building relationships and trust. The active part in the listening process can be achieved by showing interest in clients' words. Once clients notice that social workers are understanding what is said and really taking an interest, communication will be more open.

Active listening establishes trust and respect, so clients will feel comfortable confiding in social workers. Thus, it helps build a therapeutic alliance.

Active listening can also include speaking by using mirroring techniques to paraphrase and reflect back to clients what they have just said. For example, a client may say, "I hate my job and my boss yells at me all the time." An active listening response might involve saying something such as, "So you feel like your boss doesn't appreciate you or treat you with respect." Responses need to be tailored to what clients are saying to demonstrate listening and engagement in what is being said.

Although most information that a social worker uses during assessment comes from the social work interview, direct observation of interactions between family members and the client's nonverbal behavior can produce a lot of information about emotional states and interaction patterns.

Social workers also may use observation as part of macro-level intervention in order to assess the extent of a problem/issue, driving and restraining forces for change, key policy influencers, and community members who can work as part of a task group for reform.

When functioning as an observer, a social worker can take many roles, including *complete participant* (living the experience as a participant), *participant as observer* (interacting with those who are participating), *observer as participant* (limited relationship with others participating—primarily observer), or *complete observer* (removed from activity—observer only). Observation is also a method used in scientific inquiry to collect data.

VERBAL AND NONVERBAL COMMUNICATION TECHNIQUES

In order to facilitate change through the problem-solving process, a social worker must use various verbal and nonverbal communication techniques to assist clients to understand their behavior and feelings. In addition, to ensure clients are honest and forthcoming during this process, social workers must build trusting relationships with clients. These relationships develop through effective verbal and nonverbal communication. Social workers must be adept at using both forms of communication successfully, as well as understanding them, because verbal and nonverbal cues will be used by clients throughout the problem-solving process. Insight into their meaning will produce a higher degree of sensitivity to clients' experiences and a deeper understanding of their problems.

There are many verbal and nonverbal communication methods, including

- **Active listening**, in which social workers are sitting up straight and leaning toward clients in a relaxed and open manner. Attentive listening can involve commenting on clients' statements, asking open-ended questions, and making statements that show listening is occurring.

- **Silence** by social workers, which can show acceptance of clients' feelings and promotes introspection or time to think about what has been learned (*very effective when used with a client who is displaying a high degree of emotion*).

- **Questioning** using open- and closed-ended formats to get relevant information in a nonjudgmental manner.

- **Reflecting** or **validating** to show empathetic understanding of clients' problems. These techniques can also assist clients in understanding negative thought patterns.

- **Paraphrasing** and **clarifying** by social workers to rephrase what clients are saying in order to join together information. Clarification uses questioning, paraphrasing, and restating to ensure full understanding of clients' ideas and thoughts.

- **Reframing** by social workers shows clients that there are different perspectives and ideas that can help to change negative thinking patterns and promote change.

- Exhibiting desirable **facial expressions**, which include direct eye contact if culturally appropriate, warmth and concern reflected, and varied facial expressions.

- Using desirable **postures or gestures**, which include appropriate arm movements and attentive gestures.

There are many methods that social workers use to facilitate communication with clients. Central to the formation of a therapeutic alliance is displaying empathy. Empathy is distinguished from sympathy as the latter denotes pity or feeling bad for a client, whereas the former means that a social worker understands the ideas expressed, as well as the feelings of a client. To be empathetic, a social worker must accurately perceive a client's situation, perspective, and feelings, as well as communicate this understanding in a helpful (therapeutic) way.

A social worker should also display *genuineness* in order to build trust. Genuineness is needed in order to establish a therapeutic relationship. It involves listening to and communicating with clients without distorting their messages, as well as being clear and concrete in communications.

Another method is the use of *positive regard*, which is the ability to view a client as being worthy of caring about and as someone who has strengths and achievement potential. It is built on respect and is usually communicated nonverbally.

Communication is also facilitated by *listening, attending, suspending value judgments,* and *helping* clients develop their own resources. A social worker should always use *culturally appropriate communication*.

It is also essential to clearly establish *boundaries* with clients to facilitate a safe environment for change.

THE CONCEPT OF CONGRUENCE IN COMMUNICATION

Communication can be verbal and nonverbal, so an assessment of clients' communication skills must involve both. Role playing is a good way to assess and enhance clients' communication skills. It also allows a social worker to see if there is congruence between nonverbal and verbal communication.

Congruence is the matching of awareness and experience with communication. It is essential that a client is able to express himself or herself and that this communication is reflective of his or her feelings. *Congruence is essential for the vitality of a relationship and to facilitate true helping as part of the problem-solving process.*

LIMIT SETTING TECHNIQUES

Clients of all ages are frequently desperate for an environment with consistent boundaries. For this reason, it is helpful if social workers can learn limit-setting skills. Limit setting is facilitative as clients do not feel safe or accepted in a completely permissive environment.

In addition, although compassion is important for a social worker, it is important to maintain a client–social worker relationship. Understanding boundaries and being able to maintain those boundaries with clients are essential.

THE TECHNIQUE OF ROLE PLAY

Role playing is a teaching strategy that offers several advantages. Role playing in social work practice may be seen between supervisor and supervisee or social worker and client.

In all instances, role playing usually raises interest in a topic as clients are not passive recipients in the learning process. In addition, role playing teaches empathy and understanding of different perspectives as clients take on the role of another, learning and acting as that individual would in the specified setting. In role playing, participation helps embed concepts. Role playing gives clarity to information that may be abstract or difficult to understand.

The use of role playing emphasizes personal concerns, problems, behavior, and active participation. It improves interpersonal and communication skills, and enhances communication.

Role playing activities can be divided into four stages:

1. Preparation and explanation of the activity
2. Preparation of the activity
3. Role playing
4. Discussion or debriefing after the role play activity

ROLE MODELING TECHNIQUES

Role modeling emphasizes the importance of learning from observing and imitating and has been used successfully in helping clients acquire new skills, including those associated with assertiveness.

Role modeling works well when it is combined with role play and reinforcement to produce lasting change.

There are different types of modeling, including live modeling, symbolic modeling, participant modeling, or covert modeling.

Live modeling refers to watching a real person perform the desired behavior.

Symbolic modeling includes filmed or videotaped models demonstrating the desired behavior. Self-modeling is another form of symbolic modeling in which clients are videotaped performing the target behavior.

In *participant modeling*, an individual models anxiety-evoking behaviors for a client and then prompts the client to engage in the behavior.

In *covert modeling*, clients are asked to use their imagination, visualizing a particular behavior as another describes the imaginary situation in detail.

Models in any of these forms may be presented as either a coping or a mastery model. The coping model is shown as initially fearful or incompetent, and then is shown as gradually becoming comfortable and competent performing the feared behavior. The mastery model shows no fear and is competent from the beginning of the demonstration.

TECHNIQUES FOR HARM REDUCTION FOR SELF AND OTHERS

A harm reduction approach refers to any program, policy, or intervention that seeks to reduce or minimize the adverse health and social consequences associated with an illness, condition, and/or behavior, such as substance use, without requiring a client to practice abstinence, discontinue use, or completely extinguish the behavior. This definition recognizes that many clients are not unwilling or unable to abstain from behaviors or use at any given time and that there is a need to provide them with options that minimize the harm caused by their condition to themselves, to others, and to the community.

Harm reduction complements prevention approaches because it is based on the acceptance that, despite best efforts, clients will engage in behaviors such as substance use, and are unable or unwilling to stop using substances at any given time.

In addition, clients who use substances may prefer to use informal and nonclinical methods to reduce their consumption or reduce the risks associated with use. Harm reduction is practical, feasible, effective, safe, and cost-effective. Most harm reduction approaches are inexpensive, easy to implement, and have a high impact on individual and community health.

Harm reduction acknowledges the significance of ANY positive change that clients make in their lives; these interventions are designed to "meet clients where they are" currently.

Harm reduction recognizes that intervention can be seen as a continuum with the more feasible options at one end and less feasible, but desirable, ones at the other end. Though desirable, abstinence can be considered difficult to achieve. Thus, social workers should partner with clients to identify actions that can be taken to minimize impacts of their illnesses, conditions, and/or behaviors.

METHODS TO TEACH COPING AND OTHER SELF-CARE SKILLS TO CLIENTS/CLIENT SYSTEMS

Social workers assist clients in realizing how their lives can improve and/or how they can learn from mistakes that they have made. The techniques that social workers employ are a form of informal or didactic teaching.

For example, social workers may help clients see:

- How their histories have shaped them
- Needs associated with medical and/or behavioral health conditions

- Developmental issues related to various phases across the lifespan
- The workings of systems in which they operate
- Ways of coping in various situations

A social worker must use the problem-solving process to teach clients skills needed to make changes in their lives.

In addition, social workers may collaborate with or inform clients of colleagues who may also assist with more formal teaching, such as learning to read, obtaining a driver's license, and so on.

CLIENT/CLIENT SYSTEM SELF-MONITORING TECHNIQUES

Clients are encouraged to pay attention to any subtle shift in feelings. Clients frequently keep thought or emotion logs that include three components: (a) disturbing emotional states, (b) the exact behaviors engaged in at the time of the emotional states, and (c) thoughts that occurred when the emotions emerged. In cognitive behavioral therapy, homework is often done between sessions to record these encounters. This homework involves client self-monitoring, which is central to this approach.

METHODS OF CONFLICT RESOLUTION

Management of conflict entails four steps:

1. The recognition of an existing or potential conflict
2. An assessment of the conflict situation
3. The selection of an appropriate strategy
4. Intervention

When previous attempts to resolve a conflict have only escalated the conflict, a useful technique is to structure the interactions between the parties. Structuring techniques include:

1. Decreasing the amount of contact between the parties in the early stages of conflict resolution
2. Decreasing the amount of time between problem-solving sessions
3. Decreasing the formality of problem-solving sessions
4. Limiting the scope of the issues that can be discussed
5. Using a third-party mediator

CRISIS INTERVENTION AND TREATMENT APPROACHES

A state of crisis is time limited. Brief intervention during a crisis usually provides maximum therapeutic effect. Crisis intervention is a process of actively influencing the psychosocial functioning of clients during a period of disequilibrium or crisis. *A crisis does not need to be precipitated by a major life event.* The goals are to alleviate stress and mobilize coping skills, psychological capabilities and social resources.

The goals of crisis intervention are to (a) relieve the impact of stress with emotional and social resources, (b) return a client to a previous level of functioning (regain equilibrium), (c) help strengthen coping mechanisms during the crisis period, and (d) develop adaptive coping strategies.

Crisis intervention focuses on the here and now, is time limited (most crises last from 4 to 6 weeks), is directive, and requires high levels of activity and involvement from a social worker. A social worker sets specific goals and tasks in order to increase a client's sense of mastery and control.

THEORIES OF TRAUMA-INFORMED CARE

Trauma-informed care organizations, programs, and services are based on an understanding of the vulnerabilities or triggers of trauma survivors that traditional service delivery approaches may exacerbate, so that these services and programs can be more supportive and avoid retraumatization.

Trauma-informed care also can be viewed as an overarching philosophy and approach based on the understanding that many clients have suffered traumatic experiences and providers must be responsible for being sensitive to this issue, regardless of whether clients are being treated specifically for the trauma. Therefore, social workers should initially approach all of their clients as if they have a trauma history, regardless of the services for which the clients are being seen.

It is important for social workers to understand trauma and how it affects people regardless of their diagnoses or identified needs. Thus, in everyday practice, social workers need to recognize how the organizations, programs, and environments in which they practice could potentially act as trauma triggers for their clients; social workers should make every effort to minimize these triggers.

An important component of trauma-informed care is recognizing trauma's centrality to clients and how this plays into their perception of physical and emotional safety, relationships, and behaviors. When trauma goes unrecognized, it can be difficult to understand clients' behaviors or attitudes, and social workers may be tempted to assign unfounded pathologies to clients. Clients even may end up being barred from services as a result of what appears to be bizarre behavior or unfounded beliefs. Often, however, clients' otherwise challenging behavior is provoked by a legitimate trigger that easily could have been avoided.

METHODS AND APPROACHES TO TRAUMA-INFORMED CARE

Although there are many specific interventions or treatments used with clients who have suffered trauma, they all recognize that there are phases of trauma treatment. However, clients rarely proceed through them in a linear fashion. Social workers' knowledge of these phases should inform the use of specific interventions. For example, if a client is in the safety and stability phase, exposure therapies, which reduce avoidant behaviors and increase exposure to trauma-related material, are not recommended. In addition, classical psychodynamic treatment may be too destabilizing for a client inundated by flashbacks and intrusive thoughts. Thus, a trauma-informed social worker uses the three-phase model for choosing and using appropriate treatment strategies.

Phase 1: Safety and Stabilization

This initial stage is focused on establishing safety and stability, which must occur for trauma treatment to proceed. For many trauma survivors, basic needs, as described in Maslow's hierarchy of needs, are not being met. Survivors may need housing, food, and/or other essentials. In addition, survivors of complex trauma are often engaged in trauma reenactments in their lives. This means that they are frequently in relationships that are physically and/or emotionally dangerous. They may also be using substances, engaged in self-harm, and/or exhibiting risky or suicidal behaviors.

In this phase, social work interventions include case management to obtain housing, health services, transportation, and other critical supports. Crisis intervention models aimed at developing safety plans and establishing equilibrium or stability are also used. Stabilization focuses on the replacement of problematic and risky coping strategies with others that are nonharmful. At this phase of treatment, interventions that improve clients' capacities to regulate emotion, self-soothe, use relationships appropriately, and/or develop compassion for self are central.

Phase 2: Mourning and Remembrance

The second stage is when survivors acknowledge and speak about what happened and are ready to integrate experiences into a larger life context. This process allows emotional space in which the future can be constructed. Addressing what is and is not remembered is the focus of creating healing stories about the trauma experienced. Psychoeducation can be a very important component of addressing questions about the trauma experience and its effects. Trauma always results in a loss of some kind. Grief for what was, for what never was, and/or for what could have been must be addressed.

Phase 3: Reconnection and Reintegration

The third stage is marked by a commitment to move forward in life, searching for ways to use the trauma experience for empowerment. Trauma survivors may engage in new activities and/or relationships. A client moves from surviving into a new identity marked by an understanding of his or her history of trauma. Therapeutic strategies include integration of self-care strategies into everyday life and developing deepening resilience.

A good trauma-informed approach is multidimensional. The following list includes several elements that indicate a good, trauma-informed program:

Environment of Care

- Soothing colors for decor and paint
- Overall quiet; soft music
- Neutral or pleasant aroma
- Individual chairs with discrete seating areas
- Individual bathroom options

Staff Appearance

- Attire connotes professionalism; easy to identify staff members
- Clothing not sexually provocative

Staff Behavior

- Clearly demonstrate proper manners and respect
- Make every effort to minimize delays
- Speak in clear, nonthreatening tones
- Make eye contact
- Smile and demonstrate a generally pleasant demeanor
- Open physical stance, nodding
- Open to change/not rigid

Organizational Understanding

- Trauma policy/philosophy in place
- Commitment to trauma-informed care articulated

- All staff/clients/family members taught about trauma and its impact
- Universal trauma screenings for all clients
- Trauma status continually assessed
- Clear organization plan for dealing with behavioral crises
- Discrete areas for calming or crisis management identified
- Feedback valued and concerted outreach efforts made

Treatment Considerations

- Treatment goals reflect consumer preferences
- Treatment integrated across disciplines
- Offering choice of treatment provider when possible
- Everyday language used
- All statements of abuse acknowledged and addressed
- Sensitivity to seating configuration and proximity of seating options
- Co-occurring treatment needs assessed and incorporated into service provided
- Culture of origin respected and incorporated into service planning
- Recognize the importance of physical boundaries and aware that touch—sometimes even a handshake—could trigger trauma
- Avoid jokes and stories which can serve as triggers

ANGER MANAGEMENT TECHNIQUES

Although everyone gets angry, clients may come to social workers because they are not able to control their anger, causing problems. Anger can also increase risk for developing physical health problems, such as heart disease, stress-related illnesses, insomnia, digestive issues, and/or headaches.

Social workers can assist clients to develop action or treatment plans to change these behaviors. Techniques for assisting clients can include one or more of the following.

Relaxation Exercises

- Deep breathing
- Meditation or repeating calming words/phrases
- Guided imagery
- Yoga
- Stretching or physical exercise

Assisting clients to practice these techniques regularly will result in using them automatically in tense situations.

Cognitive Techniques

- Replacing destructive thoughts, such as "This is the end of the world" with healthy ones like "This is frustrating, but it will pass"
- Focusing on goals as a way of finding solutions to problems
- Using logic to get a more balanced perspective
- Not using an "all or nothing" approach
- Putting situations into perspective

Communication Skills

- Slowing down speech to avoid saying something not meant or that one will regret
- Listening to what others are saying
- Thinking about what to say before speaking
- Avoiding defensiveness
- Using humor to lighten the situation

Environmental Change

- Walking away or leaving situation
- Avoiding people or situations in the future that evoke anger
- Not starting conversations or entering situations that may cause anger when tired or rushed

STRESS MANAGEMENT TECHNIQUES

Stress is a psychological and/or physical reaction to life events, with most people experiencing it regularly in their own lives. When a life event is seen as a threat, it signals the release of hormones aimed at generating a response. This process has been labeled the "fight-or-flight" response.

Once the threat is gone, clients should return to typical relaxed states, but this may not happen if other threats are presented immediately thereafter. Thus, stress management is important because it provides tools to deal with threats and minimize the impacts of psychological and/or physical reactions.

The first step in stress management is for clients to monitor their stress levels and identify their stress triggers. These can be major life events, but also those associated with day-to-day life, such as job pressures, relationship problems, or financial difficulties. Positive life events, such as getting a job promotion, getting married, or having children, also can be stressful.

The second step in stress management is to assist clients in identifying what aspects of a situation they can control. Clients can make these changes, as well as benefit from stress-reduction techniques, such as deep breathing, exercise, massage, tai chi, or yoga, to manage those aspects of a situation that cannot be altered. Maintaining a healthy lifestyle is essential to helping manage stress.

Stress will always be a part of life, but assisting clients to manage it can increase their ability to cope with challenges and enhance their psychological and/or physical well-being.

COGNITIVE AND BEHAVIORAL INTERVENTIONS

Cognitive behavioral therapy (CBT) is a hands-on, practical approach to problem solving. Its goal is to change patterns of thinking or behavior that are responsible for clients' difficulties, and so change the way they feel. CBT works by changing clients' attitudes and their behavior by focusing on the thoughts, images, beliefs, and attitudes that are held (cognitive processes) and how this relates to behavior, as a way of dealing with emotional problems.

CBT can be thought of as a combination of psychotherapy and behavioral therapy. Psychotherapy emphasizes the importance of the personal meaning placed on things and how thinking patterns begin in childhood. Behavioral therapy pays close attention to the relationship between problems, behaviors, and thoughts.

This approach is active, collaborative, structured, time limited, goal-oriented, and problem focused. This approach lends itself to the requirements posed by managed care companies, including brief treatment, well-delineated techniques, goal and problem oriented, and empirically supported evidence of its effectiveness.

Steps in Cognitive Restructuring

Assist clients in

1. Accepting that their self-statements, assumptions, and beliefs determine or govern their emotional reaction to life's events

2. Identifying dysfunctional beliefs and patterns of thoughts that underlie their problems

3. Identifying situations that evoke dysfunctional cognitions

4. Substituting functional self-statements in place of self-defeating thoughts

5. Rewarding themselves for successful coping efforts

Foundational to this treatment is client self-monitoring. Clients are encouraged to pay attention to any subtle shift in feelings. Clients frequently keep thought or emotion logs that include three components: (a) disturbing emotional states; (b) the exact behaviors engaged in at the time of the emotional states; and (c) thoughts that occurred when the emotions emerged. Homework is often done between sessions to record these encounters.

STRENGTHS-BASED AND EMPOWERMENT STRATEGIES AND INTERVENTIONS

The primary mission of the social work profession is to enhance human well-being and help meet the basic human needs of all people, with particular attention to the needs and empowerment of people who are vulnerable, oppressed, and living in poverty (NASW Code of Ethics, 2008—Preamble).

Empowerment aims to ensure a sense of control over well-being and that change is possible. A social worker can help to empower individuals, groups, communities, and institutions.

On an individual level, social workers can engage in a process with a client aimed at strengthening his or her self-worth by making a change in life that is based on his or her desires (self-determination).

To facilitate empowerment, a social worker should:

- Establish a relationship aimed at meeting a client's needs and wishes such as access to social services and benefits or to other sources of information

- Educate a client to improve his or her skills, thereby increasing the ability for self-help

- Help a client to secure resources, such as those from other organizations or agencies, as well as natural support networks, to meet needs

- Unite a client with others who are experiencing the same issues when needed to enable social and political action

Social workers should also use an empowerment process with groups, communities, and institutions so they may gain or regain the capacity to meet human needs, enhance overall well-being and potential, and provide individuals control over their lives to the extent possible.

A social worker needs many skills that focus on the activation of resources, the creation of alliances, and the expansion of opportunities in order to facilitate empowerment.

CLIENT/CLIENT SYSTEM CONTRACTING AND GOAL-SETTING TECHNIQUES

A social worker and client work together to develop a contract (intervention or service plan), including an agreement on its implementation or the activities used to help a client attain his or her goals. Modification of the contract may be required as new information about a client's situation emerges and/or as the situation changes.

When clients seek to attain their goals, changes may need to be made to themselves, groups, families, and/or systems in the larger environment. This choice of targets is an even more complex issue than it first appears because the process of changing one system may bring about changes in others.

Change Strategies

- *Modify systems*: The decision to help a client on a one-to-one basis or in the context of a larger system must take into consideration a client's preferences and previous experiences, as well as the degree to which a client's problem is a response to forces within the larger system and whether change can be readily attained by a change in the larger system.

- *Modify individual thoughts*: A social worker may teach how to problem solve, alter his or her self-concepts by modifying self-defeating statements, and/or make interpretations to increase a client's understanding about the relationship between events in his or her life.

- *Modify individual actions*: A social worker may use behavior modification techniques, such as reinforcement, punishment, modeling, role playing, and/or task assignments. *Modeling and role modeling are very effective methods for teaching. They should be used whenever possible.*

- Thoughts can be modified by *feedback from others* and behaviors can be modified through the *actions of others* in a system (by altering reinforcements).

- A social worker can also *advocate* for a client and seek to secure a change in a system on his or her behalf.

- A social worker can be a *mediator* by helping a client and another individual or system to negotiate with each other so that each may attain their respective goals.

PARTIALIZING TECHNIQUES

During the problem-solving process, a social worker may need to assist a client to break down problems or goals into less overwhelming and more manageable components. This is known as partialization and aims to break complex issues into simpler ones.

Partialization is useful because it may assist a social worker and a client to identify the goals that are easier to achieve first, enabling a client to see results more quickly and gain some success in making harder changes. Partialization can also help individuals to order the problems or goals that need more immediate help from those that can be addressed later. A social worker can use Maslow's hierarchy of needs as one tool to assist in making decisions about more pressing needs. In addition, a client should be asked to prioritize his or her concerns or goals.

When outlining the goals for treatment, it is important that the broad overarching aims of treatment are broken down by a social worker and client into smaller, more tangible items that must be achieved in order to reach the overall goal. Behavioral objectives are the smaller, observable, and measurable intermediate steps that lead to broader long-term goals. Behavioral objectives help a social worker and client understand whether the strategies they are using to achieve the goal are resulting in change or whether they need to modify their efforts to improve the likelihood of accomplishing the desired outcome.

There are several important elements of behavioral objectives:

1. Good behavioral objectives are client-oriented and place the emphasis upon what a client will need to do in order for change to occur.

2. Good behavioral objectives are clear and understandable and contain a clearly stated verb that describes a definite action or behavior.

3. Good behavioral objectives are observable and describe an action that results in observable products.

4. Good behavioral objectives contain the behavior targeted for change, conditions under which a behavior will be performed, and the criteria for determining when the acceptable performance of the behavior occurs.

ASSERTIVENESS TRAINING

Assertiveness training is when procedures are used to teach clients how to express their positive and negative feelings and to stand up for their rights in ways that will not alienate others.

Assertiveness training typically begins with clients thinking about areas in their life in which they have difficulty asserting themselves. The next stage usually involves role plays designed to help clients practice clearer and more direct forms of communicating with others. Feedback is provided to improve responses, and the role play is repeated. Clients are asked to practice assertive techniques in everyday life.

Assertiveness training promotes the use of "I" statements as a way to help clients express their feelings. "I" statements tell others how their actions may cause clients to be upset, but are in contrast with "you" statements, which are often seen as blaming or aggressive.

Learning specific techniques and perspectives, such as self-observation skills, awareness of personal preferences, and assuming personal responsibility, are important components of the assertiveness training process.

TASK-CENTERED APPROACHES

A task-centered approach aims to quickly engage clients in the problem-solving process and to maximize their responsibility for treatment outcomes. In this modality, the duration of treatment is usually limited due to setting constraints, limitations imposed by third-party payers, or other reasons. Thus, at the outset, the expectation is that interventions from learning theory and behavior modification will be used to promote completion of a well-defined task to produce measurable outcomes. The focus is on the "here and now." This type of practice is often preferred by clients, as they are able to see more immediate results.

The problem is partialized into clearly delineated tasks to be addressed consecutively (assessment leads to goals, which lead to tasks). A client must be able to identify a precise psychosocial problem and a solution confined to a specific change in behavior or a change of circumstances. A client must also be willing to work on the problem. It is essential that a social worker and client establish a strong working relationship quickly. A social worker's therapeutic style must be highly active, empathic, and sometimes directive in this approach.

Assessment focuses on helping a client identify the primary problem and explore the circumstances surrounding the problem. Specific tasks are expected to evolve from this process. Consideration is given to how a client would ideally like to see the problem resolved. Termination, in this modality, begins almost immediately upon the onset of treatment.

PSYCHOEDUCATION METHODS (E.G., ACKNOWLEDGING, SUPPORTING, NORMALIZING)

One of the ways that social workers provide information to clients is through psychoeducation. This model allows a social worker to provide clients with information necessary to make informed decisions that will allow them to reach their respective goals. In addition to focusing on clients' education, it also provides support and coping skills development.

Psychoeducation is delivered in many service settings and with many types of client populations. It is provided to those who are experiencing some sort of issue or problem with the rationale that, with a clear understanding of the problem, as well as self-knowledge of strengths, community resources, and coping skills, clients are better equipped to deal with problems and to contribute to their emotional well-being.

The core psychoeducational principle is that education has a role in emotional and behavioral change. With an improved understanding of the causes and effects of problems, psychoeducation broadens clients' perception and interpretation of them, positively influencing clients' emotions and behavior. In other words, clients feel less helpless about the situation and more in control of themselves.

GROUP WORK TECHNIQUES AND APPROACHES (E.G., DEVELOPING AND MANAGING GROUP PROCESSES AND COHESION)

Group work is a method of working with two or more people for personal growth, the enhancement of social functioning, and/or for the achievement of socially desirable goals.

Social workers use their knowledge of group organization and functioning to affect the performance and adjustment of individuals. Individuals remain the focus of concern and the group is the vehicle of growth and change. *When individual problems arise, they should be directed to the group for possible solutions as the group is the agent of change. Social workers must remind group members that confidentiality cannot be guaranteed—though seeing an agreement among group members concerning preserving the confidentiality of information shared should be an initial goal of any group process.*

Contraindications for group: *client* who is *in crisis; suicidal;* compulsively needy for attention; actively psychotic; and/or paranoid.

There are different kinds of groups.

Open Versus Closed

Open groups are those in which new members can join at any time. Closed groups are those in which all members begin the group at the same time.

Short-Term Versus Long-Term

Some groups have a very short duration, whereas others meet for a longer duration.

A social worker takes on different roles throughout the group process, which has a beginning, middle, and end.

Beginning

A social worker identifies the purpose of the group and his or her role. This stage is characterized as a time to convene, to organize, and to set a plan. Members are likely to remain distant or removed until they have had time to develop relationships.

Middle

Almost all of the group's work will occur during this stage. Relationships are strengthened as a group so that the tasks can be worked on. Group leaders are usually less involved.

End

The group reviews its accomplishments. Feelings associated with the termination of the group are addressed.

FAMILY THERAPY MODELS, INTERVENTIONS, AND APPROACHES

Working with families has always been central to social work practice. Family interventions require treating not just an individual but all those within a family unit, with the focus of assessment and intervention directed at the interaction of family members.

In order to work effectively with families, social workers must:

1. Understand the development of, as well as the historical, conceptual, and contextual issues influencing, family functioning

2. Have awareness of the impact of diversity in working with families, particularly race, class, culture, ethnicity, gender, sexual preference, aging, and disabilities

3. Understand the impact of a social worker's family of origin, current family structure, and its influence on a social worker's interventions with families

4. Be aware of the needs of families experiencing unique family problems (domestic violence, blended families, trauma and loss, adoptive families, etc.)

Social workers use a variety of techniques to work with families. Family therapy treats the family as a unified whole—a system of interacting parts in which change in any part affects the functioning of the overall system. The family is the unit of attention for diagnosis and treatment. Social roles and interpersonal interaction are the focus of treatment. Real behaviors and communication that affect current life situations are addressed. The goal is to interrupt the circular pattern of pathological communication and behaviors and replace it with a new pattern that will sustain itself without the dysfunctional aspects of the original pattern.

Key clinical issues include:

- Establishing a contract with the family
- Examining alliances within the family
- Identifying where power resides
- Determining the relationship of each family member to the problem
- Seeing how the family relates to the outside world
- Assessing influence of family history on current family interactions
- Ascertaining communication patterns
- Identifying family rules that regulate patterns of interaction
- Determining meaning of presenting symptom in maintaining family homeostasis
- Examining flexibility of structure and accessibility of alternative action patterns
- Finding out about sources of external stress and support

Recognition of Functional Roles in Family Dynamics

Roles are extremely important in family functioning, with the establishment of clear roles directly connected to family well-being and the ability to handle crises.

Family members have both instrumental and affective functions that are essential for positive well-being. Instrumental functions are concerned with the provision of physical resources (i.e., food, clothing, and shelter) and decision making. Affective functions involve the provision of emotional support to family members.

In order for families to maintain emotional and physical health, family members must fulfill essential roles. Sometimes, these roles are assumed by multiple family members; in other instances, separate family members may meet each of these needs. Often individuals have multiple roles within family units.

Roles in Healthy Families

Provision of Resources

The provision of resources is an instrumental role that fulfills the most basic needs of the family unit: having money, food, clothing, and shelter.

Emotional Support

Supporting other family members is primarily an affective role and includes providing comfort and support.

Life Skills Development

One of the functions of families is the physical, emotional, educational, and social development of children. This role ensures that life skills development of members occurs.

Family System Management

Decision making, handling finances, and maintaining appropriate boundaries and behavioral standards are critical to maintaining a healthy family dynamic.

Intimate Relationship Maintenance

Intimate relationships, including sexual ones, are critical between partners and couples. Ensuring that quality intimate relationships are maintained is essential to meeting the emotional needs of partners and spouses.

In dysfunctional families, such as those with members who have substance use problems, members may assume codependent roles, including functioning as the *Family Hero*, the *Scapegoat*, the *Mascot*, and/or the *Lost Child*.

The *Family Hero*, often the oldest child, devotes his or her time and attention to minimizing or masking problems. By overachieving and being successful in school or work, the Family Hero tries to make up for a dysfunctional home life.

The *Scapegoat* is defiant, hostile, and angry, and gets in trouble at school or work. His or her behavior turns the focus away from dysfunction in the family.

The *Mascot* tries to get people to laugh as a way of improving the atmosphere and drawing attention away from the dysfunctional household.

The *Lost Child* becomes a loner or is very shy. He or she draws away from interactions with family members and becomes invisible in order to avoid adding to the dysfunction or stain.

The following are some types of family therapy.

Strategic Family Therapy

In strategic family therapy, a social worker initiates what happens during therapy, designs a specific approach for each person's presenting problem, and takes responsibility for directly influencing people.

It has roots in structural family therapy and is built on communication theory.

It is active, brief, directive, and task-centered. Strategic family therapy is more interested in creating change in behavior than change in understanding.

Strategic family therapy is based on the assumption that families are flexible enough to modify solutions that do not work and adjust or develop.

There is the assumption that all problems have multiple origins; a presenting problem is viewed as a symptom of and a response to current dysfunction in family interactions.

Therapy focuses on problem resolution by altering the feedback cycle or loop that maintains the symptomatic behavior. The social worker's task is to formulate the problem in solvable, behavioral terms and to design an intervention plan to change the dysfunctional family pattern.

Concepts/Techniques

- Pretend technique—encourage family members to "pretend" and encourage voluntary control of behavior

- First-order changes—superficial behavioral changes within a system that do not change the structure of the system

- Second-order changes—changes to the systematic interaction pattern so the system is reorganized and functions more effectively

- Family homeostasis—families tend to preserve familiar organization and communication patterns; resistant to change

- Relabeling—changing the label attached to a person or problem from negative to positive so the situation can be perceived differently; it is hoped that new responses will evolve

- Paradoxical directive or instruction—prescribe the symptomatic behavior so a client realizes he or she can control it; uses the strength of the resistance to change in order to move a client toward goals

Structural Family Therapy

This approach stresses the importance of family organization for the functioning of the group and the well-being of its members. A social worker "joins" (engages) the family in an effort to restructure it. Family structure is defined as the invisible set of functional demands organizing interaction among family members. Boundaries and rules determining who does what, where, and when are crucial in three ways.

1. Interpersonal boundaries define individual family members and promote their differentiation and autonomous, yet interdependent, functioning. Dysfunctional families tend to be characterized by either a pattern of rigid enmeshment or disengagement.

2. Boundaries with the outside world define the family unit, but boundaries must be permeable enough to maintain a well-functioning open system, allowing contact and reciprocal exchanges with the social world.

3. Hierarchical organization in families of all cultures is maintained by generational boundaries, the rules differentiating parent and child roles, rights, and obligations.

Restructuring is based on observing and manipulating interactions within therapy sessions, often by enactments of situations as a way to understand and diagnose the structure and provide an opportunity for restructuring.

Bowenian Family Therapy

Unlike other models of family therapy, the goal of this approach is not symptom reduction. Rather, a Bowenian-trained social worker is interested in improving the intergenerational transmission process. Thus, the focus within this approach is consistent whether a social worker is working with an individual, a couple, or the entire family. It is assumed that improvement in overall functioning will ultimately reduce a family member's symptomatology. Eight major theoretical constructs are essential to understanding Bowen's approach. These concepts are differentiation, emotional system, multigenerational transmission, emotional triangle, nuclear family, family projection process, sibling position, and societal regression. These constructs are interconnected.

Differentiation is the core concept of this approach. The more differentiated, the more a client can be an individual while in emotional contact with the family. This allows a client to think through a situation without being drawn to act by either internal or external emotional pressures.

Emotional fusion is the counterpart of differentiation and refers to the tendency for family members to share an emotional response. This is the result of poor interpersonal boundaries between family members. In a fused family, there is little room for emotional autonomy. If a member makes a move toward autonomy, it is experienced as abandonment by other members of the family.

Multigenerational transmission stresses the connection of current generations to past generations as a natural process. Multigenerational transmission gives the present a context in history. This context can focus a social worker on the differentiation in the system and on the transmission process.

An **emotional triangle** is the network of relationships among three people. Bowen's theory states that a relationship can remain stable until anxiety is introduced. However, when anxiety is introduced into the dyad, a third party is recruited into a triangle to reduce the overall anxiety. It is almost impossible for two people to interact without triangulation.

The **nuclear family** is the most basic unit in society and there is a concern over the degree to which emotional fusion can occur in a family system. Clients forming relationships outside of the nuclear family tend to pick mates with the same level of differentiation.

Family projection process describes the primary way parents transmit their emotional problems to children. The projection process can impair child functioning and increase vulnerability to clinical symptoms.

Sibling position is a factor in determining personality. Where a client is in birth order has an influence on how he or she relates to parents and siblings. Birth order determines the triangles that clients grow up in.

Societal regression, in contrast to progression, is manifested by problems such as the depletion of natural resources. Bowen's theory can be used to explain societal anxieties and social problems, because Bowen viewed society as a family—an emotional system complete with its own multigenerational transmission, chronic anxiety, emotional triangles, cutoffs, projection processes, and fusion/differentiation struggles.

COUPLES INTERVENTIONS AND TREATMENT APPROACHES

There are often reasons that couples experience problems including, but not limited to:

- Retriggering emotional trauma and not repairing it
- An inability to bond or reconnect after hurting or doing damage to one another
- Lack of skills or knowledge

Many treatment techniques are used with individuals that can be adapted in work with couples, including:

Behavior modification—Successful couples counseling methods will address and attempt to modify any dysfunctional behavior so that couples can change the way each individual behaves with the other.

Insight-oriented psychotherapy—A good deal of time is spent studying interactions between individuals in order to develop a hypothesis concerning what caused individuals to react to each other in the way they do.

There are also specific couples therapy approaches, including the *Gottman Method*, which is based on the notion that healthy relationships are ones in which individuals know each other's stresses and worries, share fondness and admiration, maintain a sense of positiveness, manage conflicts, trust one another, and are committed to one another.

The Gottman Method focuses on conflicting verbal communication in order to increase intimacy, respect, and affection; removes barriers that create a feeling of stagnancy in conflicting situations; and creates a heightened sense of empathy and understanding within relationships.

With all approaches, there are actions that a social worker can take to facilitate effective couples' treatment.

For example, when developing a collaborative alliance with each person, a social worker should validate the experience of each and explore each person's reservations about engaging in couples therapy. In addition, when developing an alliance with the couple as a unit, a social worker can reframe individual problems in relationship terms and support each person's sense of himself or herself as being part of a unit, as well as a separate individual.

PERMANENCY PLANNING

Permanency planning is an approach to child welfare that is based on the belief that children need permanence to thrive. Child protection services should focus on getting children into, and maintaining, permanent homes. Permanency planning received a lot of attention in the 1970s. Legislation in the United States, such as the Adoption Assistance and Child Welfare Act of 1980, promotes permanency planning and creates mandates related to child placements.

In permanency planning, the first goal is to get children back into their original homes. This can be achieved with a thorough investigation into child protection situations to determine if homes are safe and, if needed, exploring ideas for making them safer or more enriching for children.

Supports can include getting caregivers services for meeting needs or providing education, if needed, to ensure adequate and quality care. If children cannot return to their original homes, steps need to be made so that they can get into permanent living situations as quickly as possible with adults with whom they have continuous and reciprocal relationships, including those made available through adoption.

MINDFULNESS AND COMPLEMENTARY THERAPEUTIC APPROACHES

Social workers continue to provide the bulk of mental health services in the United States. A significant number of persons seeking services expecting providers to be aware and knowledgeable about alternatives and complements to Western medical approaches for symptom relief and healing when their medical or behavioral health is disrupted and/or compromised. An ever increasing number of people are seeking complementary and alternative medicine (CAM) or integrated health care (IHC) to address health/behavioral health issues. Not only are clients receptive to the use of complementary approaches, they often request diverse approaches that go beyond medications and psychotherapy to address their overall concerns. Thus, social workers must have knowledge mindfulness and complementary therapeutic approaches.

Interventions and remedies that some cultures and populations consider conventional others view as alternative, and what some clients assess as successful outcomes, some professionals may not concur.

Mindfulness is the practice of paying close attention to what is being experienced in the present, both inside the body and mind and in the external world. It is a conscious effort to be with whatever is going on right now, without judging or criticizing what we find. In each moment, mindfulness invites being awake, aware, and accepting of ourselves.

The practice of mindfulness is integral to efforts to reduce stress and to increase capacity to cope. Mindfulness can stand alone as a treatment tool or may be incorporated with other treatment modalities. Most settings where social workers practice would be conducive to mindfulness practice.

Social workers and other health/behavioral health providers are increasingly including the practice of mindfulness as a useful tool, not only in building a self-care routine, but also in addressing the needs of their clients.

The multitude of complementary approaches to maintaining health are vast and it is unrealistic for social workers to be informed and knowledgeable about all of them, but it is expected that social workers will be aware of the predominant practices and methods being used among the populations they are serving. Just as important, social workers need to be instilled with a respect for clients' authority in determining the best method to treat their problems when there are no indications of harm to self and/or others. Knowing how to integrate empirically tested and validated medical interventions, along with indigenous approaches preserved for generations, is essential to ensuring culturally competent, holistic treatment.

TECHNIQUES USED FOR FOLLOW-UP

The standard of practice is that social workers must involve clients and their families (when appropriate) in making their own decisions about follow-up services or aftercare. Involvement must include, at a minimum, discussion of client and family preferences (when appropriate).

Follow-up meetings are often important to ensure change maintenance. Many clients continue to progress after termination and follow-up meetings provide opportunities to acknowledge these gains and encourage continuation of such efforts.

Follow-up meetings also provide valuable interactions which can mitigate any unanticipated difficulties. Follow-up meetings provide clients with reassurance that they are not alone as they implement what they have learned. They allow for longitudinal evaluation of practice effectiveness.

It is important that social workers explain to clients that follow-up meetings may be important in the problem-solving process. Social workers must not be intrusive or send messages that clients cannot function on their own. Clients who have difficulty terminating may use follow-up meetings as ways to prolong social worker–client relationships beyond what is needed. Social workers must set clear boundaries and treat follow-up meetings with professionalism—having clearly stated goals for these sessions.

Clients who tell social workers during follow-up about new problems that have arisen should be seen for assessment. Social workers who have already assisted clients resolve issues are often the first ones to which clients disclose new problems which have emerged.

TECHNIQUES USED TO EVALUATE A CLIENT'S/CLIENT SYSTEM'S PROGRESS

Evaluating progress is a critical part of the problem-solving process. Examining with a client what has occurred and what still needs to occur involves him or her in treatment decisions.

Evaluation methods can be simple or complex. They can rely on quantitative information that shows data on reductions in target behaviors, health care improvements, or psychiatric symptom increases, and/or qualitative information in which a client and/or social worker subjectively report on progress made in various areas.

When evaluating progress, a social worker and client should gather all needed information and identify factors that helped or hindered progress. Goals outlined in the contract/service plan should be modified, if needed, based upon the outcome of the evaluation.

Social workers should assist clients to understand the progress they have made so they can clearly understand and celebrate their accomplishments, as well as identify areas that need attention. This process should ensure that clients understand why progress has happened, as well as include a dialogue about any changes that need to occur in the problem-solving process to facilitate continued growth.

THE INDICATORS OF CLIENT/CLIENT SYSTEM READINESS FOR TERMINATION

Readiness for termination may be marked when meetings between a social worker and client seem uneventful and the tone becomes one closer to cordiality rather than challenge, as well as when no new ground has been discovered for several sessions in a row.

In termination, a social worker and client (a) evaluate the degree to which a client's goals have been attained, (b) acknowledge and address issues related to the ending of the relationship, and (c) plan for subsequent steps a client may take relevant to the problem that do not involve a social worker (such as seeking out new services, if necessary).

The process of evaluation helps a client determine if his or her goals have been met and if the helping relationship was beneficial. As a result of the evaluation process, a social worker can become a more effective practitioner and provide better services. There must always be a method to evaluate the effectiveness of the services received. Evaluation measures, when compared with those taken at baseline, assist in determining the extent of progress and a client's readiness for termination.

A social worker helps a client cope with the feelings associated with termination. This process may help a client cope with future terminations.

By identifying the changes accomplished and planning how a client is going to cope with challenges in the future, a social worker helps a client maintain these changes.

CONSULTATION APPROACHES (E.G., REFERRALS TO SPECIALISTS)

Social workers are often called upon to seek consultation for a problem related to a client, service, organization, and/or policy. Consultation is the utilization of an "expert" in a specific area to assist with developing a solution to the issue. Consultation is usually time limited and the advice of the consultant can be used by a social worker in the problem-solving process. Although a consultant does not have any formal authority over a social worker, he or she has informal authority as an "expert." However, a social worker is not required to follow the recommendations of a consultant.

Four things are critical in consultation:

1. Defining the purpose of the consultation
2. Specifying the consultant's role
3. Clarifying the nature of the problem
4. Outlining the consultation process

Social workers should seek the advice and counsel of colleagues whenever such consultation is in the best interests of clients, but should only do so from colleagues who have demonstrated knowledge, expertise, and competence related to the subject of the consultation (*NASW Code of Ethics*, 2008— *2.05 Consultation*).

When seeking consultation, social workers need to get the permission of clients if any identifying or specific information will be shared. In addition, social workers should only disclose information that is absolutely necessary when interacting with consultants.

Social workers may also provide consultation. They should have the appropriate knowledge and skill to do so and should follow all ethical standards, including avoiding conflicts of interest and maintaining boundaries (*NASW Code of Ethics, 2008—3.01 Supervision and Consultation*).

METHODS TO ASSESS THE AVAILABILITY OF COMMUNITY RESOURCES

Social workers must respect the rights to self-determination of clients. In order for clients to make informed decisions, it is critical that they understand the range of services available and be informed about any opportunities they have to obtain services from other service providers. Clients should also understand their right to be referred to other professionals for assistance, as well as their right to refuse services and possible consequences of such refusals.

Throughout the problem-solving process, social workers should be assisting clients to access available resources, as well as create new ones if they do not exist or are not appropriate. In order for clients to choose between alternative resources, social workers must review the advantages and disadvantages of using each.

There are important steps, as well as ethical concerns, that must be taken when referring clients for services.

Step 1: Clarifying the Need or Purpose for the Referral

Social workers should refer clients to other professionals when the other professionals' specialized knowledge or expertise is needed to serve clients fully or when social workers believe that they are not being effective or making reasonable progress with clients and additional service is required (*NASW Code of Ethics, 2008—2.06 Referral for Services*).

Step 2: Researching Resources

When making a referral, it is critical that a social worker refers to a competent provider, someone with expertise in the problem that a client is experiencing. When researching resources, a client's right to self-determination should be paramount. In addition, if a client is already receiving services from an agency, it may be advisable to see if there are available services provided by this agency in order to avoid additional coordination and fragmentation for a client.

Step 3: Discussing and Selecting Options

Social workers are prohibited from giving or receiving payment for a referral when no professional service is provided by the referring social worker (*NASW Code of Ethics, 2008—2.06 Referral for Services*).

Step 4: Planning for Initial Contact

Social workers may want to work with a client to prepare for the initial meeting. Preparation may include helping a client to understand what to expect or reviewing needs and progress made so that it can be discussed with the new provider.

Step 5: Initial Contact

Social workers who refer clients to other professionals should take appropriate steps to facilitate an orderly transfer of responsibility. Social workers who refer clients to other professionals should disclose, with clients' consent, all pertinent information to the new service providers (*NASW Code of Ethics, 2008—2.06 Referral for Services*).

Step 6: Follow-Up to See If Need Was Met

Social workers should always follow-up to ensure that there was not a break in service and that the new provider is meeting a client's needs.

Unit **III**

Intervention Processes and Techniques for Use With Larger Systems (18%)

Program Development and Research

8

METHODS TO ESTABLISH PROGRAM OBJECTIVES AND OUTCOMES

The terms "mission," "goals," "objectives," and "outcomes" are often used interchangeably without being clearly defined.

A *mission statement* is a general, concise statement outlining the purpose guiding the practices of an organization. Outcomes eventually flow from the mission statements of an agency. *Goals* are broad, general statements of what the program intends to accomplish. Goals describe broad outcomes and concepts expressed in general terms (e.g., clear communication, problem-solving skills). Goals should provide a framework for determining the more specific objectives of a program and should be consistent with the mission of the agency. A single goal may have many specific subordinate objectives.

Objectives are brief, clear statements that describe the desired outcomes. They are distinguished from goals by the level of specificity. Goals express intended outcomes in general terms and objectives express them in specific terms.

Outcomes may be knowledge, abilities (skills), and/or attitudes (values, dispositions) that have been obtained. Outcomes are *achieved* results.

METHODS OF SERVICE DELIVERY

The context of social work practice clearly has a profound influence on the quality and standards of professional activities and the ability of social workers to practice ethically and effectively. Social work takes place in a wide variety of settings, including, but not limited to, private practices, public sector organizations (government), schools, hospitals, correctional facilities, and private nonprofit agencies.

To meet the needs of clients, social workers must have work environments that support ethical practice and are committed to standards and good quality services. A positive working environment is created where the values and principles of social workers are reinforced in agency policies and procedures.

To achieve this aim, employers must understand social work practice and provide supervision, workload management, and continuing professional development consistent with best practices.

Policies setting out standards of ethical practice should be written and clear. Social workers should never be required to do anything that would put at risk their ability to uphold ethical standards, including those in the areas of confidentiality, informed consent, and safety/risk management.

The public, including clients, should be regularly informed of agency policies and procedures and provided with information about how to raise concerns or make complaints about them.

Policies that do not tolerate dangerous, discriminatory, and/or exploitative behavior must be in place so that social workers and their clients are safe from harm.

The adoption and implementation of policies and procedures on workload and caseload management contribute greatly to the provision of quality services to clients. In addition, policies and procedures for confidential treatment and storage of records should be established.

Continuing professional development and further training enable social workers to strengthen and develop their skills. Orientation and other relevant training provided to social workers upon hire and when assuming other jobs within the setting are essential.

Good quality, regular social work supervision by professionals who have the necessary experience and qualifications in social work practice is a critical tool to ensure service quality.

Rates of pay for social workers need to be comparable with similar professionals, and the skill and qualifications of social workers must be recognized, while ensuring services are affordable to clients.

METHODS TO ESTABLISH SERVICE NETWORKS OR COMMUNITY RESOURCES

The need for services to not be duplicative and complement one another is central to meeting client needs. Social workers are often called upon to assist with developing or navigating service networks, as well as creating community resources where they are lacking. Integrating services takes sustained effort and hard work. Though the concept of service integration may seem simple, it is not and usually takes several administrative and operational strategies. Strong leadership and sound management are critical.

In order to effectively meet client needs, organizations are increasingly recognizing collaborations, networks, alliances, and/or partnerships. There are two distinct network forms—mandated network arrangements and self-organizing networks.

Within each of these forms, there may be a lead organization or a model in which all organizations share decision-making power. The former is often associated with a centralized structure, whereas the latter is more indicative of a decentralized one. Networks can also have strong and weak arrangements in which the parameters of integration may or may not be highly regulated.

The willingness and ability of social service organizations to form networks often depends on organizational size, resource dependency, and collaborative experience.

Methods of Conducting a Needs Assessment

A needs assessment is a systematic process for determining and addressing gaps between current and desired conditions. It examines strengths and weaknesses of a community, agency, and/or program with the aim of improvement. There are multiple methods for conducting needs assessments and they may be conducted by consultants, staff, and/or volunteers internal or external to the organization.

First, information is collected about a community, agency, and/or program. This data may be collected via focus groups, key informant interviews, community meetings, or through the administering of surveys. In addition, including existing data sources can be time- and cost-effective.

Using information gathered, social workers must decide what needs are being met and what resources exist in addition to the needs that are not being addressed. There are several methods for determining need—including assessing perceived, expressed, and/or relative needs. *Perceived needs* are defined by what clients think about their needs, with the standard set by each client. *Expressed needs* are defined by the number of clients who have sought help, thus taking action to address their problems. A major weakness of using expressed needs is that not all who need help seek it. *Relative needs* are concerned with equity—comparing the needs of clients with the goal of ranking them.

THE EFFECTS OF PROGRAM EVALUATION FINDINGS ON SERVICES

One of the most significant benefits that a program evaluation communicates is the need to make service improvements. Some examples of improvements that may need to be made include:

- Eliminating services that do not achieve program outcomes
- Adding services that are better designed to achieve outcomes
- Acquiring more adequate resources to support effective services
- Targeting a different group of participants to receive services

Evaluation findings should be viewed and communicated as an opportunity to make programs better. Evaluation results that indicate the need for improvement should not be communicated as an indictment of the failure of a program. Program evaluation findings should be viewed with an excitement about the possibilities of developing an even stronger set of service offerings and improving already successful efforts. An action plan aimed at improvement should be developed, based on evaluation results, and communicated widely to key stakeholders.

METHODS TO EVALUATE AGENCY PROGRAMS (E.G., NEEDS ASSESSMENT, FORMATIVE/SUMMATIVE ASSESSMENT, COST-EFFECTIVENESS, COST-BENEFIT ANALYSIS, OUTCOMES ASSESSMENT)

Program evaluation is the systematic assessment of the processes and/or outcomes of a program with the intent of furthering its development and improvement. There are many types of program evaluation including, but not limited to, the following:

- A **cost-benefit analysis** determines the financial costs of operating a program as compared with the fiscal benefits of its outcomes. A *cost-benefit ratio* is generated to determine whether, and the extent to which, the costs exceed the benefits. Program decisions can be made to eliminate or modify the program (by reducing program expenditures) based upon the findings.
- A **cost-effectiveness analysis** is similar to a cost-benefit analysis, but distinct. *It considers the benefits that are not measured in monetary terms,* such as illnesses prevented and/or lives saved. It does not produce a cost-benefit ratio, but may focus on the most financially efficient way to achieve a defined outcome or the cost for producing a specific nonmonetary outcome.

■ An **outcome assessment** is the process of determining whether a program has achieved its intended goal(s). It involves collecting evidence through assessment, analyzing the data, and then *using the findings to make programmatic changes if needed*. It is an iterative process with continual feedback loops.

THE PRINCIPLES AND FEATURES OF OBJECTIVE AND SUBJECTIVE DATA

A social worker uses both objective and subjective data throughout the problem-solving process. For example, in assessment, a social worker must understand the "facts" related to a client's situation (objective data), but also how those "facts" are perceived by the client through descriptions of his or her feelings, experiences, and perceptions (subjective data). It is not the objective facts that determine whether an event is traumatic, but a subjective emotional experience of the event. Thus, having a client describe the meaning of an event to him or her is critically important.

Treatment plans are often developed and progress is often assessed based upon objective and subjective data gathered by a social worker. For example, in health care, a **SOAP format** is often used.

S (Subjective): The subjective component is a client's report of how he or she has been doing since the last visit and/or what brought a client into treatment.

O (Objective): In health care, the objective component includes vital signs (temperature, blood pressure, pulse, and respiration), documentation of any physical examinations, and results of laboratory tests. In other settings, this section may include other objective indicators of problems such as disorientation, failing school, legal issues, and so forth.

A (Assessment): A social worker pulls together the objective and subjective findings and consolidates them into a short assessment.

P (Plan): The plan includes what will be done as a consequence of the assessment.

Lastly, in evaluation, subjective reports of a client, in conjunction with objective indicators of progress, should be used to determine when goals or objectives have been met and whether new goals or objectives should be set. Client self-monitoring (subjective data) is a good way to involve a client so he or she can see and track progress himself or herself.

BASIC AND APPLIED RESEARCH DESIGN AND METHODS

Social work research needs a design or a structure before data collection or analysis can commence. The function of a research design is to ensure that the evidence or data collected enables the research questions to be answered. Research design is different from the method by which data are collected. Many research methods texts confuse research designs with methods. It is not uncommon to see research design treated as a mode of data collection rather than as a logical structure of the inquiry.

Research design is a blueprint, with the research problem determining the type of design used. Research design will:

1. Identify the research problem clearly and justify its selection;

2. Review previously published literature associated with the problem area;

3. Clearly and explicitly specify hypotheses (i.e., research questions) central to the problem selected;

4. Effectively describe the data that will be necessary for an adequate test of the hypotheses and explain how such data will be obtained; and

5. Describe the methods of analysis that will be applied to the data in determining whether or not the hypotheses are true or false.

Types of Research

There are three broad types of research—*experimental, quasi-experimental,* and *pre-experimental*. Randomized experiments, also called experimental, are the most rigorous. When randomization of subjects or groups is neither practical nor feasible, quasi-experimental approaches can be used. Quasi-experimental research uses intervention and comparison groups, but assignment to the groups is nonrandom. Pre-experimental studies contain intervention groups only and lack comparison/control groups, making them the weakest.

Single-Subject Research

Single-subject research aims to determine whether an intervention has the intended impact on a client, or on many clients who form a group. The most common single-subject research is *pre- and post-test* or *single-case study* (AB) in which there is a comparison of behavior before treatment (baseline; denoted by an "A") and behavior after the start of treatment (intervention; denoted by a "B"). The *reversal or multiple baseline* (ABA or ABAB) is also commonly used.

In single-subject research, a client is used as his or her own control. The focus differs from experimental research, which looks at the average effect of an intervention between groups of people.

Single-subject research is ideal for studying the behavioral change a client exhibits as a result of some treatment. When done correctly and carefully, single-subject research can show a causal effect between the intervention and the outcome.

The flexibility, simplicity, and low cost of single-subject research are also beneficial. It can be more flexible and easier to plan because it is usually smaller in scale than experimental research.

Attempts should be made to maximize both internal and external validity. **Internal validity** addresses the extent to which causal inferences can be made about the intervention and the targeted behavior. **External validity** addresses how generalizable those inferences are to the general population. Due to the small number of study participants, single-subject research tends to have poor external validity, limiting the ability to generalize the findings to a wider audience.

It is important to remember that, in some cases, it would be unethical to withdraw treatment if clients would be put at risk for harm. Also, in a crisis, treatment would not be delayed in an effort to obtain baseline data.

DATA COLLECTION AND ANALYSIS METHODS

Qualitative research usually involves collecting information through unstructured interviews, observation, and/or focus groups. Data can be collected from a single individual at a time or multiple people in group settings. Qualitative data collection methods are usually very time consuming, so they are confined to smaller samples than usually found in quantitative approaches. Quantitative research mainly collects data through the input of responses to research instruments containing questions (i.e., such as questionnaires). Information can be input either by the respondents themselves (e.g., online or mail survey) or social workers can input data (e.g., phone surveys or interviews). Methods for distributing surveys are via postal mail, phone, website, or in person. However, newer technologies have created additional delivery options, including through wireless devices such as smartphones.

Social workers can also do research using secondary data, which is information that has already been collected for other purposes. Use of existing data is efficient since time and money associated with data collection are spared. However, the completeness of existing data, as well as its reliability, may be a concern as sound research practices covering its collection may not have been used.

Data analysis procedures begin with preparation that involves cleaning the data, checking it for accuracy, coding it for analysis, developing a database, and entering the data into the computer.

Once entered into the computer, *descriptive statistics* are used to describe the basic features of the data. They provide simple summaries about the sample and the measures. Together with simple graphics analysis, they form the basis of virtually every quantitative analysis of data. Descriptive statistics describe what the data shows.

Inferential statistics are used to answer research questions or test models or hypotheses. In many cases, the conclusions from inferential statistics extend beyond the immediate data. For instance, inferential statistics determine the probability that an observed difference between groups is a dependable one or one that might have happened by chance.

In most research, analyses include both descriptive and inferential statistics. Social workers must balance the level of detail that is included in a research report with the need to avoid overwhelming readers and missing the highlighting of major findings. If too much detail is included, readers may not be able to pick out the key results. Analysis details are appropriately relegated to appendices, reserving only the most critical analysis summaries for the body of the report itself.

When reading and interpreting experimental research findings, social workers must be able to identify independent variables (or those that are believed to be causes) and dependent variables (which are the impacts or results). In many studies, the independent variable is the treatment provided and the dependent variable is the target behavior that is trying to be changed.

The reliability and validity of research findings should also be assessed.

Reliability (dependability, stability, consistency, predictability): Can you get the same answer repeatedly?

Validity (accuracy): Is what is believed to be measured actually being measured or is it something else?

External validity: Can the results be generalized?

Internal validity: Is there confidence in cause/effect?

METHODS TO ASSESS RELIABILITY AND VALIDITY IN SOCIAL WORK RESEARCH

Reliability in social work research concerns the ability to get consistent assessments or data by reducing random errors associated with its collection. There are four main methods to assess reliability.

■ *Interrater or Interobserver Reliability*

Assesses the degree to which different raters/observers give consistent estimates of the same phenomenon.

■ *Test–Retest Reliability*

Assesses the consistency of a measure from one time to another.

■ *Parallel Forms Reliability*

Assesses the consistency of the results of two tests constructed in the same way from the same content domain.

■ *Internal Consistency Reliability*

Assesses the consistency of results across items within a test.

Validity is the degree to which what is being measured actually is what is claimed to be measured. It attempts to minimize systematic errors that may yield reliable results but do not actually assess the constructs of interest. There are different means to assess validity.

■ *Face Validity*

Examines whether the assessments "on their face" measure the constructs.

■ *Content Validity*

Examines whether all of the relevant content domains are covered.

■ *Criterion-Related Validity (including predictive, concurrent, convergent, and discriminant validities)*

Examines whether constructs perform as anticipated in relation to other theoretical constructs.

Predictive validity assesses whether constructs predict what they should theoretically be able to predict.

Concurrent validity assesses whether constructs distinguish between groups that should be able to be distinguished.

Convergent validity assesses the degree to which constructs are similar to (converge on) other constructs to which they should be similar.

Discriminant validity assesses the degree to which constructs are different from (diverge away from) other constructs to which they should be dissimilar.

METHODS TO DEVELOP AND EVALUATE MEASURABLE OBJECTIVES FOR CLIENT/CLIENT SYSTEM INTERVENTION, TREATMENT, AND/OR SERVICE PLANS

When social workers are creating intervention or service plans, it is essential that goals are written in observable and measurable terms. In order to achieve this aim, the following should be included in each goal contained in the intervention or service plan.

■ *Criteria:* What behavior must be exhibited, how often, over what period of time, and under what conditions to demonstrate achievement of the goal?

■ *Method for evaluation:* How will progress be measured?

■ *Schedule for evaluation:* When, how often, and on what dates or intervals of time will progress be measured?

There may also be benchmarks or the intermediate knowledge, skills, and/or behaviors that must be learned/achieved in order for a client to reach his or her ultimate goal.

Objectives break down the goals into discrete components or subparts, which are steps toward the final desired outcome.

METHODS, TECHNIQUES, AND INSTRUMENTS USED TO EVALUATE SOCIAL WORK PRACTICE

Social workers have an ethical mandate to ensure that they are providing the most efficient and effective services possible. They also must do no harm and ensure that the intervention provided enhances the well-being of clients.

These goals require the evaluation of practice. Routine practice evaluation by social workers can enhance treatment outcomes and agency decision making, planning, and accountability.

There are two main types of evaluations—formative and summative. Formative evaluations examine the process of delivering services, whereas summative evaluations examine the outcomes.

Formative evaluations are ongoing processes that allow for feedback to be implemented during service delivery. These types of evaluations allow social workers to make changes as needed to help achieve program goals. Needs assessments can be viewed as one type of formative evaluation.

Summative evaluations occur at the end of services and provide an overall description of their effectiveness. Summative evaluation examines outcomes to determine whether objectives were met. Summative evaluations enable decisions to be made regarding future service directions that cannot be made during implementation. Impact evaluations and cost-benefit analyses are types of summative evaluations.

There are ethical standards that must be followed when evaluating practice (*NASW Code of Ethics, 2008—5.02 Evaluation and Research*). Some of these guidelines include

1. Obtaining voluntary and written informed consent from clients, when appropriate, without any implied or actual deprivation or penalty for refusal to participate; without undue inducement to participate; and with due regard for participants' well-being, privacy, and dignity

2. Informing clients of their right to withdraw from evaluation and research at any time without penalty

3. Ensuring clients in evaluations have access to appropriate supportive services

4. Avoiding conflicts of interest and dual relationships with those being evaluated

EVIDENCE-BASED PRACTICE

Evidence-based social work practice combines research knowledge, professional/clinical expertise, social work values, and client preferences/circumstances. It is a dynamic and fluid process whereby social workers seek, interpret, use, and evaluate the best available information in an effort to make the best practice decisions.

The promotion of evidence-based research within social work is widespread. Evidence-based research gathers evidence that may be informative for clinical practice or clinical decision making. It also involves the process of gathering and synthesizing scientific evidence from various sources and translating it to be applied to practice.

The use of evidence-based practice places the well-being of clients at the forefront, desiring to discover and use the best practices available. The use of evidence-based practice requires social workers to only use services and techniques that were found effective by rigorous, scientific, empirical studies—that is, outcome research.

Social workers must be willing and able to locate and use evidence-based interventions. In areas in which evidence-based interventions are not available, social workers must still use research to guide practice. Applying knowledge gleaned from research findings will assist social workers in providing services informed by scientific investigation and lead to new interventions that can be evaluated as evidence-based practices.

Decisions are based on the use of many sources, ranging from systematic reviews and meta-analyses to less rigorous research designs.

Social workers often use "evidence based practice" to refer to programs that have a proven track record. However, it takes a long time for a program or intervention to be "evidence based." Thus, most interventions in social work need more empirically supported research in order to accurately apply the term. "Evidence-informed practice" may be more appropriate.

Some questions guide the selection of intervention modalities:

- How will the recommended modality assist with the achievement of the treatment goal and will it help get the outcomes desired?
- How does the recommended treatment modality promote client strengths, capabilities, and interests?
- What are the risks and benefits associated with the recommended modality?

- Is there research or evidence to support the use of this modality for this target problem?

- Is this modality appropriate and tested on those with the same or similar cultural background as the client?

- What training and experience does a social worker have with the recommended modality?

- Is the recommended modality evidence based or consistent with available research? If not, why?

- Was the recommended modality discussed with and selected by a client?

- Will the use of the recommended modality be assessed periodically? When? How?

- Is the recommended treatment modality covered by insurance? What is the cost? How does it compare to the use of other options?

Methods for Social Change

9

THEORIES OF SOCIAL CHANGE AND COMMUNITY DEVELOPMENT

There is no one way to define community development. Over the years, community development has been defined as an occupation, a movement, an approach, and a set of values. It has been labeled the responsibility of social workers because it is seen as the most practical framework for creating lasting change for clients.

Community development has been used to the benefit of communities of place, of interest, and of identity. But despite these differences, there are certain principles, characteristics, and values that underpin nearly every definition of community development—neighborhood work aimed at improving the quality of community life through the participation of a broad spectrum of people at the local level.

Community development is a **long-term** commitment. It is not a quick fix to address a community's problems, nor is it a time-limited process. It aims to address imbalances in power and bring about change founded on social justice, equality, and inclusion. Its key purpose is to build communities based on justice, equality, and mutual respect.

Community development is ultimately about getting community members **working together** in collective action to tackle problems that many individuals may be experiencing or to help in achieving a shared dream that many individuals will benefit from.

COMMUNITY ORGANIZING AND SOCIAL PLANNING METHODS

Community organizing is focused on harnessing the collective power of communities to tackle issues of shared concern. It challenges government, corporations, and other power-holding institutions in an effort to tip the power balance more in favor of communities.

It is essential for social workers to understand sources of power in order to access them for the betterment of the community. Organizing members to focus these sources of power on the problem(s) and mobilizing resources to assist is critical.

Community organization enhances participatory skills of local citizens by working with and not for them, thus developing leadership with particular emphasis on the ability to conceptualize and act on problems. It strengthens communities so they can better deal with future problems; community members can develop the capacity to resolve problems.

Social planning is defined as the process by which a group or community decides its goals and strategies relating to societal issues. It is not an activity limited to government, but includes activities of the private sector, social movements, professions, and other organizations focused specifically on social objectives.

Models of social planning in social work practice include those that are based on community participation. Rather than planning "for" communities, social workers as planners engage "with" community members. Social planning does not merely examine sociological problems that exist, but also includes the physical and economic factors that relate to societal issues.

All issues confronting those who are served by social workers are really human or social issues. Social workers can help facilitate the process of planning through all stages: organizing community members; data gathering related to the issue—including identifying economic, political, and social causes; problem identification; weighing of alternatives; policy/program implementation; and evaluation of effectiveness.

TECHNIQUES FOR MOBILIZING COMMUNITY PARTICIPATION

Community participation is critical in social work practice. Community participation informs others about needed changes that must occur. Policies, programs, and services that were effective or appropriate previously have become ineffective or inappropriate.

Community participation also creates relationships and partnerships among diverse groups who can then work together, but may not usually do so.

Community participation puts decision-making power partly or wholly with the community, ensuring that individuals will remain interested and involved over time.

When engaging in community-based decision making, individuals will typically go through various stages.

Orientation stage—Community members meet for the first time and start to get to know each other.

Conflict stage—Disputes, little fights, and arguments may occur. These conflicts are eventually worked out.

Emergence stage—Community members begin to see and agree on a course of action.

Reinforcement stage—Community members finally make a decision and justify why it was correct.

Community members are far more likely to buy into policy that has been created with their participation. Their support over time will lead to permanent change.

Community participation energizes communities to continue to change in positive directions. Once involved in a successful change effort, community members see what they can accomplish collectively and take on new challenges.

Lastly, community members must inform policy-makers and planners of the real needs of the community, so that the most important problems and issues can be addressed. They must also provide information about what has been tried before and worked or not worked.

THE IMPACT OF SOCIAL INSTITUTIONS ON SOCIETY

Many social institutions exist within our society. They have many functions including satisfying individuals' basic needs, defining and promoting dominant social values, defining and promoting individual roles, creating permanent patterns of social behavior, and supporting other social institutions.

The five basic institutions are family, religion, government, education, and economics.

Some of the functions of each of these institutions include the following.

Family

- To control and regulate sexual behavior
- To provide for new members of society (children)
- To provide for the economic and emotional maintenance of individuals
- To provide for primary socialization of children

Religion

- To provide solutions for the unexplained
- To support the normative structure of the society
- To provide a psychological diversion from unwanted life situations

■ To sustain the existing class structure

■ To promote and prevent social change

Government

■ To create norms via laws and enforce them

■ To adjudicate conflict via the courts

■ To provide for the welfare of members of society

■ To protect society from external threats

Education

■ To transmit culture

■ To prepare for jobs and roles

■ To evaluate and select competent individuals

■ To transmit functional skills

Economics

■ To provide methods for the production and distribution of goods and services

■ To enable individuals to acquire goods and services that are produced

THE IMPACT OF THE POLITICAL ENVIRONMENT ON POLICY-MAKING

Social work is unique in its dual focus on assisting clients on an individual level while also working to change the policies that adversely impact them. The personal troubles of clients are linked to the public policies which can help to prevent or address them. Social workers are charged with working with and helping individuals and their families directly, but also working within decision-making bodies to promote these policies.

Social workers must be knowledgeable about the political environment if they are to shape public policy based upon the core values of the profession. As there are always competing interest groups who would like to influence policy-makers in their favor, political advocacy is seen as an important and necessary skill.

Advocacy can be defined as attempting to influence public policy through education, lobbying, or political pressure. Social workers are often called upon to educate the general public as well as public policy-makers about the nature of problems, the legislation needed to address problems, and the funding required to provide services or conduct research.

Social workers should engage in social and political action that seeks to ensure that all people have equal access to the resources, employment, services, and opportunities they require to meet their basic human needs and to develop to their full potential. They should be aware of the impact of the political arena on practice and should advocate for changes in policy and legislation to improve social conditions in order to meet basic human needs and promote social justice (*NASW Code of Ethics—6.04 Social and Political Action*).

CONCEPTS OF SOCIAL POLICY DEVELOPMENT AND ANALYSIS

Policy analysis is a systematic approach to solving problems through policies.

It involves identifying the problem, developing alternatives, assessing the impacts of the alternatives (such as conducting a cost/benefit analysis), selecting the desired option, designing and implementing the policy, and evaluating the outcomes.

Critical to social policy analysis is the identification of alternative policy options and the evaluation of these alternatives. Analyses include developing an understanding of who "wins" and who "loses." Some of the values upon which alternatives are weighed include equity, efficiency, and liberty.

The policy analysis field has become more diversified; thus, it is highly influenced by theories from other fields. Often there are many stakeholders involved, such as federal, state, and local government agencies, community leaders, and clients, all of which will bring in their own set of values. Thus, the chosen approach will be influenced by who participates.

TECHNIQUES TO INFORM AND INFLUENCE ORGANIZATIONAL AND SOCIAL POLICY

Social policy is influenced by many factors, such as the following.

Knowledge/Innovation

Knowledge and innovation create new opportunities to change, as well as information that current practices may need to be reformed. Technological advances are often drivers of changes in policy.

Social, Political, and Economic Conditions/Resources

Good policies are often not adopted because they are proposed without the social, political, or economic resources to move them through the policy process and/or implement them.

Social norms change over time and foster or impede social policy development or revision.

Political and/or economic conditions can also promote or hinder the creation and/or revision of policy, as well as whether policy alternatives are suggested or considered for adoption.

Legal Issues/Laws

Understanding how new policies will influence or interact with existing laws is essential. Policies may not be supported if they are believed to negatively impact on existing policies that are seen as beneficial.

Institutional Influences

The structure of institutions, such as government agencies, private sector organizations, and so on, can also impact the ability to influence and efficiently or effectively implement social policies. Sometimes policies are so complex or integrated into the practices of complex institutional systems that it is difficult to understand them; therefore, change is less likely.

External Influences

The media and other external influences can be very influential. Media can be used to call attention to a problem. More media coverage of one policy alternative may influence its support as it is more familiar. Public opinion is a very salient influence as to whether policies will be proposed and/or adopted.

Social workers who want to promote certain social policies must be aware of these influences and use methods to support policies as they relate to these areas. Contrarily, social workers can decrease the desirability of policies by creating barriers or removing positive influences in these areas.

Problems are also often associated with policy implementation. Policies may not be clearly communicated, leaving implementers and others at a loss as to how to follow them in order to achieve the intended goals. Negative attitudes of service personnel, lack of resources to carry out policies, and/or the conflict with previously established procedures or structures can also be obstacles to implementation.

Cooptation has many meanings, but may be used as a strategy to influence social policy as leaders will try to quiet dissent or disturbances not only by dealing with immediate grievances, but by making efforts to channel the energies and angers of dissenters into more legitimate and less disruptive activities. When coopting, incentives are offered and other efforts are made aimed at complacency.

THEORIES AND METHODS OF ADVOCACY FOR POLICIES, SERVICES, AND RESOURCES TO MEET CLIENTS'/CLIENT SYSTEMS' NEEDS

Advocacy is one of a social worker's most important tasks. Social workers may advocate when working with an individual client to ensure that his or her needs are met. However, social workers have an ethical mandate to make systematic changes to address the problems experienced by groups of individuals who are vulnerable and/or who are unable to speak for themselves.

A social worker may engage in advocacy by convincing others of the legitimate needs and rights of members of society. Such work can occur on the local, county, state, or national levels. Some social workers are even involved in international human rights and advocacy for those in need in other countries.

Fundamental to social work is advocating to change the factors that create and contribute to problems.

Sometimes advocacy can be achieved by working through the problem-solving process as it relates to a problem, including acknowledging the problem, analyzing and defining the problem, generating possible solutions, evaluating each option, implementing the option of choice, and evaluating the outcomes.

In other instances, social workers may engage in obtaining legislative support or using the media to draw attention to a concern.

In all instances, social workers should be working with clients to have their voices heard and should not be speaking for them. *Often social workers need to help clients to advocate with third-party payers to have their needs met when resources are not adequate.* Social workers must inform clients of appeal processes when services are denied and support them as they advocate to meet their needs. When clients feel that they have not been treated fairly, social workers should empower them by providing education about appeal processes and other methods to change policies, fix services, and/or increase services to meet their needs.

The goal of social work advocacy is to assist clients to strengthen their own skills in this area. Social workers may assist by locating sources of power that can be shared with clients to make changes.

PRIMARY, SECONDARY, AND TERTIARY PREVENTION STRATEGIES

There are three major types of prevention strategies—primary, secondary, and tertiary. Optimally, all three types are needed to create comprehensive strategies of prevention and protection.

Primary Prevention

The goal is to protect people from developing a disease, experiencing an injury, or engaging in a behavior in the first place.

Examples:

- Immunizations against disease
- Education promoting the use of automobile passenger restraints and bicycle helmets
- Screenings for the general public to identify risk factors for illness
- Controlling hazards in the workplace and home
- Regular exercise and good nutrition
- Counseling about the dangers of tobacco and other drugs

Since successful primary prevention helps avoid the disease, injury, or behavior and its associated suffering, cost, and burden, it is typically considered the most cost-effective.

Secondary Prevention

Secondary prevention occurs after a disease, injury, or illness has occurred. It aims to slow the progression or limit the long-term impacts. It is often implemented when asymptomatic, but risk factors are present. Secondary prevention also may focus on preventing reinjury.

Examples:

- Telling those with heart conditions to take daily, low-dose aspirin
- Screenings for those with risk factors for illness
- Modifying work assignments for injured workers

Tertiary Prevention

Tertiary prevention focuses on managing complicated, long-term diseases, injuries, or illnesses. The goal is to prevent further deterioration and maximize quality of life because disease is now established and primary prevention activities have been unsuccessful. However, early detection through secondary prevention may have minimized the impact of the disease.

Examples:

- Pain management groups
- Rehabilitation programs
- Support groups

Supervision and Administration

10

GOVERNANCE STRUCTURES

Governance concerns those structures, functions, processes, and customs that exist within an organization to ensure it operates in a way that achieves its objectives, and does so in an effective and transparent manner. It is a framework of accountability to clients, stakeholders, and the wider community, within which organizations make decisions and control their functions and resources to achieve their objectives.

Good governance adds value by improving the performance of an organization through more efficient management, more strategic and equitable resource allocation and service provision, and other improvements that lend themselves to improved outcomes and impacts.

Social workers should advocate within and outside their agencies for adequate resources to meet clients' needs and for resource allocation procedures that are open and fair (*NASW Code of Ethics, 2008—3.07 Administration*). When not all clients' needs can be met, an allocation procedure should be developed that is nondiscriminatory, appropriate, and consistent. Social workers should take reasonable steps to ensure that adequate agency or organizational resources are available to provide appropriate staff supervision and that the working environment for which they are responsible is consistent with and encourages compliance with the 2008 *NASW Code of Ethics*.

THEORIES OF ORGANIZATIONAL DEVELOPMENT AND STRUCTURE

Classical Organizational Theories

The *scientific management theory* (Theory X) is based on (a) finding the one "best way" to perform each task; (b) carefully matching each worker to each task; (c) closely supervising workers, using reward and punishment as motivators; and (d) managing and controlling behavior.

Weber's bureaucratic theory emphasized the need for a hierarchical structure of power to ensure stability and uniformity. Weber also put forth the notion that organizational behavior is a network of human interactions, where all behavior could be understood by looking at cause and effect.

Administrative theory emphasized establishing a universal set of management principles that could be applied to all organizations.

The major deficiency with classical organizational theories was that they attempted to explain people's motivation to work strictly as a function of economic reward.

Neoclassical Theories

These theories were based upon the Hawthorne experiments and focused on workers.

The Hawthorne experiments took place at Western Electric's factory at Hawthorne, a suburb of Chicago, in the late 1920s and early 1930s. The original purpose of the experiments was to study the impacts of physical conditions on productivity. The experimenters concluded that it was not the changes in physical conditions that were affecting the workers' productivity. Rather, it was the fact that someone was actually concerned about their workplace, and the opportunities this gave them to discuss changes before they took place.

Human relations theory (Theory Y) evolved as a reaction to the tough, authoritarian structure of classical theory. It displayed genuine concern for human needs in order to produce creativity and emphasized the importance of cohesive work groups, participatory leadership, and open communication.

Modern Organizational Approaches

Systems approach considers the organization as a system composed of a set of interrelated—and thus mutually dependent—subsystems. Thus, the organization consists of components, linking processes and goals.

Sociotechnical approach considers the organization as composed of a social system, technical system, and its environment. These interact with each other, so it is necessary to balance them appropriately for effective functioning of the organization.

Contingency or situational approach recognizes that organizational systems are interrelated with their environment and that different environments require different organizational systems for effectiveness.

Organizational Structure

Organizations have formal structures, even if they are only loosely adhered to. Organizations have informal structures as well. There are times when the informal structures conflict with the formal ones, making it important to understand the difference between them.

Formal structure refers to the official hierarchy and lines of authority. Formal structure is built on division of labor and functional processes and structures. A typical organizational chart illustrates the formal structure. The hierarchical organization begins at the top with the most senior leader and cascades down to subordinate managers and employees below top-level managers. There are job titles, financial obligations, and clear lines of authority for each box on the organizational chart. It is deliberately impersonal and is often criticized for not accounting for the interactions and communication which take place informally in organizations.

Informal structure refers to the relationship between people in organizations based on personal attitudes, emotions, likes, dislikes, and so on. These relationships are not developed according to procedures and regulations laid down in the formal structure. This structure is not preplanned but develops spontaneously. These associations may be among employees on the same level of the hierarchy or on different levels.

Informal structures influence productivity and job satisfaction.

Employees rely on the informal structure if the formal structure has stopped being effective, which often happens as an organization grows or changes but does not reevaluate its hierarchy or formal structure.

Internal Controls

Internal controls are systematic measures (such as reviews, checks and balances, and procedures) instituted by a human service organization to deliver services in an orderly and efficient manner; appropriately manage its assets and resources; deter and detect errors, abuse, fraud, and theft; produce reliable and timely management information; and adhere to established policies and procedures. Internal controls are put in place to help ensure that human service organizations achieve their objectives.

Most internal controls can be classified as preventive or detective. *Preventive controls* are designed to avoid errors or irregularities from occurring, such as having managers approve expense requests to prevent inappropriate expenditures. *Detective controls* are designed to identify an error or irregularity after it has occurred. These controls are performed on a routine basis to identify issues that pose potential risks in a timely manner. A detective control can be having managers review expenditure and other fiscal reports to assure that they accurately reflect the financial transactions of the agency.

Many circumstances may compromise the effectiveness of an internal control structure, including inadequate segregation of duties, inappropriate access to assets, inadequate knowledge of agency policies, procedures which lack substance, absence of monitoring of control overrides, and so on.

Internal controls can be, but do not have to be, costly. Sometimes, there is no out-of-pocket cost to establish an adequate control—for example, creating segregation of duties such as having voided receipts approved by someone (preferably a manager) other than the person preparing the receipts. The ramifications of poor internal controls are serious, such as causing a loss of goodwill and poor public relations when it is discovered that organizations did not safeguard funds properly or follow established protocols and required policies.

THE EFFECTS OF POLICIES, PROCEDURES, REGULATIONS, AND LEGISLATION ON SOCIAL WORK PRACTICE AND SERVICE DELIVERY

Client functioning must be viewed using a "person-in-environment" (PIE) perspective. The "rules" that govern society are critical to the way in which the environment is structured, operates, and changes. They can both facilitate and hinder client functioning across time. Social workers can think of clients as part of a larger system with many layers of influence. Clients are most immediately impacted by their families, who are members of neighborhoods and communities. However, each of these contextual influences—families, neighborhood, and communities—are affected by state, national, and international forces, such as policies, procedures, regulations, and laws. They dictate who may be eligible for programs, the amount of funding received, and/or which programs are established or eliminated.

Their influence is dynamic because, using a systems perspective, changes to any one "rule" impacts all others. The creation or modification of a societal "rule" also impacts on individuals, and vice versa.

At different times, state, national, and international forces may be more or less prominent. For example, international policies may influence U.S. businesses and communities because multinational corporations make decisions about job location, outsourcing, and other restructuring. In addition, international unrest may restrict travel to other countries. Thus, policies, procedures, regulations, and laws at different levels interact with one another and can create both the opportunities and the barriers for clients in their family units, neighborhoods, and communities.

Social workers must be aware of this dynamic and the relationship of "rules" on client functioning, as well as their own professional practice, to make sure that they are delivering effective and efficient services to clients in accordance with existing rules and best practices.

Social workers should be fully informed of existing laws, policies, practices, and procedures that impact or govern service delivery.

Social workers are also expected to keep up-to-date with new public laws and policies.

Many laws affect social work practice. Although social workers may not be responsible for implementing these pieces of legislation, they provide protections or programs that are critical to those served.

Some relevant federal legislation is listed in chronological order in the following list.

1. *Title VI of the Civil Rights Act of 1964* states that no person shall "on the grounds of race, color, or national origin, be excluded from participation in, denied the benefits of, or be subjected to discrimination under any program or activity receiving federal financial assistance." It desegregated all schools and public buildings and required all agencies that receive federal funds to terminate discriminatory hiring practices. Social workers are charged with challenging discriminatory practices and upholding the belief of equal rights for all.

2. The *Older Americans Act (OAA) of 1965* offers services to older Americans. It established the Administration on Aging, which empowers the federal government to distribute funds to the states for supportive services for individuals over the age of 60. The Administration achieves its aim by awarding grants to states, which pass them along to local Area Agencies on Aging (AAA). Some programs target vulnerable older adults who need help staying in their homes. Other programs provide access services, in-home services, community services, caregiver services, and opportunities for volunteer work.

3. The *Child Abuse Prevention and Treatment Act of 1974* is key legislation for addressing child abuse and neglect. It has been amended several times and provides federal funding to states in support of prevention, assessment, investigation, prosecution, and treatment activities; it also provides grants to public agencies and nonprofit organizations for demonstration programs and projects.

4. The *Family Educational Rights and Privacy Act (FERPA) of 1974* protects the privacy of educational records. The law applies to all schools that receive funds under an applicable program of the United States Department of Education. FERPA gives parents certain rights with respect to their children's education records. These rights transfer to the student when he or she reaches the age of 18 or attends a school beyond the high school level. Prior to 18, parents have the right to inspect and review a student's education records maintained by the school. Schools are not required to provide copies of records unless, for reasons such as great distance, it is impossible for parents to

review the records. Schools may charge a fee for copies. Parents also have the right to request that a school correct records that they believe to be inaccurate or misleading. If the school decides not to amend the record, the parent or eligible student then has the right to a formal hearing. After the hearing, if the school still decides not to amend the record, the parent has the right to place a statement with the record setting forth his or her view about the contested information. Generally, schools must have written permission from the parent in order to release any information from a student's education record, though there are some exceptions related to the student's care.

5. The *Education for All Handicapped Children Act of 1975* (which is now known as the *Individuals with Disabilities Education Act [IDEA]*) guarantees a free, appropriate public education to all children with disabilities between the ages of 3 and 21. Children receiving such services should be provided with Individual Educational Programs (IEPs) which are outlined in plans that are revised annually. A team composed of a social worker, teacher, administrator, and other relevant school personnel typically create the IEP. The parents, and often the child, also participate. The IEP includes goals, means of attaining goals, and ways of evaluating goal attainment. A child who has an IEP must also be educated in the "least restrictive environment." Thus, the child should either spend part or all of his or her time in a regular classroom or in an environment that is as close to this as possible while still leading to the attainment of the educational goals. Services that are needed, such as speech therapy and others related to educational goals, are provided at no extra cost to the family.

6. The *Indian Child Welfare Act of 1978* gives American Indian/Native American/Indigenous nations or organizations jurisdiction over child welfare cases that involve an American Indian/Native American/Indigenous child in order to protect the integrity of American Indian/Native American/Indigenous families. The law specifies a hierarchical procedure for placement of an American Indian/Native American/Indigenous child: (a) verify the ethnic and tribal identity of the child; (b) allow tribal jurisdiction over case; (c) if tribe rejects jurisdiction, placement with family member; or (d) if that is impossible, placement with family of the same tribe. The last resort is placing the child in a home with a family that is not American Indian/Native American/Indigenous.

7. The *Adoption Assistance and Child Welfare Act of 1980* focuses on family preservation efforts to help keep families together and children out of foster care or other out-of-home placements. This law also focuses on family reunification or adoption if a child is removed from a home. The act requires courts to review child welfare cases more regularly and mandates that states make "reasonable efforts" to keep families together via prevention and family reunification

services. States are also required to develop reunification and preventive programs for foster care and assure that children in nonpermanent settings are seen at least every 6 months. An adoption subsidy reimbursed by the federal government is also provided through this law for children with complex needs or disabilities.

8. The *Americans with Disabilities Act (ADA) of 1990* is civil-rights legislation that prohibits discrimination on the basis of disability. It has been amended and affords similar protections as the Civil Rights Act of 1964 for discrimination based on race, religion, sex, national origin, and other characteristics. Unlike the Civil Rights Act of 1964, the ADA also requires covered employers to provide reasonable accommodations to employees with disabilities and imposes accessibility requirements on public accommodations. ADA disabilities include both mental and physical conditions. A condition does not need to be severe or permanent to be a disability.

9. The *Patient Self-Determination Act (PSDA) of 1991* introduced a new set of federal requirements intended to implement advance directive policies at all health care facilities that receive federal funding through Medicaid and Medicare programs. The Act specified that these facilities must inform clients of their rights to make decisions concerning their own health care, ask and document whether a client has an advance directive, and provide education for staff and the community.

   Advance directives are a legal way of indicating that a person has given the legal rights to a designated person to make decisions on his or her behalf about continuation of support measures should the individual be incapable physically or mentally of making wants known.

   The purpose of advance directives is to respond to judicial decisions that have been made indicating that if a person has not told someone of his or her wishes, in case of severe physical injury, the decision to remove a person from life supports or to place the person on life supports cannot be made. Therefore, it has become increasingly imperative that people indicate their wishes and identify individuals that they designate to make these decisions if needed.

   Advance directives have been paired with living wills to give people control over what happens to them in a severe illness or injury. A living will allows individuals to retain some control over what happens at the end of their lives, even if the individuals are then no longer competent to make personal choices for terminal care, by specifying their wishes while they are still healthy and at a time when there is no doubt of their mental competence.

10. The *Family and Medical Leave Act (FMLA) of 1993* requires covered employers to provide up to 12 weeks of unpaid, job-protected

leave to "eligible" employees for certain family and medical reasons with continuation of group health insurance coverage under the same terms and conditions as if the employee had not taken leave.

11. The *Multiethnic Placement Act (MEPA) of 1994* and its subsequent amendments prohibit agencies from refusing or delaying foster or adoptive placements because of a child's or foster/adoptive parent's race, color, or national origin, and prohibits agencies from considering race, color, or national origin as a basis for denying approval as a foster and/or adoptive parent. It also requires agencies to diligently recruit a diverse base of foster and adoptive parents to better reflect the racial and ethnic makeup of children in out-of-home care.

12. The *Violence Against Women Act (VAWA) of 1994* has improved the criminal justice response to violence against women by strengthening federal penalties for repeat sex offenders and creating a federal "rape shield law," which is intended to prevent offenders from using victims' past sexual conduct against them during a rape trial; keeping victims safe by requiring that a victim's protection order will be recognized and enforced in all state, tribal, and territorial jurisdictions; increasing rates of prosecution, conviction, and sentencing of offenders by helping communities develop dedicated law enforcement and prosecution units and domestic violence dockets; training law enforcement officers, prosecutors, victim advocates, and judges; and ensuring access to the services needed by victims to achieve safety and rebuild their lives.

    This law, reauthorized in 2013, now includes a landmark addition that empowers Native American tribal authorities to prosecute non-Native Americans for abuses committed on tribal lands. In addition, it includes additional protections for those who are gay, lesbian, bisexual, or transgender.

13. The *Personal Responsibility and Work Opportunity Reconciliation Act (PRWORA) of 1996* was considered to be a fundamental shift in both the method and goal of federal cash assistance to the poor. It added a workforce development component to welfare legislation, encouraging employment among the poor. PRWORA instituted Temporary Assistance for Needy Families (TANF), which became effective July 1, 1997. TANF replaced the Aid to Families With Dependent Children (AFDC) program, which had been in effect since 1935, and also supplanted the Job Opportunities and Basic Skills (JOBS) Training Program of 1988. It also imposed a lifetime 5-year limit on the receipt of benefits.

14. The *Health Insurance Portability and Accountability Act (HIPAA) of 1996* provides individuals with access to their medical records and more control over how their personal health information is used

and disclosed. It represents a uniform, federal floor of privacy protections for individuals across the country. State laws providing additional protections are not affected by HIPAA, which took effect on April 14, 2003.

15. The *Patient Protection and Affordable Care Act (ACA) of 2010* expands access to insurance, increases protections, emphasizes prevention and wellness, improves quality and system performance, expands the health workforce, and curbs rising health care costs. Key provisions of the ACA that intend to address rising health costs include providing more oversight of health insurance premiums and practices; emphasizing prevention, primary care, and effective treatments; reducing health care fraud and abuse; reducing uncompensated care to prevent a shift onto insurance premium costs; fostering comparison shopping in insurance exchanges to increase competition and price transparency; implementing Medicare payment reforms; and testing new delivery and payment system models in Medicaid and Medicare.

16. The *Workforce Innovation and Opportunity Act (WIOA) of 2014* reauthorizes the Workforce Investment Act (WIA) of 1998 with several key changes in areas such as Workforce Development Boards; One-Stop Operations; Job-Driven Training for Adults and Dislocated Workers; and Integrated Performance and Youth Services.

LEADERSHIP AND MANAGEMENT TECHNIQUES

There are many different definitions of leadership and management, with little consensus about the differences between the two terms. However, there is agreement that successful organizations need both good leadership and management. Some suggest that leadership can be viewed as a subset of management because a leadership role is inherent in a management position. Leadership is related to being focused on the future, dealing with uncertainty and instability, and prospectively considering the ways in which organizational operations need to change. Leadership also includes initiating, sustaining, and helping to maintain a certain amount of momentum through the change process. Leaders must be attentive to and help to balance stability and change. Management, on the other hand, focuses on efficiency, effectiveness, and planning.

Social work leaders need management skills and social work managers need leadership skills in order to be effective. The skill sets of leaders focus on inspiration, transformation, empowerment, trust, innovation, and creativity whereas managers are concerned with performance, planning, accountability, monitoring, evaluation, cooperation, and teamwork. Managers must govern resources and oversee the tensions between controlling, rationing, and providing needed services.

There is typically little distinction between managers and leaders because leaders are often appointed to management positions. Thus, managers and leaders within organizations are usually the same individuals.

FISCAL MANAGEMENT TECHNIQUES

Human service organizations need to be accountable in the recording and reporting of their financial transactions. Financial management refers to planning for, acquiring, allocating, controlling, and recording/reporting of financial and material resources, as well as the evaluation of methods used to achieve these aims. Financial management involves the following activities/techniques:

- **Planning**—the short- and long-term strategies used to ensure fiscal solvency

- **Acquisition**—the gathering of human, material, and economic resources through such means as fundraising, grant writing, contractual arrangements, fees, purchase of merchandise, and so on

- **Allocation**—the distribution of resources internally (such as to specific departments) or externally (such as by contracting an outside organization or using consultants)

- **Internal control**—the establishment of standardized policies and procedures relating to all transactions and events involving monetary items (including the use of generally accepted accounting principles and adherence to contractual obligations)

- **Recording/reporting**—the use of a manual, automated, or computerized system to list and classify all transactions of a fiscal nature in journals and ledgers to generate statements and reports

- **Evaluating**—the periodic review of financial activities to assess their efficiency and effectiveness at meeting the goal of financial accountability

Social work administrators need to be knowledgeable about financial management techniques because they are responsible for the oversight and operations of their programs. This responsibility includes overseeing fiscal staff and fiscal operations.

The Budgetary Process

A budget is a plan that outlines an entity's financial and operational goals. There are some similarities and differences between the budgetary processes of public entities such as federal, state, and local governments and the private social service organizations in which most social workers are employed. Understanding how budgets are developed and adopted in both the public and private sectors is critical.

Budgeting is forecasting by the government about its expenditures and revenues for a specific period of time. The budget process for the federal government of the United States involves both the executive and legislative branches of government. The president submits a budget to Congress, which then passes legislation to appropriate and authorize the funds to be spent. In state government, the governor, who is the leader of the executive branch, proposes a budget to the legislature, which then has an opportunity to modify it before voting to adopt the budget and appropriate funds. In a nonprofit agency, the executive director usually constructs the proposed budget and then works with a board of trustees to refine and adopt it.

The most reliable budgets yield the best fiscal results and are income based. *Income-based budgeting* establishes targets on realistic expectations and only includes reliable income in the budget. Expenses must be lower than the total dependable income total.

Incremental budgeting begins with prior year totals and builds the subsequent year's budget by calculating percentage increases or decreases.

Zero-based budgeting starts from scratch every year, examining the assumptions every year and allocating resources to the most important mission activities.

When looking at expenditures, it is necessary to distinguish between fixed and variable costs. *Fixed costs* are not ordinarily affected by the number of projects, programs, or clients served. Examples of fixed costs include permanent full-time staff, office rent, and payments on long-term loans. *Variable costs* are usually project-oriented and are more adjustable. *Semi-variable costs* are in between—they must occur, but can be modified (e.g., short-term rental versus purchasing equipment or engaging part-time temporary help rather than hiring full-time permanent staff).

The key to a successful budget is the generation of income. *Reliable revenue* can be counted upon from year-to-year and would include examples such as dependable annual foundation gifts or government grants for general operating and long-standing contracts with government agencies or other entities. During a recession, many revenue sources that have traditionally been dependable may become less so, moving these items from reliable toward transient. *Transient revenue* is income generated from one-time program offerings or financial gifts such as a bequest. Transient revenue can be useful for single capital purchases but cannot be counted on to sustain organizational operations over time.

FUND-RAISING AND DEVELOPMENT

Although human service organizations are often heavily reliant on government funding, philanthropic activities are critical to the operations of most nonprofit organizations. Securing private funding requires understanding of the fund-raising process and dedicated time and effort. There is fierce competition for resources, especially those that can be used for ongoing program operations.

Funding sources for human service organizations include, but are not limited to, corporate and individual donors, grants, health insurance payments, and so on. Nonprofit and service organizations often receive significant support from donors who believe in the mission of the work. Organizations reach out to such donors through donation drives, fundraising events, and by maintaining ongoing relationships with supporters.

Grants from foundations and corporations also help to support many human service organizations. Usually, grants are secured by writing applications that explain the organizational mission and operations, how funds that are being requested will be used, and how grants will help to address social problems. Some agencies also operate social enterprises or small businesses within the auspices of the organizations. The businesses can be staffed by clients who are having difficulty securing other employment. Profits from the enterprise are directed back into the budgets of the organizations operating them.

While some staff of organizations are dedicated solely to fundraising, often all staff have some role in this important work. Social workers may have a direct role such as by grant writing or they may indirectly support the activities by identifying potential donors or helping highlight agencies' success stories, illustrating the importance of donor support.

Advocacy for Resources to Meet Client Needs

Social workers struggle with many issues related to meeting the needs of clients. Needs often exceed available resources, thus requiring social workers to advocate on clients' behalf. Advocacy is taking an active, direct role on behalf of clients in need of help. It is bringing about action or change in policies, laws, and practices of influential individuals, groups, and institutions. It involves many people working together toward a shared vision of change. In order to advocate for resources to meet client needs, a social worker must:

- **Educate** about the gap between service availability and demand
- **Raise awareness** that the problem is important and needs to be addressed
- **Influence others** about the importance of the issue

- **Develop coalitions and networks** to efficiently use available resources
- **Convince legislators and private funders** to allocate money for services
- **Evaluate existing services** to ensure resources are being used in the most effective and efficient manner

ASSET-BUILDING APPROACHES (E.G., COLLABORATIVE RELATIONSHIPS, HUMAN CAPITAL, RESOURCES)

Asset building refers to strategies that increase financial and tangible assets, such as savings, a home, and businesses of all kinds. Asset-building policy focuses on long-term development of individuals, families, and communities by creating strategies for helping families escape poverty. Whereas traditional approaches to poverty alleviation emphasized increasing income, recent research has proven that income is necessary, but insufficient for solving poverty. Instead, assets—concrete and tangible resources like a home, savings, an education, or a business—must accompany income to help families move up the economic ladder.

Assets have been proven to create a financial buffer to weather emergencies, promote success in the labor market, inspire long-term thinking and planning, and enhance the economic and psychological well-being of individuals and their families.

Given a reasonable opportunity, families can save, build assets, and create a more prosperous future for themselves and their children. Policies focus on creating opportunities and addressing challenges to saving and building assets through:

- *Learning:* To participate in the mainstream economy, clients need to learn basic financial skills. They can develop these skills through formal education and financial counseling, including policies and programs that integrate savings and financial education into schools and social services.

- *Earning:* To maximize income, clients need access to quality jobs, benefits, and tax incentives.

- *Saving:* To save, households need income left over after meeting basic needs and paying down debt. They can increase savings through affordable and accessible financial products such as Individual Development Accounts and Children's Savings Accounts.

- *Investing:* To invest and grow wealth by leveraging savings through debt financing and public incentives that allow them to purchase homes, make financial investments, and/or start businesses.

- *Protecting:* To access products, services, and policies that protect them against loss of income or assets, extraordinary costs, and harmful, discriminatory, or predatory practices.

Impact of Economic Changes on Individuals, Families, Organizations, and Communities

Economic changes can dramatically impact client systems. While economic changes can be attributable to many factors, they are often associated with job loss due to business closing, downsizing, disability, and so on. Job loss is devastating given that a client's biggest asset is his or her ability to work and generate income. When losing a job, a client is faced with readjusting household budgets to account for new economic realities and determining the long-term economic impacts.

Clients experience many emotional reactions to economic change. Often, such change occurs suddenly and is accompanied with shock and disbelief. When shock and disbelief fade, clients experience fear and anxiety about paying their bills, maintaining their households, depleting their savings, losing their homes, finding new income sources, telling others about their loss, determining the impact that their situation will have on their family, and so on.

Economic changes can also undermine self-worth, personal security, and personal control, resulting in sadness and depression. In addition, clients may have to give up activities and/or certain roles, have fewer social contacts, face disruption in daily routines, and find themselves separated from roles and rewards that give meaning or purpose to their lives. These changes may result in both anger and shame. Even when caused by factors outside their control, clients may feel responsible for their changes in circumstances. There may be shame in failing as providers. With socioeconomic status viewed by society as an indicator of social status and respectability, such changes are often associated with feelings of poor self-worth.

Economic changes also impact families, organizations, and communities. Economic changes are associated with shifts in family roles, relationships, and responsibilities that can result in stress. Economic recession can cause citizens to be cautious as they do not know if the overall economy will improve. People may be fearful of spending money or engaging in activities that may have financial implications. Declines can be seen in moving, marriages, car purchases, and so on. Also, enrollment in higher education often edges up during a recession as individuals graduate with their bachelor's degrees and there are no jobs available. Thus, they decide to pursue master's or some other kinds of professional degrees until they become employed. A recession does not necessarily impact on the rich and poor equally. Those who are low-income prior to a recession are likely to be more adversely affected, thus widening the income gap between these groups.

THE RELATIONSHIP BETWEEN FORMAL AND INFORMAL POWER STRUCTURES IN THE DECISION-MAKING PROCESS

Formal power is received in accordance with position in an organization and the authority associated with that position. Conversely, informal power stems from the relationships built and respect earned from coworkers.

Formal Power

Organizations typically have organizational charts that list the relationship and ranks of positions. The charts detail the lines of authority and responsibilities and outline the formal power structures of the organizations. Formal power may refer to position in the organizational hierarchy, corporate structure, or even job function. A chief executive officer, for example, has decision-making power in many areas. Even in small agencies without official organizational charts, employees can easily recognize formal power because of job roles, titles, and functions.

Informal Power

The most powerful person in an organizational unit is not necessarily a supervisor. Instead, persons with the most influence, who can lead others to achieve goals or accomplish tasks, may have the greatest influence. Informal power refers to the ability to lead, direct, or achieve without official authority. It is derived from relationships that are built. Employees with informal power may be the most experienced or knowledgeable or the most respected because of personality traits.

All forms of power within an organization are beneficial when used appropriately. Formal power is necessary to achieve goals. Informal power can be equally useful. Workers may be more apt to accept criticism or take direction when they receive guidance from a colleague that is respected and trusted. It is often easier to get employee "buy-in" when suggestions come from those with informal power.

EDUCATIONAL COMPONENTS, TECHNIQUES, AND METHODS OF SUPERVISION

There are three components of supervision—administrative, educational, and supportive. *Administrative supervision* aims to ensure that a social worker is accountable to the public as well as to his or her organization's policies. The major responsibility is to make sure that the work is performed in an acceptable manner. *Educational supervision* establishes a learning alliance between a supervisor and a social worker with the aim of teaching new skills or refining existing ones. *Supportive supervision* is focused on increasing performance by decreasing job-related stress that interferes with functioning.

For a social worker to learn job-related material and develop as a skilled professional, he or she must make appropriate and effective use of educational supervision. The educational component of supervision is concerned with teaching a social worker what he or she needs to know in order to do his or her job and helping him or her through the learning process. In essence, the educational component relates to the transmission of knowledge, skills, attitudes, and values needed by social workers.

In order for learning to occur, a supervisee must be cooperative (willing to work and learn new skills), willing to follow directions (initially doing what he or she told until able to complete routines without direction), and knowledgeable (about agency procedures). A supervisee also must show initiative (seeking out learning opportunities and applying new knowledge) and accepting of criticism (trying to improve and accepting feedback when it is justified and constructive).

Supervisors also have responsibilities in educational supervision. They must provide education and training (formal and informal opportunities to ensure supervisees have the knowledge and skills needed to do their jobs competently) and feedback (explanations on what is going well and what needs improvement). Identifying the learning needs of supervisees should be done at hire and regularly thereafter. Changes in the field must always be considered. Lastly, supervisors should be aware of supervisees' learning styles and ensure that education is delivered via methods that are most effective. There are three main cognitive learning styles: visual (uses visual objects such as graphs and charts to learn), auditory (retains information through hearing and speaking), and kinesthetic (likes to use hands-on approaches to acquire knowledge).

METHODS TO IDENTIFY LEARNING NEEDS AND DEVELOP LEARNING OBJECTIVES FOR SUPERVISEES

Supervision is an essential way in which social workers acquire knowledge and skills needed for professional practice. It is often the bridge between the classroom and the field. Supervision is necessary to improve client care, develop professionalism, and maintain ethical standards in the field. Supervision has also become the cornerstone of quality improvement and assurance.

Quality supervision is founded on a positive supervisor–supervisee relationship that promotes client welfare and the professional development of the supervisee. A supervisor is a teacher, coach, consultant, mentor, evaluator, and administrator. *Ultimately, effective supervision ensures that clients are competently served.* Supervision ensures that social workers continue to increase their skills, which in turn increases service effectiveness.

Some of the skills that social work supervisors must have in order to effectively teach supervisees include the ability to:

- Identify learning needs and styles
- Write learning goals and objectives
- Devise instructional strategies to accommodate needs and learning styles
- Present material in a didactic manner, using modeling
- Match learning styles to developmental levels (e.g., provide more instruction to junior supervisees and use guided discovery for those who are senior)
- Explain the rationales for interventions
- Evaluate supervisees' learning
- Give constructive feedback to supervisees

Learning needs of supervisees may result from gaps in knowledge about practice modalities; effective communication strategies; setting, funding, or legal requirements; self-care strategies; and so on. Social work supervisors should be knowledgeable about the skills supervisees acquired from previous professional training and experience, as well as gaps in learning, such as those related to diagnostic assessment and treatment; ethical standards of practice; state and federal laws and rules; record keeping; cultural competence; methods for establishing treatment relationships with clients; methods for including family members in clients' treatment when appropriate; communication with other professionals in developing diagnosis and treatment plans and assuring continuity of care; and so on. Lastly, social work supervisors should solicit input from supervisees about what they view as their greatest learning needs and develop learning objectives to meet these needs in partnership with supervisees. Identifying learning needs and developing learning objectives is a collaborative process between social work supervisors and supervisees.

CASE RECORDING FOR PRACTICE EVALUATION OR SUPERVISION

Case records are often an excellent source of information for evaluating the impacts of services. They are existing sources of data, so there is no additional cost or time associated with their collection. However, there are a few limitations. If looking at records completed by multiple workers, there may be inconsistencies in recording styles or details that may impact on the evaluation. Also, information of interest may not be contained in the records;

evaluations would need to be limited to only information that is explicitly stated, which may not reflect all progress that has been made.

In addition, the opinions about how a client views both the process and outcome of service delivery are also critical and may not be fully captured in the record. Ensuring that a client's views are the center of any practice evaluation is critical. Thus, a social worker may want to use the case record as one source of information, but include others as well, to ensure all aspects of a client's care, including satisfaction with services, are included.

Social workers engaged in formal evaluation beyond that used to determine individual client progress should obtain voluntary and written informed consent from clients regarding the use of their records without any penalty for refusal to participate or undue inducement to participate (*NASW Code of Ethics, 2008—5.02 Evaluation and Research*).

Review of case records by supervisors is also essential. This review will ensure that a social worker is documenting properly and recording information in an unbiased manner. Clients must understand and consent to supervisory review of records.

When reviewing information, supervisors should adhere to the same standards of confidentiality as a social worker. The supervisor should not review the records unless it is for the betterment of a client and only within the supervisory context to ensure the quality of services. If the supervisor is a consultant, a client must consent unless there is a compelling need for such disclosure.

METHODS TO CREATE, IMPLEMENT, AND EVALUATE POLICIES AND PROCEDURES FOR SOCIAL WORKER SAFETY

Social workers provide services in increasingly complex, dynamic social environments with many client populations. The number and variety of people to whom social workers provide services and the variety of settings in which these services are provided contribute to an increasingly unpredictable, and often unsafe, environment for social work practice. Social workers have been the targets of verbal and physical assaults in agencies, as well as during field visits with clients. Tragically, some social workers have also been permanently injured or have lost their lives.

Most clients and families that social workers serve do not present threats or pose danger. In cases where threats are present, most employers address these issues appropriately. There are, however, social work settings where social workers face increased risks of violence.

Social workers have the right to work in safe environments and to advocate for safe working conditions. Social workers who report concerns regarding their personal safety, or who request assistance in assuring their safety, should not fear retaliation, blame, or questioning of their competency from their supervisors or colleagues. Social workers should routinely practice universal safety precautions in their work. Violence occurs in every economic, social, gender, and racial group. To avoid stereotyping particular groups of people and to promote safety, social workers should practice safety assessment and risk reduction with all clients and in all settings. A thorough understanding of the risk factors associated with elevated risk for violence can inform safety assessments. Social workers should also be aware of the potential that their personal information on the Internet, particularly social networking sites, can be accessed by anyone. Universal safety precautions also include the establishment of safety plans as a matter of routine planning. The adoption of universal safety precautions should not preclude agencies from establishing particular safeguards when social workers are asked to perform dangerous tasks. In those situations, agencies should establish specific policies to reduce the risk of harm.

MODELS OF SUPERVISION AND CONSULTATION (E.G., INDIVIDUAL, PEER, GROUP)

There are many and varied supervision models, each with its own benefits and limitations. In order for supervision to be effective, it is necessary to take into account both the needs of social workers and the requirements and constraints of organizations when considering the model to be utilized.

Individual supervision has traditionally been the cornerstone of professional skill development. Supervision can be provided in groups, peer-led or facilitated by professional leaders. Group and peer supervision, as well as intensive case consultation on a case-by-case basis, are useful and less costly additions to individual supervision, but they may be inadequate as substitutes for one-on-one support.

Individual

Benefits

- Full attention on the skill development, strengths, challenges, and professional enhancement of the individual supervisee
- More time and potentially safer environment in which to explore supervisee's interpersonal dynamics with clients and the impact of the work (e.g., countertransference issues, secondary trauma, compassion fatigue, burnout)
- Less exposure to poor practices of peers, which could be inappropriately modeled or interfere with supervision process

Challenges

- Potential for supervisee to feel intimidated by the supervisor, with no one else present to observe, or break up the intensity of the one-to-one focus
- Costly and time-consuming
- No input from others outside the dyad
- No opportunity for supervisee to compare self with others, or gain support from peers

Peer Group

Benefits

- Each group member can offer and receive wisdom, experience and ideas (i.e., enjoy both "teacher" and "student" roles)
- Shared influence and responsibility regarding how the group is run
- Avoids chance of getting stuck with an unwanted supervisor
- Opportunities for personal growth via group dynamics
- Participants as equals encourages lateral help and peer support

Challenges

- Potential for unconscious designation of more experienced/skilled members as "de facto" supervisors
- Success is dependent upon how group members exercise their responsibilities
- Mutual trust, openness, and respect are essential
- Usually requires that groups remain closed, at least for a period of time
- Competition, defensiveness, and criticism between peers can occur
- Clinical case discussion frequency, depth, and intensity is limited by the time available and the number of members participating in the group

Facilitated Group

Benefits

- Learning occurs from others' practice examples and ways of working
- Self-confirmation occurs through giving feedback

- Opportunities for role play and other action techniques are present
- Less expensive and time consuming than individual supervision
- Opportunities for personal growth via group dynamics

Challenges

- Supervisor must be skilled in working systemically with groups and must be able to facilitate while also supervising (dual tasks)
- Supervisor's anxiety about his or her own competence may pose a barrier, as there is greater exposure of the supervisor's abilities and experience
- Less time for each supervisee, as the group must balance the needs of each member
- Group needs to have a high level of trust in order for supervisees to feel safe

THE SUPERVISEE'S ROLE IN SUPERVISION (E.G., IDENTIFYING LEARNING NEEDS, SELF-ASSESSMENT, PRIORITIZING, ETC.)

The short-term objectives of supervision are to increase a social worker's capacity to work more effectively, to provide a work context conducive to productivity, and to help a social worker take satisfaction in his or her work. The ultimate objective is to assure the delivery of the most effective and efficient client services.

Social workers who are administrators should take reasonable steps to ensure that adequate agency or organizational resources are available to provide appropriate staff supervision.

Competence is essential for ethical social work practice and social workers must be competent in the services that they are providing (*NASW Code of Ethics, 2008–1.04 Competence*). In order to be competent, they must keep abreast of new developments in the field and obtain supervision.

Social workers should provide services and represent themselves as competent only within the boundaries of their education, training, license, certification, consultation received, supervised experience, or other relevant professional experience (*NASW Code of Ethics, 2008–1.04 Competence*).

Social workers should provide services in substantive areas or use intervention techniques or approaches that are new to them only after engaging in appropriate study, training, consultation, and supervision from people who are competent in those interventions or techniques (*NASW Code of Ethics, 2008–1.04 Competence*).

When generally recognized standards do not exist with respect to an emerging area of practice, social workers should exercise careful judgment and take responsible steps (including appropriate education, research, training, consultation, and supervision) to ensure the competence of their work and to protect clients from harm (*NASW Code of Ethics*, 2008–1.04 Competence).

If a supervisor needs to talk with a social worker about a problem situation, he or she should meet privately with the social worker to discuss the matter.

EMPLOYEE RECRUITMENT, TRAINING, RETENTION, PERFORMANCE APPRAISAL, EVALUATION, AND DISCIPLINE

Employment and human resources law can be very complicated. Social work administrators should be familiar with federal, state, and local regulations. They must ensure that human service organizations operate legally and they must make ethical decisions with regard to employee recruitment, training, retention, performance appraisal, evaluation, and discipline. Social work administrators must also ensure that employment policies and practices are not discriminatory based on race, ethnicity, national origin, color, sex, sexual orientation, gender identity or expression, age, marital status, political belief, religion, immigration status, or mental or physical disability.

Employee recruitment can be difficult as it involves finding the best candidates for positions. Bad recruitment practices may lead to unqualified people being selected. Although there is no perfect method for hiring, it is best to start well in advance of a hiring need. A pool of candidates should be recruited using a detailed job description and an established background check policy. Interviews should use standard questioning which complies with legal and ethical standards.

Once hired, employees need to be initially trained and should receive ongoing development opportunities to ensure that they have the skills needed to fulfill the mission of an organization. There are several options for training and education related to employees' official duties. These include doing training within an agency or having employees go to other entities to be trained. Training may be paid solely by an employer or an employee, or split between the two parties. In addition, time spent in training may or may not be compensated by an employer, depending upon the policy of an agency.

Once employees are hired and trained, retaining them should also be a top priority. Many good retention practices are inexpensive to implement. Employee retention is positively linked to career development opportunities and a chance to advance within an agency, opportunities for regular feedback and recognition, flexible work schedules that recognize the need for work/life balance, and good salaries and benefits.

Employee performance should be periodically evaluated to ensure that employees are meeting expected standards, as well as to inform them of their status. In order to ensure the delivery of effective and efficient client services, social workers' performance should be reviewed and evaluated. Such reviews and evaluations should occur regularly as part of the administrative task of supervision. Performance appraisal should be both formal and informal so that employees can get immediate feedback if they are doing something good or bad.

Evaluations provide information to facilitate sound administrative decision making on employment matters (pay increases, promotions, terminations), as well as contribute to social workers' professional development and job performance.

The most important objective, however, is to ultimately improve the outcome of service delivery, thereby being accountable to a client and the public at large.

Evaluations should include a review of both the quality and quantity of the work performed. Some of the areas to be included in a social work appraisal or evaluation are the following:

- The ability to establish and maintain meaningful, effective, appropriately professional relationships with clients
- Knowledge and skills (i.e., data-gathering, diagnostic, treatment/ intervention, interviewing, and recording skills)
- Ability to adhere to agency objectives, policies, and procedures
- Use of supervision
- Staff and community relationships
- Professional attributes and attitudes, including adherence to the *NASW Code of Ethics*
- Cultural competence

Evaluations should identify both strengths and weaknesses and should be specific and individualized. Evaluations should focus on recurrent patterns of behavior, not atypical, isolated examples. Supervisors should consider factors that may have affected performance, such as a heavy caseload or the unavailability of needed support.

Social workers are responsible for conducting evaluations on their employees in a responsible and ethical manner. They also should ensure that evaluations of their services are completed in order to provide feedback on their work.

Supervisors should notify supervisees in advance of when evaluations will occur, what information and standards will be used, who will see the results, and how the results will be used. When conducting evaluations, supervisors and supervisees should prepare by reviewing all materials, including evaluation tools, supervision notes, and employee reports. Supervisors and supervisees should have a chance to discuss their perceptions, followed by written documentation of the supervisee performance and suggestions for improvement. This documentation should be given to the supervisee with the opportunity for revision if the supervisor agrees with objections raised. Objections that the supervisor does not accept should be documented and placed in his or her file.

There are a number of evaluation formats/methods including, but not limited to, the use of ordinal rating scales and evaluation outlines.

Supervisors need to be aware of and guard against biases, such as a central tendency bias, halo effect, and leniency bias, which may impact on ratings.

Positive reinforcement is a powerful force for employees who are doing a good job. For problem employees, specific work-quality issues can be pointed out. Evaluations should make employees feel empowered, not micromanaged. After employees have been evaluated, goals for development and/or improvement should be established.

Sometimes discipline, including termination, becomes necessary. Social work administrators must be knowledgeable about both laws and agency policies that impact disciplinary actions. When employees have performed illegal acts, termination is justified. Breaking agency policies can also be grounds for termination. However, there are situations where termination can be considered "wrongful" or inappropriate, such as when an employee is fired for reporting wrongdoing or for taking time off when covered by the Family Medical Leave Act (FMLA).

THE IMPACT OF TRANSFERENCE AND COUNTERTRANSFERENCE WITHIN SUPERVISORY RELATIONSHIPS

Transference and countertransference within supervisory relationships can be a parallel process of what is occurring between a social worker and a client. The transference occurs when a social worker recreates, within a supervisory relationship, a presenting problem and emotions occurring in a therapeutic relationship. Countertransference occurs when a supervisor responds to a social worker in the same manner that a social worker responds to a client. Thus, a supervisory interaction replays, or is parallel with, a social worker–client interaction. In essence, the processes at work in the relationship between a social worker and a client are reflected in the relationship between a social worker and his or her supervisor.

Parallel process is an unconscious identification with a client and can be used as an important part of the supervisory process. Examining it will assist a social worker and his or her supervisor in identifying issues that exist in a therapeutic relationship and allow for techniques to resolve these issues to be identified and discussed.

THE COMPONENTS OF A SAFE AND POSITIVE WORK ENVIRONMENT

To practice effectively and ethically, social workers need a working environment that upholds ethical practice and is committed to standards and good quality services. A positive working environment is created where the values and principles of employers and social workers are consistent with each other and mutually reinforcing. There is substantial evidence that the most effective social work services are provided in situations where employers understand social work practice, respect their employees, and are committed to implementing professional values.

A framework for supporting good practice needs to take account of ethical principles and ensure effective induction, supervision, workload management, and continuing professional development.

The following are some elements which enable social workers to practice ethically:

- Written policies setting out standards of ethical practice provide clarity and protection for clients, social workers, and agencies. Social workers should never be required to do anything that would put at risk their ability to uphold such ethical standards, including policies on confidentiality, equal opportunities, and risk management.

- Quality social work services draw on research and practice evidence. Policies should be informed by research and practice evidence.

- The public, including clients, should be regularly informed about these standards, policies, and procedures and provided with information about how to raise concerns or make complaints about standards of practice.

- People employed as social workers must be suitable to enter the workforce, hold appropriate recognized qualifications that entitle them to practice as social workers, provide references (including evidence that they are not a risk to clients), and demonstrate that they understand their roles and responsibilities, including their ethical duties.

- Dangerous, discriminatory, or exploitative behavior and practice must be dealt with promptly through the implementation of policies and procedures. Such policies should provide measures to prevent and minimize violence, making it clear to staff, social workers, and clients that violence, threats, or abusive behavior is not acceptable.

- Social workers have a right for their health and occupational safety to be protected. Social workers frequently experience trauma or violence in their work and they are vulnerable to work-related stress and burnout due to the nature of their work.

- The adoption and implementation of policies on workload management make a major contribution to the provision of quality services to clients. Workload practices must consider the basic tenets of social work intervention, including the centrality of human relationships, the need to manage risk and complexity, and the duty to highlight unmet need.

■ The physical working environment has an important part to play in the support of effective and ethical practice including, for example, the physical arrangements and procedures required for confidential interviewing and storage of confidential records.

■ Continuing professional development and further training enable social workers to strengthen and develop their skills and knowledge and ensure that agencies adapt to the changing needs of clients and changing organizational realities. Orientation and induction training provided to new employees and those changing jobs are essential, including the management of risk, making complex professional judgments, and the fulfillment of statutory obligations such as the protection of minors and vulnerable adults.

■ Good quality, regular social work supervision by people who have the necessary experience and qualifications in social work practice is an essential tool to ensure accountable and ethical practice. Research has confirmed that supervision is an important vehicle for supporting the management function in promoting creative and reflective practice, supporting staff resilience and well-being, and continuous professional development.

■ Systematic reviews of services and practice, led by social workers who have experience of the field, should be held regularly. These activities identify needed support, training, and action when poor or unethical practice is identified.

■ Career development opportunities for social workers wishing to develop advanced practice skills need to be available. These not only meet the individual needs of social workers, but can also constitute an effective tool for retaining valuable practice knowledge and experience and for preventing high staff turnover and difficulties in recruitment that are typical challenges constantly being faced by social work services.

■ Rates of pay or fees for social work practice need to be comparable with similar professionals and recognize the skill and qualifications of social workers.

THE COMPONENTS OF CASE MANAGEMENT

Case management has been defined in many ways. However, all models are based on the belief that clients often need assistance in accessing services in today's complex systems, as well as the need to monitor duplication and gaps in treatment and care.

Although there may be many federal, state, and local programs available, there are often serious service gaps. A client might have a specific need met in one program and many related needs ignored because of the lack of coordination. Systems are highly complex, fragmented, duplicative, and uncoordinated.

Social workers provide case management services to different client populations in both nonprofit and for-profit settings.

The primary goal of social work case management is to optimize client functioning and well-being by providing and coordinating high-quality services, in the most effective and efficient manner possible, to individuals with multiple complex needs *(NASW Standards for Social Work Case Management, 2013).*

Five case management activities are (a) assessment, (b) planning, (c) linking, (d) monitoring, and (e) advocacy.

Fragmentation presents one of the biggest service delivery challenges for clients and those who are assisting them, such as social workers. Clients can fall through the cracks because the connections between services are either absent or problematic, or needed services are missing altogether.

The purpose of coordinating services for clients is to improve outcomes. The assumption is that collaborative activity can facilitate access to services, reduce unnecessary duplication of effort, and produce a more effective and efficient social service system.

Social workers are uniquely positioned to coordinate services.

Coordination is achieved through the *integration of services* in which services are combined and provided simultaneously. Such an approach is often used with mental health and substance use interventions in which they are combined within a primary treatment relationship or service setting.

Another method of coordination is *wrap-around services* in which multiple providers and services may overlap in some ways, but are not combined to the same degree as integrated services.

In addition, "roundtables" or *interdisciplinary team approaches* also are useful in ensuring that all professionals are brought together to stay informed of total client care and work together to avoid fragmentation and/or duplication.

THE ELEMENTS OF A CASE PRESENTATION

When a social worker communicates with others in order to ensure comprehensive and complete care for clients, he or she completes a case presentation. Case presentations are also used in professional development and learning to provide input into options for treatment and to ensure services are being delivered effectively and efficiently.

There is no universal format for a case presentation in social work practice. However, there are some standard elements, including:

- Identifying data (demographics, cultural considerations)
- History of the presenting problem (family history)
- Significant medical/psychiatric history (diagnoses)
- Significant personal and/or social history (legal issues, academic/work problems, crisis/safety concerns)
- Presenting problem (assessment, mental status, diagnosis)
- Impressions and summary (interview findings)
- Recommendations (treatment plan/intervention strategies, goals, theoretical models used)

Content areas can be added or eliminated based on the reasons for the case presentation and input sought. Information for a case presentation is usually information that a social worker has obtained directly from a client during an interview and/or observation, as well as that collected from collateral contacts, other professionals, and/or case records.

TIME MANAGEMENT APPROACHES

Time management is planning and consciously controlling the amount of time spent on specific activities, especially to increase effectiveness, efficiency, or productivity. Though time management initially focused on business or work activities, it is now increasingly used to control personal activities as well.

Most time management approaches focus on creating conducive or effective environments, modifying behaviors, setting priorities, and/or reducing time spent on nonpriorities.

The approaches to time management have evolved. Initially, approaches consisted of checklists and notes to recognize the demands on time. These then evolved into calendars and appointment books that focused on looking ahead to anticipate future events. The third approach, often used today, examines efficiency with the focus on prioritizing, planning, controlling, and taking steps toward a goal.

The last approach requires the categorization of daily activities by importance and urgency. Those activities that are urgent and important can be stressful and require immediate action; those who deal with these exclusively will think they are just "putting out fires." Activities that are not urgent or important require little or no attention, and time spent on these activities will result in feelings of disengagement. Activities that are urgent but not important often take up a lot of attention but tend to yield little difference or progress. The last grouping—those things that are important but not urgent—are likely to be put aside yet are critical to personal fulfillment. Time management should include minimizing time spent on activities that are not important and ensuring those that are not urgent but are important, such as building relationships, recreation and leisure, and so on, are also prioritized.

METHODS OF NETWORKING

The importance of networking has been stressed heavily in business, but it has received far less attention in social work practice. This void is interesting, because it is critical to the effective delivery of services. Networking involves building relationships with other professionals who share areas of interest. It is about creating a community around common interests and building alliances. It is also about creating opportunities to work with others toward the achievement of mutual goals.

Although networking in business is a way to attract patrons/customers or to get jobs, it has a broader, and more altruistic, focus in social work.

For example, learning about others who do similar or complementary work can result in a sharing of resources and expertise, which could be beneficial to clients by keeping the cost of services contained and/or increasing the skills of practitioners. Learning about the skills of others and establishing professional relationships through networking can also provide resources for clients who may need referrals to other professionals.

Networking helps improve social skills and the ability to relate to others in a variety of settings. It puts social workers "out there" so that others can be aware of the important work that they do. Educating others about social problems is an important part of making systematic changes. Lastly, networking can identify individuals who would be good candidates for jobs. Recruiting qualified individuals into the agencies where social workers are employed results in clients receiving quality care.

THE PROCESS OF INTERDISCIPLINARY AND INTRADISCIPLINARY TEAM COLLABORATION

Social workers often work together with others from various professions. This is known as an interdisciplinary approach. Some interdisciplinary teams interface daily, whereas others may only meet periodically. Sometimes social workers form interdisciplinary relationships that do not constitute team practice but are nevertheless necessary for effective service. These relationships may be with legal or educational professionals. To practice effectively, social workers must be prepared to work with professionals from all other disciplines that may be needed by a client. In turn, social work knowledge is influenced by, and in turn influences, other disciplines, including family studies, medicine, psychiatry, sociology, education, and psychology.

Interdisciplinary teams are often seen as advantageous to clients because they do not have the burden of navigating multiple service systems and communicating to multiple professionals involved in their care. Interdisciplinary teams can also be cost effective and can increase positive outcomes.

An interdisciplinary approach may also have benefits for social workers as they:

1. Provide peer support, especially when working with stressful problems associated with involuntary service delivery, violence, suicide, and so on

2. Allow for work to be assigned across multiple professionals

3. Fulfill professional goals by ensuring all aspects of a client's biopsychosocial–spiritual–cultural care are delivered

4. Create cross-fertilization of skills between professionals

5. Facilitate decision making related to all aspects of client care, which can lead to increased job satisfaction

6. Streamline work practices through sharing of information

Interdisciplinary collaboration is a rewarding, yet challenging, social work activity. Collaboration, a learned skill that can be improved through practice, is a vehicle for improving services for all clients. It means working with others for the betterment of a client. Collaborative teams are more likely to develop important new and innovative approaches to dealing with problems.

Collaboration goes beyond people sitting around a table. It includes pre-meeting work (i.e., making telephone calls), how members typically conduct themselves (i.e., being friendly), and how meetings proceed (i.e., choosing to ignore minor irritations in order to get on with the agenda).

Social workers must understand their own styles and focus on their own behavior as part of a group, rather than on how other members should change.

Collaboration involves strong interpersonal communication and group process skills, as well as being able to understand the perspectives of others. It can be discrete (distinct or separate; limited to single occurrence or action) or continuous (ongoing or repetitive).

The following list provides some guidelines that can be helpful when social workers participate in such collaboration.

1. Social workers should clearly articulate their roles on interdisciplinary teams.

2. Social workers should understand the roles of professionals from other disciplines on these teams.

3. Social workers should seek and establish common ground with these professionals, including commonalities in professional goals.

4. Social workers should acknowledge the differences within the field and across other disciplines.

5. Social workers should address conflict within teams so that it does not interfere with the collaborative process and the teams' outcomes.

6. Social workers should establish and maintain collegial relationships.

There are also ethical guidelines that must be followed when social workers are part of interdisciplinary collaboration (*NASW Code of Ethics, 2008—2.03 Interdisciplinary Collaboration*).

1. Social workers who are members of an interdisciplinary team should participate in and contribute to decisions that affect the well-being of clients by drawing on the perspectives, values, and experiences of the social work profession. Professional and ethical obligations of the interdisciplinary team as a whole and of its individual members should be clearly established.

2. Social workers for whom a team decision raises ethical concerns should attempt to resolve the disagreement through appropriate channels. If the disagreement cannot be resolved, social workers should pursue other avenues to address their concerns consistent with client well-being.

Intradisciplinary teams are composed exclusively of social workers who may have different levels of training and skill within the profession. Intradisciplinary teams are often referred to as unidisciplinary. Unfortunately, the terms "intradisciplinary," "multidisciplinary," and "interdisciplinary" are often used interchangeably, causing confusion. Intradisciplinary teams in social work practice can be useful in professional development, mentorship, and the provision of supervision. However, working on a team with others in the profession has advantages and disadvantages. Members share the same professional orientation and values, which can facilitate consensus and cohesion within the group, but the ability to generate alternative solutions to problems when viewing problems from multiple professional perspectives can be reduced.

THE BASIC TERMINOLOGY OF PROFESSIONS OTHER THAN SOCIAL WORK (E.G., LEGAL, EDUCATIONAL)

Social workers should maintain access to professional case consultation. Often, this consultation may be from qualified professionals in other disciplines. Each discipline has its own set of assumptions, values, and priorities; in order to ensure that the assessment of a client's problems consider all possible root causes (including medical) and all needs of a client are met, the social worker should consult with experts in other fields, as well as refer a client to them when needed.

Social workers often work together with others from various professions. This is known as an interdisciplinary approach. Some interdisciplinary teams interface daily, whereas others may only meet periodically.

Sometimes social workers form interdisciplinary relationships that do not constitute team practice, but are nevertheless necessary for effective service. These relationships may be with legal or educational professionals. To practice effectively, social workers must be prepared to work with professionals from all other disciplines that may be needed by a client.

In turn, social work knowledge is influenced by, and in turn influences, other disciplines, including family studies, medicine, psychiatry, sociology, education, and psychology.

METHODS TO CREATE, IMPLEMENT, AND EVALUATE POLICIES AND PROCEDURES THAT MINIMIZE RISK FOR INDIVIDUALS, FAMILIES, GROUPS, ORGANIZATIONS, AND COMMUNITIES

Social workers should create, implement, and evaluate policies that minimize risk for clients, workers, and practice settings. One critical feature of implementing a comprehensive risk management strategy is conducting a comprehensive ethics audit. An ethics audit entails examining risks through the following steps:

1. Appointing a committee or task force of concerned and informed staff and colleagues

2. Gathering information from agency documents, interviews with staff and clients, accreditation reports, and other sources to assess risks associated with client rights; confidentiality and privacy; informed consent; service delivery; boundary issues; conflicts of interest; documentation; client records; supervision; staff development and training; consultation; client referral; fraud; termination of services; professional impairment; misconduct, or incompetence; and so on

3. Reviewing all collected information

4. Determining whether there is no risk, minimal risk, moderate risk, or high risk in each area

5. Preparing action plans to address each risk, paying particular attention to policies that need to be created to prevent risk in the future and steps needed to mitigate existing risk

6. Monitoring policy implementation and progress made toward reducing existing risk, as well as ensuring that procedures adhere to social work's core ethical principles

Risk management is an ongoing process and must consist of preventive strategies as well as corrective actions that result from audits done routinely or in response to particular concerns or complaints.

METHODS TO DEVELOP, REVIEW, AND IMPLEMENT CRISIS PLANS

A crisis is defined as an acute *disruption of psychological homeostasis (steady state) in which usual coping mechanisms fail* and there exists evidence of distress and functional impairment. The subjective reaction to a stressful life is a compromised stability and ability to cope or function.

Given such a definition, it is imperative that social workers have a framework or blueprint to guide them in responding. When confronted by clients in crisis, social workers need to address their distress, impairment, and instability by operating in a logical and orderly process. Social workers can easily exacerbate crises with well-intentioned, but haphazard responding. Comprehensive plans allow for responses that are active and directive, but do not take problem ownership away from clients. Finally, plans should meet clients where they are at, assessing their levels of risk, mobilizing client resources, and moving strategically to stabilize the crisis and improve functioning.

The development, review, and implementation of crises plans require actions aimed at crisis stabilization, resolution, and mastery. Social workers should:

1. Plan and conduct a thorough biopsychosocial and lethality/imminent danger assessment

2. Make psychological contact and rapidly establish the collaborative relationship

3. Identify the major problems, including crisis precipitants

4. Encourage an exploration of feelings and emotions

5. Generate and explore alternatives and new coping strategies

6. Restore functioning through implementation of an action plan

7. Plan follow-up and "booster" sessions

QUALITY ASSURANCE, INCLUDING PROGRAM REVIEWS AND AUDITS BY EXTERNAL SOURCES

Historically, quality assurance systems have focused on auditing case records to monitor and report on the extent of compliance with state and federal requirements. This focus paralleled federal approaches that often were directed toward assessing compliance with procedural requirements. Usually a small number of quality assurance staff within organizations focused on this auditing function and their reports often had minimal impact on the services delivered by the agency.

Today, many agencies are developing systems that move beyond compliance monitoring. These systems attempt to gather and assess a range of information on quality, and they work to implement needed improvements on an ongoing basis. As a way of differentiating these efforts from traditional compliance monitoring, the new approaches are called continuous quality improvement systems. These systems require that agencies adopt the following steps:

Step 1: Adopting outcomes and standards

Step 2: Incorporating quality assurance standards and processes throughout their work

Step 3: Gathering data and information

Step 4: Analyzing data and information

Step 5: Using analyses and information to make improvements

Funders and accreditors support and encourage the move toward continuous quality improvement processes. This new approach improves upon compliance monitoring in three ways. First, quality improvement programs are broader in scope, assessing practice and outcomes, as well as compliance. Second, they attempt to use data, information, and results to affect positive changes in policy and case practice, along with compliance with federal, state, and agency requirements. Third, these programs engage a broad range of internal and external partners in the quality improvement process, including top managers, staff at all levels, clients, and other stakeholders.

ACCREDITATION AND/OR LICENSING REQUIREMENTS

Administrative reviews, such as annual reviews from public and private social service organizations, are critical to the fulfillment of the social work mission. They provide accountability to the public about the number of people served, the services delivered, and how funds were allocated. They also may be used by social workers to document unmet needs that should be addressed.

Social workers may be required to engage in grant monitoring, evaluations, program inspections, and accreditation reviews. While each of these reviews serves a different purpose, they all require social workers to use critical thinking/analysis to help clients directly or indirectly.

PROFESSIONAL DEVELOPMENT ACTIVITIES TO IMPROVE PRACTICE AND MAINTAIN CURRENT PROFESSIONAL KNOWLEDGE (E.G., IN-SERVICE TRAINING, LICENSING REQUIREMENTS, REVIEWS OF LITERATURE, WORKSHOPS)

Professions enjoy a high social status, regard, and esteem conferred upon them by society. This high esteem arises primarily from the higher social function of their work, which is regarded as vital to society as a whole and, thus, special and valuable in nature. All professions involve technical, specialized, and highly skilled work, often referred to as "professional expertise." Training for this work involves obtaining degrees and professional qualifications (i.e., licensure) without which entry to the profession is barred. Training also requires regular updating of skills through continuing education.

Professional development refers to skills and knowledge attained for effective service delivery and career advancement. Professional development encompasses all types of learning opportunities, ranging from formal coursework and conferences to informal learning opportunities situated in practice. There are a variety of approaches to professional development, including consultation, coaching, communities of practice, mentoring, reflective supervision, and technical assistance.

Social workers often go through various stages of professional development, including:

1. Orientation and job induction

2. Autonomous worker

3. Member of a service team (independence to interdependence)

4. Development of specialization

5. Preparation to be mentor or supervisor

Record-Keeping and Reporting

THE PRINCIPLES OF CASE RECORDING, DOCUMENTATION, AND MANAGEMENT OF PRACTICE RECORDS

Documentation in social work practice is critical because it forms the basis of assessment, planning, intervention, and evaluation of services. It is used to memorialize what has occurred and to hold social workers accountable for their services to clients, third-party payers, employers, and others. It also is used for supervision to ensure that clients receive the most effective and efficient services possible. Social workers should always document services appropriately and must never tamper with or alter records to mislead, omit, or falsify information.

There are many issues with regard to the management of practice records, including, but not limited to, that they have sufficient and credible content, they are prepared and stored correctly, and they are protected and accessed only by those who are authorized to do so. It is essential that there are written protocols with regard to the management of practice records and that these protocols are reviewed and revised regularly. Training on these protocols should be regularly conducted so that social workers know what is expected and how to address routine situations, as well as those that are not anticipated, such as the receipt of a subpoena or court order.

Management of practice records must be in accordance with federal laws such as the Family Educational Rights and Privacy Act (FERPA) or Health Insurance Portability and Accountability Act (HIPAA), state laws, and agency policies. Funders may also have requirements with regard to necessary documentation and/or the retention of records. Social workers should be knowledgeable about standards related to practice records that appear in the *NASW Code of Ethics (2008)*.

The protection of confidential information also requires great care. Social workers should know the exceptions to confidentiality and how to handle practice records when working with court-ordered clients or those who are involved in divorce or child custody proceedings. Social workers who are providing treatment to children whose parents are divorced should be aware of legal custody determinations and the respective rules that govern release of information in these arrangements.

The proper documentation of client services is paramount to competent practice. Without proper case recording or record-keeping, the quality of service may be compromised, the continuity of service may be disrupted, there may be misinterpretation that can cause harm, client confidentiality may be breached, and a client's confidence in the integrity of a social worker may be impacted.

In addition to client harm, a social worker, as well as his or her agency, if applicable, may be at risk of liability due to malpractice, negligence, and/or breach of confidentiality.

In order to ensure that all communications are written in a professional manner that will assist clients, social workers should ensure that:

- The purpose of the written communication is clear and concise
- Arguments and opinions are logical, with recommendations well supported
- Client confidentiality is addressed ethically
- Grammar is correct
- Assessments and recommendations are not based on assumptions or generalizations
- The format is clear and headings are appropriate
- The content is easily understood
- Jargon is not included
- Person-first language is used
- Language is culturally appropriate
- Content is based on value-free, objective descriptions

Written communications of social workers may be harmful to clients if they are not prepared correctly with care and skill. Social workers should understand the "audience" for documents that are prepared and ensure that they are written so that they can be used effectively.

It should also include only information that is directly relevant to the delivery of services.

The release and storage of case recordings is also critical. Social workers must make sure that records are not released without proper client consent and records are properly stored during and following the termination of services. Records should be maintained for the number of years required by state statutes and regulations and relevant contracts.

THE ELEMENTS OF CLIENT/CLIENT SYSTEM REPORTS

There is no one way to organize information or client files. Some client information and files are obtained and stored in paper format. However, increasingly client records are kept electronically with software to assist professionals in organizing and accessing data.

Whether paper or electronic, client files are usually stored with the following in separate sections or folders:

1. Demographic information and intake materials

2. Assessments, quarterly reviews, and reassessments

3. Service plan(s) with goals

4. Discharge plan

5. Releases of information and referrals

6. Correspondence

Social workers should keep psychotherapy notes in a secure location outside of client files to provide added confidentiality protection.

Often agency policies or requirements imposed by funders dictate the organizational structure for client files. However, regardless of the schema, it is essential that files are secure, up-to-date, and complete, with a format that makes locating information easy and evident.

Social workers are expected to communicate effectively, including in the preparation of written reports for external organizations. Poorly written reports or the inclusion of irrelevant or inappropriate information can have an adverse impact on a client. In the preparation of reports, including those for the courts, social workers are expected to communicate accurately and professionally. Reports generated by social workers must be taken seriously and will not be treated legitimately if there are spelling or grammatical mistakes, or the content is not based on critical thought and analysis.

Social workers also must develop reports as requested or needed, adhering to the standards of confidentiality, as failure to provide professional observations may hinder opportunities for clients. Often, social workers are reluctant to generate reports even when requested by clients and legally allowed to do so.

Critical to developing reports is the knowledge that they must be understandable and useful to recipients with a wide range of educational backgrounds and literacy levels. In addition, social workers must have a keen awareness of the purposes of reports, who they are being written for, and how they should be presented differently depending on the purposes and the audience.

Social workers should avoid irrelevant and inappropriate information, meaningless phrases or slang words, and illogical conclusions in the preparation and writing of reports. Social workers should plan what should and should not be included in the final documents prior to starting to develop them. It is also helpful to prepare drafts for later editing. Having others review draft reports can help catch errors and ensure the clarity of all material.

Social workers' competence and the value of social work services are often judged by the quality of written reports. Thus, it is essential that thought and care be taken in their preparation, and that they adhere to best practices and standards.

Administrative reports, such as annual reports from public and private social service organizations, are critical to the fulfillment of the social work mission. They provide accountability to the public about the number of people served, the services delivered, and how funds were allocated. They also may be used by social workers to document unmet needs which should be addressed.

Social workers may be required to prepare grant reports, evaluations, program proposals, and accreditation reports. While each of these documents serves a different purpose, they all require social workers to use their written communication skills and critical thinking/analysis to help clients directly or indirectly.

For example, a program proposal sets forth a plan of activities needed to begin or modify services in order to (better) meet clients' needs. It includes recommendations to organize or arrange a program in an effective and efficient manner. It describes and recommends procedures and ways to organize services for maximum client benefit. To ensure that it is implemented as intended, it must be clear, accurate, and well-written.

THE PRINCIPLES AND PROCESSES FOR DEVELOPING FORMAL DOCUMENTS (E.G., PROPOSALS, LETTERS, BROCHURES, PAMPHLETS, REPORTS, EVALUATIONS)

Social workers are expected to communicate effectively and be able to prepare formal documents. Being able to provide quality services is not the only important aspect of social work; all work is undermined by poor recording or documentation.

A good document begins with careful planning—jotting down the report's purpose and some notes about key content to be contained. Many times, drafts need to be made to ensure that the formal document meets its purpose and is written clearly, without punctuation and other mistakes. Editing is usually required before finalizing for dissemination. Typing reports is always preferred for a more professional appearance and to avoid "illegible" handwriting.

From court reports, to grant proposals, to public relations pamphlets, social workers are expected to communicate accurately with others. Poor English skills can affect the quality of reports. Social workers need to be able to write reports that can be taken "seriously" by others.

Quality of content is just as critical as spelling and punctuation. Time must be allotted to be able to do critical analyses which many formal reports require. It is easy to describe something, but much harder to indicate its significance. Repeating facts may not provide needed professional opinions and observations.

Formal documents will only count if they get to the right people. Social workers must be aware of the purpose of documents to be prepared and to whom they are being written, and then write accordingly. Social workers should avoid irrelevant, inappropriate information; meaningless phrases; and illogical conclusions.

Social workers should expect that their documents may be scrutinized. Thus, they should write just enough to make their points, but not "overdocument" with irrelevant details. Social workers should be specific and avoid characterizations such as "poor outcome," "good result," "moderate compliance," "drunk," "aggressive," and "combative." They should also avoid acronyms and abbreviations and use precise description and specific language (not "it seems," "I suppose," "it appears," "I believe," "I feel," and so on).

Social workers must prepare documents in a timely fashion and consider ethical issues that can be related to their preparation and distribution. Documents should not contain bias wording. Social workers should not alter documents after they are written unless it is appropriate to do so. Social workers must know when communication is "privileged" and should not share information with those without a need to know.

Unit IV

Professional Relationships, Values, and Ethics (27%)

Professional Values and Ethical Issues

12

LEGAL AND/OR ETHICAL ISSUES RELATED TO THE PRACTICE OF SOCIAL WORK, INCLUDING RESPONSIBILITY TO CLIENTS/CLIENT SYSTEMS, COLLEAGUES, THE PROFESSION, AND SOCIETY

Social workers frequently encounter ethical and legal issues. In most instances, ethical and legal standards complement each other. However, in some circumstances, ethical and legal standards conflict. The ethical standards for social workers are outlined in the *NASW Code of Ethics* (2008). With regard to legal mandates, social workers must be aware of five distinct sets of requirements: constitutional law, statutory law, regulatory law, court-made/common law, and executive orders.

Ethical and legal issues encountered by social workers fall into four distinct categories:

1. Actions that are compatible with both legal and ethical standards in social work (legal and ethical)

2. Actions that are neither legal nor ethical in social work according to prevailing standards (not legal and not ethical)

3. Actions that are legal, but not ethical according to prevailing standards (legal, but not ethical)

4. Actions that are ethical, but not legal according to standards and laws (ethical, but not legal)

When there are conflicts between ethical and legal standards, a social worker should identify the mandates that conflict. A social worker should also identify the individuals, groups, and organizations that are likely to be affected by the outcome of the conflict. All possible courses of action and the benefits and risks of each alternative should be considered, including the reasons supporting and in opposition to each possibility. Resolution of conflicts should not be done in a vacuum and a social worker should consult with colleagues and appropriate experts. All steps in the decision-making process should be documented. Once a decision is made, the results should be monitored and evaluated.

PROFESSIONAL VALUES AND PRINCIPLES (E.G., COMPETENCE, SOCIAL JUSTICE, INTEGRITY, AND DIGNITY AND WORTH OF THE PERSON)

The mission of the social work profession is rooted in a set of core values. These core values are the foundation of social work practice:

- Service
- Social justice
- Dignity and worth of the person
- Importance of human relationships
- Integrity
- Competence

Professional ethics are based on these basic values and guide social workers' conduct. These standards are relevant to all social workers, regardless of their professional functions, the settings in which they work, or the populations they serve.

Professional ethics are "rules" based on the core values of the profession that should be adhered to by social workers. They are statements to the general public about what they can expect from a social worker. These standards tell new social workers what is essential for practice based on the profession's core values. Social workers are judged with regard to competency based on these standards.

Professional standards are also helpful in guiding social workers when they are unsure about a course of action or conflicts arise.

The social work profession is based on the belief that every person has dignity and worth. It is essential that social workers respect this value and treat everyone in a caring and respectful fashion. Social workers should also be mindful of individual differences, as well as cultural and ethnic diversity.

Social workers should promote clients' right to self-determination and act as a resource to assist clients to address their own needs. Social workers have a dual responsibility to clients and to the broader society and must resolve any conflicts, in a socially responsible and ethical manner, that arise due to this dual mandate.

TECHNIQUES TO IDENTIFY AND RESOLVE ETHICAL DILEMMAS

An ethical dilemma is a predicament when a social worker must decide between two viable solutions that seem to have similar ethical value. Sometimes two viable ethical solutions can conflict with each other. Social workers should be aware of any conflicts between personal and professional values and deal with them responsibly.

In instances where social workers' ethical obligations conflict with agency policies or relevant laws or regulations, they should make a responsible effort to resolve the conflict in a manner that is consistent with ethical values, principles, and standards.

In order to resolve this conflict, ethical problem solving is needed.

Essential Steps in Ethical Problem Solving

1. Identify ethical standards, as defined by the professional code of ethics, that are being compromised (always go to the *NASW Code of Ethics* first—do not rely on supervisor or coworkers)

2. Determine whether there is an ethical issue or dilemma

3. Weigh ethical issues in light of key social work values and principles as defined by the *NASW Code of Ethics*

4. Suggest modifications in light of the prioritized ethical values and principles that are central to the dilemma

5. Implement modifications in light of prioritized ethical values and principles

6. Monitor for new ethical issues or dilemmas

CLIENT/CLIENT SYSTEM COMPETENCE AND SELF-DETERMINATION (E.G., FINANCIAL DECISIONS, TREATMENT DECISIONS, EMANCIPATION, AGE OF CONSENT, PERMANENCY PLANNING)

Self-determination, the concept that clients are qualified to make their own decisions about their lives, is a central concept in the social work profession. It is described in the *NASW Code of Ethics* as one of a social worker's primary ethical responsibilities. Using a strengths-based perspective, all clients are assumed to be competent to make their own decisions, including those about financial matters and treatment options.

When working with clients, there may be, at times, some concerns about their cognitive or functional abilities to perform life tasks. For example, clients who are not able to complete activities of daily living independently may need services to assist them in these areas. The need to rely on others to assist may limit clients' independence. An assessment which can assist social workers in determining assistance needed in functional life domains is the *World Health Organization Disability Assessment Schedule 2.0 (WHODAS 2.0)* which was added to the *Diagnostic and Statistical Manual of Mental Disorders* (5th ed.; *DSM-5*) in "Section III, Emerging Measures and Models," under Assessment Measures.

When limitations are not physical, but involve mental processes, there may be some unease about clients' abilities to provide consent related to financial, medical, and/or legal treatment. All those over the age of majority (adults) are presumed to be competent to provide consent unless legal proceedings have found otherwise. When clients lack the capacity to provide consent, social workers should protect clients' interests by seeking permission from an appropriate third party and informing clients in a manner consistent with the clients' level of understanding. In such instances, social workers should seek to ensure that the third party acts in a manner consistent with clients' wishes and interests. Social workers should take reasonable steps to enhance such clients' ability to give informed consent (*NASW Code of Ethics*, 2008—1.03 Informed Consent).

Emancipation and Age of Consent

Treating minors requires social workers to be well versed in state and federal laws related to consent and confidentiality. The age at which minors can obtain services without parental/guardian permission varies by state and the type of service being delivered. Minors also do not have the same legal rights to confidentiality in some instances because parents/guardians may have access to minors' records.

Even when parental/guardian consent is needed for treatment, social workers should provide explanations to minors of all elements required in a consent procedure, using language that can easily be understood. Social workers should also seek the minor's assent or willingness to participate.

During the problem-solving process, social workers treating minors must make clear to them all the limits to their self-determination imposed by legal, financial, and other constraints.

Within our society, minors do not have the same rights as adults. Emancipation is a legal process that ends the rights and responsibilities of parents or guardians over minor children. However, there can be either a partial or complete emancipation. Emancipation involves decision-making authority. Upon achieving emancipation, the minor assumes the rights, privileges, and duties of adulthood before actually reaching the "age of majority" (adulthood). An emancipated minor can enter into a contract, sue others, make health care decisions, and so on. However, the emancipated minor still has to follow other laws and still cannot get a driver's license or drink alcohol prior to the legal age to do so.

All states have laws dealing with the emancipation of minors; that is, laws that specify when and under what conditions children can become independent of their parents or guardians for important legal purposes. Approximately half of the states regulate emancipation by statutes specifically designed for that purpose. These statutes set forth the conditions required or the procedures for seeking emancipation. Statutes vary considerably from state to state, but most states allow for the possibility of court-reviewed emancipation. The age at which minors can apply for or petition for emancipation varies between states.

Under normal circumstances, a minor is presumed to become emancipated from his or her parents upon reaching the age of majority. In most states, the age of majority is 18.

TECHNIQUES FOR PROTECTING AND ENHANCING CLIENT/ CLIENT SYSTEM SELF-DETERMINATION

Social workers respect and promote the right of clients to self-determination and assist clients in their efforts to identify and clarify their goals. Social workers may limit clients' right to self-determination when, in social workers' professional judgment, clients' actions or potential actions pose serious, foreseeable, and imminent risk to themselves or others (*NASW Code of Ethics, 2008—1.02 Self-Determination*).

THE CLIENT'S/CLIENT SYSTEM'S RIGHT TO REFUSE SERVICES (E.G., MEDICATION, MEDICAL TREATMENT, COUNSELING, PLACEMENT, ETC.)

Social workers should provide services to clients only in the context of a professional relationship based, when appropriate, on valid informed consent. Social workers should use clear and understandable language to inform clients of the purpose of the services, risks related to the services, limits to services because of the requirements of a third-party payer, relevant costs, reasonable alternatives, clients' right to refuse or withdraw consent, and the time frame covered by the consent. Social workers should provide clients with an opportunity to ask questions (*NASW Code of Ethics, 2008—1.03 Informed Consent*).

In instances when clients are receiving services involuntarily, social workers should provide information about the nature and extent of services and about the extent of clients' right to refuse service (*NASW Code of Ethics, 2008—1.03 Informed Consent*).

PROFESSIONAL BOUNDARIES IN THE SOCIAL WORKER–CLIENT/ CLIENT SYSTEM RELATIONSHIP (E.G., POWER DIFFERENCES, CONFLICTS OF INTEREST, ETC.)

Many standards speak to the professional boundaries that social workers should maintain with clients. These include those related to sexual relationships, physical contact, and sexual harassment.

The standards that govern social work practice address the use of physical contact with clients. Setting clear, appropriate, and sensitive boundaries that govern physical contact are essential for professional practice (*NASW Code of Ethics, 2008—1.10 Physical Contact*). Social workers should not engage in physical contact with clients when there is a possibility of psychological harm to a client as a result of the contact (such as cradling or caressing clients).

Physical contact or other activities of a sexual nature with clients are clearly not allowed by social workers.

Social workers should under no circumstances engage in sexual activities or sexual contact with current clients, whether such contact is consensual or forced (*NASW Code of Ethics, 2008—1.09 Sexual Relationships*).

Social workers should not engage in sexual activities or sexual contact with clients' relatives or other individuals with whom clients maintain a close personal relationship when there is a risk of exploitation or potential harm to a client. Sexual activity or sexual contact with clients' relatives or other individuals with whom clients maintain a personal relationship has the potential to be harmful to a client and may make it difficult for a social worker and client to maintain appropriate professional boundaries. Social workers—not their clients, their clients' relatives, or other individuals with whom a client maintains a personal relationship—assume the full burden for setting clear, appropriate, and culturally sensitive boundaries (*NASW Code of Ethics, 2008— 1.09 Sexual Relationships*).

Social workers should not engage in sexual activities or sexual contact with former clients because of the potential for harm to a client. If social workers engage in conduct contrary to this prohibition or claim that an exception to this prohibition is warranted because of extraordinary circumstances, it is social workers—not their clients—who assume the full burden of demonstrating that the former client has not been exploited, coerced, or manipulated, intentionally or unintentionally (*NASW Code of Ethics, 2008—1.09 Sexual Relationships*).

Social workers should not provide clinical services to individuals with whom they have had a prior sexual relationship. Providing clinical services to a former sexual partner has the potential to be harmful to the individual and is likely to make it difficult for a social worker and individual to maintain appropriate professional boundaries (*NASW Code of Ethics, 2008—1.09 Sexual Relationships*).

In addition, social workers should not sexually harass clients, including sexual advances, sexual solicitation, requests for sexual favors, and other verbal or physical conduct of a sexual nature (*NASW Code of Ethics, 2008—1.11 Sexual Harassment*).

ETHICAL ISSUES RELATED TO DUAL RELATIONSHIPS

Social workers must ensure that they do not engage in dual or multiple relationships that may impact on the treatment of clients. The standards related to this area provide guidelines that can assist social workers if such relationships emerge (*NASW Code of Ethics, 2008—1.06 Conflicts of Interest*).

Social workers should be alert to and avoid conflicts of interest that interfere with the exercise of professional discretion and impartial judgment. Social workers should inform clients when a real or potential conflict of interest arises and take reasonable steps to resolve the issue in a manner that makes clients' interests primary and protects clients' interests to the greatest extent possible. In some cases, protecting clients' interests may require termination of the professional relationship with proper referral of clients (*NASW Code of Ethics, 2008—1.06 Conflicts of Interest*).

Social workers should not take unfair advantage of any professional relationship or exploit others to further their personal, religious, political, or business interests (*NASW Code of Ethics, 2008—1.06 Conflicts of Interest*).

Social workers should not engage in dual or multiple relationships with clients or former clients in which there is a risk of exploitation or potential harm to a client. In instances when dual or multiple relationships are unavoidable, social workers should take steps to protect clients and are responsible for setting clear, appropriate, and culturally sensitive boundaries. Dual or multiple relationships occur when social workers relate to clients in more than one relationship, whether professional, social, or business. Dual or multiple relationships can occur simultaneously or consecutively (*NASW Code of Ethics, 2008—1.06 Conflicts of Interest*).

When social workers provide services to two or more people who have a relationship with each other (e.g., couples, family members), social workers should clarify with all parties which individuals will be considered clients and the nature of social workers' professional obligations to the various individuals who are receiving services. Social workers who anticipate a conflict of interest among the individuals receiving services or who anticipate having to perform in potentially conflicting roles (e.g., when a social worker is asked to testify in a child custody dispute or divorce proceedings involving clients) should clarify their role with the parties involved and take appropriate action to minimize any conflict of interest (*NASW Code of Ethics, 2008—1.06 Conflicts of Interest*).

In addition, social workers engaged in evaluation or research should be alert to and avoid conflicts of interest and dual relationships with participants, should inform participants when a real or potential conflict of interest arises, and should take steps to resolve the issue in a manner that makes participants' interests primary (*NASW Code of Ethics, 2008—5.02 Evaluation and Research*).

PROFESSIONAL OBJECTIVITY IN THE SOCIAL WORKER–CLIENT/CLIENT SYSTEM RELATIONSHIP

Social worker communication should not be burdened with emotional investment; instead, social workers should be interested, genuinely concerned, and encouraging, while neither condemning nor praising.

The relationship between a social worker and a client must be productive, and must have certain characteristics. There must be mutual acceptance and trust. A client must feel he or she is understood and valued as a person, though his or her performance may be unsatisfactory. If a client feels judged, he or she will not speak freely, and his or her response will be to find ways to defend himself or herself and his or her acts.

A social worker accepts and understands a client's problems, recognizes the demands and the requirements of the situation, and assists a client to examine alternatives and potential consequences. A social worker does not tell a client what he or she should do. Only a client can and will decide, because he or she acts upon his or her feelings, insights, and/or understanding of himself or herself and the problem.

The social worker–client relationship is a social microcosm where clients' interpersonal behavioral and conditioned patterns of perceiving and feeling are manifested. This relationship allows social workers to see for themselves the interaction patterns and methods of communication that have caused difficulties for clients in their everyday lives.

Social workers should use various intervention techniques to assist clients in identifying distorted perceptions and communication patterns and replacing them with healthy, more constructive ones.

For example, social workers who observe that clients have poor boundaries with them and/or engage in behaviors that interfere with productive interactions during the problem-solving process can use limit setting. Limit setting can be facilitative because clients do not feel safe or accepted in a completely permissive environment. In addition, it is important for clients to learn the importance of appropriate boundaries.

Social workers may also observe in the helping relationship that clients are not assertive. Thus, they may use assertiveness training to teach clients how to express their positive and negative feelings and to stand up for their rights in ways that will not alienate others.

Learning self-observation skills and awareness of personal preferences, as well as assuming personal responsibility, are important components of the assertiveness training process.

One of the best ways that a social worker can assist a client when observing a maladaptive behavior is by modeling, along with role play and reinforcement, to produce behavioral change.

Social workers and clients should view the therapeutic environment as a place to learn and practice new skills and relationship patterns that can be used outside of this setting with others.

SELF-DISCLOSURE PRINCIPLES AND APPLICATIONS

The decision about whether to disclose personal information by a social worker often arises in practice because the social worker–client relationship involves the discussion of intimate topics. Some self-disclosure by a social worker may be harmless and even therapeutically useful as it can help clients connect during engagement and/or realize that they are not the only ones who have experienced similar problems.

However, some self-disclosure is exploitative, self-serving, and harmful to clients. Many boundary violations begin as a result of social workers discussing personal information with clients. Though not intended to be the start of friendships or more intimate relationships, self-disclosure by social workers, perhaps well meaning, can blur the boundaries between professional and personal relationships.

Sometimes social workers disclose personal information because they have experienced trauma or other problems which have not been adequately addressed and they are looking to connect with others in order to cope with their own challenges. Social workers may also self-disclose about problems because they think that clients can help them in some way, such as giving them legal advice if the clients are lawyers.

Sometimes clients learn personal information about social workers unexpectedly. For example, a social worker may run into a client at his or her children's activities. These events cannot be anticipated and provide personal information to a client about a social worker that he or she would prefer not to have been revealed.

Most therapeutic situations require no self-disclosure by a social worker. In fact, a client having information about a social worker's family, personal interests, and/or relationship status can be an indication of a potential boundary violation.

Prior to disclosing any information about themselves, social workers should engage in consultation or supervision about why such disclosure is being considered and why it is professionally justified in this instance. Only when it will clearly assist clients and there are no other methods for achieving the same outcome should it be contemplated. Better understanding by social workers about their own desire to self-disclose is necessary in order to prevent boundary crossings which are harmful to clients.

LEGAL AND/OR ETHICAL ISSUES REGARDING DOCUMENTATION

In addition to maintaining confidentiality of client records, there are many other obligations related to documentation that social workers must consider in order to follow legal and/or ethical standards.

It is important to document the purpose, goals, plans, services, interventions, and referrals offered and provided to clients. Assessments, evaluations, recommendations, and circumstances of termination should also be documented in the case record. Consultations with supervisors and other professionals and rationale for case-related decisions should be documented as well. Case records should include informed consent and release of information documents. All information relevant to client contact should be stated in clear, accurate terms. False, inaccurate, or misleading information in a client record is unethical and may be potentially harmful to clients and pose a liability risk to social workers. It is unethical to alter case notes after the fact. If necessary, social workers should add new notes with current dates indicating that, in review, past entries were found to be inaccurately documented and correction of those inaccuracies should be clearly stated.

In an effort to ensure continuity of service, it is imperative that client contact be documented in a timely, thorough, and accurate manner. Timely documentation is required for optimal service continuity when clients are transferred from one staff member to another in an agency or when clients are referred out of the agency to collaborating agencies. In addition, accurate and timely records are required by insurers, funding agencies, and so on. Lastly, documentation of significant aspects of client contact is also critical to protecting social workers in the event of lawsuits or ethics complaints.

Client contact documentation should include social history, assessment, treatment plans, intervention strategies, dates and times of contacts, methods of evaluation of progress, reasons for termination, documentation of informed consent and release of information signatures, contacts with all third parties, consultation with collaborating professionals, explanation of social worker's reasoning regarding decisions, recommendations, interventions, and referrals and documentation of any critical incidents. Documentation should be completed as soon as possible after contact so as to ensure accuracy and to maintain up-to-date information in the record in the event of an emergency or the social workers' absence or incapacitation that would require another professional to intervene.

Social workers should only include relevant information that is directly related to client issues for the purpose of service provided. Case records should not include subjective or speculative observation, or any extraneous and irrelevant information.

Social workers must be familiar with legal and ethical protections available for clients—including keeping psychotherapy notes in locations which are secure, but separate from clients' files to provide additional confidentiality protections.

LEGAL AND/OR ETHICAL ISSUES REGARDING TERMINATION

Social workers should terminate services to clients and professional relationships with them when such services and relationships are no longer required or no longer serve client needs or interests (*NASW Code of Ethics, 2008—1.16 Termination of Services*).

Social workers should take reasonable steps to avoid abandoning clients who are still in need of services. Social workers should withdraw services precipitously only under unusual circumstances, giving careful consideration to all factors in the situation and taking care to minimize possible adverse effects. Social workers should assist in making appropriate arrangements for continuation of services when necessary (*NASW Code of Ethics, 2008—1.16 Termination of Services*).

Social workers in fee-for-service settings may terminate services to clients who are not paying an overdue balance if the financial contractual arrangements have been made clear to a client, if a client does not pose an imminent danger to self or others, and if the clinical and other consequences of the current nonpayment have been addressed and discussed with a client (*NASW Code of Ethics, 2008—1.16 Termination of Services*).

Social workers should not terminate services to pursue a social, financial, or sexual relationship with a client (*NASW Code of Ethics, 2008—1.16 Termination of Services*).

Social workers who anticipate the termination or interruption of services to clients should notify clients promptly and seek the transfer, referral, or continuation of services in relation to client needs and preferences (*NASW Code of Ethics, 2008—1.16 Termination of Services*).

Social workers who are leaving an employment setting should inform clients of appropriate options for the continuation of services and of the benefits and risks of the options (*NASW Code of Ethics, 2008—1.16 Termination of Services*).

It is unethical to continue to treat clients when services are no longer needed or in their best interests.

Another standard also relevant to termination of services mandates that social workers should make reasonable efforts to ensure continuity of services in the event that services are interrupted by factors such as unavailability, relocation, illness, disability, or death (*NASW Code of Ethics, 2008—1.15 Interruption of Services*).

LEGAL AND/OR ETHICAL ISSUES RELATED TO DEATH AND DYING

There are many legal and/or ethical issues related to death and dying. Some legal issues involved with dying include, but are not limited to, clients' right to have informed consent to receive or refuse treatment, advance directives, and establishing living wills. Treating professionals, by law, must give clients the opportunity for informed consent. It involves explaining the options for treatment, the possible benefits as well as risks for each treatment, and any recommendations, with rationales, for one treatment over another. Furthermore, clients must know that they have the right to choose whatever treatment they want or to choose to refuse treatment. Particularly when discussing chronic or terminal illness, conditions over which there is little control over the ultimate outcome of care provided, having clients feel as much control over their treatment options as possible is of great importance.

Clients can give written directions, called advance directives, about the type of care they do and do not want to receive when dying. Advance directives are legal written agreements that will be honored in the future when people can no longer communicate their wishes. For example, advance directives can prohibit resuscitation (the act of trying to revive a person whose heart has stopped) or tube feeding, if clients wish. Advance directives may be in the form of living wills, which express clients' preferences for medical care; a durable power of attorney, in which clients designates other people to make health care decisions; or both.

Clients whose death may occur soon should also have Physician Orders for Life-Sustaining Treatment (POLST) documents. These documents are written doctors' orders that reflect preferences for medical care (particularly whether to receive care or not). The documents are kept in clients' medical records and in the home and are used to direct emergency medical personnel in following the clients' preferences. For example, these documents may contain the doctors' orders as to whether people should receive cardiopulmonary resuscitation (CPR), transportation to hospitals, or aggressive treatments (such as blood transfusions or chemotherapy) to relieve symptoms even if death is inevitable.

Although very few people actually take any steps toward causing their own death, many clients who are dying at least consider suicide. Discussing suicide may help sort out the issues and often correct certain problems that prompted consideration of suicide. Pain medicine can be prescribed if clients are uncomfortable and spiritual guidance can help clients find meaning in the remainder of their lives. Making decisions to forgo life-sustaining treatment, forgo food and fluids when near death, or take many drugs or large doses of drugs to relieve symptoms is not considered suicide. Several states have passed laws which allow those who are terminally ill to receive lethal combinations of drugs to take when they decide to die.

RESEARCH ETHICS (E.G., INSTITUTIONAL REVIEW BOARDS, USE OF HUMAN SUBJECTS, INFORMED CONSENT)

Social workers have an ethical mandate to monitor and evaluate policies, the implementation of programs, and practice interventions. They also must promote and facilitate evaluation and research to contribute to the development of knowledge. In addition to doing research themselves, social workers must keep current with emerging knowledge relevant to social work and fully use evaluation and research evidence in their professional practice.

When doing research and evaluation, social workers must consider possible consequences and should follow guidelines developed for the protection of evaluation and research participants. Social workers must protect participants from unwarranted physical or mental distress, harm, danger, or deprivation (*NASW Code of Ethics, 2008—5.02 Evaluation and Research*). Appropriate institutional review boards should be consulted.

For example, social workers engaged in evaluation or research should obtain voluntary and written informed consent from participants, when appropriate, without any implied or actual deprivation or penalty for refusal to participate or without undue inducement to participate. Informed consent should include information about the nature, extent, and duration of the participation requested and disclosure of the risks and benefits of participation in the research (*NASW Code of Ethics, 2008—5.02 Evaluation and Research*). When evaluation or research participants are incapable of giving informed consent, social workers should provide an appropriate explanation to the participants, obtain the participants' assent to the extent they are able, and obtain written consent from an appropriate proxy (*NASW Code of Ethics, 2008—5.02 Evaluation and Research*).

Social workers should never design or conduct evaluation or research that does not use consent procedures, such as certain forms of naturalistic observation and archival research, unless rigorous and responsible review of the research has found it to be justified because of its prospective scientific, educational, or applied value and unless equally effective alternative procedures that do not involve waiver of consent are not feasible (*NASW Code of Ethics, 2008—5.02 Evaluation and Research*).

Social workers should inform participants of their right to withdraw from evaluation and research at any time without penalty (*NASW Code of Ethics, 2008—5.02 Evaluation and Research*).

Social workers should take appropriate steps to ensure that participants in evaluation and research have access to appropriate supportive services (*NASW Code of Ethics, 2008—5.02 Evaluation and Research*).

Social workers engaged in evaluation or research should ensure the anonymity or confidentiality of participants and of the data obtained from them. Social workers should inform participants of any limits of confidentiality, the measures that will be taken to ensure confidentiality, and when any records containing research data will be destroyed (*NASW Code of Ethics, 2008—5.02 Evaluation and Research*).

Social workers engaged in evaluation or research should be alert to and avoid conflicts of interest and dual relationships with participants, should inform participants when a real or potential conflict of interest arises, and should take steps to resolve the issue in a manner that makes participants' interests primary (*NASW Code of Ethics, 2008—5.02 Evaluation and Research*).

ETHICAL ISSUES IN SUPERVISION AND MANAGEMENT

Social workers must follow all ethical standards when providing and receiving supervision, as well as engaging in management tasks. These include, but are not limited to, those regarding commitment to clients, self-determination, informed consent, competence, cultural competence and social diversity, conflicts of interest, privacy and confidentiality, access to records, sexual relationships, physical contact, sexual harassment, derogatory language, payments, clients who lack decision-making capacity, and interruption or termination of services.

Social workers who provide supervision should have the necessary knowledge and skill to supervise or consult appropriately, and they should do so only within their areas of competence. They should also evaluate supervisees' performance in a manner that is fair and respectful (*NASW Code of Ethics, 2008—3.01 Supervision and Consultation*). Social workers who are in managerial roles should take reasonable steps to ensure that adequate agency resources are available to provide appropriate staff supervision (*NASW Code of Ethics, 2008—3.07 Administration*).

Social workers who provide supervision are responsible for setting clear, appropriate, and culturally sensitive boundaries. They should not engage in any dual or multiple relationships with supervisees when there is a risk of exploitation of or potential harm to the supervisee (*NASW Code of Ethics, 2008—3.01 Supervision and Consultation*).

Social workers in managerial roles should advocate within and outside their agencies for adequate resources to meet clients' needs and ensure resource allocation procedures are open, fair, and nondiscriminatory. Social work managers should ensure that working environments are consistent with the *NASW Code of Ethics* and eliminate conditions which are not (*NASW Code of Ethics, 2008—3.07 Administration*).

Sometimes in practice, ethical issues can arise related to the payment of services. These standards indicate what rules social workers should follow in these situations.

When setting fees, social workers should ensure that the fees are fair, reasonable, and commensurate with the services performed. Consideration should be given to clients' ability to pay (*NASW Code of Ethics, 2008—1.13 Payment for Services*).

Social workers should avoid accepting goods or services from clients as payment for professional services. Bartering arrangements, particularly involving services, create the potential for conflicts of interest, exploitation, and inappropriate boundaries in social workers' relationships with clients. Social workers should explore and may participate in bartering only in very limited circumstances when it can be demonstrated that such arrangements are an accepted practice among professionals in the local community, considered to be essential for the provision of services, negotiated without coercion, and entered into at a client's initiative and with a client's informed consent. Social workers who accept goods or services from clients as payment for professional services assume the full burden of demonstrating that this arrangement will not be detrimental to a client or the professional relationship (*NASW Code of Ethics, 2008—1.13 Payment for Services*).

Social workers should not solicit a private fee or other remuneration for providing services to clients who are entitled to such available services through social workers' employers or agencies (*NASW Code of Ethics, 2008—1.13 Payment for Services*).

Social workers should obtain information on procedures for using insurance coverage when a client wants to use an employee benefit package for behavioral health services.

Confidentiality

13

THE PRINCIPLES AND PROCESSES OF OBTAINING INFORMED CONSENT

In instances when clients are not literate or have difficulty understanding the primary language used in the practice setting, social workers should take steps to ensure clients' comprehension. This may include providing clients with a detailed verbal explanation or arranging for a qualified interpreter or translator whenever possible (*NASW Code of Ethics, 2008—1.03 Informed Consent*).

In instances when clients lack the capacity to provide informed consent, social workers should protect clients' interests by seeking permission from an appropriate third party, informing clients consistent with clients' level of understanding. In such instances, social workers should seek to ensure that the third party acts in a manner consistent with the clients' wishes and interests. Social workers should take reasonable steps to enhance such clients' ability to give informed consent (*NASW Code of Ethics, 2008—1.03 Informed Consent*).

Social workers who provide services via electronic media (such as computer, telephone, radio, and television) should inform recipients of the limitations and risks associated with such services (*NASW Code of Ethics, 2008—1.03 Informed Consent*).

Social workers should obtain clients' informed consent before audiotaping or videotaping clients or permitting observation of services to clients by a third party (*NASW Code of Ethics, 2008—1.03 Informed Consent*).

When social workers act on behalf of clients who lack the capacity to make informed decisions, social workers should take reasonable steps to safeguard the interests and rights of those clients (*NASW Code of Ethics, 2008—1.14 Clients Who Lack Decision-Making Capacity*).

In order to obtain informed consent, social workers must use clear and understandable language related to service purpose, risks, limits due to third-party payers, time frame, and right of refusal or withdrawal. If the client lacks capacity or is a minor, informed **consent** must be obtained by a responsible third party and **assent** must be obtained from the client.

THE USE OF CLIENT/CLIENT SYSTEM RECORDS

Social workers should provide clients with reasonable access to their records. Social workers who are concerned that clients' access to their records could cause serious misunderstanding or harm to a client should provide assistance in interpreting the records and consultation with a client regarding the records. **Social workers should limit clients' access to their records, or portions of their records, only in exceptional circumstances when there is compelling evidence that such access would cause serious harm to a client.** Both clients' requests and the rationale for withholding some or all of the records should be documented in clients' files (*NASW Code of Ethics, 2008—1.08 Access to Records*).

When providing clients with access to their records, social workers should take steps to protect the confidentiality of other individuals identified or discussed in such records.

The *NASW Code of Ethics* **states that a social worker should only solicit information essential for providing services (minimum necessary to achieve purpose).**

LEGAL AND/OR ETHICAL ISSUES REGARDING CONFIDENTIALITY, INCLUDING ELECTRONIC INFORMATION SECURITY

Social workers should respect clients' right to privacy. Social workers should not solicit private information from clients unless it is essential to providing services or conducting social work evaluation or research. Once private information is shared, standards of confidentiality apply (*NASW Code of Ethics, 2008–1.07 Privacy and Confidentiality*).

Social workers may disclose confidential information when appropriate with valid consent from a client or a person legally authorized to consent on behalf of a client (*NASW Code of Ethics, 2008—1.07 Privacy and Confidentiality*).

Social workers should protect the confidentiality of all information obtained in the course of professional service, except for compelling professional reasons. The general expectation that social workers will keep information confidential does not apply when disclosure is necessary to prevent serious, foreseeable, and imminent harm to a client or other identifiable person. In all instances, social workers should disclose the least amount of confidential information necessary to achieve the desired purpose; only information that is directly relevant to the purpose for which the disclosure is made should be revealed (*NASW Code of Ethics, 2008—1.07 Privacy and Confidentiality*).

Social workers should inform clients, to the extent possible, about the disclosure of confidential information and the potential consequences, when feasible, before the disclosure is made. This applies whether social workers disclose confidential information on the basis of a legal requirement or client consent (*NASW Code of Ethics, 2008—1.07 Privacy and Confidentiality*).

Social workers should discuss with clients and other interested parties the nature of confidentiality and limitations of clients' right to confidentiality. Social workers should review circumstances with clients where confidential information may be requested and where disclosure of confidential information may be legally required. This discussion should occur as soon as possible in a social worker–client relationship and as needed throughout the course of the relationship (*NASW Code of Ethics, 2008–1.07 Privacy and Confidentiality*).

When social workers provide counseling services to families, couples, or groups, social workers should seek agreement among the parties involved concerning each individual's right to confidentiality and obligation to preserve the confidentiality of information shared by others. Social workers should inform participants in family, couples, or group counseling that social workers cannot guarantee that all participants will honor such agreements (*NASW Code of Ethics, 2008—1.07 Privacy and Confidentiality*).

Social workers should inform clients involved in family, couples, marital, or group counseling of a social worker's, employer's, and agency's policy concerning a social worker's disclosure of confidential information among the parties involved in the counseling (*NASW Code of Ethics, 2008—1.07 Privacy and Confidentiality*).

Social workers should not disclose confidential information to third-party payers unless clients have authorized such disclosure (*NASW Code of Ethics, 2008—1.07 Privacy and Confidentiality*).

Social workers should not discuss confidential information in any setting unless privacy can be ensured. Social workers should not discuss confidential information in public or semipublic areas such as hallways, waiting rooms, elevators, and restaurants (*NASW Code of Ethics, 2008—1.07 Privacy and Confidentiality*).

Social workers should protect the confidentiality of clients during legal proceedings to the extent permitted by law. When a court of law or other legally authorized body orders social workers to disclose confidential or privileged information without a client's consent and such disclosure could cause harm to a client, social workers should request that the court withdraw the order or limit the order as narrowly as possible or maintain the records under seal, unavailable for public inspection (*NASW Code of Ethics, 2008—1.07 Privacy and Confidentiality*).

A subpoena and court order are not the same. When receiving a subpoena, a social worker should respond and claim privilege, but not turn over records unless the court issues a subsequent order to do so. As stated, when a social worker gets a court order, he or she should try to limit its scope and/or ask that the records be sealed.

Social workers should protect the confidentiality of clients when responding to requests from members of the media (*NASW Code of Ethics, 2008—1.07 Privacy and Confidentiality*).

Social workers should protect the confidentiality of clients' written and electronic records and other sensitive information. Social workers should take reasonable steps to ensure that clients' records are stored in a secure location and that clients' records are not available to others who are not authorized to have access (*NASW Code of Ethics, 2008—1.07 Privacy and Confidentiality*).

Social workers should take precautions to ensure and maintain the confidentiality of information transmitted to other parties through the use of computers, electronic mail, facsimile machines, telephones and telephone answering machines, and other electronic or computer technology. Disclosure of identifying information should be avoided whenever possible (*NASW Code of Ethics, 2008—1.07 Privacy and Confidentiality*).

Social workers should transfer or dispose of clients' records in a manner that protects clients' confidentiality and is consistent with state statutes governing records and social work licensure (*NASW Code of Ethics, 2008—1.07 Privacy and Confidentiality*).

Social workers should take reasonable precautions to protect client confidentiality in the event of a social worker's termination of practice, incapacitation, or death (*NASW Code of Ethics, 2008—1.07 Privacy and Confidentiality*).

Social workers should not disclose identifying information when discussing clients for teaching or training purposes unless a client has consented to disclosure of confidential information (*NASW Code of Ethics, 2008—1.07 Privacy and Confidentiality*).

Social workers should not disclose identifying information when discussing clients with consultants unless a client has consented to disclosure of confidential information or there is a compelling need for such disclosure (*NASW Code of Ethics, 2008–1.07 Privacy and Confidentiality*).

Social workers should protect the confidentiality of deceased clients consistent with the preceding standards (*NASW Code of Ethics, 2008–1.07 Privacy and Confidentiality*).

If a client sues a social worker, a social worker has the right to defend himself/herself and may need to release client information as part of this defense. A social worker should limit this disclosure only to information required for defense.

Confidentiality of minor records can be challenging, especially if a parent wants access to them and/or consents to their release. Social workers must be knowledgeable about ethical standards and laws that relate to the protection and release of minor records. Parents may have access to these records depending upon the age of the minor and the type of treatment or setting. Social workers treating minors with parents who may have joint or limited custody must also be aware of the rights of all parties to access and/or consent to their release.

LEGAL AND/OR ETHICAL ISSUES REGARDING MANDATORY REPORTING (E.G., ABUSE, THREAT OF HARM, IMPAIRED PROFESSIONALS, ETC.)

Social workers are required to disclose confidential information, sometimes against a client's wishes, to comply with mandatory reporting laws. Laws not only require social workers to report suspected cases of abuse and neglect, but there can be varying levels of civil and criminal liability for failing to do so.

This mandate causes ethical issues for social workers who have a commitment to their clients' interests as well as a responsibility to the larger society.

The majority of all reports of abuse and/or neglect came from professionals including medical personnel, law enforcement agents, educators, lawyers, and social workers.

Social workers who have direct knowledge of a social work colleague's impairment that is due to personal problems, psychosocial distress, substance abuse, or mental health difficulties and that interferes with practice effectiveness should consult with that colleague when feasible and assist the colleague in taking remedial action. Social workers who believe that a social work colleague's impairment interferes with practice effectiveness and that the colleague has not taken adequate steps to address the impairment should take action through appropriate channels established by employers, agencies, NASW, licensing and regulatory bodies, and other professional organizations (*NASW Code of Ethics, 2008—2.09 Impairment of Colleagues*).

Professional Development and Use of Self

14

THE COMPONENTS OF THE SOCIAL WORKER–CLIENT/CLIENT SYSTEM RELATIONSHIP

A social worker–client relationship is an emotional or connecting bond. The relationship is the communication bridge whereby messages pass over the bridge with greater or lesser difficulty, depending on the nature of the emotional connection or alliance.

A positive relationship is an important tool of helping. Social workers must create a warm, accepting, trustworthy, and dependable relationship with clients.

In working with a client, a social worker must convey a sense of respect for a client's individuality, as well as his or her right and capacity for self-determination and for being fully involved in the helping process from beginning to end.

The most consistent factor associated with beneficial outcomes of a helping relationship is a positive relationship between a social worker and a client, but other factors, such as a social worker's competence and the motivation and involvement of a client, are also influential.

THE SOCIAL WORKER'S ROLE IN THE PROBLEM-SOLVING PROCESS

Social worker roles in the problem-solving process include consultant, advocate, case manager, catalyst, broker, mediator, facilitator, instructor, mobilizer, resource allocator, and so on.

Key social work practice roles include:

Advocate

In the advocate role, social workers champion the rights of others with the goal of empowering the client system being served. Social workers speak on behalf of clients when others will not listen or when clients are unable to do so. Social workers have a particular responsibility to advocate on behalf of those disempowered by society.

Broker

In the role of broker, social workers are responsible for identifying, locating, and linking client systems to needed resources in a timely fashion. Once client needs are assessed and potential services identified, the broker assists in choosing the most appropriate service option and assists in negotiating the terms of service delivery. Social workers are concerned with the quality, quantity, and accessibility of services.

Change Agent

A change agent participates as part of a group or organization seeking to improve or restructure some aspect of service provision. A change agent, working with others, uses the problem-solving model to identify the problem, solicit input, and plan for change. A change agent acts in a coordinated manner to achieve planned change at multiple levels that helps to shift the focus of institutional resources to meet identified goals.

Counselor

The role of the counselor focuses on improving social functioning. Social workers help client systems articulate their needs, clarify their problems, explore resolution strategies, and apply intervention strategies to develop and expand the capacities of client systems to deal with problems more effectively. A key function of this role is to empower clients by affirming their personal strengths and their capacities to deal with problems more effectively.

Mediator

When dispute resolution is needed in order to accomplish goals, social workers will carry out the role of mediator. Social workers intervene in disputes between parties to help them find compromises, reconcile differences, and reach mutually satisfying agreements. The mediator takes a neutral stance among the involved parties.

The primary role of social workers is to act as a resource—assuming various roles depending upon the nature of client problems.

METHODS TO CLARIFY THE ROLES AND RESPONSIBILITIES OF THE SOCIAL WORKER AND CLIENT/CLIENT SYSTEM IN THE INTERVENTION PROCESS

A social worker can be supportive in these roles, but is not supposed to be the client's support system. Instead, a social worker should assist the client to mobilize or build his or her own natural supports. People generally like to give advice. It gives them the feeling of being competent and important. Hence, social workers may easily fall into this inappropriate role without taking into account the abilities, the fears, and the interests of clients and/or their circumstances.

Social workers should also not be insensitive to clients' resistance. When a client does not claim any difficulties, is unable or refuses to talk, explains that it is someone else's fault, and/or denies what has happened, a social worker may try to argue or in other ways exert pressure. This response tends to increase a client's resistance. This approach does nothing for a client.

A social worker may also confuse the situation and hinder clarification of the problem. In an effort to establish a relationship, a social worker may overpraise or fail to confront a client. A client must look at his or her own role in the situation and recognize his or her own limitations.

THE PRINCIPLES AND TECHNIQUES FOR BUILDING AND MAINTAINING A HELPING RELATIONSHIP

Helping is based on acceptance of a client's situation and the ability of him or her to make changes only if desired. In a helping relationship, a social worker is trying to constructively assist a client—that is, to have an impact on or to influence his or her thinking and acting. The influence is further presumed to be in the direction of increasing the autonomy, understanding, effectiveness, and skill of a client.

Helping is distinguished from the more common concepts of advice giving, reprimanding, or punishing. These often involve threats and seldom result in more than outward conformity or superficial change. They generally do not increase strength or willingness and ability to carry responsibility.

The core of the helping process is the relationship between a social worker and a client.

The relationship between a social worker and a client is expressed through interaction. This interaction is commonly thought of in terms of verbal communication, which is natural, because the greater part of treatment consists of talking. However, nonverbal behavior is also very important. Body posture, gestures, facial expressions, eye movements, and other reactions often express feelings and attitudes more clearly than do spoken words. It is often for these reasons that a social worker must be aware of his or her own feelings, attitudes, and responses, as well as those of a client if he or she is to understand what is taking place and be of assistance.

A social worker cannot be useful in helping others unless he or she understands and is willing to accept the difficulties that all human beings encounter in trying to meet their needs. A social worker must know that the potential for all the weaknesses and strengths known to humanity exists at some level in every person. Social workers must also understand that human beings become more capable of dealing with their problems as they feel more adequate. Social workers recognize positive, as well as negative, aspects of a client, which will influence efforts to change and successful achievement of goals.

The interaction between a social worker and a client that takes place about a problem involves and is affected by the relationship between the two persons. Human beings act in terms of their feelings, attitudes, and understandings; hence, these must be taken into account and explored if the helping process is to result in change. Both a social worker and a client have objectives; a social worker's perceived objective is to be of assistance. Clarification and definition of these objectives often become important parts of the helping process. Both a social worker and a client have a degree of power (i.e., ability to influence the situation and the results).

The therapeutic process calls for several basic conditions.

There must be trust with a social worker. Unless this condition exists, facts will be withheld and there will be no real exploration of problems. Trust grows as clients talk about themselves and their circumstances, revealing things they do not ordinarily disclose, and discovering that social workers do not condemn them. Trust does not come quickly.

There must be recognition that *the therapeutic process is a joint exploration.* Both a social worker and client must be willing to examine problems, attitudes, and feelings.

There must be listening on both sides. However, a social worker must listen more than a client does. There is no movement when a social worker is doing all the talking and a client listens passively. A social worker must behave in a manner that makes it easier for a client to speak freely by listening attentively, by *accepting what is said in a nonjudgmental manner*, and by giving occasional support or encouragement.

A social worker may be encouraging by simply repeating reflectively or paraphrasing what a client has said. A social worker may, without other comment, say, "Tell me more" or show acceptance when a client reveals ideas, attitudes, or behaviors that are generally viewed unfavorably. A social worker may also point out that other persons also have such attitudes or make similar mistakes. By assisting a client to speak more freely, a social worker not only furthers mutual exploration of the problem, but also frees a client of anxieties that stand in the way of readiness to accept suggestions. A social worker is also obligated to respect the confidence a client has placed in him or her and to refrain from sharing the information with others.

Process of Engagement in Social Work Practice

The beginning of the problem-solving process includes activities of a social worker and a client to be helped that are directed at (a) becoming engaged with each other (engagement), (b) assessing a client's situation in order to select appropriate goals and the means of attaining them (assessment), and (c) planning how to employ these means (planning). During engagement, the limits to confidentiality must be explicitly stated at the beginning of this stage. Social workers must also explain their roles and how they can assist clients in addressing their problems.

It is important to consider how a client feels about coming for help and to deal with any negative feelings a client may feel (particularly if a client is involuntarily seeking help). A social worker must be open to discussing these feelings openly, because very little in a client can be changed until negative feelings are addressed. If a social worker is empathic with a client, it may be possible to find a common ground between what a client wishes and what a social worker can legitimately do.

A social worker and a client establish a therapeutic alliance in which a client views himself or herself as an ally of a social worker. A working alliance or a willingness by a client to work with a social worker should be established. A working alliance is sometimes referred to as a treatment alliance.

A social worker should express hopefulness that change can occur.

Resistance may occur during this stage. If clients are resistant to engage, social workers should clarify the process or specify what will happen and discuss this ambivalence.

THE CONCEPT OF ACCEPTANCE AND EMPATHY IN THE SOCIAL WORKER–CLIENT/CLIENT SYSTEM RELATIONSHIP

Empathic understanding involves being nonjudgmental, accepting, and genuine.

Empathic Communication

- Establishes rapport with clients—empathic communication is one means of bridging the gap between a social worker and client
- Starts where a client is and stays attuned to a client throughout the encounter (being perceptive to changes in frame of mind)
- Increases the level at which clients explore themselves and their problems
- Responds to a client's nonverbal messages (a social worker can observe body language and make explicit a client's feelings)
- Decreases defensiveness and engages a client in processing and testing new information
- Defuses anger that represents obstacles to progress

Empathic responding encourages more rational discussion and sets the stage for problem solving. For those clients who have learned to cope with feelings of helplessness and frustration by becoming angry and/or violent, an empathic response may be the first step in engaging in helping relationships.

THE DYNAMICS OF POWER AND TRANSPARENCY IN THE SOCIAL WORKER–CLIENT/CLIENT SYSTEM RELATIONSHIP

Social workers have power and privileges associated with their roles, titles, and education. Being conscious of these privileges is critical because there is a responsibility to challenge hierarchical assumptions and power dynamics inherent in social worker–client relationships. Social workers should use egalitarian and collaborative approaches that give clients choices, decision-making power, and opportunities for honest feedback.

If social workers are transparent and honest about their positions of privilege, they help to undercut the power differentials. Transparency about the process and intent of social work interventions is essential. Role expectations should be discussed and power differences should be acknowledged.

Transparency and power are linked. If clients are not informed about what is going to occur in each stage of the problem-solving process and do not understand the theoretical models which help explain their situations, they cannot be full participants in the change process. Thus, transparency or the provision of all available information is the underpinning of the therapeutic relationship. If social workers deliberately withhold observations or knowledge from clients, they are reinforcing the power differential which inherently exists and disempowering clients. This is not helpful to clients or in accordance with the values of social work practice.

THE IMPACT OF TRANSFERENCE AND COUNTERTRANSFERENCE IN THE SOCIAL WORKER–CLIENT/CLIENT SYSTEM RELATIONSHIP

Transference refers to redirection of a client's feelings for a significant person to a social worker. Transference was first described by Sigmund Freud, who acknowledged its importance for a better understanding of a client's feelings.

Transference is often manifested as an erotic attraction toward a social worker, but can be seen in many other forms such as rage, hatred, mistrust, parentification, extreme dependence, or even placing a social worker in an esteemed status.

When Freud initially encountered transference in his therapy with clients, he felt it was an obstacle to treatment success. But what he learned was that the analysis of the transference was actually the work that needed to be done. The focus in psychoanalysis is, in large part, a social worker and a client recognizing the transference relationship and exploring the relationship's meaning.

Since the transference between a client and a social worker happens on an unconscious level, a social worker doing psychoanalysis uses transference to reveal unresolved conflicts a client has with childhood figures.

Countertransference is defined as redirection of a social worker's feelings toward a client, or more generally as a social worker's emotional entanglement with a client. A social worker's recognition of his or her own countertransference is nearly as critical as understanding a client's transference. Not only does this help a social worker regulate his or her emotions in the therapeutic relationship, but it also gives a social worker valuable insight into what a client is attempting to elicit in him or her.

For example, a social worker who is sexually attracted to a client must understand this as countertransference, and look at how a client may be eliciting this reaction. Once it has been identified, a social worker can ask a client what his or her feelings are toward a social worker, and/or explore how they relate to unconscious motivations, desires, or fears.

THE IMPACT OF DOMESTIC, INTIMATE PARTNER, AND OTHER VIOLENCE ON THE HELPING RELATIONSHIP

A type of trauma is that resulting from intimate partner abuse (heterosexual, gay, lesbian, dating, married, cohabitating). The common thread in all abusive

344 IV PROFESSIONAL RELATIONSHIPS, VALUES, AND ETHICS (27%)

relationships is the abuser's need for power and control over his or her partner. Domestic violence occurs across all racial, cultural, and socioeconomic groups and can involve physical, sexual, psychological/emotional, and economic/financial abuse.

Signs of abuse are varied.

- Suspicious injury (not consistent with history of injury, unusual locations, various stages of healing, bites, repeated minor injuries, delay in seeking treatment, old scars, or new injuries from weapons)
- Somatic complaints without a specific diagnosis (such as chronic pain—head, abdomen, pelvis, back, or neck)
- Behavioral presentation (crying, minimizing, no emotional expression, anxious or angry, defensive, fearful eye contact)
- Controlling/coercive behavior of partner (partner hovers, overly concerned, won't leave client unattended, client defers to partner, fear of speaking in front of partner, or disagreeing with him or her)

Cycle of Violence

Phase I:	Tension building
Phase II:	Battering incident—shortest period of the cycle, lasts a brief time
Phase III:	"Loving–contrition" (absence of tension or "honeymoon" phase)—batterer offers profuse apologies; assures attacks will never happen again; and declares love and caring

Batterers often learn abusive behavior from their families of origin, peers, and media, as well as from personal experience of being abused as children. Batterers view their victims as "possessions" and treat them like objects. Victims are dehumanized to justify the battering. Batterers are very self-centered and feel entitled to have their needs (physical, emotional, sexual) met "no matter what." Batterers have control over their impulses and give themselves permission to be abusive.

Some of the reasons that clients stay in abusive relationships are:

- Hope that the abuser will change. If the batterer is in a treatment program, the client hopes the behavior will change; leaving represents a loss of the committed relationship
- Isolation and lack of support systems
- Fears that no one will believe the seriousness of abuse experienced
- Abuser puts up barricades so client won't leave the relationship (escalates threats of violence, threatens to kill, withholds support, threatens to seek custody of children, threatens suicide, etc.)

- Dangers of leaving may pose a greater danger than remaining with the batterer
- Client may not have the economic resources to survive on his or her own

Leaving is a process. Over time, the client comes to the conclusion that the abuser will not change; each time the client tries to leave, he or she gathers more information that is helpful.

Social exchange theory is based on the idea of totaling potential benefits and losses to determine behavior. People make decisions about relationships based on the amount of rewards they receive from them. A client remains in an abusive relationship because the high cost of leaving lowers the attractiveness (outweighs the benefits) of the best alternative. A client will leave when the best alternative promises a better life (rewards outweigh the costs).

Guidelines for Interventions

- **According to most literature on domestic violence, traditional marital/couples therapy is not appropriate in addressing abuse in the family. It puts victims in greater danger of further abuse.**
- Medical needs and safety are priorities. Note: Consider domestic violence in the context of Maslow's hierarchy of needs.
- In working with a victim of abuse, trust is a major issue in establishing a therapeutic alliance.

THE DYNAMICS OF DIVERSITY IN THE SOCIAL WORKER–CLIENT/ CLIENT SYSTEM RELATIONSHIP

A social worker's self-awareness about his or her own attitudes, values, and beliefs about cultural differences and a willingness to acknowledge cultural differences are critical factors in working with diverse populations. A social worker is responsible for bringing up and addressing issues of cultural difference with a client and is also ethically responsible for being culturally competent by obtaining the appropriate knowledge, skills, and experience.

Social workers should:

1. Move from being culturally unaware to being aware of their own heritage and the heritage of others

2. Value and celebrate differences of others rather than maintaining an ethnocentric stance

3. Have an awareness of personal values and biases and how they may influence relationships with clients

4. Demonstrate comfort with racial and cultural differences between themselves and clients

5. Have an awareness of personal and professional limitations

6. Acknowledge their own racial attitudes, beliefs, and feelings

Although experiences will differ, many individuals have experienced racism, oppression, or discrimination in some form and are very sensitive to being treated with disrespect or to being exploited. They will be skeptical and cautious about seeking help for fear of being mistreated or misunderstood.

Trust is an important element in establishing a therapeutic alliance. Clients want to know if a social worker can be trusted and is competent to help them solve their problems. Clients regard and treat social workers as experts and authority figures.

Matching clients and social workers of the same race and ethnicity may decrease dropout rates and increase utilization of services, but the quality of the therapeutic relationship remains the most important factor in predicting the outcome of treatment.

Clients will ascribe credibility to a social worker using their cultural norms as a reference point (i.e., role, age, education, gender).

Understanding the cultural heritage of a client is important to working with him or her. Conflict between older and younger generations is often a common occurrence. Younger members assume the values and traditions of the majority, which can conflict with the more traditional values of the original culture that are held by an older generation.

Power and role reversals that threaten and undermine parental authority and leadership can also occur in families as parents rely on younger members of the family to become cultural interpreters. Role reversals may also occur if a woman becomes the main breadwinner because her husband cannot find employment. In a traditional marital relationship with strict gender roles, men may have difficulty dealing with this role reversal.

Although no culture condones child abuse or neglect, there are cultural variations about what constitutes child abuse and neglect, as well as acceptable disciplinary measures.

There are greater incidences of domestic violence in cultures where women have lower statuses than men.

Cultural groups have various explanations for an illness, particularly mental illness, and also have different ideas of what will help (often depends on the identified cause of the illness).

Impact of Diversity in Styles of Communicating

Communication styles may be strongly influenced by culture, race, and/or ethnicity.

Communication is far more than an exchange of words. Facial expressions, hand gestures, posture, eye contact, and even silence are constantly sending messages about attitudes, emotions, status, and relationships.

Nonverbal cues are critical. For example, personal space or the distance two people keep between themselves in order to feel comfortable is culturally based. Personal space may be influenced by gender or status. It can also be influenced by intimacy of a relationship.

Eye contact is also influenced by culture. For some, direct eye contact is very brief, with the gaze then sliding away to the side, especially with superiors or members of the opposite sex, whereas others may engage in more direct eye contact.

Speaking volume can be nearly as important as the words themselves. Normal baseline volumes also vary among cultures and among individuals in these cultures.

The appropriateness of physical touch is also important to understand. In some cultures, individuals rarely touch each other, limiting themselves to handshakes and occasional pats on the shoulder or arm in business relationships, or hugs in closer friendships. In other cultures, however, physical touch, such as hugging, is part of many interactions, even those that are casual.

Smiling, facial expressions, time, and silence are also communication factors that vary among those from different cultures, races, or ethnic groups.

In order to be effective with those from diverse cultural, racial, and/or ethnic groups, social workers must:

1. Recognize direct and indirect communication styles

2. Demonstrate sensitivity to nonverbal cues

3. Generate a wide variety of verbal and nonverbal responses and strategies

4. Use language that is culturally appropriate

5. Identify his or her own professional style and recognize limitations and strengths

6. Identify and reduce barriers that will inhibit engagement with persons who are culturally different

THE EFFECT OF THE CLIENT'S DEVELOPMENTAL LEVEL ON THE SOCIAL WORKER–CLIENT RELATIONSHIP

Social workers must be sensitive to the developmental levels of clients. Development levels refer to the functional abilities at which clients find themselves at given moments. The problem-solving process must take these developmental levels into account. Social workers should not rely on chronological age as clients may be functioning at very different developmental levels. Social workers must use engagement and intervention strategies which are appropriate given clients' developmental functioning. Assessments should include determining the psychosocial levels of clients. Clients' development may be delayed or advanced across all domains or inconsistent with some areas more behind than others. Understanding causes for discrepancies between chronological and developmental age also may be important for insight into clients' problems.

SOCIAL WORKER SELF-CARE PRINCIPLES AND TECHNIQUES

Self-care is essential for social workers so that they can practice effectively and honor their professional and personal commitments. Self-care refers to activities and practices that are done on a regular basis to reduce stress and maintain and enhance short- and longer-term health and well-being.

Practicing self-care helps social workers:

- **Identify and manage the general challenges** that hard-working professionals face, such as the potential for stress and burnout or interpersonal difficulties
- **Become aware of personal vulnerabilities** such as the potential for retraumatization (if trauma history exists), vicarious or secondary traumatization (if working with individuals who report their own traumatic experiences), and compassion fatigue (which can be developed from a combination of burnout and vicarious traumatization)
- **Achieve balance in life** by maintaining and enhancing the attention paid to different domains of life in a way that meets personal needs

Self-care is not simply about limiting or addressing professional stressors. It is also about **enhancing overall well-being**. There are common aims to almost all self-care efforts including:

- Taking care of physical and psychological health
- Managing and reducing stress
- Honoring emotional and spiritual needs

- Fostering and sustaining relationships
- Achieving an equilibrium between meeting personal needs and school/work demands

BURNOUT, SECONDARY TRAUMA, AND COMPASSION FATIGUE

Burnout, secondary trauma, and compassion fatigue have been used interchangeably to express adverse impacts that result from constantly working with those who are experiencing problems or trauma or are in crisis.

Burnout is a state of physical, emotional, psychological, and/or spiritual exhaustion. It can be manifested by cynicism or a lack of satisfaction in working with clients to resolve their problems. Burnout is characterized by emotional fatigue and feeling inadequate due to not being able to change clients' life circumstances. Many factors can contribute to burnout, including client, organizational, and/or contextual variables.

Secondary trauma relates to the behaviors and emotions that result from knowledge about traumatizing events experienced by clients and the stress resulting from helping or wanting to help them. Secondary trauma results from engaging in empathic relationships with clients who have had traumatic experiences and witnessing the effects of those experiences. The symptoms of secondary trauma mirror those experienced by the primary victim of trauma, including, but not limited to, insomnia, chronic irritability or angry outbursts, fatigue, difficulty concentrating, and/or avoidance.

Compassion fatigue is best defined as a syndrome consisting of a combination of the symptoms of secondary trauma and burnout. It usually represents the overall experience of emotional and physical fatigue that social workers can experience due to the prevalent use of empathy when treating clients who are distraught and experiencing emotional pain. Social workers also encounter bureaucratic hurdles that exacerbate agency stress and upset the balance between practice and administrative demands. Much like burnout, compassion fatigue tends to occur cumulatively over time, whereas secondary trauma may have a more immediate onset. Social workers may develop empathy or compassion fatigue as they repeatedly see little or no improvement in client situations. Social workers who treat victims of trauma can find that secondary trauma may contribute to overall compassion fatigue. However, social workers who do not treat those who have experienced trauma may experience compassion fatigue without experiencing secondary trauma.

In order to manage the effects of burnout and secondary trauma, and in an attempt to prevent compassion fatigue, social workers must engage in *self-care* activities which should include, but not be limited to, receiving support from mentors or peers, obtaining therapy, engaging in relaxation and personal endeavors that are nonprofessional activities, and balancing work demands with one's personal life.

THE INFLUENCE OF THE SOCIAL WORKER'S OWN VALUES AND BELIEFS ON THE SOCIAL WORKER–CLIENT/CLIENT SYSTEM RELATIONSHIP

Social workers must recognize values that may inhibit the therapeutic relationship.

1. **Universalism—There is one acceptable norm or standard for everyone** versus there are other valid standards that have been developed by people that they have determined to be most useful to them.

2. **Dichotomous "either-or" thinking; differences are inferior, wrong, bad** versus differences are just different and coexist.

3. **Heightened ability/value on separating, categorizing, numbering, "left-brain"** versus "right-brain" or "whole picture." Mental activity is highly valued to the exclusion of physical and spiritual experiences. Persons are studied in isolation, not as part of a group or interrelated with their environment.

4. **High value on control, constraint, restraint** versus value on flexibility, emotion/feelings, expressiveness, spirituality. What cannot be controlled and definitively defined is deemed nonexistent, unimportant, unscientific, or deviant/inferior. Reality is defined with the assumption of objectivity; subjective reality is viewed as invalid because it cannot be consistently replicated by many people.

5. **Measure of self comes from outside, and is only in contrast to others** versus value comes from within—you are worthwhile because you were born, and you strive to live a life that is in harmony with others and the environment. Worth is measured by accumulation of wealth or status (outside measures)—therefore, one can only feel good if one is better than someone else, or accumulates more than someone else, or has a higher status.

6. **Power is defined as "power over" others, mastery over environment** versus "power through" or in harmony with others; by sharing power, power can be expanded, and each becomes more powerful.

THE INFLUENCE OF THE SOCIAL WORKER'S OWN VALUES AND BELIEFS ON INTERDISCIPLINARY COLLABORATION

Social workers are increasingly recognized as beneficial members of interdisciplinary teams in addressing the complex needs of clients. A social worker may be on the team because he or she is a direct service provider (counselor, case manager), an administrator, and/or a consultant.

Interdisciplinary teams can compromise those from many professions including law, psychology, and education. When working collaboratively, social workers can work "hand-in-hand" or "side-by-side" with others. In the former, social workers and others work together on most issues, whereas in the latter, each discipline works separately to accomplish what needs to be done.

Often when working with others, there can be potential conflicts in both personal and professional values of the team members involved. In order to mitigate these conflicts, it is important to:

- Outline the parameters that will govern the functioning of the collaborative team, including frequency of contact, other forms of communication, delineation of responsibilities, and leadership positions
- Understand and define the roles of those who are collaborating
- Understand and articulate the professional values of each member
- Agree upon methods of decision making
- Determine means for resolving disagreements

The importance of role boundaries, role maintenance, and role clarity are essential in collaborative relationships. These issues should be openly discussed among team members, and obstacles to effective team functioning should be identified and addressed.

In all instances, it is the responsibility of a social worker to understand and reflect upon his or her own values, ensure that they do not interfere with the collaborative process, and that they are always aligned with ensuring outcomes in the best interest of a client. Areas of sensitivity that require self-reflection include beliefs about differing status among team members, unequal benefits for participation, different levels of personal and time commitments, insecurity about the value of the team approach, and/or lack of administrative support.

Practice Test

170-Question Practice Test

This practice test contains 170 questions, but remember that your score on the actual examination will be based on 150 questions because 20 items are being piloted. As you won't know which items will be scored and determine whether or not you pass, you will need to complete all 170 questions. Thus, this test has 170 questions so that you can gauge the length of time that it takes you to complete an equivalent number of questions. The questions in each domain or area are in random order on this practice test, as they are on the actual examination, and there is a similar distribution of questions from each section as will appear on your actual examination.

Human Development, Diversity,
and Behavior in the Environment

39 Questions

Intervention Processes and Techniques for
Use Across Systems

54 Questions

Intervention Processes and Techniques for
Use With Larger Systems

31 Questions

Professional Relationships, Values, and Ethics

46 Questions

The best way to use this practice test is as a mock examination, which means:

a. Take it AFTER you have completed your studying—do not memorize answers to these questions.

b. Do not apply the answers to these questions to the actual examination or you may miss subtle differences in each question that can distinguish the correct from the incorrect answer.

c. Take it in its entirety during a 4-hour block of time to show yourself that you can finish in the allotted time period for the examination.

d. Do not look up the answers until you are completely finished with the entire practice test, and do not worry if you get incorrect answers. Remember, this examination is not one in which you can expect to get all of the answers correct. **The number of questions that you will need to answer correctly generally varies from 93 to 106 correct of the 150 scored items.**

1. Which of the following is NOT a secondary prevention strategy?

   A. Regular screenings of those with risk factors for an illness or disease
   B. Regular exercise and good nutrition
   C. Modification of work assignments for those who are injured
   D. Taking low doses of aspirin for those with heart conditions

2. All of the following may be viewed as indicators of resistance EXCEPT:

   A. A client engaging in small talk about irrelevant topics during a session
   B. A client who limits the amount of information communicated to a social worker during treatment
   C. A client who is silent during appointments
   D. A client who was originally referred by another person

3. A client abruptly stopped coming to sessions after 6 weeks. He calls the social worker and asks for a copy of his record about a month later. There is nothing in the record that is harmful to the client, but the social worker refuses to give it to him. In this situation, the social worker's actions are:

   A. Ethical because he did not terminate with the social worker prior to not coming anymore
   B. Ethical because the request must come in writing with the reason that a copy of the record is needed
   C. Unethical because the social worker has a duty to give the client a copy of his record in this situation
   D. Unethical because the social worker has a duty to give the client a copy of his or her record under all circumstances

4. When a social worker has direct knowledge of a social work colleague's impairment that interferes with effective practice, the social worker should FIRST:

   A. Design a short-term intervention to stabilize the situation
   B. Notify the agency director so that employee assistance services can be accessed
   C. Report the situation to the social work licensing board
   D. Consult with that colleague when feasible and assist the colleague in taking remedial action

5. A client is extremely upset because her 14-year-old son is not helping around the house, independently doing his homework, or arriving to school on time. The son states that his mother watches over him too closely and does not give him needed privacy. This problem is best understood as:

   A. A communication problem
   B. Role discomplementarity
   C. Progressive discipline
   D. Developmental processes

6. Which of the following is NOT true about conflict theory?

   A. Constant competition between groups forms the basis for the ever-changing nature of society.
   B. Society is fragmented into groups that compete for social and economic resources.
   C. Social order is maintained by those with the greatest political, economic, and social resources.
   D. There is a strong emphasis on consensus and conformity.

7. A client has just been fired from his job and he is focusing solely on the stress associated with the financial challenges that he is facing. Using a systems approach, the social worker can expect his unemployment to:

   A. Result in a negative impact on his financial well-being
   B. Affect other areas of his life such as his physical and mental health
   C. Cause him to be worried about finding another job
   D. Build resiliency that can be used to deal with other life crises

8. Which of the following medications is NOT typically prescribed for the treatment of Attention-Deficit/Hyperactivity Disorder?

   A. Adderall
   B. Ritalin
   C. Dexedrine
   D. Tofranil

9. A client has dilated pupils, appears jittery, and complains that "he just needs to get some sleep." The client is MOST likely using which of the following substances?

   A. Cocaine
   B. Heroin
   C. Marijuana
   D. Painkillers

10. According to the Tarasoff decision, social workers must:

    A. Notify both the authorities and intended victims of imminent danger
    B. Seek inpatient hospitalization if dangerousness exists
    C. Inform only the intended victims of imminent danger
    D. Identify the risk factors that are linked to dangerousness of others

11. Which of the following is NOT associated with low ego strength?

    A. Viewing challenges as something to avoid
    B. Feeling overwhelmed by reality
    C. Finding new ways to deal with struggles
    D. Using wishful thinking or fantasies

12. In couples development, which of the following stages describes when partners try to please each other; place few demands on one another; and begin initially bonding on cognitive, emotional, physical, and behavioral levels?   page 98-100

    A. Practicing
    B. Rapprochement
    C. Mutual interdependence
    D. Symbiosis

13. Which of the following is NOT one of the therapeutic advantages of injectable antipsychotic medications?

    A. They reduce medication noncompliance because they are needed less frequently than oral medications.
    B. They are less likely to be used for suicide or result in overdose because the dosing is controlled.
    C. They are associated with decreased hospitalizations due to fewer symptom relapses.
    D. They are less expensive than oral medications.

14. When making level of care determinations, which criterion is primarily used in behavioral health settings?

    A. Capitation
    B. Medical necessity
    C. Managed risk
    D. Diagnostic groupings

15. A social worker has joined the board of directors of a domestic violence agency where she was formally a volunteer. Which of the following activities would NOT be ethical for the social worker to engage in?

    A. Raising money for the organization through direct solicitation
    B. Receiving referrals for clients leaving their shelter program for her private practice who will be treated for a reduced rate
    C. Educating the public about the risks of domestic violence
    D. Making the executive director aware of funding opportunities in the local area

16. Which of the following is an objective outcome that might be associated with a foster care program?

    A. Proportion of children served who are reunified with their biological families
    B. Satisfaction of foster parents with the program
    C. Perceived safety of children
    D. Number of children served in the program

17. All of the following are associated with Borderline Personality Disorder EXCEPT:

   A. Poor impulse control
   B. Control of aggressive drives
   C. Dichotomous thinking
   D. Emotional dysregulation

18. Which of the following is the FIRST goal of assisting clients who have suffered a life crisis?

   A. Helping them to develop coping skills to deal with similar crises in the future
   B. Identifying the cause of the crisis in order to prevent it from reoccurring in the future
   C. Assisting them to establish a sense of equilibrium and return to prior levels of functioning
   D. Linking them with others who have experienced a similar crisis to build a network of support

19. A social worker suspects that a child receiving services from her agency is being psychologically abused and neglected. She discusses the reasons for her belief and her serious concerns about the child's home environment with her social work supervisor. After a lengthy conversation, the social work supervisor does not agree with the social worker and tells the social worker to monitor the situation for a while before deciding whether to make a report to the child protection agency. The social worker should:

   A. Make an anonymous report to the child protection agency
   B. Contact the child protection agency immediately while informing the supervisor of the need to do so
   C. Schedule another appointment to speak to the supervisor and try to collect additional information that supports the social worker's concerns
   D. Continue to collect information and follow up regularly with the supervisor to seek direction

20. A social worker is seeing a family for therapy. During a session, the 17-year-old daughter states that her father molested her when she was 6 years old. She says that it happened twice and has not occurred since that time. The father confirms the daughter's account and says that he is remorseful about his actions. He assures the social worker and his family that it will never happen again. In this situation, the social worker should:

   A. Not contact the child protection agency given the length of time that has occurred since the incidents
   B. Not contact the child protection agency because these were isolated incidents and the father realizes the inappropriateness of his actions

C. Contact the child protection agency after telling the family of the need to do so because the social worker is a mandated reporter

D. Contact the child protection agency, but do not tell the family in order to preserve the therapeutic relationship

21. A client recently started a new job and reports fighting with his boss. The boss tells the client repeatedly that he is not "doing what he is supposed to," but the client claims that he does everything that the boss asks. In order to BEST understand the situation, the social worker should:

A. Recommend that the client speak to the boss's supervisor to request assistance with mediating the situation

B. Ask the client to explain his work responsibilities as they relate to the official job description and his boss's feedback

C. Explore with the client his underlying feelings about being criticized by his boss and its impact on his job performance

D. Assess why the client initially accepted this position and his willingness to complete the required tasks

22. Which of the following contains thoughts, feelings, desires, and memories of which a client has no awareness, even though they influence his or her daily life?

A. Preconscious

B. Conscious

C. Superego

D. Unconscious

23. A client whose husband is very controlling has used newly learned assertiveness skills in the home. She reports that her husband is reacting by placing more restrictions on her actions. Which of the following is the BEST explanation for the husband's actions?

A. The husband's behavior is caused by a suprasystem.

B. The husband is trying to reject homeostasis.

C. The husband's behavior is attributable to negative entropy.

D. The husband is trying to maintain homeostasis.

24. After an assessment is completed, what follows according to the problem-solving process?

A. Intervention

B. Evaluation

C. Planning

D. Engagement

25. A client shows a social worker a large tattoo on his arm dedicated to his mother who recently died. He begins to cry and states that it always

makes him very emotional when he sees it because it reminds him of her bravery in fighting her illness. The tattoo is a form of:

A. Symbolization
B. Substitution
C. Sublimation
D. Splitting

26. Which of the following is NOT true about the relationship between research and policy in social work practice?

A. There must be a reciprocal relationship between research and policy with each informing the other.
B. Policy-makers need to receive full research articles and reports so that they can make informed decisions.
C. Policy decisions must be based on research findings to ensure that scarce resources are efficiently allocated.
D. Policy-makers and researchers often have different professional backgrounds, causing communication challenges.

27. A social worker who is a director of a residential substance abuse facility sees a former client who left the program about 5 years ago at a community event. The former client tells the social worker that he has always been attracted to her and would like to go on a date with her now that he has left the program and is no longer in need of services. The social worker, who also has romantic feelings toward the client, should:

A. Accept his invitation as it is ethical based on the length of time that he has been out of services
B. Accept his invitation as the professional code of ethics does not address relationships with former clients
C. Decline his invitation as it is unethical to date him until more time passes following his leaving the program
D. Decline his invitation as it is unethical to date him at all given these circumstances

28. Which of the following BEST describes the benefit of peer supervision in social work practice?

A. It is less expensive than individual supervision.
B. It can occur as needed, anytime and anywhere.
C. It is a reciprocal learning relationship aimed at skill acquisition.
D. It does not require "experts" in the field.

29. Which of the following is NOT a "deficiency need" according to Maslow?

A. Self-actualization
B. Safety

C. Esteem

D. Physiological

30. Which of the following is the MOST important factor in choosing an appropriate intervention or treatment strategy?

   A. It is currently being used by a social worker to assist clients with similar problems.
   B. It results from the biopsychosocial–spiritual–cultural assessment of a client.
   C. It is approved as medically necessary by third-party payers.
   D. It is not constrained by agency practices and/or time limits for treatment.

31. A social worker is asked to determine the need for a new parenting support group within his agency. In order to determine how many people might be interested, the social worker looks at existing case files to identify the number of clients with children who cite child-rearing difficulties on their intake applications. What is the PRIMARY concern of using this data collection method to determine need?

   A. Clients who could benefit from this group may not be identified.
   B. Informed consent procedures are not being used to select service recipients.
   C. Clients outside of the agency should have been surveyed.
   D. The need for a service should be based on subjective assessments, not empirical data.

32. Which of the following is NOT true about data analysis in social work practice?

   A. It is a sequential process which begins with cleaning the data and checking it for accuracy.
   B. It involves using either descriptive or inferential statistics.
   C. It involves a balance between generating too little and too much information.
   D. It is usually performed electronically by a computer once the data is coded and entered.

33. According to the family life cycle, which of the following is NOT generally a task in families with young children?

   A. Adjusting to children taking a more central role in family maintenance
   B. Adopting and developing parenting roles
   C. Assisting children to develop peer relationships
   D. Realigning relationships with families of origin to include parenting and grandparenting roles

34. Which of the following is TRUE about risk factors for violence?

    A. They are present only at the individual level.
    B. They predict with certainty who will engage in aggressive acts.
    C. They are positively associated with protective factors to predict violence.
    D. They increase the likelihood that a community will be affected by, or a client will be a perpetrator of, violence.

35. Which of the following is NOT a core value in social work as stated in the preamble of the professional code of ethics?

    A. Social justice
    B. Importance of human relationships
    C. Minimizing risk to self and others
    D. Service

36. A social worker receives a call from a former girlfriend who is now married and is having trouble dealing with the recent death of her mother. The former girlfriend would like to see the social worker for counseling. The social worker has not seen the former girlfriend in more than 10 years. The social worker should:

    A. Begin treatment immediately because more than a decade has passed since the presence of an intimate relationship
    B. Gather more information about why the former girlfriend wants the social worker to provide therapy
    C. Contact the social work licensing board to determine if regulation prohibits this treatment
    D. Inform the former girlfriend that the social worker cannot treat her

37. Which of the following is the MOST important function of service networks?

    A. Service networks share resources that strengthen their member agencies.
    B. Service networks increase ease of service billing because payments are managed centrally.
    C. Service networks reduce duplication and increase integration of client services.
    D. Service networks increase agency referrals because they have a single point of entry.

38. When clients sue social workers for malpractice, social workers fulfill their ethical obligations by:

    A. Not releasing any information about treatment, including whether clients were even served

B. Providing all information obtained during treatment so the court can get a complete picture of clients' concerns, issues, and problems
C. Not responding to the courts because the information is privileged
D. Releasing only information related to the nature of the lawsuits

39. Social workers are allowed to terminate services when:

A. They wish to pursue social relationships with clients.
B. They are leaving employment settings to pursue other opportunities.
C. They believe that clients are making poor choices that negatively affect their well-being.
D. They are owed money for services even if the consequences for nonpayment have not been discussed.

40. What type of relationship exists between resilience and compassion fatigue?

A. Positive
B. Negative
C. Curvilinear
D. Linear

41. Which of the following is NOT a diagnostic criterion in the *DSM-5* for Gambling Disorder?

A. Lying to conceal gambling
B. Loss of relationship, job, or opportunity due to gambling
C. Legal problems associated with gambling
D. Preoccupation with gambling

42. Which of the following diagnoses is MOST likely to be given as the result of mental status examinations?

A. Delirium
B. Schizophrenia
C. Oppositional Defiant Disorder
D. Avoidant Personality Disorder

43. A social worker is worried that he does not have all the necessary information to make a practice decision, so he uses multiple sources to collect data. This approach is known as:

A. Cooptation
B. Triangulation
C. Social exchange
D. Twinning

44. A social worker is asked to do a case presentation for her supervisor. She presents basic demographic information, client and family history, and the presenting problem. The supervisor would consider this presentation to be:

   A. Satisfactory because it contains all information needed to develop a treatment plan
   B. Satisfactory because it should only include objective data
   C. Unsatisfactory because it does not contain the social worker's impressions and treatment recommendations
   D. Unsatisfactory because it should only include information on the client and not the client's family

45. A social worker employed in a hospital is using a SOAP documentation format. Which of the following is NOT usually included in this record?

   A. A plan of care
   B. Insurance coverage limits
   C. Assessment of the client's current needs
   D. Subjective reports of client well-being

46. Which BEST describes the role of a social worker when engaged in crisis intervention?

   A. Short-term support focused on restoring clients' psychological capacities
   B. Long-term support to ensure clients are able to address all aspects of trauma
   C. Passively involved acting as a resource for any concerns or problems
   D. Highly involved and focused on meeting the clients' basic needs

47. A social worker is a facilitator of a group for clients diagnosed as having Anorexia Nervosa. Over several weeks, clients talk about their diverse backgrounds, including their varied early childhood experiences. The social worker comments that this disorder is caused by many different factors. The concept mentioned by the social worker is:

   A. Homeostasis
   B. Equifinality
   C. Subsystems
   D. Diagnostic-related groups

48. An elderly client has been diagnosed with a terminal illness and wants to make sure that his financial affairs are in order. He would like to divide his assets equally among his children upon his death. The client is worried that choosing one of his children to serve as executor of his

estate will be a burden. The social worker volunteers to take on this role as long as there is no financial compensation. The social worker is acting:

A. Ethically as there is no financial remuneration for this responsibility
B. Unethically since it was the social worker who suggested assuming this role and not at the client's initial request
C. Unethically as it represents a dual relationship between the client and the social worker
D. Ethically as it helps the client have self-determination about how his assets will be divided after his death

49. A social worker is seeing a 69-year-old client who is a former cigarette smoker and has chronic obstructive pulmonary disease (COPD), which makes it hard to breathe. She takes several medications, including one to regulate her blood pressure. Her primary prevention needs include:

A. Participation in a support group for others with COPD
B. Monitoring her blood pressure to modify her medications as needed
C. Reducing strenuous activity that causes heavy breathing
D. Receiving an annual influenza immunization

50. Which is the MOST important reason that self-monitoring is used as a social work technique?

A. Clients are the most reliable sources of information.
B. It is an effective and efficient data collection method, saving time and money.
C. It allows clients to better understand the causes and frequency of the problem behaviors.
D. It is based on the principles of self-determination.

51. A social worker receives a referral to provide case management to a family who just came to the United States from another country and needs to be linked to services to meet their basic needs. The 13-year-old daughter in the family speaks English in addition to her native language, which is exclusively spoken by the parents. The social worker, who only understands and speaks English, accepts the referral. This action is:

A. Ethical because the daughter will be available to translate for the parents
B. Unethical because the social worker has not determined if the daughter is willing to translate
C. Ethical because the services are time limited and nonclinical in nature
D. Unethical because the social worker cannot speak to or understand all family members

52. A recognition that all people who could benefit from assistance do not seek help implies that using which type of need is NOT adequate justification for program development?

    A. Relative
    B. Perceived
    C. Expressed
    D. Absolute

53. Tardive dyskinesia is a side effect of taking antipsychotic medications that affects which of the following?

    A. Nervous system
    B. Circulatory system
    C. Respiratory system
    D. Muscular system

54. A social worker in an agency setting who determines that an ethical dilemma exists should select an appropriate course of action based on:

    A. Past practices
    B. Agency policies and procedures
    C. Funding requirements
    D. Social work values and principles

55. A client reports to a social worker that he is having problems with his wife because he feels that she does not care about him. The social worker discovers that this belief stems from her perceived distraction when the husband is talking. The social worker challenges this thought and helps him replace it with an alternative one that she "does care, but just has a lot of other demands for her attention." The approach used by the social worker is:

    A. Operant conditioning
    B. Cognitive behavioral therapy
    C. Classical conditioning
    D. Ego psychology

56. A man is seeing a social worker because he is struggling to "find himself" as his children have become adults and left the family home. He feels that his job has become mundane and he is feeling "bored with life." This client is MOST likely in which stage of psychosocial development?

    A. Generativity versus stagnation
    B. Industry versus inferiority

C. Initiative versus guilt

D. Intimacy versus isolation

57. A social worker observes that a client is having trouble communicating with her husband, so she often confides in her sister-in-law about her fears and concerns, hoping that the sister-in-law will be able to assist. The sister-in-law finds that she is becoming increasingly "in the middle" of the problems that exist between her brother and his wife. This situation is known as:

A. Joining

B. Differentiation

C. Familial regression

D. Triangulation

58. A married couple comes in to see a social worker because they are having problems in their relationship. They report feeling disconnected and having little intimacy. The husband admits that his drinking recently caused him to be fired from his job and he is currently unemployed. The wife reports that she is fearful of her husband because he often is loud when he drinks and spends a lot of time out of the house. They have not had sex for several months and are behind in their mortgage payments. The FIRST issue that the social worker should help the couple address is:

A. The couple's lack of emotional intimacy

B. The wife's absence from the home

C. The husband's alcohol use

D. The couple's financial problems

59. Which of the following is NOT true about normal and abnormal client behavior?

A. There are many influences on client behavior including individual, interpersonal, institutional, and community factors.

B. Client behavior should not be viewed through an ecological perspective.

C. There are many theoretical perspectives which help explain client behavior.

D. Client behavior can be explained using social constructivism.

60. A hospital social worker is charged with completing a biopsychosocial–spiritual–cultural assessment on a client upon admission. In the biological section of the assessment, the social worker lists the client's current medications, weight, height, blood pressure, and subjective

assessment of well-being. The social worker then moves on to the psychological section of the assessment. When the social worker's supervisor looks at the biological section, it will be viewed as:

A. Complete because it gives critical information about the client's current physical well-being

B. Accurate and useful in understanding the current functioning of the client

C. Incorrect because it should contain only objective data and not subjective information

D. Incomplete because it does not contain the client's current medical problems and history, including developmental milestones

61. A social worker, who has been court-ordered to release information about a client, feels strongly that providing this information will place the client and the client's family in grave danger. The social worker refuses to comply with the court order. In this situation, the actions by the social worker are:

A. Illegal and unethical

B. Legal, but unethical

C. Illegal, but ethical

D. Legal and ethical

62. What is the MOST important reason for proper case recording of social work services?

A. Demonstrating services adhere to professional standards and agency policies

B. Identifying issues to be discussed in supervision or consultation

C. Assisting in making practice decisions about client treatment

D. Ensuring public accountability to efficient and effective service delivery

63. When working with an involuntary client, which of the following actions is likely to be MOST effective during engagement?

A. Reviewing the court order so the client understands why services are mandated

B. Discussing mandates of confidentiality as per the *Code of Ethics*

C. Explaining the professional standards to be upheld by the social worker

D. Listening to the client to understand his or her feelings and current situation

64. A social worker is seeing a client in private practice. The client has not paid the social worker for many weeks, accumulating a substantial balance, despite receiving and acknowledging the social worker's

payment policy. The social worker has told the client repeatedly that he will be terminated if he does not pay his bill and decides to do so at the next session. The client comes into this session visibly upset and crying because he doesn't think "he can go on" without the social worker. The social worker tells the client that he can come back to see her once the balance is paid. The actions of the social worker are:

A. Ethical because the social worker has given the client notice of the nonpayment consequences, as well as the payment policy
B. Ethical because the social worker is allowing the client to return when the balance is paid
C. Unethical because the professional code of ethics does not allow termination based upon nonpayment of services
D. Unethical because the client may be a danger to himself

65. A school social worker is employed part time in a mental health agency. A mother brings her daughter into the agency and asks that the social worker provide counseling because she has been impressed by the social worker's ability to "relate to" her daughter in school. The school social worker has taken the lead in developing her daughter's Individual Education Plan (IEP) and meets with the daughter regularly in school to assess her progress. In this situation, the social worker should:

A. Complete only the intake and assessment of the daughter at the mental health agency before proceeding to determine whether she could benefit from seeing the school social worker in this alternate setting
B. Serve the daughter in both settings to ensure continuity of treatment outside of the school setting
C. Ask another social worker to be the primary treating professional in the mental health agency and agree to be a consultant as needed to provide information on problems or issues in school
D. Not counsel the daughter in the mental health agency because this poses a conflict of interest

66. In which of the following situations would it be ethical for a social worker to breach privilege?

A. A social worker needs to tell a client's family about poor choices being made.
B. An insurance company is suing a client for fraud and needs behavioral health information.
C. A social worker is contacted by the police who are investigating a crime that may have been committed by a client.
D. A client is suing a social worker and information is needed for the social worker's defense.

67. A social work supervisor is asked by a supervisee in her agency for a written recommendation for a graduate program in a related discipline. The supervisor agrees to provide it. In this situation, the supervisor's actions are:

    A. Unethical because writing this recommendation for a supervisee creates a potential conflict of interest or dual relationship
    B. Ethical since the supervisor would be aware of the supervisee's strengths and learning needs
    C. Unethical since the graduate program is not in social work, but in a related field
    D. Ethical because it would benefit the agency to have employees with higher academic credentials

68. A social worker asks her current clients to write testimonial endorsements to assist with attracting others to her private practice. These requests are:

    A. Ethical because clients can decide whether they will write them
    B. Ethical if she agrees not to identify them by name
    C. Unethical because she did not also solicit former clients
    D. Unethical because they are vulnerable due to their circumstances

69. Which of the following are predominantly used by younger people to define themselves?

    A. Social roles
    B. Emotional relationships
    C. Intellectual abilities
    D. Personal characteristics

70. During the first session, a client becomes very upset and hostile about his need to seek treatment. He blames others for his situation and yells in a loud manner. In order to facilitate the problem-solving process, the social worker should FIRST:

    A. Listen to the client as he explains his concerns
    B. Tell the client that he needs to calm down in order for the social worker to best understand his issues
    C. Develop a plan to help him deal with his anger and blame of others
    D. Assess why the client is so upset and unwilling to accept responsibility for his problems

71. Which of the following would be an UNETHICAL use of identifying client data?

    A. Releasing information to a targeted victim under duty to warn
    B. Notifying child protective services of suspected neglect

C. Seeking assistance from a supervisor or consultant concerning critical treatment issues

D. Using it in a grant application for emergency funding due to significant budget cuts

72. Social work intervention with offenders is MOST effective when focused on:

   A. Dynamic risk factors
   B. Genetic predispositions to violence
   C. Static risk factors
   D. Arrest records and past legal involvement

73. While meeting with a client and her child, a social worker becomes suspicious of markings on the child's arms and legs. After asking the client about them, the social worker believes that they are the result of physical abuse in the home. In order to appropriately address the situation, the social worker should FIRST:

   A. Inform the client of the need to make a report to the child protection agency
   B. Wait for the client to leave the office
   C. Gather information about the length and severity of the abuse
   D. Interview the child alone to see if the suspicion of abuse is corroborated

74. In instances in which clients lack the capacity to provide informed consent, social workers must do all of the following EXCEPT:

   A. Seek permission from appropriate third parties
   B. Help identify appropriate third parties for full guardianship of clients
   C. Inform clients consistent with their understanding
   D. Ensure third parties act in a manner consistent with clients' interests and wishes

75. A couple comes to see a social worker because they feel that they have suffered discrimination. They are blind and would like to adopt a child, but have been told by an adoption agency that it is not possible because of their visual impairments. They are distraught, but do not think that they will be able to fight the agency bias. In order to BEST assist this couple, the social worker should:

   A. Assist them to identify other methods to become parents
   B. Help them cope with their disappointment from being denied
   C. Support them in fighting the agency bias
   D. Connect them with others who have experienced similar discrimination

76. Which of the following BEST describes most older adults with regard to their typical mental functioning?

    A. They continue to learn, but may experience declines in memory skills.
    B. They are at their peak with regard to problem-solving and mental processes.
    C. They do not learn and may experience declines in memory skills.
    D. They are not able to acquire new skills or solve problems.

77. A client reports to a social worker that she was often criticized by her parents when she was in elementary and middle school and now has poor self-esteem and doubts her abilities. According to Erikson's stages of psychosocial development, the client experienced a crisis in which of the following stages?

    A. Identity versus role confusion
    B. Generativity versus stagnation
    C. Industry versus inferiority
    D. Integrity versus despair

78. A social worker believes that there may be an ethical dilemma in his agency. According to steps in ethical problem solving, the social worker should FIRST consult:

    A. His supervisor
    B. The professional code of ethics
    C. The policies and procedures of the agency
    D. A colleague who has worked in the agency longer

79. A social worker is charged with evaluating the effectiveness of a mental health outpatient treatment program. He constructs an evaluation strategy that consists of collecting data on the quality of services by holding focus groups with current clients so that they can relay their firsthand experiences. In addition, he uses existing agency data to compute the proportion of clients who have been rehospitalized since admission. The social worker is conducting what type of evaluation?

    A. Qualitative
    B. Quantitative
    C. Quasi-experimental
    D. Mixed method

80. Which of the following is an example of a role reversal?

    A. A 14-year-old boy told by his mother that he has to work to financially contribute to household expenses
    B. A 13-year-old girl physically and emotionally taking care of her father who was permanently injured in an accident

C. A 10-year-old boy yelling at his mother that she is not doing enough work around the house

D. A 12-year-old girl staying out later than allowed by her parents

81. Which of the following is a protective factor for dangerousness to others?

A. Violence at an early age
B. Drug and/or alcohol use
C. Clinical services for physical and behavioral care
D. Exposure to violent acts

82. Therapy sessions conducted by social workers in an agency are frequently audiotaped for review by their supervisors. These tapes are destroyed upon client terminations and are used only for supervisory purposes, not shared with others outside the agency. The standard consent form used by the agency states that social workers will receive supervision and client information may be disclosed with supervisors to ensure service quality. In order to avoid making clients feel uncomfortable, taping is not discussed with them, but consent forms are read by the social worker to clients who sign them. The audiotaping of these sessions is:

A. Ethical because it is done as part of supervision to ensure service quality
B. Unethical because clients should receive the names of the supervisors before signing the consent forms
C. Unethical because informed consent for audiotaping has not been obtained
D. Ethical because the tapes are destroyed upon termination

83. A social worker finds that she has a lot in common with a client. The client suggests seeing another professional because the client feels she "would be a better friend than client." The social worker agrees, but states that she cannot have contact with the client for several months after termination to allow time for her to get engaged in treatment with a new social worker. The social worker's actions are:

A. Ethical because there will be several months after the ending of the therapeutic relationship before contact occurs
B. Unethical because the time period after termination, but before contact occurs, is not long enough
C. Ethical because it respects the client's self-determination
D. Unethical because the social worker cannot terminate services for this reason

84. After several months of treating a client, a social worker learns that the client goes to the same church as the social worker. The social worker

continues to go to the church, seeing the client occasionally across the room. The social worker has no contact with the client at church. This situation is:

A. Unethical because a referral should have been made to another social worker once this issue was discovered

B. Ethical because the conflict was not known initially and has been minimized by avoiding contact

C. Unethical because the social worker should have started attending another church

D. Ethical because religious participation is not considered in the evaluation of dual relationships

85. A client is having trouble achieving a treatment goal, so the social worker breaks it down into small successive steps and rewards the client after achieving each one. This behavioral technique is known as:

A. Shaping
B. Biofeedback
C. Modeling
D. Flooding

86. All of the following are methods to address resistance during engagement EXCEPT:

A. Clarifying what will occur in treatment
B. Instilling hope that change is possible
C. Explaining the limits of confidentiality
D. Partializing action steps so clients can make incremental progress toward change

87. A social worker regularly refers clients to a colleague because he has expertise in treating Substance-Related and Addictive Disorders. The colleague is very appreciative of the social worker's confidence in his abilities and offers his season football tickets each time a referral is received. The social worker takes the tickets so as not to "hurt his feelings," but donates them to a local charity. The social worker's actions are:

A. Ethical because the tickets are donated to charity
B. Unethical because the social worker should not accept the tickets
C. Ethical because there is no additional cost to the colleague because he has already purchased season tickets
D. Unethical because the social worker should only refer clients to practitioners that she does not know

88. A man is court-ordered to receive an evaluation by a social worker. Although initially agreeable to participating, the client states at the conclusion of his meetings with the social worker that he "changed

his mind" and wished that he had never agreed to be interviewed. He asks the social worker not to release any information to the court. The social worker should:

A. Respect the client's wishes and not provide any information to the court
B. Inform the court that the client rescinded his consent and ask the court to advise the social worker of next steps
C. Complete the evaluation based on all of the information gathered
D. Release only notes from the meetings and not complete a formal evaluation based on the wishes of the client

89. A social worker advises a 16-year-old client who has often been bullied in public by a group of peers to walk away each time such an incident occurs in the future. In the past, the boy would often cry when teased, causing the peers to laugh at his reaction. The social worker is hoping to reduce the teasing through:

A. Systematic desensitization
B. Aversion therapy
C. Extinction
D. Time out

90. Which of the following is TRUE of youth who are not heterosexual and/or gender conforming?

A. They go through different developmental stages than their peers.
B. They are challenged to develop identities with few role models.
C. They do not have greater social isolation and poorer self-image than their peers.
D. They are not at greater risk for mental and physical health complications compared with their peers.

91. An agency is required by its funder to make extensive modifications to its human resource policies. The agency director is worried about the financial health of the agency and reports that the agency does not have the money to hire someone to complete this task. The social worker's wife is a human resource manager at a large corporation and agrees to work with the agency for a few weeks at a deeply discounted rate in order to meet the requirements. According to the *Code of Ethics*, this situation is:

A. Ethical because the wife is being hired as a consultant and is not an employee of the agency
B. Ethical because the agency has no other means to fulfill the funding requirement
C. Unethical because it represents a conflict of interest
D. Unethical because the wife is charging for her services

92. A client in crisis comes to a social worker for critically needed services. The social worker decides to use a single-subject design to determine service efficacy. Which of the following is most appropriate in determining the internal validity of these services?

    A. ABAB
    B. BAB
    C. AB
    D. A

93. Which of the following is NOT part of termination in social work practice?

    A. Identifying other issues that may need to be addressed in the future
    B. Reviewing accomplishments that occurred during treatment
    C. Anticipating how to address subsequent reoccurrences of the problem
    D. Recognizing loss on the part of the client and social worker

94. A social worker is completing an intake with a family who recently immigrated from another country. They are in need of basic resources such as rental and nutrition assistance. The children appear neat and clean. The social worker observes the mother mixing a small amount of alcohol into her infant's bottle and is told that this "soothes" the child as she is teething. During the intake, the family discloses that they do not believe in Western medicine and think sickness is caused by the presence of evil demons. They report that they spend much of their day engaged in prayer and meditation because one of their children is gravely ill. In order to BEST assist this family, the social worker should:

    A. Prioritize them for services provided by the agency
    B. Respect their cultural traditions and work with the family to prioritize their needs
    C. Inform them that it is necessary to get the child protection agency involved and contact the agency immediately
    D. Seek consultation to learn more about the cultural practices of this family

95. A client reports that he was just diagnosed with Hodgkin's disease. This cancer is associated with which of the major body systems?

    A. Lymphatic
    B. Circulatory
    C. Digestive
    D. Endocrine

96. A social worker in a mental health agency is very upset by the passage of legislation that, in his opinion, will be detrimental to some of his clients.

He is asked by an advocacy organization to join a protest that he does on his own time and without identifying his employer. His agency director is very upset by his participation because the board of directors of the mental health agency supported this legislation. The social worker's actions are:

A. Unethical because the social worker is considered a representative of his employer
B. Ethical because he acted as a private individual
C. Unethical because he should have gotten permission from his agency director first
D. Ethical because he is allowed to take any and all actions in instances where policies are considered detrimental to clients

97. A client in a group facilitated by a social worker has a red face and appears visibly upset when he talks about his current relationship with his family. When the social worker states that he can see how the client is not happy about his current situation based upon his physical symptoms, the client says, "Everything is fine." The client is MOST likely exhibiting:

A. Lack of congruence in communication
B. Denial of his underlying psychic conflict
C. Desire to please the social worker
D. Symptomatology of a psychiatric diagnosis

98. A social worker receives a request for detailed treatment summaries from a client's insurance company. In the correspondence, it is made clear that the insurance company will cease funding for treatment unless the summaries are received immediately. In order to best serve the client, the social worker should:

A. Prepare the summaries, but review them with the client and get his or her approval before sending
B. Write to the insurance company and ask why they are needed
C. Send only the diagnosis and prognosis, citing confidential mandates
D. Send the treatment summaries as soon as possible so that funding for treatment will not stop

99. A social worker is working with a family who has become homeless after a fire destroyed their home. The 10-year-old daughter begins to use "baby talk" and suck her thumb, behaviors that were not present before the fire. The mother reports that the daughter now always wants to sit on her lap and clings to her side when they go out in public. The daughter is MOST likely using the defense mechanism of:

A. Undoing
B. Reaction formation

    C. Regression

    D. Splitting

100. Which of the following is NOT a limitation of using existing case records as the basis for practice evaluations?

    A. Records may not contain consistent and/or complete information.

    B. There is no additional time or cost associated with their use.

    C. Evaluations have to be limited to only topics contained in the case records.

    D. The client's opinions about service quality are not considered.

101. What is the PRIMARY goal of permanency planning?

    A. Living in stable and long-term homes

    B. Including all parties in case conferencing

    C. Improving educational outcomes

    D. Ensuring treatment decisions are individually based

102. A man comes to see a social worker because he is sexually attracted to those of the same gender and is deeply distressed by the thought that he may be homosexual. The feelings experienced by this client are:

    A. Ego alien

    B. Ego-syntonic

    C. Coping skills

    D. Fixations

103. Which of the following Personality Disorders is clustered with Antisocial Personality Disorder in a grouping characterized by dramatic, emotional, and erratic behavior?

    A. Schizoid Personality Disorder

    B. Narcissistic Personality Disorder

    C. Obsessive-Compulsive Personality Disorder

    D. Paranoid Personality Disorder

104. A social worker in a substance abuse treatment facility is attracted to one of her supervisees and asks him out on a date. After several months of dating, they get married and the supervisee finds a job at another agency. The behavior of the social worker is:

    A. Unethical because she engaged in a dual relationship with a supervisee

    B. Ethical because the supervisee found another job once they were married

    C. Unethical because the relationship led to marriage

    D. Ethical because the sexual contact prohibition only applies to social workers and clients

105. A family seeks treatment with a social worker. During the assessment process, the social worker learns that the parents expect their children to follow strict rules and the children are severely punished if they do not. When the social worker asks the children why they have to follow several of the rules, the children are not sure why and respond "just because we do." The parents in this family are MOST likely using which of the following parenting styles?

    A. Authoritative
    B. Punitive
    C. Corporal
    D. Authoritarian

106. All of the following are key concepts in individual psychology EXCEPT:

    A. Psychosexual urges
    B. Compensation
    C. Inferiority
    D. Perfection

107. A client reports that she is very upset by her 17-year-old daughter's behavior. She has not been completing her homework and is showing up late for her classes. The client reports that she recently took away the daughter's cell phone until her behavior changes. Which of the following behavioral techniques is the mother using?

    A. Positive reinforcement
    B. Negative reinforcement
    C. Positive punishment
    D. Negative punishment

108. In order to ethically obtain informed consent, social workers must use clear and understandable language to review all of the following EXCEPT:

    A. Agency mission
    B. Service purpose and risks
    C. Limits due to third-party payers
    D. Right to refuse or withdraw from services

109. Which of the following is NOT true about a task-centered approach in social work practice?

    A. There is no assessment phase.
    B. It is highly structured and time limited.
    C. Termination usually begins in the first session.
    D. The client takes a very active role in making change.

110. Which of the following is TRUE with regard to confidentiality in group work?

    A. Group members have the same protection of confidentiality that they receive in individual counseling.
    B. Group members have a legal duty not to disclose information that is shared.
    C. Social workers can discuss information shared in groups with others because it is not confidential.
    D. Social workers cannot guarantee to group members that information disclosed in groups will be kept confidential because it may be disclosed by other members.

111. A social worker develops a survey instrument to assess client well-being. The social worker has clients complete this new survey, as well as one that is currently being used by the agency to reliably measure the same construct. The social worker then compares the consistency of the findings produced by these two separate tests. This social worker is using which of the following methods to assess the reliability of the new survey instrument?

    A. Test–retest
    B. Interrater
    C. Parallel forms
    D. Internal consistency

112. A client tells a social worker that she "feels like a failure" because she cannot seem to meet the multiple daily demands of working and parenting. The social worker states that "many people in your situation experience the same feelings." The technique used by the social worker is known as:

    A. Validating
    B. Reflecting
    C. Paraphrasing
    D. Clarifying

113. Which of the following statements about social work interviews is NOT true?

    A. They aim to serve the best interest of clients.
    B. They are uniform in nature in order to collect consistent information on all clients.
    C. They can be informational, diagnostic, or therapeutic.
    D. They focus on collecting important information to be used in the problem-solving process.

114. A client tells a social worker that he "can't stand it anymore," but does not believe that he can make needed changes in his life. He engages with the social worker in the discussions about what his life would be like without his problem behaviors. The client is MOST likely at which stage of change?

   A. Contemplation
   B. Precontemplation
   C. Preparation
   D. Maintenance

115. Which of the following statements is TRUE about research ethics in social work?

   A. A client does not need a separate informed consent process for research participation and service receipt if they are done by the same agency.
   B. Naturalistic observation is a preferred method for social work research as it does not require a consent procedure.
   C. Social workers do not have an ethical mandate to promote and facilitate research.
   D. Social workers must ensure that a research participant has access to supportive services.

116. Which of the following perspectives on human behavior is based on the belief that clients have the capacity to change themselves and actions are driven by a desire for growth, personal meaning, and competence?

   A. Humanistic
   B. Developmental
   C. Psychodynamic
   D. Rational choice

117. A client shows up for the initial session with a coworker. The BEST response for a social worker is to:

   A. Tell the client that confidentiality policies preclude the coworker from sitting in on sessions, so the coworker should sit in the waiting area until the session is over
   B. Have the coworker also complete the intake paperwork and releases because the coworker is regarded as a client if he or she sits in on the initial session
   C. Complete an assessment in the waiting area to determine why the client brought the coworker to the session and the appropriateness of him or her being there
   D. Leave it up to the client to determine the extent to which the coworker attends or participates in sessions

118. What is the BEST definition of empowerment?

    A. Helping clients obtain services needed to solve their problems
    B. Providing clients with training and education to improve their coping skills
    C. Assisting clients to realize that they have strengths and resources to solve their own problems
    D. Developing a relationship with clients based on mutual respect and trust

119. Which BEST describes the ethical mandates about social and political action by social workers?

    A. Social and political action is strictly prohibited by social workers.
    B. Social workers should only engage in social and political action if they are not compensated for these activities.
    C. Social workers should engage in social and political action that seeks to ensure that clients have equal access to and expanded choice for needed resources.
    D. Social and political action must be done by all clients in order to change the conditions that have contributed to their problems.

120. Which of the following is NOT an indicator of ego strength?

    A. Taking responsibility for actions
    B. Dealing with mood changes
    C. Accepting limitations and being accountable
    D. Blaming others

121. Which of the following are stages of group development in sequential order?

    A. Preaffiliation, differentiation, intimacy, power and control, and separation/termination
    B. Differentiation, power and control, preaffiliation, intimacy, and separation/termination
    C. Preaffiliation, power and control, intimacy, differentiation, and separation/termination
    D. Differentiation, preaffiliation, power and control, intimacy, and separation/termination

122. A client tells a social worker that she was denied housing based upon her ethnic/racial background. She feels hopeless and depressed due to this discrimination, despite having found alternative housing. She states that she "would not like this treatment to happen to others," but

she does not think "anything will change." Treatment goals for the client should focus on:

A. Determining whether the alternative housing located is safe and affordable
B. Referring her to a psychiatrist to see if antidepressant medication needs to be prescribed
C. Helping her cope with the hopelessness and depression experienced
D. Assisting her to fight the housing discrimination

123. Which of the following is the BEST definition of referent power?

A. It is derived from position within an organization.
B. It is derived from interpersonal relationships and charisma, as well as connections with those in leadership positions.
C. It results from possessing knowledge or expertise that is highly valued.
D. It arises from the ability to influence the allocation of incentives, including salary increments, positive appraisals, and/or promotions.

124. A social worker finds that clients are showing improved social skills, but he is worried that the changes may be due to typical human development instead of program participation. The concerns of the social worker focus on:

A. Instrumentation
B. External validity
C. Reliability
D. Internal validity

125. A client who reports that she repeatedly feels the urge to physically strike her child when angry tells the social worker that she is having trouble moving her arm. The client is MOST likely exhibiting the defense mechanism of:

A. Introjection
B. Reaction formation
C. Conversion
D. Projective identification

126. An agency is concerned with the recidivism of its clients and hires a consultant to provide recommendations about service modifications that may have to occur. The consultant has a doctorate and extensive experience in the field. After several weeks, the consultant generates a report advising of service changes that, in the social worker's professional opinion, would be detrimental to clients. The social worker should:

A. Implement them as the consultant is an "expert" in the field
B. Not implement them, citing the reasons for the concerns

C. Speak to the agency director and let him or her decide whether or not to implement them

D. Have another consultant examine the report to see if he or she concurs with the recommendations

127. What is the PRIMARY difference between common and statutory law?

A. Common law is voluntary and does not need to be followed whereas statutory law requires compliance.

B. Common law governs federal rules whereas statutory law applies to state policies.

C. Statutory law is time limited, requiring revision or readoption at specified intervals whereas common law can be in effect for an indefinite period.

D. Statutory law is made by a legislative body whereas common law is made by judges.

128. The following do not violate state laws when performed outside the social work context, but are unethical when engaged in by a social worker EXCEPT:

A. Writing a recommendation for a current adult client

B. Dating a current adult client

C. Borrowing money from a current adult client

D. Having a business relationship with a current adult client

129. A social worker decides to use a pretest-posttest study design to determine whether services positively impacted a client as intended. This design is denoted as:

A. A

B. B

C. ABA

D. AB

130. Which of the following is NOT true about the Substance-Related and Addictive Disorders in the *DSM-5*?

A. Substance Use and Substance Abuse are combined into a single continuum measured from severe to mild.

B. Drug craving has been added and legal problems have been eliminated from the diagnostic criteria.

C. Caffeine Use Disorder is included as a new disorder.

D. Gambling Disorder is the sole disorder under a new category of Non-Substance-Related Disorders.

131. Which of the following is NOT true of attachment and bonding?

   A. Attachment and bonding are best viewed separately from a client's culture because the theoretical approaches are universal.
   B. Some theories of connectedness are understood within an evolutionary context.
   C. Attachment can be viewed as a set of learned behaviors involving both classical and operant conditioning.
   D. Insecure attachment systems have been linked to psychiatric disorders and aberrant behaviors.

132. A school social worker asks the parents of a boy who is Asian to come in for a conference because he has been experiencing problems at school. These problems include not obeying rules and deliberately annoying others. The grandparents of the boy come to the meeting with the parents. Their presence MOST likely can be viewed by the social worker as an indication that:

   A. The boy is having problems at home and the grandparents are needed by the parents to assist with the behaviors.
   B. The grandparents are an important part of the boy's support system and should be incorporated into the treatment plan.
   C. The parents lack the skills needed to make changes in the boy's behavior and they have shifted the responsibility for change to the grandparents.
   D. The boy will only listen to the grandparents and they will be needed in the treatment process in order for him to stop the behaviors in school.

133. A client tells a social worker that he has been screamed at by his boss on a daily basis for the last month. He is very angry, but has not said anything for fear of being fired. He also reports that he is having problems with his wife and children because he has not been able to control his temper in the last few weeks at home. This client's behavior is MOST likely represented by which of the following defense mechanisms?

   A. Displacement
   B. Incorporation
   C. Denial
   D. Compensation

134. Which is the PRIMARY reason for filing court-ordered legal documents "under seal"?

    A. It prevents the submission of any information that can be used for prosecution.
    B. It allows sensitive information not to become public record.
    C. It avoids the need to issue a subpoena for the same information.
    D. It expedites the legal process, minimizing adverse impacts due to delays.

135. The social worker ends a family session with, "During the last hour, each of you has had a chance to discuss your frustrations with one another and how sometimes your own actions have been perceived by each other as hurtful, though they were not intended to be so." The social worker's statement is MOST likely aimed at:

    A. Clarifying to the family that the social worker is being objective since each member got a chance to talk
    B. Demonstrating that the family members are overreacting to each other's actions because they are not intentional
    C. Summarizing what occurred in the session in order for family members to gain a new understanding of their actions
    D. Praising the family members for their openness and participation in the session

136. Entropy is BEST defined as:

    A. Randomness or disorder in a system, leading to decline
    B. Forward motion, leading toward goal achievement
    C. Specialization in system function and purpose
    D. Openness in a system with good information exchange

137. Which of the following is TRUE about the relationship between race and ethnicity?

    A. Individuals who are the same race are always part of the same ethnic group.
    B. Individuals who are the same race may or may not be part of the same ethnic group.
    C. Individuals who are the same race are never part of the same ethnic group.
    D. Race and ethnicity are synonymous.

138. A social worker needs to evaluate the behavior of a client who is living in a group home. The social worker asks two staff to each record the frequency of the behavior independently and to submit their tracking

sheets to her without sharing them with one another. The social worker is using which of the following approaches to ensure reliability of the data collected?

A. Alternate or parallel forms
B. Test–retest
C. Interrater
D. Internal consistency

139. A social worker employed to work with juvenile offenders has developed an innovative program that has yielded very positive outcomes. She approaches the agency director about using the same approach with adult offenders. The director is skeptical about its ability to achieve the same outcomes. The director is expressing concerns about:

A. Internal validity
B. Multicollinearity
C. External validity
D. Measurement error

140. Upon intake, a client states that she "feels like hurting herself, but will be fine." She assures the social worker that she will not act on her feelings. In order to best assist the client, the social worker should FIRST:

A. Conduct a safety assessment
B. Acknowledge the client's feelings and concerns
C. Refer the client to a psychiatrist for a medication evaluation
D. Determine the reasons that have caused the client to feel this way

141. When two or more people share the same delusion or delusional system, it is called:

A. Folie à deux
B. Rumination Disorder
C. Conversion Disorder
D. Comorbid psychosis

142. A social worker is seeing a mother and her 6-year-old child for therapy. They have made substantial progress and the social worker is seeing dramatic improvements in their relationship. During a session, the social worker observes what appear to be burns on the child's neck and arm. She asks the mother about what caused them and the mother's explanation does not seem plausible. The social worker is concerned

and feels that physical abuse may have occurred. In order to BEST address this situation, the social worker should:

A. Express her concerns to the mother and ask the mother to come back with the child in a few days so that the social worker can assess the situation

B. Wait until the mother and child leave the office and contact the child protection agency

C. Tell the mother that the social worker will need to contact the child protection agency and involve her in making the report immediately

D. Tell the mother that the social worker will need to report her concerns to the child protection agency in the future if further signs of physical abuse are seen

143. Theories of human development in social work have stressed all of the following EXCEPT:

A. A systems approach
B. An ecological orientation
C. A focus on preventing mental deficiency
D. A lifespan perspective

144. A social worker receives a subpoena for a former client's record. The social worker should FIRST:

A. Respond to the court by claiming privilege
B. Provide the record because it is for a former client
C. Send the subpoena and record to the client so he or she can respond to the court
D. Ignore the subpoena because the information is confidential

145. According to Erikson, psychosocial development follows which sequence of relationship formation?

A. Attachment–autonomy–intimacy
B. Intimacy–attachment–autonomy
C. Autonomy–attachment–intimacy
D. Intimacy–autonomy–attachment

146. A client reports to a social worker that she is thinking of ending her marriage and would like to get guidance from her priest about her desire. In response to the client's request, the social worker should FIRST:

A. Determine why the client thinks that speaking to her priest will help
B. Assess, in conjunction with the client, whether going to her priest will be helpful

C. Inform the client that this is a good idea as the priest should handle religious/spiritual concerns

D. Determine what support is needed to prepare the client for this meeting with her priest

147. In social work practice, assent and consent are:

A. Identical because both give legal authorization to participate in treatment

B. Distinct, with only consent providing legal authorization to participate in treatment

C. Sequential, with consent needed first and assent required later in the problem-solving process

D. Required of all clients, even those who are court-mandated

148. Which of the following is NOT true about feedback in social work practice?

A. Client consent is not needed if consultation is related to client care.

B. The best insight can often be gained from those who are critical of care.

C. Feedback is especially important at key decision points in service development and implementation.

D. Clarity should always be given about why feedback is needed and what will be done with the information.

149. When a social worker and client are NOT from the same ethnic or racial group, it is essential that the social worker:

A. Engage in supervision and/or consultation with a member of that ethnic or racial group

B. Recognize the differences and understand how they may impact on the treatment process

C. Understand the customs and beliefs that are universal to those from that ethnic or racial group

D. Ask the client if this is a problem prior to starting treatment

150. A social worker is asked by a community governing body to assist with developing youth programs aimed at reducing youth violence, school truancy, vandalism, and drug usage. In order to be most effective, the social worker should FIRST:

A. Work with the community to prioritize the youth problems to be addressed

B. Educate community leaders and members about youth programs that have been effective nationally

C. Collect data on the magnitude of the need that has to be addressed in program design

D. Determine why youth problems are now seen as a priority for the community governing body

151. A social worker is struggling with treating a client with Pica. This disorder is not common among those served by her agency. The social worker believes that it is in the best interest of the client for her to obtain consultation. A colleague in the agency has shown interest in the situation and agrees to advise because she has known the social worker for many years and they both became employed at the agency immediately after graduation. In order to best assist the client, the social worker should:

A. Decline the offer because a consultant with more experience in treating this disorder is needed

B. Accept the offer because the colleague is immediately available to assist

C. Accept the offer because the colleague is knowledgeable about the social worker's skills, which may be valuable in making treatment recommendations

D. Decline the offer because it would be a conflict of interest to use a colleague who is employed by the same agency

152. A woman is court-ordered to receive an evaluation and services from an agency. After completing the evaluation, the client stops coming to appointments so the findings are not reviewed with her and services are not rendered. The social worker has been unable to reach her by phone. The court has requested a copy of the evaluation report. In this instance, the social worker should:

A. Notify the court by submitting the report and information about the client not coming to appointments

B. Claim privilege and not release the report to the court as it is confidential

C. Request that the court get a signed release from the client prior to submitting it

D. Send the client a registered letter with a copy of the court's request in an effort to motivate her to contact the social worker

153. All of the following are reasons that social workers should seek agency accreditation EXCEPT:

A. Accreditation provides accountability to the public.

B. Accreditation justifies higher salaries for agency workers.

C. Accreditation involves objective evaluation of agency processes and outcomes.

D. Accreditation assists with professional development of agency personnel.

154. A couple is seeing a social worker for marriage counseling. After several months, they decide to end their marriage and ask the social worker to make a child custody recommendation to the court because they feel that she is best suited to make suggestions since she has worked with the couple for so long. The social worker should:

    A. Decline because it is not appropriate since they are both current counseling clients
    B. Accept because both clients agree that it would produce the best child custody recommendation
    C. Decline until the social worker is contacted by the court directly
    D. Accept, but with the understanding that further sessions will be needed to collect the information needed by the courts

155. A social worker completes an assessment report after several meetings with the client. The report begins by describing the social worker's observations with regard to the client's appearance, orientation, and affect. It refers to using educational, legal, and psychological documents shared by the client during the sessions. The assessment contains presenting problems in addition to treatment recommendations. The social worker's supervisor who reviews this assessment would consider it to be inadequate because it:

    A. Relies on educational, legal, and psychological sources to make recommendations
    B. Contains subjective observations with regard to the client's appearance, orientation, and affect
    C. Omits the strengths and resources of the client and his/her community
    D. Includes treatment recommendations in the assessment document

156. Which of the following BEST describes summative evaluation criteria for a prisoner reentry program?

    A. Reincarceration rates
    B. Program satisfaction
    C. Criminal history
    D. Length of services

157. A couple comes in to see a social worker because of their destructive pattern of fighting. The husband complains that his wife is always nagging him to do things around the house and suggests that he will get them done if she just stops complaining. The husband is stating that his behavior will improve if which of the following behavioral techniques is used?

    A. Positive reinforcement
    B. Positive punishment

C. Negative reinforcement

D. Negative punishment

158. Which of the following is TRUE about a client who is transgender?

A. The client is likely to undergo sexual reassignment surgery in the future.

B. The client is likely to be gay or lesbian.

C. The client is likely to be a cross dresser.

D. The client is likely to experience stigma, bias, and/or discrimination as a result of his or her gender identity.

159. A client reports that she is under the surveillance of the police and that they have been following her for days, as well as listening in on her phone conversations. There is no other evidence to support this belief. The client's report is MOST likely resulting from a:

A. Dissociation

B. Delusion

C. Hallucination

D. Hypomanic state

160. After completing an assessment, a client states that she would like to work on being more assertive at work. In order to best assist the client, the social worker should FIRST:

A. Provide the client with communication strategies aimed at self-expression

B. Assist the client with identifying classes aimed at assertiveness training

C. Gather information on issues at her current and past jobs that have resulted from communication barriers

D. Identify the outcome that she hopes to attain from this behavioral change

161. During the first session, a young woman sobs as she states that she does not think that she will ever get through the recent dissolution of her marriage. She ends by saying that she "is alone and nobody understands how I feel." In order to instill hope, the social worker should:

A. Talk about how she felt the same way during her own divorce and is now happily remarried

B. Assure her that she will have the opportunity to express her feelings and work through them in the coming weeks

C. Refer her to a support group with other women who are going through divorce

D. Evaluate whether she is at risk for self-harm

162. A client is being discharged from an inpatient hospitalization. Upon admission, he slept most of the time, reported extreme despair, and felt hopeless. Several days later, while hospitalized, he appeared jittery and agitated. His speech was rambling and he wandered around the unit, talking to others for hours. He also had trouble sleeping. This client is MOST likely going to be prescribed which of the following medications upon discharge?

   A. Lithium
   B. Elavil
   C. Ativan
   D. Haldol

163. Which of the following is generally TRUE about self-image during the life cycle?

   A. Self-esteem declines during adolescence due to body image concerns, puberty, and academic/social challenges.
   B. Self-esteem generally increases in older adulthood because individuals have fewer demands placed upon them in retirement.
   C. Self-esteem gradually declines during adulthood, leveling off around age 60.
   D. Young children have relatively low self-esteem, but it gradually increases over childhood.

164. A client starts to miss appointments with a social worker after achieving her goals. Prior to these absences, she had very good attendance and had made substantial progress. These missed appointments are MOST likely an indication of:

   A. Readiness to terminate from services
   B. Emergence of a new problem that needs to be addressed
   C. Dissatisfaction with achieved outcomes
   D. Codependency that needs to be addressed as a treatment issue

165. A client has just been diagnosed with Stage 4 cancer and is referred to a pain management group to minimize the discomfort associated with her illness. The provision of this service is BEST represented as which of the following?

   A. Tertiary prevention
   B. Primary prevention
   C. Secondary prevention
   D. Hospice

166. A school social worker is seeing a 14-year-old girl who confides that she is struggling with gender identity issues and is being teased by peers. Several weeks later, the principal asks the social worker what is

"going on" with her client because she was involved in an altercation with other students. The principal asks to see her file in order to better understand her issues because she is facing out-of-school suspension for her behavior. The principal thinks that the information contained in the file will help reduce her punishment. The social worker should:

A. Share the file with the principal since it will potentially assist the client

B. Refrain from letting the principal see the file, but explain the client's situation

C. Prepare a written summary of the client's struggles to share with the principal

D. Tell the principal that the information is confidential and cannot be released

167. If social workers engage in appropriate physical contact with clients, all of the following must be present in the boundaries that govern such contact EXCEPT:

A. Contact should not occur with those for which such contact could cause psychological harm.

B. Contact should only occur with adult clients and not children.

C. Contact should be culturally sensitive, considering the customs, beliefs, and traditions of clients.

D. Rules for the use of contact should be able to be clearly articulated by both social workers and their clients.

168. Acculturation is BEST defined as which of the following?

A. One culture seeking ways to establish its own identity from others that exist

B. One culture incorporating elements, such as attitudes, beliefs, or behaviors, of another culture into its own ways

C. One culture wanting to dominate another as a way of obtaining social rewards

D. One culture trying to work with others despite differences

169. A social worker is contacted by a man who is very distraught. He is aware that his mother was a client of the social worker because she has recently passed away and he has found bills for services in her belongings. He had little contact with her in the last years of her life as she seemed "to pull away." He is trying to understand her behavior and would like to make an appointment to see the social worker. The social worker should:

A. Reassure the son that his mother's behavior was not related to him in any way

B. Explain to the son that the social worker cannot talk to him about his mother

C. Ask him to put his questions in writing so the social worker can see whether the information can be released

D. Schedule a session to try to assist

170. Which of the following uses "person-first language"?

A. The disabled

B. Individuals with disabilities

C. Disabled people

D. Disabled population

Practice Test

Answers

1. B

Regular exercise and good nutrition are actions that are classified as primary prevention, helping to avoid developing diseases, injuries, and/or illnesses. The other three response choices are secondary prevention strategies that occur after diseases, injuries, and/or illnesses have developed to mitigate or slow their progression/impacts.

Knowledge Area

Unit III—Intervention Processes and Techniques for Use With Larger Systems (Content Area); Methods for Social Change (Competency); Primary, Secondary, and Tertiary Prevention Strategies (KSA)

2. D

All of the options, except the last response choice, are actions taken by a client during treatment. Indicators of resistance can also include engaging in intellectual talk by using technical terms or abstract concepts, asking questions of a social worker that are not related to his or her issues or problems, being preoccupied with past events instead of current issues, false promising, and/or flattering a social worker in an attempt to "soften" him or her so as not to be pushed.

A client who was referred by another person may not necessarily be apprehensive about change, but instead may not have known where to seek help. Behaviors that occur after a client has seen a social worker are better indicators of resistance.

Knowledge Area

Unit II—Intervention Processes and Techniques for Use Across Systems (Content Area); Assessment Methods and Techniques (Competency); The Indicators of Motivation, Resistance, and Readiness to Change (KSA)

3. C

Social workers should provide clients with reasonable access to their records. Social workers who are concerned that clients' access to their records could cause serious misunderstanding or harm to a client should provide assistance in interpreting the records and consultation with a client regarding the records. Social workers should limit clients' access to their records, or portions of their records, only in exceptional circumstances when there is compelling evidence that such access would cause serious harm to a client.

In this case vignette, there was not a risk of harm due to the release, so the social worker should have provided access; however, information can be withheld in some circumstances, as described, as long as the request and the reason for the denial is documented in the client's file.

Knowledge Area

Unit IV—Professional Relationships, Values, and Ethics (Content Area); Confidentiality (Competency); The Use of Client/Client System Records (KSA)

4. D

The *NASW Code of Ethics* states social workers who have direct knowledge of colleague impairment that is due to personal problems, psychosocial distress, substance abuse, or mental health difficulties that interfere with practice effectiveness should consult with the colleague when feasible and assist the colleague in taking remedial action. Going to the agency director may be appropriate, but only after the social worker has gone to the colleague FIRST.

Knowledge Area

Unit IV—Professional Relationships, Values, and Ethics (Content Area); Confidentiality (Competency); Legal and/or Ethical Issues Regarding Mandatory Reporting (e.g., Abuse, Threat of Harm, Impaired Professionals, etc.) (KSA)

5. B

Role discomplementarity occurs when role expectations are not being met and activities associated with these expectations are not carried out in an expected manner. In this case vignette, the client's belief about what her son should be doing is not consistent with his behavior. In addition, the son is dissatisfied with the fulfillment of the role expectations that he has for his mother. This case vignette solely involves role issues and not communication, discipline, or developmental problems.

Knowledge Area

Unit I—Human Development, Diversity, and Behavior in the Environment (Content Area); Effects of the Environment on Systems' Behavior (Competency); Role Theories (KSA)

6. D

Conflict theory posits that society is fragmented into groups that compete for social and economic resources (B). Social order is maintained by those with the greatest political, economic, and social resources (C). Inequality exists because those in control of a disproportionate share of society's resources actively defend their advantages.

Conflict theorists challenge the status quo, encourage social change, and believe rich and powerful people force social order on the poor and the weak. This constant competition between groups forms the basis for the ever-changing nature of society (A).

The masses are bound by coercion by those in power. This perspective emphasizes social control, NOT consensus and conformity (D).

Knowledge Area

Unit I—Human Development, Diversity, and Behavior in the Environment (Content Area); Human Growth and Development (Competency); Theories of Conflict (KSA)

7. B

The case vignette requires the social worker to view the unemployment "using a systems approach." Although the job loss is causing financial concerns, it would also have an impact on other aspects of the client's life, such as his physical and mental health. Systems theory indicates that a change to one part of a client's life will impact on others.

Knowledge Area

Unit II—Intervention Processes and Techniques for Use Across Systems (Content Area); Biopsychosocial History and Collateral Data (Competency); Biopsychosocial Factors Related to Mental Health (KSA)

8. D

Adderall, Ritalin, and Dexedrine are stimulants that are used for the treatment of Attention-Deficit/Hyperactivity Disorder. Tofranil is an antidepressant and is used primarily to treat Depressive Disorders. However, it is also used at times for the treatment of Anxiety Disorders.

Knowledge Area

Unit II—Intervention Processes and Techniques for Use Across Systems (Content Area); Biopsychosocial History and Collateral Data

(Competency); Common Psychotropic and Non-Psychotropic Prescriptions and Over-the-Counter Medications and Their Side Effects (KSA)

9. A

Cocaine use is indicated by dilated pupils, hyperactivity, euphoria, anxiety, and/or excessive talking.

Heroin use is indicated by contracted pupils, sleeping at unusual times, sweating, vomiting, twitching, and/or loss of appetite. Marijuana use is indicated by glassy, red eyes; inappropriate laughter; and/or loss of interest/motivation. Painkiller addiction is indicated by sleepiness, inattention, constipation, and/or loss of appetite.

Knowledge Area

Unit II—Intervention Processes and Techniques for Use Across Systems (Content Area); Biopsychosocial History and Collateral Data (Competency); The Indicators of Addiction and Substance Abuse (KSA)

10. A

Since the Tarasoff case in 1974, duty to warn has become an important concept in social work. Being able to protect potential victims from harm and protecting clients from self-harm are ethical obligations. Duty to warn means that social workers must verbally tell intended victims that there is a foreseeable danger of violence. In addition, social workers have a duty to protect, so social workers who determine that their clients present a serious danger of violence to others have an obligation to use reasonable care to protect the intended victims against danger. This may entail police notification or other necessary steps.

Knowledge Area

Unit II—Intervention Processes and Techniques for Use Across Systems (Content Area); Assessment Methods and Techniques (Competency); Risk Assessment Methods (KSA)

11. C

Those with high ego strength approach problems with a sense that they can overcome problems and even grow as a result. They try to find new ways to cope with struggles and handle challenges without losing their sense of self. On the contrary, those with low ego strength view challenges as something to avoid. Reality seems overwhelming and they may try to avoid it through wishful thinking, fantasies, and/or substance use.

Knowledge Area

Unit II—Intervention Processes and Techniques for Use Across Systems (Content Area); Assessment Methods and Techniques (Competency); Methods to Assess Ego Strengths (KSA)

12. D

Couples development follows the stages of Margaret Mahler, who chronicled the experiences of parents and children. There are five developmental stages—symbiosis, differentiation, practicing, rapprochement, and mutual interdependence. Symbiosis, the first stage, is when partners are passionate, nurturing, and selflessly attentive to each other's needs (D). They place few demands on one another and create enduring attachment, which is the foundation that allows couples to move to the second stage, differentiation. Differentiation occurs when partners begin to notice annoyances with issues that were previously unnoticed; it is reemergence of the self in relation to the partner. Practicing, the third stage, is the time when autonomy and individuality become primary (A). Rapprochement, which follows, occurs when openness and vulnerability begin to reemerge (B); partners feel comfortable with their own individuality in the relationship. The last stage, mutual interdependence, is marked by constancy; each partner is able to value and respect the separateness of the other (C).

Knowledge Area

Unit I—Human Development, Diversity, and Behavior in the Environment (Content Area); Functioning of Various Systems (Competency); Theories of Couples Development (KSA)

13. D

Clients who receive their antipsychotic medications via injection are more likely to continue their medications than those who take them orally. Since injectable medications are usually only needed once or twice per month, it may be easier to remember these appointments than taking pills several times a day. This consistency in medication compliance may result in fewer hospitalizations and few symptom relapses. Those on injectable medications are also less likely to overdose or use their medications for suicide. The cost of the medications is not a therapeutic consideration.

Knowledge Area

Unit II—Intervention Processes and Techniques for Use Across Systems (Content Area); Biopsychosocial History and Collateral Data (Competency); Common Psychotropic and Non-Psychotropic Prescriptions and Over-the-Counter Medications and Their Side Effects (KSA)

14. B

Medical necessity is a criterion used to determine whether treatments and services are justified as reasonable, necessary, and/or appropriate, based on evidence-based clinical standards of care. Payment for services, as well as whether levels of care are justified, uses medical necessity to assess whether treatment and service requests are "reasonable and necessary" given clients' diagnoses and/or presenting problems.

Knowledge Area

Unit III—Intervention Processes and Techniques for Use With Larger Systems (Content Area); Supervision and Administration (Competency); The Effects of Policies, Procedures, Regulations, and Legislation on Social Work Practice and Service Delivery (KSA)

15. B

All of the described activities are routinely expected of board members of human service organizations with the exception of using an agency as a referral source for a social worker's private practice. Serving former agency clients is a conflict of interest, and it is unethical for the social worker to arrange to have them referred to her, even if the rate is reduced.

Knowledge Area

Unit IV—Professional Relationships, Values, and Ethics (Content Area); Professional Values and Ethical Issues (Competency); Ethical Issues Related to Dual Relationships (KSA)

16. A

Program evaluation usually relies on both subjective and objective data. The "facts" or objective outcomes include days incarcerated, number of subsequent hospitalizations, and so forth. Subjective information, such as how the "facts" are perceived by clients through descriptions of their feelings, experiences, and perceptions, is equally important. Subjective outcomes often provide valuable information about how the service experience was viewed by those served. The satisfaction of foster parents and perceived safety of children are subjective, not objective, outcomes of a foster care program. The number of children served is not an outcome. The proportion of children reunified is the only objective outcome in the response choices provided.

Knowledge Area

Unit III—Intervention Processes and Techniques for Use With Larger Systems (Content Area); Program Development and Research (Competency); The Principles and Features of Objective and Subjective Data (KSA)

17. B

Clients with Borderline Personality Disorder tend to view the world in black and white, all-or-nothing, dichotomous thinking. These polarized thoughts lead to intense emotional reactions that are unable to be regulated. Clients with Borderline Personality Disorder often engage in self-destructive behavior and act impulsively.

Knowledge Area

Unit II—Intervention Processes and Techniques for Use Across Systems (Content Area); Assessment Methods and Techniques (Competency); The Use of the Diagnostic and Statistical Manual of the American Psychiatric Association (KSA)

18. C

The FIRST goal is to immediately relieve the stress experienced, return clients to previous levels of functioning, and assist them with regaining equilibrium. A social worker may want to work with clients to identify precursors, develop coping skills, and/or link with others for mutual support, but these actions would occur after the crisis has subsided.

Knowledge Area

Unit II—Intervention Processes and Techniques for Use Across Systems (Content Area); Intervention Planning and Implementation (Competency); Crisis Intervention and Treatment Approaches (KSA)

19. B

Social workers are mandated reporters. Despite the supervisor's assessment not reaching the same conclusion, the social worker still must make a report because she has "a reasonable suspicion." It would not be appropriate to delay to collect more information and/or try to convince the supervisor of the need. In addition, the social worker should be forthcoming with her supervisor about her actions and not anonymously report.

Knowledge Area

Unit IV—Professional Relationships, Values, and Ethics (Content Area); Confidentiality (Competency); Legal and/or Ethical Issues Regarding Mandatory Reporting (e.g., Abuse, Threat of Harm, Impaired Professionals, etc.) (KSA)

20. C

Social workers are mandated reporters. In this instance, the social worker should not be making an assessment about these being isolated incidents or the likelihood that they would happen again. The *NASW Code of Ethics* states that clients should be informed whenever possible of such reports. Not telling the family would not be warranted as they are likely to find out that the social worker contacted the child protection agency and will feel betrayed without being told that such a report was being made.

The social worker should have reviewed the limits of confidentiality with this family upon intake.

Knowledge Area

Unit IV—Professional Relationships, Values, and Ethics (Content Area); Confidentiality (Competency); Legal and/or Ethical Issues Regarding Mandatory Reporting (e.g., Abuse, Threat of Harm, Impaired Professionals, etc.) (KSA)

21. B

The conflict between the client and his boss focuses on the completion of tasks associated with the job. In order for the client to successfully function in his new employment role, he must start with a clear understanding of what is expected of him by his boss. Disputes, such as the one described, often arise because clients are unclear about role expectations (*role ambiguity*) or have different role expectations than others (*role discomplementarity*). These disputes lead to incompatible or conflicting expectations (*role conflicts*). Thus, determining whether the client's understanding of his duties differ from those in his job description and/or the expectations of his boss would be helpful in understanding whether his problems stem from a lack of clarity or agreement with regard to his role (B).

Obtaining mediation assistance (A) will not help the social worker *understand the situation* as presented in the question. There is no indication that the criticism by his boss is affecting his job performance (C) or that he is unwilling to complete the work (D). Thus, they are not the likely causes of the problem.

Knowledge Area

Unit I—Human Development, Diversity, and Behavior in the Environment (Content Area); Effects of the Environment on Systems' Behavior (Competency); Role Theories (KSA)

22. D

The *unconscious* contains thoughts, feelings, desires, and memories of which clients have no awareness, but that influence every aspect of their day-to-day lives.

The *preconscious* contains all the information outside of a client's attention, but that is readily available, if needed.

The *conscious* contains all the information that a client is paying attention to at any given time.

The *superego* is the moral component of personality. It causes clients to feel guilty when they go against society's rules.

Knowledge Area

Unit I—Human Development, Diversity, and Behavior in the Environment (Content Area); Human Growth and Development (Competency); Psychoanalytic and Psychodynamic Approaches (KSA)

23. D

A social worker must view a couple or family as a system, with actions of each member affecting the others. Couples and families try to maintain homeostasis or stability in their relationships so that they do not have to change as a result of actions exhibited outside the "norm" of members. This can be problematic if one member of the couple or family is learning new coping skills because others are likely to fight the healthy changes.

The husband is trying to maintain *homeostasis* (D). A *suprasystem* is an entity that is served by a number of component systems organized in interacting relationships. It is a high-level system in which other systems play subsystem roles. It is a way to describe the relationship between systems and is not a cause of the husband's behavior. *Negative entropy* is the exchange of energy and resources between systems that promote growth and transformation. It is an open system and is not the reason for the husband's behavior.

Knowledge Area

Unit I—Human Development, Diversity, and Behavior in the Environment (Content Area); Human Growth and Development (Competency); Systems and Ecological Perspectives and Theories (KSA)

24. C

The problem-solving process consists of engaging, assessing, planning, intervening, evaluating, and terminating. Thus, planning is done after an assessment is complete.

Knowledge Area

Unit II—Intervention Processes and Techniques for Use Across Systems (Content Area); Intervention Planning and Implementation (Competency); Problem-Solving Models and Approaches (e.g., Brief, Solution-Focused Methods or Techniques) (KSA)

25. A

Symbolization occurs when emotional feelings are associated with an object or, in this instance, the client's tattoo. The tattoo represents internal ideas, attitudes, and/or feelings of the client's mother. It evokes emotions that were present during her illness and represents her bravery.

Knowledge Area

Unit I—Human Development, Diversity, and Behavior in the
Environment (Content Area); Effects of the Environment on Systems'
Behavior (Competency); Psychological Defense Mechanisms and Their
Effects on Behavior and Relationships (KSA)

26. B

There is a strong relationship between research and policy in social work.
Research findings are very useful to inform policy development, and
research agendas must be driven by issues and problems facing clients
(A). Resources are scarce, so ensuring that services are efficient and
effective is critical. Allocations of funds are made based upon evaluation
outcomes (C). Researchers and policy-makers do not speak the same
professional language (D). Thus, report findings must be jargon free and
presented in a manner that a lay person can understand.

    Policy-makers often have to digest a lot of information. Research
articles in academic journals are not easily understandable. Social workers
should highlight research results in formats that are useful to those with
decision-making authority and power, NOT give them the full reports
(B) in which key findings may be difficult to identify.

Knowledge Area

Unit III—Intervention Processes and Techniques for Use With Larger
Systems (Content Area); Methods for Social Change (Competency);
Techniques to Inform and Influence Organizational and Social Policy (KSA)

27. D

Social workers should not engage in sexual activities or sexual contact
with former clients because of the potential for harm to a client (D). If a
social worker engages in conduct contrary to this prohibition or claims
that an exception to this prohibition is warranted because of extraordinary
circumstances, it is the social worker—not the client—who assumes the
full burden of demonstrating that the former client has not been exploited,
coerced, or manipulated, either intentionally or unintentionally.

    Given the high relapse potential in substance abuse, the social worker
in this case vignette should decline the invitation because the former
client may need to use the residential facility again. Having a romantic
relationship with the former client would preclude use of the residential
facility in the future, resulting in fewer service options or harm to the
client. In addition, there is a potential for unintentional exploitation,
coercion, or manipulation given the nature of the services provided.

Knowledge Area

Unit IV—Professional Relationships, Values, and Ethics (Content Area);
Professional Values and Ethical Issues (Competency); Professional

Boundaries in the Social Worker–Client/Client System Relationship (e.g., Power Differences, Conflicts of Interest, etc.) (KSA)

28. C

The primary benefit of peer supervision is the reciprocal learning through the sharing of experiences.

Peer supervision is based on the use of feedback to assist with self-directed learning and evaluation. Peer supervision is not always associated with cost savings and this is not its biggest benefit if they do occur. In order for peer supervision to be effective, it should occur regularly and be scheduled, not just happen "on the fly."

Knowledge Area

Unit III—Intervention Processes and Techniques for Use With Larger Systems (Content Area); Supervision and Administration (Competency); Models of Supervision and Consultation (e.g., Individual, Peer, Group) (KSA)

29. A

Maslow's hierarchy of needs can be divided into basic (or deficiency) needs (i.e., physiological, safety, social, and esteem) and growth needs (i.e., self-actualization). "Deficiency needs" arise due to deprivation, according to Maslow.

Knowledge Area

Unit I—Human Development, Diversity, and Behavior in the Environment (Content Area); Human Growth and Development (Competency); Basic Human Needs (KSA)

30. B

Social work interventions or treatments MUST be selected based upon the biopsychosocial–spiritual–cultural assessments of clients, which include the strengths that they possess, as well the identification of feasible and desired outcomes within larger service contexts.

Knowledge Area

Unit II—Intervention Processes and Techniques for Use Across Systems (Content Area); Intervention Planning and Implementation (Competency); The Criteria Used in the Selection of Intervention/Treatment Modalities (e.g., Client/Client System Abilities, Culture, Life Stage) (KSA)

31. A

This social worker is assessing need using secondary data, which is information that has already been collected for other purposes. Use of existing data is efficient since time and money associated with data collection are spared. However, the completeness of existing data, as well as its reliability, may be a concern. Thus, clients who could benefit from this group may not be identified (A) if they did not disclose that they had children or issues with child-rearing on their intake applications—even if both are true. Data collection is only being done to assess the need for developing this service, and since clients are not actually being selected for the group, B is not a primary concern. Data to determine whether clients can benefit from an additional service can be collected within an agency and need is best assessed using objective or empirical data, so C and D are not reasons for alarm.

Knowledge Area

Unit III—Intervention Processes and Techniques for Use With Larger Systems (Content Area); Program Development and Research (Competency); Data Collection and Analysis Methods (KSA)

32. **B**

Data analysis procedures begin with preparation that involves cleaning the data and checking it for accuracy (A). It is eventually coded for analysis and entered into a computer database given that data analysis is usually now done electronically (D). Social workers must balance the level of detail that is generated by data analysis to avoid its being so overwhelming as to increase the likelihood that major findings will be missed (C).

In most research, analyses include use of both descriptive AND inferential statistics, making B incorrect. Descriptive statistics provide information about the basic features of the data, such as simple summaries about the sample and the measures. However, inferential statistics are also important and are used to answer research questions or test models or hypotheses.

Knowledge Area

Unit III—Intervention Processes and Techniques for Use With Larger Systems (Content Area); Program Development and Research (Competency); Data Collection and Analysis Methods (KSA)

33. **A**

The main tasks in families with young children include realigning the family system to make space for children, adopting and developing parenting roles, realigning relationships with families of origin to include parenting and grandparenting roles, and facilitating children to develop peer relationships. Adjusting to children taking a more central role in family maintenance is usually associated with later family life when children are adults.

Knowledge Area

Unit I—Human Development, Diversity, and Behavior in the Environment (Content Area); Functioning of Various Systems (Competency); The Family Life Cycle (KSA)

34. D

Risk factors are associated with an increased likelihood that a client or community will be affected by, or become a perpetrator of, violence. Risk factors can occur at the individual, family, school, and community levels. Not everyone who is identified as being "at risk" becomes involved in violence. Risk factors are negatively associated with protective factors (i.e., the more likely that risk factors are present, the less likely that there are existing protective factors).

Knowledge Area

Unit II—Intervention Processes and Techniques for Use Across Systems (Content Area); Biopsychosocial History and Collateral Data (Competency); The Indicators and Risk Factors of the Client's/Client System's Danger to Self and Others (KSA)

35. C

The mission of the social work profession is rooted in a set of core values. These core values are the foundation of social work's unique purpose and perspective. The values stated in the preamble of the *NASW Code of Ethics* are service, social justice, dignity and worth of the person, importance of human relationships, integrity, and competence.

Knowledge Area

Unit IV—Professional Relationships, Values, and Ethics (Content Area); Professional Values and Ethical Issues (Competency); Professional Values and Principles (e.g., Competence, Social Justice, Integrity, and Dignity and Worth of the Person) (KSA)

36. D

Social workers should not provide clinical services to individuals with whom they have had prior intimate relationships. Providing clinical services to a former girlfriend has the potential to be harmful to her and it may be difficult for the social worker and the former girlfriend to maintain appropriate professional boundaries.

Knowledge Area

Unit IV—Professional Relationships, Values, and Ethics (Content Area); Professional Values and Ethical Issues (Competency); Professional Boundaries in the Social Worker–Client/Client System Relationship (e.g., Power Differences, Conflicts of Interest, etc.) (KSA)

37. C

The need for services to complement one another and not be duplicative is central to meeting client needs. Although several of the response choices may be correct, the development of service networks must directly help clients navigate the delivery system. Service networks ensure that duplication is reduced and integration is increased (C).

All of the other response choices focus on benefits for agencies or payers, which are not the MOST important function of service networks.

Knowledge Area

Unit III—Intervention Processes and Techniques for Use With Larger Systems (Content Area); Program Development and Research (Competency); Methods to Establish Service Networks or Community Resources (KSA)

38. D

Social workers are allowed to defend themselves when sued by clients. Such a defense usually involves releasing information related to treatment. However, social workers should limit the information released to that which is relevant to the allegations in the lawsuit.

Knowledge Area

Unit IV—Professional Relationships, Values, and Ethics (Content Area); Confidentiality (Competency); Legal and/or Ethical Issues Regarding Confidentiality, Including Electronic Information Security (KSA)

39. B

Social workers should not terminate services to pursue social, financial, or sexual relationships with clients or when they believe that clients are making poor choices.

Social workers in fee-for-service settings may terminate services to clients who are not paying overdue balances if the financial contractual arrangements have been made clear, if clients do not pose an imminent danger to self or others, and if the clinical and other consequences of the current nonpayment have been addressed and discussed.

Social workers who are leaving employment settings can terminate with clients after informing them of appropriate options for the continuation of services and the benefits and risks of the options.

Knowledge Area

Unit IV—Professional Relationships, Values, and Ethics (Content Area); Professional Values and Ethical Issues (Competency); Legal and/or Ethical Issues Related to Termination (KSA)

40. B

Compassion fatigue is associated with burnout and compassion satisfaction. Resilience is negatively correlated with compassion fatigue and with burnout. A negative relationship means that as resilience increases, compassion fatigue decreases as they are inversely related. Contrarily, compassion satisfaction and resilience are positively related.

Knowledge Area

Unit IV—Professional Relationships, Values, and Ethics (Content Area); Professional Development and Use of Self (Competency); Burnout, Secondary Trauma, and Compassion Fatigue (KSA)

41. C

Legal involvement was removed as a diagnostic criterion from the Substance-Related and Addictive Disorders category of the *DSM-5*.

Knowledge Area

Unit II—Intervention Processes and Techniques for Use Across Systems (Content Area); Assessment Methods and Techniques (Competency); The Use of the Diagnostic and Statistical Manual of the American Psychiatric Association (KSA)

42. A

A mental status examination is a structured way of observing and describing a client's current state of mind, under the domains of appearance, attitude, behavior, mood and affect, speech, thought processes, thought content, perception, cognition, insight, and judgment. It is NOT a psychiatric evaluation aimed at diagnosing disorders. Many disorders or conditions cause delirium such as alcohol/drug abuse or withdrawal and infections. Delirium involves a quick change between mental states (e.g., from lethargy to agitation and back to lethargy). Symptoms that can be detected by a mental status examination include changes in alertness (usually more alert in the morning, less alert at night), awareness, orientation to time or place, memory, recall, and mood (personality changes).

Knowledge Area

Unit II—Intervention Processes and Techniques for Use Across Systems (Content Area); Biopsychosocial History and Collateral Data (Competency); The Components and Function of the Mental Status Examination (KSA)

43. B

In social work, triangulation indicates that multiple sources or methods are used to gather information and/or check results. A social worker may be more confident that he or she has the information needed or is accurate with conclusions drawn if different sources/methods lead to the same result. By using multiple sources or methods, a social worker can hope to overcome the weakness or intrinsic biases and the problems that come from a single source or method.

Knowledge Area

Unit II—Intervention Processes and Techniques for Use Across Systems (Content Area); Assessment Methods and Techniques (Competency); Methods of Involving Clients/Client Systems in Problem Identification (e.g., Gathering Collateral Information) (KSA)

44. C

Case presentations are also used in professional development and learning to provide input into options for treatment and to ensure services are being delivered effectively and efficiently. Although there is no universal format for a case presentation, it should contain demographic information, client and family history, and the presenting problem. In addition, a case presentation should contain the social worker's impressions and treatment recommendations. Thus, the summary described is unsatisfactory because it does not contain these elements (B).

Knowledge Area

Unit III—Intervention Processes and Techniques for Use With Larger Systems (Content Area); Supervision and Administration (Competency); The Elements of a Case Presentation (KSA)

45. B

SOAP stands for Subjective, Objective, Assessment, and Plan. In the Subjective and Objective sections, a client's subjective and objective well-being are reported by the social worker. In the Assessment section, a social worker pulls together these subjective and objective findings and consolidates them into a short assessment. A Plan is then made based upon the assessment. The SOAP format does not outline cost and/or payment for services or insurance coverage.

Knowledge Area

Unit III—Intervention Processes and Techniques for Use With Larger Systems (Content Area); Program Development and Research (Competency); The Principles and Features of Objective and Subjective Data (KSA)

46. D

Crisis intervention focuses on the here and now, is time limited (most crises last from 4 to 6 weeks), is directive, and requires high levels of activity and involvement from social workers. Social workers' primary goal is to return clients to equilibrium and meet their immediate needs. Although the first response choice indicates that the support is short term, it is incorrect because social workers focus on meeting basic needs, not "restoring clients' psychological capacities."

Knowledge Area

Unit II—Intervention Processes and Techniques for Use Across Systems (Content Area); Intervention Planning and Implementation (Competency); Crisis Intervention and Treatment Approaches (KSA)

47. B

Equifinality refers to the concept that similar outcomes may stem from different experiences. Different early experiences in life (i.e., parental divorce, physical abuse, parental substance abuse) can lead to similar outcomes (i.e., diagnoses). In other words, there are many different experiences that can lead to the same problems, behaviors, and/or disorders.

Knowledge Area

Unit I—Human Development, Diversity, and Behavior in the Environment (Content Area); Human Growth and Development (Competency); Systems and Ecological Perspectives and Theories (KSA)

48. C

The social worker has agreed to be an executrix, a woman legally named to carry out the provisions of a will. This is a conflict of interest or dual relationship and is unethical (C). Despite the social worker agreeing not to be compensated, which often occurs when assuming this role, there is a risk that these responsibilities may interfere or conflict with those that are critical to social work services. For example, the social worker's duties as executrix may lead to discussions with the client that focus on financial matters, overshadowing the emotional feelings that the client may need to address as a result of his terminal illness diagnosis.

In addition, the social worker's education and training do not necessarily include the handling of legal and financial matters, leading to questions of competence as an executrix. Lastly, the social worker should not assume the legal authority to make decisions with regard to a client's personal or financial affairs, such as being his or her guardian or executrix, as these roles create a power differential between the two parties and can easily be conflicting, especially as related to matters of client self-determination.

Knowledge Area

Unit IV—Professional Relationships, Values, and Ethics (Content Area); Professional Values and Ethical Issues (Competency); Ethical Issues Related to Dual Relationships (KSA)

49. D

The receipt of an influenza immunization is the only response choice aimed at disease prevention. Participation in a support group and reducing strenuous activity are associated with managing or living with her COPD. Such actions are tertiary prevention. Monitoring her medication is an activity aimed to slow the progression or long-term impacts of her conditions, including high blood pressure. Thus, medication monitoring is a secondary prevention activity.

Knowledge Area

Unit III—Intervention Processes and Techniques for Use With Larger Systems (Content Area); Methods for Social Change (Competency); Primary, Secondary, and Tertiary Prevention Strategies (KSA)

50. C

Self-monitoring consists of clients systematically observing their own behavior. Most clients are not entirely aware of the extent to which they engage in various behaviors and/or antecedents or consequences of their actions. When clients are provided with the opportunity to observe their own behaviors carefully, dramatic changes often occur by the mere monitoring of the behaviors themselves.

Knowledge Area

Unit II—Intervention Processes and Techniques for Use Across Systems (Content Area); Intervention Planning and Implementation (Competency); Client/Client System Self-Monitoring Techniques (KSA)

51. D

Because the parents do not speak or understand English, the social worker should arrange for a qualified interpreter or translator. The use of the daughter to translate for her parents is not appropriate because the parents may be apprehensive to identify the family's true needs to their daughter. In addition, the social worker will only hear what the parents say as per the daughter. Valuable information may be omitted or lost. The daughter also may not communicate what the social worker is saying in a manner that is appropriate or accurate.

Knowledge Area

Unit II—Intervention Processes and Techniques for Use Across Systems (Content Area); Intervention Planning and Implementation (Competency); The Principles and Techniques of Interviewing (e.g., Supporting, Clarifying, Focusing, Confronting, Validating, Feedback, Reflecting, Language Differences, Use of Interpreters, Redirecting) (KSA)

52. C

Expressed needs (C) are defined by the number of clients who have sought help. A major weakness of using expressed needs to justify program development is that it assumes that all those with needs seek help.

Social workers may want to use other methods for determining need to avoid this problem. Relative needs (A) are concerned with equity or comparing the needs of clients with the goal of ranking them. Perceived needs (B) are defined by what clients think about their needs, with the standard set by each client. Absolute needs (D) are those which are needed for basic survival or well-being, such as food, shelter, clothing, and so on.

Knowledge Area

Unit III—Intervention Processes and Techniques for Use With Larger Systems (Content Area); Program Development and Research (Competency); Methods to Establish Service Networks or Community Resources (KSA)

53. A

Tardive dyskinesia is a neurological disorder of involuntary movements caused by long-term use of antipsychotic drugs. These medications may be used to treat Schizophrenia Spectrum and Other Psychotic Disorders. Symptoms include tongue protrusion, grimacing, lip smacking, or other involuntary movements of the head, face, neck, and tongue muscles.

Knowledge Area

Unit II—Intervention Processes and Techniques for Use Across Systems (Content Area); Biopsychosocial History and Collateral Data (Competency); Common Psychotropic and Non-Psychotropic Prescriptions and Over-the-Counter Medications and Their Side Effects (KSA)

54. D

Regardless of setting, a social worker who identifies that an ethical dilemma exists should determine an appropriate action in light of key social work values and principles as defined by the *NASW Code of Ethics* (D). After implementation, the social worker should continue to monitor the situation and make further changes based upon these values and principles.

Knowledge Area

Unit IV—Professional Relationships, Values, and Ethics (Content Area); Professional Values and Ethical Issues (Competency); Techniques to Identify and Resolve Ethical Dilemmas (KSA)

55. B

Cognitive behavioral therapy aims to change patterns of thinking or behavior that are responsible for clients' difficulties. In this approach, the social worker assists the client to change attitudes and his or her behavior by focusing on the thoughts, images, beliefs, and attitudes that are held (cognitive processes) and replacing distorted thinking patterns with healthy ones (cognitive restructuring).

Knowledge Area

Unit II—Intervention Processes and Techniques for Use Across Systems (Content Area); Intervention Planning and Implementation (Competency); Cognitive and Behavioral Interventions (KSA)

56. A

During middle adulthood, individuals establish careers, settle down within relationships, begin families, and develop a sense of being a part of the bigger picture. They give back to society through raising children, being productive at work, and becoming involved in community activities and organizations. By failing to achieve these objectives, individuals become stagnant and feel unproductive.

Knowledge Area

Unit I—Human Development, Diversity, and Behavior in the Environment (Content Area); Human Growth and Development (Competency); Theories of Human Development Throughout the Lifespan (e.g., Physical, Social, Emotional, Cognitive, Behavioral) (KSA)

57. D

Triangulation occurs when there is anxiety and tension between two individuals that may cause them not to communicate directly. In this situation, they communicate through a third person, leading to the formation of a triangle. Often the two people try to get the third to take each of their sides when disagreements arise.

Knowledge Area

Unit II—Intervention Processes and Techniques for Use Across Systems (Content Area); Intervention Planning and Implementation (Competency); Family Therapy Models, Interventions, and Approaches (KSA)

58. C

Many of the problems reported by the couple appear to be caused by the alcohol use of the husband, including his unemployment, their financial problems, and her absence from the home. The social worker should FIRST determine the husband's willingness to address his drinking because many of the reported problems will not change if this behavior continues. Treating substance abuse and medical issues always comes first because they are often the etiological causes of negative impacts on psychosocial well-being.

Knowledge Area

Unit II—Intervention Processes and Techniques for Use Across Systems (Content Area); Intervention Planning and Implementation (Competency); Couples Interventions and Treatment Approaches (KSA)

59. B

There are many influences on client behavior including individual, interpersonal, institutional, and community factors (A). In addition, human behavior can be explained through many theoretical perspectives, such as systems, conflict, rational choice, psychodynamic, developmental, social behavioral, and humanistic perspectives (C). Client behavior can also be explained using social constructivism which sees individuals as social beings who interact with each other and the physical world based on shared meanings (D).

Most importantly, social workers assess the interactions of clients with their environments and view all behavior using an ecological perspective, making B NOT true.

Knowledge Area

Unit I—Human Development, Diversity, and Behavior in the Environment (Content Area); Human Growth and Development (Competency); Systems and Ecological Perspectives and Theories (KSA)

60. D

The biopsychosocial–spiritual–cultural assessment provides critical information on the current/presenting issue or issues, including a client's past and present physical health and developmental milestones.

In order to be complete, the biological section should contain a client's medical history, developmental history, current medications, substance abuse history, and family history of medical illnesses. The information that was collected from the social worker in the case vignette is acceptable, but is not adequate or sufficient for a thorough assessment.

Knowledge Area

Unit II—Intervention Processes and Techniques for Use Across Systems (Content Area); Biopsychosocial History and Collateral Data (Competency); The Components of a Biopsychosocial Assessment (KSA)

61. C

Legal practices refer to processes and policies to abide by laws dictated by government. Ethical practices refer to behavioral guidelines that result from personal morals and values, as well as standards of conduct that are set by social work professionals for those who are practicing within the field.

In this case vignette, the social worker is acting illegally, but ethically (C). The social worker is legally required to comply with the terms of the court order. By not providing the information, the social worker is breaking the law. However, by not placing the client and the client's family in danger, the social worker is fulfilling the primary mission of the profession: the enhancement of human well-being. Thus, the social worker is behaving ethically.

Knowledge Area

Unit IV—Professional Relationships, Values, and Ethics (Content Area); Confidentiality (Competency); Legal and/or Ethical Issues Regarding Confidentiality, Including Electronic Information Security (KSA)

62. C

Case recording helps social workers be accountable for their actions and decision making, as well as demonstrates their integrity as professionals. Case records help social workers understand what has happened in treatment so that practice decisions are made based on information that is up-to-date, accurate, and relevant. While some of the incorrect answers may be accurate, the most important reason for all social workers' actions is to ensure that clients get the most effective services, which can only be done with proper documentation.

Knowledge Area

Unit III—Intervention Processes and Techniques for Use With Larger Systems (Content Area); Record-Keeping and Reporting (Competency); The Principles of Case Recording, Documentation, and Management of Practice Records (KSA)

63. D

Engagement is aimed at starting to build the therapeutic alliance. When a client is involuntary, he or she may be reluctant to trust the social worker and may think that the social worker does not understand his or her life circumstances. Thus, listening is the most effective action because it begins to build rapport. It shows the client that the social worker cares about what is being said and is nonjudgmental.

Knowledge Area

Unit II—Intervention Processes and Techniques for Use Across Systems (Content Area); Intervention Planning and Implementation (Competency); Methods to Engage and Work With Involuntary Clients/Client Systems (KSA)

64. D

Social workers in fee-for-service settings may terminate services to clients who are not paying overdue balances if the financial contractual arrangements have been made clear to clients, *if clients do not pose an imminent danger to self or others*, and if the clinical and other consequences of the current nonpayment have been addressed and discussed. In the case vignette, the client appears upset and states that he cannot "go on." Such a statement may be an indication of suicide risk. The social worker must assess this risk and provide appropriate supports/referrals prior to termination.

Knowledge Area

Unit IV—Professional Relationships, Values, and Ethics (Content Area); Professional Values and Ethical Issues (Competency); Legal and/or Ethical Issues Related to Termination (KSA)

65. D

The social worker should NOT begin the problem-solving process, including the intake or assessment, because she already has a prior relationship with the daughter in the school setting. The *NASW Code of Ethics* states that social workers should take appropriate action to minimize any conflict of interest. An agreement for the social worker to be a consultant from the onset is also a conflict because the school social worker will then be serving her in different roles in both settings.

Knowledge Area

Unit IV—Professional Relationships, Values, and Ethics (Content Area); Professional Values and Ethical Issues (Competency); Ethical Issues Related to Dual Relationships (KSA)

66. D

In *Jaffe v. Redmond* (1996), the U.S. Supreme Court ruled that the clients of clinical social workers have the right to privileged communication in federal courts. In various rulings, courts have identified numerous exceptions to clients' right of privileged communication. One of these exceptions is when a social worker's testimony about a client is required so that the social worker can defend himself or herself against a lawsuit filed by the client (D).

Disclosure of privileged information may also be permissible when a client threatens to commit suicide, has been abused or neglected, and/or may pose a threat to the public. Whether a social worker must disclose privileged information without a client's consent is often a matter of dispute and subject to relevant statutes, regulations, and judicial opinions.

Knowledge Area

Unit IV—Professional Relationships, Values, and Ethics (Content Area); Confidentiality (Competency); Legal and/or Ethical Issues Regarding Confidentiality, Including Electronic Information Security (KSA)

67. B

Social workers who provide supervision are responsible for setting clear, appropriate, and culturally sensitive boundaries. They should not engage in any dual or multiple relationships with supervisees when there is a risk of exploitation of or potential harm to the supervisee.

However, in this case vignette, providing a written recommendation is an appropriate task for the social work supervisor as she would be aware of the supervisee's strengths and learning needs (B). It is critical that the recommendation be fair, accurate, and reflects only those areas of which the supervisor has direct knowledge. There is no inherent conflict of interest or dual relationship. She is instead promoting the professional development of the supervisee—an appropriate aim of a supervisor. The supervisor should not write the recommendation solely because it will benefit the agency, making D incorrect.

Knowledge Area

Unit IV—Professional Relationships, Values, and Ethics (Content Area); Professional Values and Ethical Issues (Competency); Ethical Issues in Supervision and Management (KSA)

68. D

Social workers should not engage in solicitation of testimonial endorsements (including solicitation of consent to use a client's prior statement as a testimonial endorsement) from current clients or from other people who, because of their particular circumstances, are vulnerable to undue influence.

Knowledge Area

Unit IV—Professional Relationships, Values, and Ethics (Content Area); Professional Values and Ethical Issues (Competency); Professional Boundaries in the Social Worker–Client/Client System Relationship (e.g., Power Differences, Conflicts of Interest, etc.) (KSA)

69. D

Self-image or how a client views himself or herself is critical to understand. Typically, younger people describe themselves more in terms of personal traits, such as physical characteristics (D), whereas older people feel defined to a greater extent by their social roles (A). Emotional relationships (B) are critical during Erikson's early adulthood stage of intimacy versus isolation. Intellectual abilities (C) are described by Piaget as the formal operations stage, taking place age 11 through maturity, which is marked by abstract thinking and assumption of adult roles. Thus, cognitive aptitudes are associated with positive self-image in adulthood.

Knowledge Area

Unit I—Human Development, Diversity, and Behavior in the Environment (Content Area); Human Growth and Development (Competency); Factors Influencing Self-Image (e.g., Culture, Race, Religion/Spirituality, Age, Disability, Trauma) (KSA)

70. A

The client's actions are occurring during the first session. There is no indication that his outbursts are dangerous to himself or the social worker. Upon intake, clients are often upset and angry (even at themselves) for their current situations. The problem-solving process starts with engagement.

Because the case vignette is asking what the social worker should do FIRST, the answer should be directly related to engagement. Listening to the client as a way of building rapport will help facilitate change. The other answers will interfere with development of the therapeutic alliance and/or may come later in the process.

Knowledge Area

Unit IV—Professional Relationships, Values, and Ethics (Content Area); Professional Development and Use of Self (Competency); The Principles and Techniques for Building and Maintaining a Helping Relationship (KSA)

71. D

Releasing information is mandated under duty to warn and child abuse and neglect protections. A social worker should inform the client when seeking supervision and/or consultation and get the client's permission to release information. However, in instances in which disclosure is needed to prevent serious, foreseeable, and imminent harm to a client, the social worker can release only the minimum amount of information necessary to prevent such harm. The last response choice, using it for a grant application, is unethical because it is not directly tied to client safety or duty to warn. Identifying client data should never be used in a grant application.

Knowledge Area

Unit IV—Professional Relationships, Values, and Ethics (Content Area); Confidentiality (Competency); Legal and/or Ethical Issues Regarding Confidentiality, Including Electronic Information Security (KSA)

72. A

Risk factors can be categorized in a number of ways, but the most common distinctions in forensic risk assessments are between static and dynamic factors.

Static risk factors are historical factors that do not frequently fluctuate (i.e., genetic predisposition). Static risk factors include characteristics such as number of previous convictions, age, offense type, age at first conviction, and marital status. Many risk assessment tools are based entirely, or almost entirely, on static risk factors. A problem with such assessments is that it is virtually impossible for the offender to alter his or her risk assessment for the better.

Dynamic risk factors are those that can be changed by interventions such as change in living situation, treatment of psychiatric symptoms, abstaining from drug and alcohol use, or access to weapons. Each client presents with a unique set of risk factors that require an individualized plan.

Knowledge Area

Unit II—Intervention Processes and Techniques for Use Across Systems (Content Area); Biopsychosocial History and Collateral Data (Competency); The Characteristics of Perpetrators of Abuse, Neglect, and Exploitation (KSA)

73. A

The social worker is mandated to report this suspicion of child abuse. This question focuses on the FIRST action to be taken. According to the *NASW Code of Ethics*, social workers should inform clients, to the extent possible, about the disclosure of confidential information and the potential consequences, when feasible, before the disclosure is made (A). This applies whether social workers disclose confidential information on the basis of a legal requirement or client consent.

In this case vignette, not telling the client about the need to report the suspected abuse prior to leaving the office will greatly affect the ongoing social worker–client trust. There also should be no delays due to any efforts to gather more information. The social worker should leave the interviewing of the youth to child protection agency staff who are trained in appropriate methods.

Knowledge Area

Unit IV—Professional Relationships, Values, and Ethics (Content Area); Confidentiality (Competency); Legal and/or Ethical Issues Regarding Mandatory Reporting (e.g., Abuse, Threat of Harm, Impaired Professionals, etc.) (KSA)

74. B

According to the *NASW Code of Ethics*, in instances when clients lack the capacity to provide informed consent, social workers should protect clients' interests by seeking permission from an appropriate third party (A) and informing clients consistent with the clients' level of understanding (C). In such instances, social workers should seek to ensure that the third party acts in a manner consistent with the clients' wishes and interests (D).

Clients' lack of capacity to provide informed consent may NOT require guardianship by others (B). In addition, there are many types of guardianship, including full and limited. Full guardianship means that another individual makes all legal, financial, and medical decisions, whereas limited guardianship only allows another individual to make decisions in certain specified areas.

Knowledge Area

Unit IV—Professional Relationships, Values, and Ethics (Content Area); Confidentiality (Competency); The Principles and Processes of Obtaining Informed Consent (KSA)

75. C

Social workers are charged with helping clients who have experienced discrimination by making policy and/or system changes. The social worker should not be seeking alternative methods to assist the couple to become parents because they have the right to adopt and desire to do so. Although they may need support, developing coping skills or connecting them with others will not BEST assist the couple because these actions do not help them ultimately realize parenthood through adoption.

Knowledge Area

Unit III—Intervention Processes and Techniques for Use With Larger Systems (Content Area); Methods for Social Change (Competency); Theories and Methods of Advocacy for Policies, Services, and Resources to Meet Clients'/Client Systems' Needs (KSA)

76. A

The mental development of older adults (age 65–79) and elders (age 80 and above) is characterized by being active learners and thinkers, but with declines in memory. In the oldest years, confusion may signal illness and/or medication problems. Older adults do continue to learn, but are not at their peak with regard to problem solving due to some declines associated with age.

Knowledge Area

Unit I—Human Development, Diversity, and Behavior in the Environment (Content Area); Human Growth and Development (Competency); The

Indicators of Normal and Abnormal Physical, Cognitive, Emotional, and Sexual Development Throughout the Lifespan (KSA)

77. C

From age 6 to puberty, children begin to develop a sense of pride in their accomplishments. If they are encouraged and reinforced for their initiative, they begin to feel industrious and feel confident in their ability to achieve goals. If this initiative is not encouraged, it produces feelings of inferiority.

Knowledge Area

Unit I—Human Development, Diversity, and Behavior in the Environment (Content Area); Human Growth and Development (Competency); Theories of Human Development Throughout the Lifespan (e.g., Physical, Social, Emotional, Cognitive, Behavioral) (KSA)

78. B

The first step in ethical problem solving is to identify ethical standards, as defined by the professional code of ethics, which may be compromised. The social worker should not rely on his supervisor or coworker to determine whether there is an ethical issue or dilemma. By referring directly to the professional code of ethics, the social worker can better weigh ethical issues in light of key social work values and principles, which are explicitly stated in this document.

Knowledge Area

Unit IV—Professional Relationships, Values, and Ethics (Content Area); Professional Values and Ethical Issues (Competency); Techniques to Identify and Resolve Ethical Dilemmas (KSA)

79. D

Evaluation methods can be classified as either qualitative or quantitative. In qualitative evaluations, data are collected through observations and/ or interviews. Findings are generated via identification of themes in the language used and content contained in the communication observed or generated. The focus groups employed by the social worker are qualitative in nature.

Contrarily, quantitative evaluations are conducted by making numerical comparisons and statistical inferences. The social worker's comparison of the number of clients rehospitalized versus the number who were not is a quantitative approach. Since both qualitative and quantitative methods are being used, the social worker is using a mixed method approach to evaluation.

Knowledge Area

Unit III—Intervention Processes and Techniques for Use With Larger Systems (Content Area); Program Development and Research (Competency); Data Collection and Analysis Methods (KSA)

80. B

A role reversal is when two individuals switch roles. The 13-year-old girl has become the caregiver for her father, who is dependent due to his permanent injury. This is a role reversal because a parent would usually be meeting the physical and emotional needs of a child. The other response choices are all role issues, but none contain a reversal in a parent–child relationship.

Knowledge Area

Unit I—Human Development, Diversity, and Behavior in the Environment (Content Area); Effects of the Environment on Systems' Behavior (Competency); Role Theories (KSA)

81. C

Protective factors are attributes that are associated with NOT engaging in dangerous behaviors. They are the opposite of risk factors. All of the options are associated with an increased likelihood of engaging in violence except the provision of clinical services for physical and behavioral care, which is a protective factor.

Knowledge Area

Unit II—Intervention Processes and Techniques for Use Across Systems (Content Area); Biopsychosocial History and Collateral Data (Competency); The Indicators and Risk Factors of the Client's/Client System's Danger to Self and Others (KSA)

82. C

Social workers should obtain clients' informed consent before audio or video recording clients or permitting observation of services to clients by a third party. The consent forms should explicitly state that the sessions will be audiotaped and have information about who will listen to the recordings, how they will be stored, what will happen to the tapes after treatment has ended, and so forth. The risks and benefits associated with audio or video recording should also be reviewed with clients in order to get their informed consent. The permission of the client to make these recordings cannot be assumed or taken for granted as part of standard language about supervision on a consent form.

Knowledge Area

Unit IV—Professional Relationships, Values, and Ethics (Content Area); Confidentiality (Competency); The Principles and Processes of Obtaining Informed Consent (KSA)

83. D

Social workers should not terminate services to pursue a *social*, financial, or sexual relationship with a client.

Knowledge Area

Unit IV—Professional Relationships, Values, and Ethics (Content Area); Professional Values and Ethical Issues (Competency); Ethical Issues Related to Dual Relationships (KSA)

84. B

The social worker was not aware of this potential conflict of interest upon the start of treatment. Once it was discovered, steps, such as minimizing contact and sitting across the room, were taken to mitigate its existence. The client does not have to be referred to another social worker unless it is more comfortable for the client to do so. In addition, the social worker does not have to leave the church. However, the existence of this unanticipated conflict should be discussed so that the client is aware of its existence and strategies for minimizing its impact can be established.

Knowledge Area

Unit IV—Professional Relationships, Values, and Ethics (Content Area); Professional Values and Ethical Issues (Competency); Ethical Issues Related to Dual Relationships (KSA)

85. A

Shaping is used when it may be, or has been, difficult to achieve a goal or demonstrate a behavior. Shaping allows the goal or behavior to be achieved in steps, with each step positively reinforced. After a client achieves each successive step of the behavior or goal, a reward is received and the next step is presented until the desired end result is reached. If the client is having difficulty completing the steps, they should be broken down into smaller increments.

Knowledge Area

Unit II—Intervention Processes and Techniques for Use Across Systems (Content Area); Intervention Planning and Implementation (Competency); Cognitive and Behavioral Interventions (KSA)

86. D

Partialization is a good technique to assist clients in breaking down problems or goals into less overwhelming and more manageable components. However, it does not happen during engagement, but rather during planning and/or intervention. The remaining response choices do occur during engagement and are useful for helping alleviate the fears of resistant clients.

Knowledge Area

Unit II—Intervention Processes and Techniques for Use Across Systems (Content Area); Intervention Planning and Implementation (Competency); Partializing Techniques (KSA)

87. B

Because the receipt of the tickets by the social worker is clearly linked to the referrals, this is a form of "fee splitting," which is not allowed in social work practice. Social workers cannot receive incentives or remuneration for making referrals. The donation of the tickets to a local charity does not justify acceptance of these gifts. Although there is no additional cost to the colleague, the football tickets clearly have monetary value.

Knowledge Area

Unit IV—Professional Relationships, Values, and Ethics (Content Area); Professional Values and Ethical Issues (Competency); Ethical Issues Related to Dual Relationships (KSA)

88. C

The evaluation is court ordered and, therefore, the social worker does not need to get the consent of the client to perform services and/or release information to the court. However, it is essential that the social worker inform the client at the onset about what he has control over and what information will/will not be released. The client not wanting the social worker to release the information does not change the legal duty to do so.

Knowledge Area

Unit II—Intervention Processes and Techniques for Use Across Systems (Content Area); Intervention Planning and Implementation (Competency); Methods to Engage and Work With Involuntary Clients/Client Systems (KSA)

89. C

Extinction is withholding a reinforcer that normally follows a behavior. Since the behavior no longer is reinforced, it will eventually cease. In this case vignette, the boy's reaction of crying is desired by the bullies, so removal of this response by walking away will hopefully reduce the incidents in the future.

Knowledge Area

Unit I—Human Development, Diversity, and Behavior in the Environment (Content Area); Human Growth and Development (Competency); Theories of Human Development Throughout the Lifespan (e.g., Physical, Social, Emotional, Cognitive, Behavioral) (KSA)

90. B

Youth who are not heterosexual and/or gender conforming face the same developmental tasks as their peers. However, they also face additional challenges that are different from their peers, such as the need to develop an identity with few role models. They may have poor self-image; experience harassment, family rejection, stigma, or social isolation; or engage in self-harm or risky behavior. They are often taunted and bullied, resulting in greater risk for mental and physical health complications compared with their peers.

Knowledge Area

Unit I—Human Development, Diversity, and Behavior in the Environment (Content Area); Diversity, Discrimination, and Stereotypes (Competency); The Effect of Discrimination and Stereotypes on Behaviors, Attitudes, and Identity (KSA)

91. C

The NASW *Code of Ethics* indicates that consultation should follow all ethical standards, including avoiding conflicts of interest and maintaining boundaries. In the case vignette, the social worker's wife making changes to the agency's personnel policies that impact her husband is clearly a conflict of interest. Breaching this standard should not be justified because the situation appears desperate and other resources are not evident. It remains a conflict of interest whether the wife charges for her services or not.

Knowledge Area

Unit IV—Professional Relationships, Values, and Ethics (Content Area); Professional Values and Ethical Issues (Competency); Ethical Issues Related to Dual Relationships (KSA)

92. B

Single-subject designs aim to determine if an intervention has the intended impact on a client. Data collected before the start of or during the withdrawal of services is a baseline (denoted by an "A") and is compared to that collected during service delivery (denoted by a "B"). Internal validity is the confidence that the social worker has that behavioral change is caused by an intervention. Thus, ABAB (A) is a design which is more effective in establishing internal validity than AB

(C) because it provides two opportunities, rather than one, to observe changes in the target behavior once an intervention is introduced. D is only a baseline measure with no intervention—denoted by a single "A"—so there is no ability to assess internal validity.

BAB (B) is the correct answer because it is the only design that begins with an intervention. Since the client in this case vignette is in crisis, it would be unethical to delay treatment to collect baseline data. The social worker must choose the design that begins with an intervention rather than a baseline assessment.

Knowledge Area

Unit III—Intervention Processes and Techniques for Use With Larger Systems (Content Area); Program Development and Research (Competency); Basic and Applied Research Designs and Methods (KSA)

93. A

Termination is focused on reviewing accomplishments, anticipating how to address the problem if it arises in the future, and recognition of the loss on the part of the client and social worker because the relationship is ending. Identifying *new* problems is NOT appropriate during termination.

Knowledge Area

Unit II—Intervention Processes and Techniques for Use Across Systems (Content Area); Intervention Planning and Implementation (Competency); The Indicators of Client/Client System Readiness for Termination (KSA)

94. C

Although the beliefs and behaviors of the family may be culturally based, there may be some adverse impacts to the children that threaten their well-being. It is not the responsibility of the social worker to determine the reasons for or impact of their actions. The social worker should get the child protection agency involved so they can investigate the situation further. There also may be some resources available to this family by the child protection agency.

Knowledge Area

Unit IV—Professional Relationships, Values, and Ethics (Content Area); Confidentiality (Competency); Legal and/or Ethical Issues Regarding Mandatory Reporting (e.g., Abuse, Threat of Harm, Impaired Professionals, etc.) (KSA)

95. A

Hodgkin's disease is a type of lymphoma, a cancer of the lymphatic system. The first sign of Hodgkin's disease is often an enlarged lymph node. The disease can spread to nearby lymph nodes. Later, it may spread to the lungs, liver, or bone marrow. The exact cause is unknown.

Knowledge Area

Unit II—Intervention Processes and Techniques for Use Across Systems (Content Area); Biopsychosocial History and Collateral Data (Competency); Basic Medical Terminology (KSA)

96. B

Social workers should make clear distinctions between statements made and actions engaged in as private individuals as opposed to those as representatives of their employing agencies. In the case vignette, the social worker did not protest on agency time or identify himself in any way as an employee of the agency. He acted as a private individual and, therefore, his actions are ethical.

Knowledge Area

Unit III—Intervention Processes and Techniques for Use With Larger Systems (Content Area); Methods for Social Change (Competency); Theories and Methods of Advocacy for Policies, Services, and Resources to Meet Clients'/Client Systems' Needs (KSA)

97. A

Congruence is the matching of awareness and experience with communication. It is essential that a client is able to express himself/ herself and that this communication is reflective of his or her feelings. Congruence is essential for the vitality of a relationship and to facilitate true helping as part of the problem-solving process.

   The client in the case vignette is saying that the relationship is "fine," but his physical symptoms clearly indicate that it is not. This is an example of a lack of congruence in his communication.

Knowledge Area

Unit II—Intervention Processes and Techniques for Use Across Systems (Content Area); Intervention Planning and Implementation (Competency); The Concept of Congruence in Communication (KSA)

98. A

Social workers should not disclose confidential information to third-party payers, including insurance companies, unless clients have authorized such disclosures. Only the first response choice includes reviewing the information requested with the client and getting his or her permission to submit.

Knowledge Area

Unit IV—Professional Relationships, Values, and Ethics (Content Area); Confidentiality (Competency); Legal and/or Ethical Issues Regarding Confidentiality, Including Electronic Information Security (KSA)

99. C

Regression occurs when someone returns to an early state of being. In this instance, the daughter is using more infantile actions, such as "baby talk" and sucking her thumb. Because she did not do them immediately prior to the family's crisis, she may be relieving some of the anxiety of the situation through her dependency, which is further evidenced by clinging and wanting to be physically close to her mother.

Knowledge Area

Unit I—Human Development, Diversity, and Behavior in the Environment (Content Area); Effects of the Environment on Systems' Behavior (Competency); Psychological Defense Mechanisms and Their Effects on Behavior and Relationships (KSA)

100. B

Case records are often an excellent source of information for evaluating the impacts of services. They are existing sources of data so there is no additional cost or time associated with their collection. However, there are a few limitations. If looking at records completed by multiple workers, there may be inconsistencies in recording styles or detail that may impact on evaluations. Also, information of interest may not be contained in the records and evaluations would need to be limited to only information that is explicitly stated, which may not reflect all progress that has been made.

   In addition, the opinions about how a client views both the process and outcomes of service delivery are also critical and may not be fully captured in the record.

Knowledge Area

Unit II—Intervention Processes and Techniques for Use Across Systems (Content Area); Assessment Methods and Techniques (Competency); Methods to Assess Organizational Functioning (e.g., Agency Assessments) (KSA)

101. A

Permanency planning is an approach to child welfare that is based on the belief that children need permanence to thrive. Child protective services should focus on getting children into and maintaining permanent homes.

Knowledge Area

Unit II—Intervention Processes and Techniques for Use Across Systems (Content Area); Intervention Planning and Implementation (Competency); Permanency Planning (KSA)

102. A

When the ego is comfortable with feelings and/or behaviors, a client is said to be ego-syntonic. However, if a client is bothered by some of his or her feelings and/or behaviors, he or she would be ego-dystonic (ego alien).

Knowledge Area

Unit I—Human Development, Diversity, and Behavior in the Environment (Content Area); Human Growth and Development (Competency); Psychoanalytic and Psychodynamic Approaches (KSA)

103. B

Cluster B includes the Personality Disorders that are characterized by dramatic, emotional, and erratic behavior. It includes Borderline Personality Disorder, Narcissistic Personality Disorder, Histrionic Personality Disorder, and Antisocial Personality Disorder. Schizoid Personality Disorder and Paranoid Personality Disorder are in Cluster A (odd and eccentric behavior) and Obsessive-Compulsive Personality Disorder is in Cluster C (anxious and fearful behavior).

Knowledge Area

Unit II—Intervention Processes and Techniques for Use Across Systems (Content Area); Assessment Methods and Techniques (Competency); The Use of the Diagnostic and Statistical Manual of the American Psychiatric Association (KSA)

104. A

The *NASW Code of Ethics* prohibits social workers who function as supervisors or educators from engaging in sexual activities or contact with supervisees, students, trainees, or other colleagues over who they exercise professional authority.

The social worker engaged in a dual relationship with her supervisee, which is unethical.

Knowledge Area

Unit IV—Professional Relationships, Values, and Ethics (Content Area); Professional Values and Ethical Issues (Competency); Ethical Issues Related to Dual Relationships (KSA)

105. D

In authoritarian parenting, children are expected to follow the strict rules established by the parents. Failure to follow such rules usually results in punishment. Authoritarian parents fail to explain the reasoning behind these rules. Like authoritarian parents, those with an authoritative parenting style establish rules and guidelines that their children are expected to follow. However, this parenting style is much more democratic. Authoritative parents are responsive to their children and willing to listen to questions. When children fail to meet the expectations, these parents are more nurturing and forgiving rather than punishing.

Knowledge Area

Unit I—Human Development, Diversity, and Behavior in the Environment (Content Area); Human Growth and Development (Competency); Parenting Skills and Capacities (KSA)

106. A

Individual psychology is a theory of human behavior emphasizing the drive to overcome feelings of inferiority by compensation and the need to achieve personal goals that have value for society.

Alfred Adler believed that the main motives of human thought and behavior were a striving for superiority and power, partly in compensation for feelings of inferiority.

Adler believed that the main motivations for human behavior were not sexual or aggressive urges, but striving for perfection.

Knowledge Area

Unit I—Human Development, Diversity, and Behavior in the Environment (Content Area); Human Growth and Development (Competency); Psychoanalytic and Psychodynamic Approaches (KSA)

107. D

Negative punishment is when a desirable stimulus is removed following an undesirable behavior for the purpose of decreasing or eliminating the behavior. In the case vignette, the client takes away her daughter's cell phone (a desirable stimulus) with the desire to decrease her homework incompletion and tardiness (targeted behaviors).

Knowledge Area

Unit I—Human Development, Diversity, and Behavior in the Environment (Content Area); Human Growth and Development (Competency); Theories of Human Development Throughout the Lifespan (e.g., Physical, Social, Emotional, Cognitive, Behavioral) (KSA)

108. A

According to the *Code of Ethics*, to obtain informed consent social workers must use clear and understandable language with clients to review service purpose and risks (B), limits due to third-party payers (C), and right of refusal or withdrawal (D).

Although it would be helpful for clients to receive information about the setting in which services are to be provided, reviewing the agency's mission (A) is not required. In addition, not all services are delivered in agency settings, but informed consent elements must be reviewed universally, even when services are rendered in private practices or government offices.

Knowledge Area

Unit IV—Professional Relationships, Values, and Ethics (Content Area); Confidentiality (Competency); The Principles and Processes of Obtaining Informed Consent (KSA)

109. A

A task-centered approach aims to quickly engage clients in the problem-solving process and to maximize their responsibility for treatment outcomes. The focus is on the "here and now." The problem is partialized into clearly delineated tasks to be addressed consecutively (*assessment* leads to goals, which lead to tasks). Termination, in this modality, begins almost immediately upon the onset of treatment.

Knowledge Area

Unit II—Intervention Processes and Techniques for Use Across Systems (Content Area); Intervention Planning and Implementation (Competency); Task-Centered Approaches (KSA)

110. D

When social workers engage in group work, they should seek agreement among group members concerning preserving the confidentiality of information shared. However, social workers should inform members that they cannot guarantee that all group members will honor such agreements. Group members do not have the same legal obligations that social workers do to keep information private and protected. However, social workers engaged in group work should use the same professional standards with regard to their own conduct.

Knowledge Area

Unit II—Intervention Processes and Techniques for Use Across Systems (Content Area); Intervention Planning and Implementation (Competency); Group Work Techniques and Approaches (e.g., Developing and Managing Group Processes and Cohesion) (KSA)

111. C

There are four main methods to assess reliability. The social worker is comparing the results of two tests that are believed to assess the same domain—client well-being. This method is used to establish parallel forms reliability (C).

Test–retest reliability (A) involves determining whether an assessment yields the same data in two separate administrations. Interrater or interobserver reliability (B) occurs when assessments of different raters or observers are found to be consistent. Internal consistency reliability (D) is confirmed when items within a single survey or test, thought to measure the same construct, yield consistent results.

Knowledge Area

Unit III—Intervention Processes and Techniques for Use With Larger Systems (Content Area); Program Development and Research (Competency); Methods to Assess Reliability and Validity in Social Work Research (KSA)

112. A

Validation shows empathic understanding of the client's problems. It lets the client know that she is not alone and others are experiencing the same feelings or difficulties. By realizing that her belief is one that is shared by those in similar situations, the client feels less isolated and gains strength by the realization that others have worked through the problem(s) that she is experiencing.

Knowledge Area

Unit II—Intervention Processes and Techniques for Use Across Systems (Content Area); Intervention Planning and Implementation (Competency); The Principles and Techniques of Interviewing (e.g., Supporting, Clarifying, Focusing, Confronting, Validating, Feedback, Reflecting, Language Differences, Use of Interpreters, Redirecting) (KSA)

113. B

Social work interviews are always purposeful and involve verbal and nonverbal communication between social workers and clients during which ideas, attitudes, and feelings are exchanged. The aim is to gather important information used in the problem-solving process.

Social work interviews are designed to serve the interest of clients. Questions in a social work interview should be *tailored* to the specifics of a client, *not generic*, "one size fits all" inquiries.

The purpose of the social work interview can be informational, diagnostic, or therapeutic.

Knowledge Area

Unit II—Intervention Processes and Techniques for Use Across Systems (Content Area); Intervention Planning and Implementation (Competency); The Principles and Techniques of Interviewing (e.g., Supporting, Clarifying, Focusing, Confronting, Validating, Feedback, Reflecting, Language Differences, Use of Interpreters, Redirecting) (KSA)

114. A

Behavior change is best understood as a process with different stages of readiness. For most clients, behavior change occurs gradually over time, with a client progressing from being uninterested, unaware, or unwilling to make a change (precontemplation), to considering a change (contemplation), to deciding and preparing to make a change (preparation). This is followed by definitive action and attempts to maintain the new behavior over time (maintenance).

Contemplation is the first time that there is some movement toward change because a client, while ambivalent about changing, may weigh the benefits versus costs (i.e., time, expense, effort) of change. The client in the case vignette is willing to examine what his life would be like if change occurred. This is contemplation.

Knowledge Area

Unit II—Intervention Processes and Techniques for Use Across Systems (Content Area); Assessment Methods and Techniques (Competency); Methods to Assess Motivation, Resistance, and Readiness to Change (KSA)

115. D

Social workers should take appropriate steps to ensure that participants in research have access to appropriate supportive services (D).

The remaining response choices are NOT true for the following reasons. Social workers engaged in research must always obtain voluntary and written informed consent from participants, even when they are clients of their agencies. When research participants are clients, separate informed consent (A) is essential because of the risk of perceived or actual coercion to participate or the belief by clients that their participation is linked to service receipt. Social workers should never design or conduct research that does not use consent procedures—such as certain forms of naturalistic observation (B) and archival research—unless rigorous and responsible review of the research has found it to be justified by its prospective scientific, educational, or applied value and equally effective alternative procedures that do not involve waiver of consent are not feasible. Lastly, social workers must promote and facilitate research to contribute to the development of knowledge (C).

Knowledge Area

Unit IV—Professional Relationships, Values, and Ethics (Content Area); Professional Values and Ethical Issues (Competency); Research Ethics (e.g., Institutional Review Boards, Use of Human Subjects, Informed Consent) (KSA)

116. A

In social work, human behavior of clients is often explained using systems, conflict, rational choice, social constructionist, psychodynamic, developmental, social behavioral, and humanistic perspectives. Rational choice believes clients behave in a manner that tries to maximize rewards and minimize costs. A psychodynamic perspective is based on the view that unconscious, as well as conscious, mental activity serves as the motivating force in human behavior. A developmental perspective sees human development as occurring in defined, age-related stages, which build upon one another and are distinct. However, the humanistic perspective is based on seeing each client as unique and responsible for choices made. Accordingly, clients have the capacity to change themselves as human behavior is driven by a desire for growth, personal meaning, and competence.

Knowledge Area

Unit I—Human Development, Diversity, and Behavior in the Environment (Content Area); Human Growth and Development (Competency); Personality Theories (KSA)

117. D

Cultural competence involves working in conjunction with natural, informal support and helping networks (i.e., neighborhoods, coworkers, churches, spiritual leaders, healers). The coworker is probably a member of the client's support network and can be useful in the problem-solving process. It is the client's decision of whether information can be shared. The social worker should use the coworker as a valuable source of information about the problem as the coworker is a collateral source.

Knowledge Area

Unit II—Intervention Processes and Techniques for Use Across Systems (Content Area); Assessment Methods and Techniques (Competency); Methods of Involving Clients/Client Systems in Problem Identification (e.g., Gathering Collateral Information) (KSA)

118. C

Empowerment is a multidimensional social work process that helps clients gain control over their lives. It fosters clients to use their strengths and skills to make changes that they desire. Only C focuses on clients solving their own problems, a fundamental concept in empowerment.

Knowledge Area

Unit II—Intervention Processes and Techniques for Use Across Systems (Content Area); Intervention Planning and Implementation (Competency); Strengths-Based and Empowerment Strategies and Interventions (KSA)

119. C

Social and political action involves a social worker's ethical responsibility to broader society. Social workers should engage in social and political action that seeks to ensure that people have equal access to and expanded choice for needed resources (C). Social workers should promote conditions that encourage respect for cultural and social diversity.

Although empowering clients and educating them about the value of social and political action are important, the *NASW Code of Ethics* does not mandate client behavior, but serves as a guide for social workers' actions—making D incorrect.

Knowledge Area

Unit III—Intervention Processes and Techniques for Use With Larger Systems (Content Area); Methods for Social Change (Competency); Theories and Methods of Advocacy for Policies, Services, and Resources to Meet Clients'/Client Systems' Needs (KSA)

120. D

Ego strength is the ability of the ego to effectively deal with the demands of the id, the superego, and reality. It is a basis for resilience and helps maintain emotional stability by coping with internal and external stress.
Indicators of positive ego strength include clients:
- Not getting overwhelmed by their moods
- Using painful events to strengthen themselves
- Taking responsibility for actions
- Holding themselves accountable
- NOT blaming others
- Accepting themselves with their limitations

Knowledge Area

Unit II—Intervention Processes and Techniques for Use Across Systems (Content Area); Assessment Methods and Techniques (Competency); Methods to Assess Ego Strengths (KSA)

121. C

Group development can be characterized by the sequential steps of forming (preaffiliation), storming (power and control), norming (intimacy), performing (differentiation), and adjourning (separation/termination).

Knowledge Area

Unit I—Human Development, Diversity, and Behavior in the Environment (Content Area); Functioning of Various Systems (Competency); Theories of Group Development and Functioning (KSA)

122. D

The client has experienced discrimination. Although the social worker must be concerned about the impacts of this discrimination, such as feelings of hopelessness and depression (C), he or she has an ethical mandate to assist the client to fight the housing discrimination (D) or the root cause of the problem.

Advocacy is essential to meeting the client's goal because she is discouraged and thinking that change cannot occur but "would not like this treatment to happen to others." The social worker must work with the client to have her voice heard and educate her about tangible steps that can be taken to end such practices. A, B, and C may be included or addressed in treatment, but her goals have to "focus on" the discrimination because the feelings and alternative housing resulted from this core problem.

Knowledge Area

Unit III—Intervention Processes and Techniques for Use With Larger Systems (Content Area); Methods for Social Change (Competency); Theories and Methods of Advocacy for Policies, Services, and Resources to Meet Clients'/Client Systems' Needs (KSA)

123. B

Referent power is derived from interpersonal relationships with others (B). It arises from charisma, as well as personal connections with key people who have decision-making authority and are influential.

Legitimate power (A) is also known as positional power. It comes from one's position within an organizational hierarchy. Expert power (C) arises from possessing knowledge or expertise in a particular area. Those with expert power perform critical tasks, are deemed indispensable, and are held in high regard. Reward power (D) results from the ability to influence the allocation of incentives, such as salary increments, positive appraisals, and/or promotions.

Knowledge Area

Unit III—Intervention Processes and Techniques for Use With Larger Systems (Content Area); Supervision and Administration (Competency); The Relationship Between Formal and Informal Power Structures in the Decision-Making Process (KSA)

124. D

Internal validity addresses the extent to which causal inferences can be made about the intervention and the targeted behavior. There are many threats to internal validity, including history, maturation (client behavior changing because of maturational occurrences in the life course and not as a result of the intervention), selection biases, testing, statistical regression, instrumentation (use of revised or alternate scales causing differential results rather than the intervention itself causing the noted changes), and mortality/attrition.

In this case scenario, the social worker is concerned with maturation of clients (a threat to internal validity) being responsible for the change instead of program effects.

Knowledge Area

Unit III—Intervention Processes and Techniques for Use With Larger Systems (Content Area); Program Development and Research (Competency); Basic and Applied Research Designs and Methods (KSA)

125. C

Conversion is when mental conflict or disturbance is transferred into a physical symptom to relieve anxiety. The loss of movement in her arm may have resulted from the desire to strike her child.

Knowledge Area

Unit I—Human Development, Diversity, and Behavior in the Environment (Content Area); Effects of the Environment on Systems' Behavior (Competency); Psychological Defense Mechanisms and Their Effects on Behavior and Relationships (KSA)

126. B

If the social worker has concerns about the consultant's recommendations and thinks they will be detrimental to clients, he or she cannot ethically implement them, but must make clear why such a decision is being made. It would be advisable for the social worker to speak to his or her supervisor and even the agency director or the consultant, if permitted and appropriate, to discuss the concerns. However, the social worker should not implement them because of the consultant's educational background and expertise or let the agency director decide. The social worker is also not responsible for hiring another consultant because the first one was contracted by the agency. In instances like the one described, the recommendations of consultants may not ultimately be implemented by the organization, may be modified based on the concerns, and/or may be studied further for their appropriateness.

Knowledge Area

Unit II—Intervention Processes and Techniques for Use Across Systems (Content Area); Intervention Planning and Implementation (Competency); Consultation Approaches (e.g., Referrals to Specialists) (KSA)

127. D

Statutory law is set by "statutes" or laws made by legislatures, locally or on the state or federal levels. Common law is made by judges. It is created by the courts deciding cases. When a court decides a case, it sets a "precedent" or binding example that other courts follow. When a large number of judges decide the same kind of case or question of law in the same way, the decision becomes "common law."

Knowledge Area

Unit III—Intervention Processes and Techniques for Use With Larger Systems (Content Area); Supervision and Administration (Competency); The Basic Terminology of Professions Other Than Social Work (e.g., Legal, Educational) (KSA)

128. A

None of the behaviors listed in the response choices, when engaged in by social workers, are illegal (unless they violate state statute or regulation related to the practice of social work). Adults can legally write recommendations, date other adults, borrow money, and/or have business relationships. However, dating, borrowing money, and/or having a dual (business) relationship with clients are prohibited by the *NASW Code of Ethics.*

A social worker can certainly write a recommendation for a current (or even former) client as long as the content is based on information collected as part of service delivery and the social worker is not making assertions or drawing conclusions beyond the scope of the therapeutic relationship.

Knowledge Area

Unit IV—Professional Relationships, Values, and Ethics (Content Area); Professional Values and Ethical Issues (Competency); Legal and/or Ethical Issues Related to the Practice of Social Work, Including Responsibility to Clients/Client Systems, Colleagues, the Profession, and Society (KSA)

129. D

Pretest–posttest single-subject designs are widely used in social work, principally for measuring change resulting from treatment/service delivery. The definitive characteristic of this study design is that (at least) two measurements are made on a client system: the pretest measurement (baseline) made prior to the administration of a treatment or intervention and the posttest measurement made at a point in time reasonably afterward (intervention). A baseline is denoted by an "A" and an intervention is denoted by a "B." A pretest–posttest design would be AB.

Knowledge Area

Unit III – Intervention Processes and Techniques for Use With Larger Systems (Content Area); Program Development and Research (Competency); Basic and Applied Research Designs and Methods (KSA)

130. C

DSM-5 does not include Caffeine Use Disorder, although research shows that as little as two to three cups of coffee can trigger a withdrawal effect marked by tiredness or sleepiness. There is sufficient evidence to support this as a condition, but it is not yet clear to what extent it is a clinically significant disorder. To encourage further research on the impact of this condition, Caffeine Use Disorder is included in Section III of the *DSM-5*.

Knowledge Area

Unit II—Intervention Processes and Techniques for Use Across Systems (Content Area); Assessment Methods and Techniques (Competency); The Use of the Diagnostic and Statistical Manual of the American Psychiatric Association (KSA)

131. A

Connectedness between human beings can be understood within an *evolutionary* context. Children come into the world biologically preprogrammed to form attachments with others, because this will help them to survive. In addition, some theories suggest that attachment is a set of *learned behaviors*. Insecure attachment systems have been linked to psychiatric disorders and can result in clients reacting in a hostile and rejecting manner. Cultural influences impact on attachment. Thus, attachment and bonding must be viewed, keeping in mind a client's cultural background and traditions.

Knowledge Area

Unit I—Human Development, Diversity, and Behavior in the Environment (Content Area); Human Growth and Development (Competency); The Principle of Attachment and Bonding (KSA)

132. B

In the Asian culture, there is usually respect for elders and a hierarchical family structure with strictly prescribed roles and rules of behavior. The family and extended kinship network is often involved in treatment. The grandparents are traditionally viewed as the most knowledgeable and their opinions are held in high esteem.

Knowledge Area

Unit I—Human Development, Diversity, and Behavior in the Environment (Content Area); Diversity, Discrimination, and Stereotypes

(Competency); The Effect of Culture, Race, and Ethnicity on Behaviors, Attitudes, and Identity (KSA)

133. A

Displacement is directing an impulse, wish, or feeling toward a less threatening object. The client is getting angry at his family instead of expressing this emotion with his boss.

Knowledge Area

Unit I—Human Development, Diversity, and Behavior in the Environment (Content Area); Effects of the Environment on Systems' Behavior (Competency); Psychological Defense Mechanisms and Their Effects on Behavior and Relationships (KSA)

134. B

Social workers should protect the confidentiality of clients during legal proceedings to the extent permitted by law. When a court of law orders social workers to disclose confidential or privileged information without client consent, especially that which can be harmful, social workers should request that the court maintain the records "under seal." Filing "under seal" allows sensitive or confidential information to be filed with a court without becoming a matter of public record (B).

Knowledge Area

Unit IV—Professional Relationships, Values, and Ethics (Content Area); Confidentiality (Competency); Legal and/or Ethical Issues Regarding Confidentiality, Including Electronic Information Security (KSA)

135. C

Summarization seeks to bring together the important points of a discussion and to heighten awareness of progress made. It omits irrelevant information and organizes pertinent aspects of the interaction. It provides a sense of closure at the completion of a discussion. During summarization, social workers and clients strive to grasp the significance of what has been said, to formulate the meaning of the information, and to achieve new understandings.

In this case vignette, the social worker uses summarization at the end of a session to pull together the meaning of what has been said by each family member. This technique allows the family to better understand the common theme in session discussions and perhaps gain a new understanding about the behaviors of others.

Knowledge Area

Unit II—Intervention Processes and Techniques for Use Across Systems (Content Area); Intervention Planning and Implementation (Competency); Verbal and Nonverbal Communication Techniques (KSA)

136. A

Entropy is associated with disorder in a system. Higher entropy means higher disorder and lower availability of the system's energy to do useful work. Although the concept of entropy originated in thermodynamics, it is applicable to communications, psychology, and sociology. The term is often used in systems theory.

Knowledge Area

Unit I—Human Development, Diversity, and Behavior in the Environment (Content Area); Human Growth and Development (Competency); Systems and Ecological Perspectives and Theories (KSA)

137. B

Ethnicity refers to the idea that one is a member of a particular cultural group that may share some of the following elements: religion, language, customs, and/or beliefs. Two people can share the same race, but have different ethnicities. Their customs and beliefs, as well as traditions, may be very different. However, individuals in a racial group may also be in the same cultural group.

Knowledge Area

Unit I—Human Development, Diversity, and Behavior in the Environment (Content Area); Diversity, Discrimination, and Stereotypes (Competency); The Principles of Culturally Competent Social Work Practice (KSA)

138. C

There are four different ways to assess reliability or consistency. Interrater reliability uses different independent raters/observers to see if there are consistent estimates of the behavior. Alternative or parallel forms use two means of data collection constructed in the same way to see if they yield the same result. Test–retest reliability determines if assessments fluctuate from one time to another. Internal consistency looks at measurements within a test or assessment to see if they yield comparable results. Only establishing interrater reliability requires two or more independent staff to record the data.

Knowledge Area

Unit III—Intervention Processes and Techniques for Use With Larger Systems (Content Area); Program Development and Research (Competency); Methods to Assess Reliability and Validity in Social Work Research (KSA)

139. C

External validity is concerned with the ability to generalize the results. In this case vignette, the director agency is worried about the effectiveness of the program with adults versus children.

Knowledge Area

Unit III—Intervention Processes and Techniques for Use With Larger Systems (Content Area); Program Development and Research (Competency); Methods to Assess Reliability and Validity in Social Work Research (KSA)

140. A

Despite the client's report that she will not act on her thoughts, she is at risk because she has these feelings. The case vignette does not describe the social worker taking any action yet. A safety assessment will determine the severity of the depression and whether she is at risk for a suicide attempt. It must be done FIRST before any other action is taken.

Knowledge Area

Unit II—Intervention Processes and Techniques for Use Across Systems (Content Area); Biopsychosocial History and Collateral Data (Competency); The Indicators and Risk Factors of the Client's/Client System's Danger to Self and Others (KSA)

141. A

Folie à deux is very rare and describes when identical or similar psychiatric disorders affect two or more people, who usually have a close relationship. Often these disorders involve delusions, especially those that are paranoid.

Knowledge Area

Unit II—Intervention Processes and Techniques for Use Across Systems (Content Area); Biopsychosocial History and Collateral Data (Competency); The Indicators of Mental and Emotional Illness Throughout the Lifespan (KSA)

142. C

The "reasonable suspicion" of the social worker makes reporting to the child protection agency necessary. This report should not be delayed to monitor the situation and/or collect additional information. The social worker should tell the mother of her need to report and support the mother and child through the process. Having the mother present when the social worker contacts the child protection agency may alleviate the mother's fears about what is being disclosed and the social worker can help the mother to understand the next steps after such a report is made.

Knowledge Area

Unit IV—Professional Relationships, Values, and Ethics (Content Area); Confidentiality (Competency); Legal and/or Ethical Issues Regarding Mandatory Reporting (e.g., Abuse, Threat of Harm, Impaired Professionals, etc.) (KSA)

143. C

Human development in social work uses a strengths-based approach to understand how humans develop and grow throughout the life course. It does NOT pathologize or describe development in terms of problems that focus on deficit. Such an approach is often used in a medical model of medicine. Social work focuses on resiliency and adaptation.

Knowledge Area

Unit I—Human Development, Diversity, and Behavior in the Environment (Content Area); Human Growth and Development (Competency); Theories of Human Development Throughout the Lifespan (e.g., Physical, Social, Emotional, Cognitive, Behavioral) (KSA)

144. A

A subpoena is a request by the court for information. The social worker must respond. When receiving a subpoena, a social worker should claim privilege and not turn over records unless the court issues a subsequent court order to do so. A subpoena and a court order are not the same. When a social worker gets a court order, he or she should try to limit its scope and/or ask that the records be sealed.

Knowledge Area

Unit IV—Professional Relationships, Values, and Ethics (Content Area); Confidentiality (Competency); Legal and/or Ethical Issues Regarding Confidentiality, Including Electronic Information Security (KSA)

145. A

Erikson's first stage, which occurs in the first year of life, focuses on children learning the ability to trust others. They learn whether their needs can be met by others, and insecurities can develop if these attachments are not nurturing. Children then go through three states (autonomy vs. shame/doubt, initiative vs. guilt, and industry vs. inferiority) that all focus on autonomy and exertion of independence. In adulthood, there is a need to begin to connect with others as part of intimacy versus isolation.

Knowledge Area

Unit I—Human Development, Diversity, and Behavior in the Environment (Content Area); Human Growth and Development (Competency); Theories of Human Development Throughout the Lifespan (e.g., Physical, Social, Emotional, Cognitive, Behavioral) (KSA)

146. D

Cultural competence involves working in conjunction with natural, informal support, as well as helping networks (i.e., neighborhoods, churches, spiritual leaders, and healers). The social worker should help prepare the client for the meeting and provide other support as needed. The social worker should not be evaluating the client's reasons for seeking guidance from her priest. In addition, the biopsychosocial–spiritual–cultural functioning of the client is the focus of treatment; the client should not feel that the social worker is not interested or able to address and consider her religious/spiritual concerns.

Knowledge Area

Unit I—Human Development, Diversity, and Behavior in the Environment (Content Area); Diversity, Discrimination, and Stereotypes (Competency); The Effect of Culture, Race, and Ethnicity on Behaviors, Attitudes, and Identity (KSA)

147. B

Consent is the agreement of clients or their authorized representatives, who have legal authority to make decisions for them, to participate in treatment.

Assent is a term used to express willingness to participate in treatment by clients who are too young to give consent or have been deemed by the courts as incapable of making legal decisions. Assent by itself is not sufficient. If assent is given, social workers must still obtain consent from clients' parents or guardians.

Court-mandated services do not require clients' consent, but clients should be advised at the onset what they have control over and what they do not in these situations. In some states, children can access limited services without parental consent, but the terms still have distinct meanings.

Knowledge Area

Unit IV—Professional Relationships, Values, and Ethics (Content Area); Confidentiality (Competency); The Principles and Processes of Obtaining Informed Consent (KSA)

148. A

When social workers involve consultants or others in the feedback process related to client care, clients should provide consent.

Social workers should ask for feedback in difficult circumstances—not just when circumstances appear neutral or positive. Sometimes the best learning can come from those who will be critical. Feedback is especially important at key decision points. Social workers must always be clear about why feedback is needed and what will be done with the information.

Knowledge Area

Unit II—Intervention Processes and Techniques for Use Across Systems (Content Area); Intervention Planning and Implementation (Competency); Methods to Obtain and Provide Feedback (KSA)

149. B

A social worker's self-awareness about his or her own attitudes, values, and beliefs concerning cultural differences and a willingness to acknowledge racial/cultural differences are critical factors in working with diverse populations. Supervision and consultation are important, but a client is the expert of his or her experiences. There are more intragroup differences than intergroup ones, so no customs or beliefs are universal. Asking a client if this is a problem from the onset may make a client feel that a social worker cannot assist or will not understand his or her problems because of the ethnic or racial differences.

Knowledge Area

Unit IV—Professional Relationships, Values, and Ethics (Content Area); Professional Development and Use of Self (Competency); The Dynamics of Diversity in the Social Worker–Client/Client System Relationship (KSA)

150. A

Community organization and development are methods of intervention that focus on addressing social problems. Social workers assist communities in identifying problems, causes, and solutions aimed at improving the lives of community members. Basic tenets of these activities require full participation of community members in the change and development efforts.

In the case vignette, there are many broad reasons cited for the development of youth programs. In order to be most effective, the social worker should FIRST help community members prioritize the youth problems to be addressed; without a more defined focus, the program will not be successful. It would be impossible for a single youth program to positively address all the problems noted, so the social worker should initially work to narrow the goals of the program, thereby increasing its likelihood of success.

Knowledge Area

Unit III—Intervention Processes and Techniques for Use With Larger Systems (Content Area); Methods for Social Change (Competency); Theories of Social Change and Community Development (KSA)

151. A

Social workers should seek the advice and counsel of colleagues whenever such consultation is in the best interests of clients, but should only do so from colleagues who have demonstrated knowledge, expertise, and competence related to the subject of the consultation.

Although willing, the colleague probably does not have expertise and competence related to the disorder because both social workers began working at the agency upon graduation and this disorder is not commonly treated in this setting. There is no conflict of interest in having a colleague in the same agency provide consultation if the colleague has the requisite knowledge and skills.

Knowledge Area

Unit II—Intervention Processes and Techniques for Use Across Systems (Content Area); Intervention Planning and Implementation (Competency); Consultation Approaches (e.g., Referrals to Specialists) (KSA)

152. A

The woman is court-ordered to receive an evaluation and services from an agency. As this client is involuntary, the social worker should have told her at the initial meeting that information would be shared with the court and the scope of what was to be submitted. In this instance, the client does not have privilege (B) and a signed release is not needed (C). Trying to outreach to the client via other means of communication (D) is a good idea, but the social worker is required to submit the report, which is not mentioned in this response choice.

The protection of confidential information requires great care. Social workers should know the exceptions to confidentiality and how to handle practice records when working with court-ordered clients. In this case vignette, the social worker should send the court the report and information about the client not coming to appointments (A).

Knowledge Area

Unit IV—Professional Relationships, Values, and Ethics (Content Area); Confidentiality (Competency); Legal and/or Ethical Issues Regarding Confidentiality, Including Electronic Information Security (KSA)

153. B

Accreditation should not be used to justify higher salaries for agency workers (B), but instead to ensure that clients get the most effective services possible and resources are used appropriately and efficiently.

Accreditation provides accountability to the public (A) by having agency practices and outcomes reviewed (C) by an external entity which is objective. Accreditation reviews help social workers and other agency personnel learn more about best practices and how to critically think and analyze service delivery. Thus, accreditation aids in professional development of those involved (D).

Knowledge Area

Unit III—Intervention Processes and Techniques for Use With Larger Systems (Content Area); Supervision and Administration (Competency); Accreditation and/or Licensing Requirements (KSA)

154. A

The process and goals for completion of a child custody evaluation are vastly different than those used in marriage counseling. Making child custody recommendations would be inappropriate because both parties were not informed from the onset that discussions and information collected would be used for this purpose. In addition, both parties are current counseling clients. Often child custody evaluation recommendations are not favorable and/or acceptable to both parents. Providing such a recommendation may, therefore, not be in the best interest or promote positive well-being for one or both of the current clients.

Knowledge Area

Unit IV—Professional Relationships, Values, and Ethics (Content Area); Professional Values and Ethical Issues (Competency); Ethical Issues Related to Dual Relationships (KSA)

155. C

Social work assessments must contain the strengths and resources of a client, as well as the communities of which they are a part. These elements are key as they will be used to improve client conditions. Most information comes from direct reports, but social workers can add to information gathered via interviews by consulting important documents such as psychiatric, educational, vocational, and medical records. Sources used for assessments should be documented. While there is no standard format, many assessments begin with descriptions of a client's personal appearance including appropriate dress, personal hygiene, ability to maintain eye contact, and mental orientation (awareness of person, place, time, and event). Treatment recommendations based on gathered information are appropriately contained in the assessment, though some formats may keep these separate. All social work assessments must contain client strengths and resources.

Knowledge Area

Unit III—Intervention Processes and Techniques for Use With Larger Systems (Content Area); Record-Keeping and Reporting (Competency); The Elements of Client/Client System Reports (KSA)

156. A

Summative evaluations examine the outcomes of programs. Since prisoner reentry programs attempt to ease the transition of those who are leaving jail or prison and provide support to avoid rearrest, reincarceration (A) is a good indicator of service effectiveness.

Program satisfaction (B) and length of services (D) are formative evaluation criteria because formative evaluations focus on the process of delivering services. Understanding clients' feelings and experiences is useful feedback that can help drive program improvements. It is also critical to assess whether clients stay in services or drop out.

Criminal history (C) is an extraneous variable that has to be controlled when assessing outcomes because it can be related to client success; however, it is not an outcome measure.

Knowledge Area

Unit III—Intervention Processes and Techniques for Use With Larger Systems (Content Area); Program Development and Research (Competency); Methods, Techniques, and Instruments Used to Evaluate Social Work Practice (KSA)

157. C

Negative reinforcement is the removal of an aversive (negative) stimulus with the goal of increasing the targeted behavior. In the case vignette, the husband says that he will do more around the house (targeted behavior) if the wife stops (removes) the nagging (negative stimulus).

Knowledge Area

Unit I—Human Development, Diversity, and Behavior in the Environment (Content Area); Human Growth and Development (Competency); Theories of Human Development Throughout the Lifespan (e.g., Physical, Social, Emotional, Cognitive, Behavioral) (KSA)

158. D

Most individuals who are transgender do not undergo sexual reassignment surgery. Gender identity is distinct from sexual orientation and those who are transgender can be heterosexual, homosexual, bisexual, pansexual, polysexual, or asexual. A cross dresser is someone who enjoys dressing in the opposite gender's clothing, but may not identify with that gender. Those who are transgender often experience stigma, bias, or discrimination due to myths and misconceptions.

Knowledge Area

Unit I—Human Development, Diversity, and Behavior in the Environment (Content Area); Diversity, Discrimination, and Stereotypes (Competency); The Impact of Transgender and Transitioning Process on Behaviors, Attitudes, Identity, and Relationships (KSA)

159. B

A delusion is a false or erroneous belief that usually involves a misinterpretation of perceptions or experiences. A delusion is a belief that is held despite evidence to the contrary. A hallucination involves the senses. An auditory hallucination—hearing something that is not said—is the most common type. In this case vignette, the client had a false, fixed belief despite a lack of supporting evidence, but there was no indication that it resulted from actually seeing or hearing anything that would support these beliefs.

Knowledge Area

Unit II—Intervention Processes and Techniques for Use Across Systems (Content Area); Biopsychosocial History and Collateral Data (Competency); The Indicators of Mental and Emotional Illness Throughout the Lifespan (KSA)

160. D

The client and social worker are in the planning stage of the problem-solving process. Planning comes after engagement and assessment. The first two response choices are interventions. However, in order to determine their appropriateness, the social worker must clarify with the client the desired outcomes and what she means by "being more assertive." Clearly defining the problem and how it relates to positive and negative aspects of the client's life will assist in the formation of an appropriate intervention, treatment, or service plan.

Knowledge Area

Unit II—Intervention Processes and Techniques for Use Across Systems (Content Area); Intervention Planning and Implementation (Competency); Methods to Involve Clients/Client Systems in Intervention Planning (KSA)

161. B

Most practice situations are best handled with no self-disclosure by the social worker. In the case vignette, the social worker should not discuss her own marital breakup and remarriage. Instead, she should instill hope by providing the client with a feeling that she will be heard by the social worker and have the opportunity to address her feelings. The woman may benefit from meeting others who are going through similar experiences, but referring her at this point in the problem-solving process is not an appropriate method for instilling hope. The client's comments are indicative of those who are in this situation and do not alone indicate risk for self-harm.

Knowledge Area

Unit IV—Professional Relationships, Values, and Ethics (Content Area); Professional Development and Use of Self (Competency); The Principles and Techniques for Building and Maintaining a Helping Relationship (KSA)

162. A

The client's behavior is consistent with Bipolar Disorder. He was depressed upon admission and then appeared to be manic during the hospitalization. Only lithium, out of those medications listed, is a mood stabilizer. Elavil is an antidepressant, Ativan is an antianxiety agent, and Haldol is an antipsychotic medication.

Knowledge Area

Unit II—Intervention Processes and Techniques for Use Across Systems (Content Area); Biopsychosocial History and Collateral Data (Competency); Common Psychotropic and Non-Psychotropic Prescriptions and Over-the-Counter Medications and Their Side Effects (KSA)

163. A

Self-esteem is relatively high in childhood, drops during adolescence, rises gradually throughout adulthood, and then declines sharply in old age.

Declines during adolescence are perhaps due to a decrease in body image and other problems associated with puberty, as well as the increasing ability to think abstractly, coupled with more academic and social challenges.

Self-esteem is relatively high in childhood, drops during adolescence, rises gradually throughout adulthood, and then declines sharply in old age.

Declines during adolescence are perhaps due to a decrease in body image and other problems associated with puberty, as well as the increasing ability to think abstractly, coupled with more academic and social challenges.

Knowledge Area

Unit I—Human Development, Diversity, and Behavior in the Environment (Content Area); Human Growth and Development (Competency); Factors Influencing Self-Image (e.g., Culture, Race, Religion/Spirituality, Age, Disability, Trauma) (KSA)

164. A

Sometimes missing appointments after achieving stated goals can be an indicator that the client is ready to terminate. The client may want to practice her new skills independently and does not think that she needs to continue to see the social worker. There is no indication that a new problem has emerged or the client is dissatisfied. Codependency occurs when a client does not want to end the therapeutic relationship despite having achieved goals. The client's behavior most likely means that she is ready to stop seeing the social worker.

Knowledge Area

Unit II—Intervention Processes and Techniques for Use Across Systems (Content Area); Intervention Planning and Implementation (Competency); The Indicators of Client/Client System Readiness for Termination (KSA)

165. A

Tertiary prevention focuses on managing complicated, long-term diseases, injuries, or illnesses. The goal is to prevent further deterioration and maximize quality of life because the disease is now established. Other types of prevention strategies are aimed at preventing the development of a disease and/or slowing its progression or minimizing its long-term impacts. Hospice is associated with care as a result of a life-limiting illness. The case vignette does not indicate that the cancer is terminal, so the management of the pain may be associated with treatment that is occurring.

Knowledge Area

Unit III—Intervention Processes and Techniques for Use With Larger Systems (Content Area); Methods for Social Change (Competency); Primary, Secondary, and Tertiary Prevention Strategies (KSA)

166. D

The client file cannot be shared with the principal even if it will assist the client. Social workers should not be sharing information without consent unless necessary to prevent harm to self or others.

Knowledge Area

Unit IV—Professional Relationships, Values, and Ethics (Content Area); Confidentiality (Competency); Legal and/or Ethical Issues Regarding Confidentiality, Including Electronic Information Security (KSA)

167. B

The standards that govern social work practice address the use of physical contact with clients. Setting clear, appropriate, and culturally sensitive boundaries that govern physical contact are essential for professional practice. Social workers should not engage in physical contact with clients when there is a possibility of psychological harm as a result of the contact (such as cradling or caressing clients).

Physical contact or other activities of a sexual nature with clients are clearly not allowed by social workers.

The *Code of Ethics* does not limit physical contact to only adult clients. However, social workers must clearly evaluate the appropriateness of having physical contact with children, especially because many of the youth served have experienced trauma.

Knowledge Area

Unit IV—Professional Relationships, Values, and Ethics (Content Area); Professional Values and Ethical Issues (Competency); Professional Boundaries in the Social Worker–Client/Client System Relationship (e.g., Power Differences, Conflicts of Interest, etc.) (KSA)

168. B

Acculturation is a process in which members of one cultural group adopt the beliefs and behaviors of another. Although acculturation is usually in the direction of a minority group adopting habits and language patterns of the majority, acculturation can be reciprocal with the majority also adopting patterns typical of the minority group.

Knowledge Area

Unit I—Human Development, Diversity, and Behavior in the Environment (Content Area); Diversity, Discrimination, and Stereotypes (Competency); The Principles of Culturally Competent Social Work Practice (KSA)

169. B

Social workers should protect the confidentiality of deceased clients consistent with the same standards that apply to those who are living. In this case vignette, the social worker should not disclose any information about the client. There is no reason to have the son put his questions in writing or to schedule a session to see him.

Knowledge Area

Unit IV—Professional Relationships, Values, and Ethics (Content Area); Confidentiality (Competency); Legal and/or Ethical Issues Regarding Confidentiality, Including Electronic Information Security (KSA)

170. B

Person-first language names the person before a diagnosis, disability, or condition to avoid defining him or her by this trait. Its use began in the disability self-advocacy community but is now used universally. It is the belief that a person is not his or her disability and that by referring to those with varying physical and cognitive abilities as "the disabled," society is dehumanizing them. Thus, sentence structure should be used that names the person first and the condition second to avoid perceived and subconscious dehumanization when discussing people with diagnoses, disabilities, or conditions.

"Individuals with disabilities" (B) is the only response choice that lists individuals first and the presence of disabilities second.

Knowledge Area

Unit I—Human Development, Diversity, and Behavior in the Environment (Content Area); Diversity, Discrimination, and Stereotypes (Competency); The Effects of Discrimination and Stereotypes on Behaviors, Attitudes, and Identity (KSA)

Practice Test

Evaluation of Results

These tables assist in identifying the content areas and competencies needing further study. Within each of the competencies, there are specific KSAs that social workers should reference to assist with locating appropriate study resources. As there is tremendous overlap in the material that could be contained across the KSAs within a given competency, all KSAs for the competency should be reviewed to make sure of an adequate breadth of knowledge in the content area.

The results of this evaluation should be the basis of the development of a study plan. Social workers should get to a level of comfort with the material so that they can summarize relevant content, including key concepts and terms. Social workers do not need to be experts in all of the KSAs, but should understand their relevancy to social work practice. They should be able to describe how each of the KSAs specifically impact assessment, as well as decisions about client care.

Analysis of Advanced Generalist Practice Test Unit I: Human Development, Diversity, and Behavior in the Environment (23%)					
Competency	**Question Numbers**	**Number of Questions**	**Number Correct**	**Percentage Correct**	**Area Requiring Further Study?**
1. Human Growth and Development	6, 22, 23, 29, 47, 56, 59, 69, 76, 77, 89, 102, 105, 106, 107, 116, 131, 136, 143, 145, 157, 163	22	__/22	__%	
2. Functioning of Various Systems	12, 33, 121	3	__/3	__%	
3. Effects of the Environment on Systems' Behavior	5, 21, 25, 80, 99, 125, 133	7	__/7	__%	
4. Diversity, Discrimination, and Stereotypes	90, 132, 137, 146, 158, 168, 170	7	__/7	__%	

Analysis of Advanced Generalist Practice Test Unit II: Intervention Processes and Techniques for Use Across Systems (32%)					
Competency	**Question Numbers**	**Number of Questions**	**Number Correct**	**Percentage Correct**	**Area Requiring Further Study?**
5. Biopsychosocial History and Collateral Data	7, 8, 9, 13, 34, 42, 53, 60, 72, 81, 95, 140, 141, 159, 162	15	__/15	__%	
6. Assessment Methods and Techniques	2, 10, 11, 17, 41, 43, 100, 103, 114, 117, 120, 130	12	__/12	__%	
7. Intervention Planning and Implementation	18, 24, 30, 46, 50, 51, 55, 57, 58, 63, 85, 86, 88, 93, 97, 101, 109, 110, 112, 113, 118, 126, 135, 148, 151, 160, 164	27	__/27	__%	

Analysis of Advanced Generalist Practice Test					
Unit III: Intervention Processes and Techniques for Use With Larger Systems (18%)					
Competency	**Question Numbers**	**Number of Questions**	**Number Correct**	**Percentage Correct**	**Area Requiring Further Study?**
8. Program Development and Research	16, 31, 32, 37, 45, 52, 79, 92, 111, 124, 129, 138, 139, 156	14	__/14	__%	
9. Methods for Social Change	1, 26, 49, 75, 96, 119, 122, 150, 165	9	__/9	__%	
10. Supervision and Administration	14, 28, 44, 123, 127, 153	6	__/6	__%	
11. Record-Keeping and Reporting	62, 155	2	__/2	__%	

Analysis of Advanced Generalist Practice Test Unit IV: Professional Relationships, Values, and Ethics (27%)					
Competency	**Question Numbers**	**Number of Questions**	**Number Correct**	**Percentage Correct**	**Area Requiring Further Study?**
9. Professional Values and Ethical Issues	3, 4, 19, 20, 38, 61, 66, 71, 73, 74, 82, 94, 98, 108, 134, 142, 144, 147, 152, 166, 169	21	__/21	__%	
10. Confidentiality	15, 27, 35, 36, 39, 48, 54, 64, 65, 67, 68, 78, 83, 84, 87, 91, 104, 115, 128, 154, 167	21	__/21	__%	
11. Professional Development and Use of Self	40, 70, 149, 161	4	__/4	__%	

Overall Results of Advanced Generalist Practice Test				
	Content Area	**Number of Questions**	**Number Correct**	**Percentage Correct**
Unit I (23%)	Human Development, Diversity, and Behavior in the Environment	39	—/39	—%
Unit II (32%)	Intervention Processes and Techniques for Use Across Systems	54	—/54	—%
Unit III (18%)	Intervention Processes and Techniques for Use Across Larger Systems	31	—/31	—%
Unit IV (27%)	Professional Relationships, Values, and Ethics	46	—/46	—%
Overall Knowledge	ASWB® Advanced Generalist Examination	170	—/170	—%

Index